BLACKWELL READERS IN AMERICAN SOCIAL AND CULTURAL HISTORY

Series Editor: Jacqueline Jones, Brandeis University

The *Blackwell Readers in American Social and Cultural History* series introduces students to well-defined topics in American history from a socio-cultural perspective. Using primary and secondary sources, the volumes present the most important works available on a particular topic in a succinct and accessible format designed to fit easily into courses offered in American history or American studies.

American Radicalism

Edited by
Daniel Pope

BLACKWELL
Publishers

Copyright © Blackwell Publishers Ltd 2001; editorial matter and organization copyright
© Daniel Pope 2001

First published 2001

2 4 6 8 10 9 7 5 3 1

Blackwell Publishers Inc.
350 Main Street
Malden, Massachusetts 02148
USA

Blackwell Publishers Ltd
108 Cowley Road
Oxford OX4 1JF
UK

Library of Congress Cataloging-in-Publication Data is available for this book

ISBN 0-631-21898-X (hardback); 0-631-21899-8 (paperback)

British Library Cataloguing in Publication Data
A CIP catalogue record for this book is available from the British Library.

This book is printed on acid-free paper.

Contents

Series Editor's Preface

The purpose of the Blackwell Readers in American Social and Cultural History is to introduce students to cutting-edge historical scholarship that draws upon a variety of disciplines, and to encourage students to "do" history themselves by examining some of the primary texts upon which that scholarship is based.

Each of us lives life with a wholeness that is at odds with the way scholars often dissect the human experience. Anthropologists, psychologists, literary critics, and political scientists (to name just a few) study only discrete parts of our existence. The result is a rather arbitrary collection of disciplinary boundaries enshrined not only in specialized publications but also in university academic departments and in professional organizations.

As a scholarly enterprise, the study of history necessarily crosses these boundaries of knowledge in order to provide a comprehensive view of the past. Over the last few years, social and cultural historians have reached across the disciplines to understand the history of the British North American colonies and the United States in all its fullness. Unfortunately, much of that scholarship, published in specialized monographs and journals, remains inaccessible to undergraduates. Consequently, instructors often face choices that are not very appealing – to ignore the recent scholarship altogether, assign bulky readers that are too detailed for an undergraduate audience, or cobble together packages of recent articles that lack an overall contextual framework. The individual volumes of this series, however, each focus on a significant topic in American history, and bring new, exciting scholarship to students in a compact, accessible format.

The series is designed to complement textbooks and other general readings assigned in undergraduate courses. Each editor has culled particularly innovative and provocative scholarly essays from widely scattered books and journals, and provided an introduction summarizing the major themes of the essays and documents that follow. The essays reproduced here were chosen because of the authors' innovative (and often interdisciplinary) methodology and their ability to reconceptualize historical issues in fresh and insightful ways. Thus students can appreciate the rich complexity of an historical topic and the way that scholars have explored the topic from different perspectives, and in the process transcend the highly artificial disciplinary boundaries that have served to compartmentalize knowledge about the past in the United States.

Also included in each volume are primary texts, at least some of which have been drawn from the essays themselves. By linking primary and secondary material, the editors are able to introduce students to the historian's craft, allowing them to explore this material in depth, and draw additional insights – or interpretations contrary to those of the scholars under discussion – from it. Additional teaching tools, including study questions and suggestions for further reading, offer depth to the analysis.

Jacqueline Jones
Brandeis University

Introduction: The Nature and Significance of Radicalism in American History

Defining Radicalism in the American Past

In this volume, we will meet women rioters demanding price controls during the American Revolution and earnest young students trying to combine spiritualism with social change. We'll encounter German immigrant anarchists in Chicago and African-American sharecroppers and steelworkers in Alabama. After studying those who conspired to launch a revolution against slavery, we can turn to women textile workers demanding "Bread and Roses" in New England. What does it mean to label all of these groups as radical?

Although the word "radical" dates back to the Middle Ages, the term "radicalism" is younger than the American nation, making its linguistic debut around 1820. As an "ism" or system of belief, it is notoriously hard to pin down and assign a consistent meaning. The wit who said that a conservative is someone who admires radicals long after they're dead made the valid point that radicalism is about change, and the radicalism of one era may bolster the status quo in another. Any definition of radicalism should be bounded chronologically. And a definition of *American* radicalism should not pretend to cover the entire world.[1]

With those provisos, a first approximation of a definition that is broad but not all-encompassing would point to *equality* as a central objective and core value of American radical movements and ideas. But equality is not enough, for mainstream groups and individuals can plausibly claim a desire for greater equality. Radicals, however, are willing to employ *illegitimate means* to achieve that goal. Again, context counts; "illegitimate" does not necessarily mean either illegal or violent. Dominant religious and social views in mid-nineteenth-century America considered it improper for women to speak in public to mixed audiences, and women who lectured about abolitionism or women's rights radically challenged those precepts. African-American men, though supposedly guaranteed equal rights by the Fourteenth and Fifteenth Amendments to the Constitution, threatened the white supremacist order of the South at the turn of the century by exercising those rights and taking part in local politics (see chapter 5). The theatrical protests of AIDS activists late in the twentieth century offended upholders of the status quo whether or not they violated any laws (see chapter 9).

Complicating the Definition

But a definition of American radicalism based on equality as a goal and willingness to use illegitimate means invites probing questions. What did equality consist of? In the century or more after the American Revolution, radical movements generally took "equality" to mean equality of opportunity and contended that a true realization of the Declaration of Independence's noble phrase "All men are created equal" would come in allowing equal freedom for all. Whatever different circumstances in life resulted, equal freedom would affirm the moral equality of all before God. That concept still resonates today. The African-American struggle for civil rights in the South invoked the ideals of equality before the law and an equal chance to participate in the blessings of American life. However, by the late nineteenth century, many radicals asserted that formal equality in a capitalist society was a sham. The anarchists of Chicago in the 1880s spoke of freedom, but they also claimed that capitalist interests controlled society and destroyed that freedom. For them, as for later radical groups, the overthrow of an economic system deemed exploitative became the primary goal. Equality of condition, not opportunity, was what counted. And to complicate the issue of equality further, is the use of government power to promote equality consistent with the freedom that radicals have also called for?

Another challenge to our definition comes from social movements that seem to affirm difference as much as or more than they claim equality. By the mid-1960s, for example, the civil rights movement was transforming itself into a movement for Black Power and pride. Black Power activists asked why African Americans would want to be integrated into a burning house, a corrupt, racist society. Some feminists have asserted that, rather than push for equal access to power in a patriarchal society, women should strive to develop and protect a women's culture in which specifically female values of nurturance, peace, and community would be valued. (Jokingly, it has been said that "Women who seek to be equal with men lack ambition.") Radical movements may demand drastic change, but they also seek unity based on traditions and common experiences and respect for who they are. We can see this in case after case, ranging from the crowds demanding fairness in the revolutionary era to immigrant women in the Lawrence textile strike of 1912, to ACT UP, the radicals who fought stigmatization of people with Acquired Immune Deficiency Syndrome, in the late 1980s. We must recognize that radicals often scorn equality when it is taken to mean the submergence of individual or group identity, and becoming "just like" the dominant order.

Finally, this is a book about the radical "left." What about the so-called "radical right?" And is the distinction still valid? The metaphor of a left–right spectrum of political views, with the far left as radical and the far right as reactionary, has persisted since the French Revolution, when members of the National Assembly sat themselves in this pattern. But moderates have often claimed that both ends of the spectrum are similar in their disrespect for stability and gradual progress, their intolerance of democratic processes, and their attachment to violent means. Indeed, whether or not these characterizations are fair, there are real parallels. The anarchists who fought the power of capitalists (historically the left wing's mission) also rejected the power of governments (a stance that today is usually associated with the political right wing). Populists who railed against corporate control in the name of a more humane, democratic economy sometimes also blamed their woes on conspiracies of foreigners, Jews, or Englishmen. Some radical groups in recent decades have refused to be placed on the left–right continuum at all. "Neither left nor right but straight ahead" was a motto of the militant environmentalist American Green Party in the 1980s and early 1990s.

The left–right continuum may be an imperfect device for locating social movements and ideologies, but it has a certain utility. By positing equality as a core radical goal, we exclude movements which exalted order and discipline, claimed the superiority of one group or people to another, or strove for individual choice and opportunity (often through unregulated market capitalism) as their main objective. There are ambiguities in the left-wing/right-wing metaphor, but it gives us a method of clustering similar movements together and analyzing them separately from those with drastically different aims. But consider where the "New Social Movements" of the late twentieth century, as reflected in the militant theatrics of ACT UP (see chapter 9), belong on the spectrum, or whether ACT UP's focus on identity, pride, and respect makes the question irrelevant.

Persistent Dilemmas in American Radicalism

The movements and individuals this book presents are a diverse lot, but many of them faced the same challenges and strategic choices. Briefly, we will discuss four of these recurrent dilemmas below. First, what is the relationship between – to put it starkly – reform and revolution? Next, what are the opportunities and pitfalls in working through the established means of democratic participation: voting, running for office, pressing for legislation, etc.? Third, what role, both positive and negative, has violence played in the history of American radicalism? Can violence be used to further the humane ends that radicals profess? Equally important, how should radicals respond to the repressive violence that they have historically encountered? Finally, radicals confront a cluster of issues about how to build and maintain social movements.

Almost all movements for social change maintain an ideal of a profoundly transformed society. Almost all of them, too, operate in the here-and-now, working for immediate gains: winning higher wages, enacting favorable legislation, ending unjust policies. They have found themselves confronting the relationship between short-term goals and their broader hopes for social transformation. Did radical labor movements advance or betray their aspirations for the overthrow of the capitalist system by fighting for wage increases or shorter hours? (See chapters 4 and 6.) Were the legal reforms contemplated by the participants at the Seneca Falls Convention a worthwhile first step on the road to the full equality they sought? (See chapter 2.) Did AIDS activists' fury and confrontational style alienate others and prevent them from winning tangible improvements in the treatment of people with the disease? Or did their unrelenting, "in-your-face" approach jolt their audiences into re-examining their biases and fears about homosexuality and AIDS? (See chapter 9.) Whether consciously or not, almost all movements for social change have had to make choices about the ethics and politics of compromise and intransigence, between half a loaf now and their dreams of their full portion in the future.

Another issue American radicals have often confronted is their relationship to electoral democracy. By early in the nineteenth century, the vast majority of white adult men had won the right to vote; radicals and others fought battles to extend the franchise to white women and people of color for well over a century thereafter. Throughout most of that century, campaigns, parties and elections absorbed the interest and energies of untold millions of Americans – predominantly white male Americans who could vote, to be sure. Yet American radicals have seldom been comfortable with electoral politics. In part, the objection has been philosophical. Many have shared Henry David Thoreau's distrust: "All voting," he wrote, "is a sort of gaming, like checkers or backgammon, with a slight moral tinge to it, a playing with right and wrong, with moral questions." Numerical majorities could not be trusted on the great moral issues such as slavery. Thus Thoreau's adage, "Any man more right than his neighbors constitutes a majority of one." Would a racist white majority eliminate racism? Would a cowed or complacent populace recognize the oppression all around them, even their own oppression, and vote to end it? America's foremost anarchist, Emma Goldman, herself radicalized by the Haymarket tragedy (see chapter 4), wrote that "the majority represents a mass of cowards."

Although most American radicals have placed more faith in the underlying goodness of the masses, the structure of American politics has also cast doubt on electoral strategies. From the women at Seneca Falls through the African-American Communists in the Depression-era South, lacking the effective right to vote meant that any success at the ballot box would have to come from others' votes (see chapters 2 and 7). Even the male workers attracted to the Industrial Workers of the World were frequently non-citizen immigrants or unable to meet state residency requirements and therefore effectively denied the right to vote. No wonder the Wobblies scorned party politics as a capitalist trick (see chapter 6). The two-party system, dominant throughout most of the last two centuries, has discouraged voters from "wasting" their ballots on independent or minor-party candidates and has induced radicals to give their votes to "lesser evil" moderates. The dominance of big money in campaigns and its ability to wield potent influence in legislation and administration may be more blatant now but was no less real a century ago. If, as Thoreau stated, voting is like gaming, the game seems stacked against radical movements. However (and this is the heart of the radical dilemma) often electoral politics appeared to be "the only game in town," worth fighting to get into and playing with fervor once inside. The dilemma remains unresolved.

Working through the legal, socially-approved means of electoral politics has been problematic for American radicals. What role, then, has violence played in movements for social change? In the first place, we need to emphasize that American radicals have more often been the victims of violence than its perpetrators. However we judge the wisdom or morality of John Brown's raid on Harper's Ferry (see chapter 3), his attempt to overthrow slavery by violent means and all the other violent revolts against slavery combined are negligible compared to the centuries of institutionalized violence inherent in the enslavement of African Americans. The chapters on Haymarket, the suppression of

Populism in Grimes County, Texas, the Lawrence textile workers, and African-American radicals in the 1930s, all indicate that repressive violence is (to borrow the phrase of 1960s Black Power advocate H. Rap Brown) "as American as cherry pie" (see chapters 4 through 7).

Nevertheless, radical responses to the threat and reality of repression have sometimes themselves been violent. (Definitions are tricky here. Are attacks on property rather than persons violent? Are threats, harassment and humiliation, as opposed to physical assault, to be labeled violent?) John Brown's raid in 1859 punctuated a decade in which slavery's opponents lost faith in the strategy of abolition through "moral suasion" or conventional politics alone (see chapter 3). Chicago's anarchists in the 1880s talked about violence far more than they engaged in it, but they were hardly pacifists (see chapter 4). They were convinced that violent means would be needed for revolution. The Industrial Workers of the World seldom followed through on their threats of sabotage but they also believed that the ruling class would not yield to peaceful protest alone (see chapter 6). American radicals have generally been aware that the prospects for violent overthrow of the existing order were quite dismal. Small groups of militants could hardly hope to take on an increasingly powerful military and police apparatus. Moreover, radical violence might provoke conservative backlash and alienate potential supporters.

Finally, it is clear that we cannot discuss violence merely in terms of its efficacy or futility in achieving radical goals. For some radical movements in the nation's past, violence has been something beyond simply a tool for achieving political goals. The food rioters during the American Revolution employed force to symbolize their beliefs in community and mutual obligations and to punish those who violated those ideals (see chapter 1). Suffering and martyrdom as the victims of repressive violence, as in the case of John Brown or the Haymarket anarchists, could be a way of building emotional solidarity and commitment among those who carried on the fight (see chapters 3 and 4).

In an influential study of the 1960s New Left, Wini Breines sets forth the concept of *prefigurative politics*. Suspicious of structure and conventional organizational forms, the New Left's prefigurative politics aimed to "create and sustain within the live practice of the movement, relationships and political forms that 'prefigured' and embodied the desired society." Breines contrasts prefigurative politics with a strategic politics of organization building to "achieve major structural changes in the political, economic and social orders."[2] Chapter 8 on the origins of the New Left at the University of Texas indicates that the emerging movement would have difficulty balancing the deeply felt spiritual and psychological impulses toward community with its aspirations for effectiveness in the "real world." The tension between a prefigurative and a strategic politics was perhaps most visible in the New Left, but others faced the same dilemma. For example, abolitionists yearned for the company of those who shared their moral principles when white society seemed obvious to the sinfulness of human bondage. At the same time, they had to worry about how best to craft a movement capable of influencing the nation's policy toward slavery.

A related question: Can social movements thrive without formal leadership and internal hierarchies? Conversely, at what point does a division between leaders and followers contradict professed goals of equality? People, it seems, join radical movements not only to achieve changes in society but also for the satisfactions of working with like-minded souls who share their values and aspirations. Organizations that failed to recognize and nurture these emotional bonds weakened their members' allegiance. Those which concentrated on internal cohesion might turn out to be ill-equipped to achieve their broader goals of social change.

To outline the persistent dilemmas of American radicalism is not to resolve them or to pass historical judgment on how radicals should have responded. Context always matters. Party politics, say, may be effective sometimes and futile at others. In some cases reforms can set the stage for more fundamental changes whereas at other junctures they may deflect dissent and stifle the energy of radical social movements. Yet the same kinds of questions recur, even though the answers have always depended on time, place, and circumstances.

The Significance of American Radicalism in American History

The history of American radicalism is full of dramatic stories and vivid personalities. This can be reason enough to study it. But some would contend that radical movements and individuals are fringe elements of little significance in understanding the broader dimensions of American history. They point out that radicals throughout American history have consistently failed to gain majority support, have found themselves marginalized, and have sometimes indeed deserved the scorn and ostracism they encountered. Some historians celebrate radical weakness. For them, the nation's success, its expansive prosperity and political freedoms, have made radicalism superfluous at best. The distinguished historian Daniel Boorstin claimed approvingly, "Here the number of people who do not accept the predominant values of our society is negligible."[3] Others have contended the weakness of American radicalism is the result less of national success than of America's intellectual impoverishment. In this interpretation, Americans, trapped by their own optimistic, individualistic assumptions about their society, have been unable to think imaginatively about alternatives to the "American way of life."[4] These "consensus" interpretations of the American past, highly influential in the decades immediately following World War II, made little room for a radical tradition in American history.

Admittedly, the history of American radicalism demands a capacity for irony and an understanding of futility. Left-wing movements have often fragmented in absurdly hair-splitting internal debates while their opponents have stayed focused on maintaining power and wealth. Radical demands have often transmuted into social change that strengthened established interests and power relationships. The women and men who gathered at Seneca Falls in 1848 and demanded women's suffrage as an emblem of equal rights for all could live to see a suffrage movement that all too frequently called for votes for women as a counterbalance to the "dangers" posed by black and immigrant male voters (see chapter 2). Southern Populists who wanted a coalition of poor whites and African Americans based on their common exploitation within a few years could see (and in some cases take part in) Jim Crow's clampdown and substantial political disenfranchisement of poor whites as well as blacks (see chapter 5). Marxists worked to build industrial unions in the 1930s which brought their members not to the barricades but to suburban ranch homes and shopping malls in the 1950s. Conservatives of the 1980s and 1990s turned the New Left's suspicion of oppressive government into a call for dismantling the welfare state. The sixties' radical slogan "Power to the People" was an ancestor, however distant, of the conservative call for "empowerment." If we direct our attention to these transformations, we might even conclude that the main impact of radical movements has turned out to be buttressing the status quo.

Yet consideration of the variety of radical movements in this volume should dispel the notion that American radicalism is a mere sideshow on the fringes of the nation's history. Movements of those who suffered exploitation and discrimination, and of others who sympathized with them, wrought major changes in American society – though, as Karl Marx noted in another context, "Men make their own history, but they do not make it as they please." (Women, too, we might add, as chapters 1, 2, and 6 in particular indicate.) Radicals' impact did not always match their intent, but they did affect the course of American history. Beyond this, American radicals deserve our attention and at least a degree of respect for their ideas and their ideals. We can, sometimes at least, hear (borrowing Abraham Lincoln's phrase) "our better angels" speaking to us in the words of the dissenters, protesters, and revolutionaries in the American past.

Radicals at times in American history have been forerunners, pressing demands treated as outlandish or subversive at the time, but eventually accepted as practical and just. Politicians such as Abraham Lincoln were appalled at John Brown's anti-slavery raid on Harper's Ferry (see chapter 3). A year and a half later Lincoln was Commander-in-Chief in the effort to subdue the Confederacy. Military victory, Lincoln's Emancipation Proclamation of 1863, and the Thirteenth Amendment of 1865 brought about the end to bondage that Brown and others had died for. The eight-hour day movement which mobilized hundreds of thousands of workers in 1886 set the scene for the Haymarket incident and repression of radical labor, but in the longer run corporate and public policies recognized workers' demands for shorter hours (see chapter 4). Mainstream politicians ridiculed the Populists' 1892 Omaha Platform, but in the twentieth century much of their program came to fruition in popular legislation (see chapter 5). The civil rights movement against segregation and legalized discrimination in the 1950s and 1960s encountered fierce resistance, but its demands for equal rights became law, its principles became rhetorical commonplaces among liberals and even conservatives, and its leaders – at least those no longer alive to disturb the establishment's peace – celebrated as national heroes.

Yet the role of path-breaker has usually been bittersweet. The price of eventual victories has been high, and the triumphs have often been tinged with defeat. Those who fought for independence from Great Britain in a revolutionary war in order to escape old world corruptions and challenge concentrated power wondered about their accomplishment as the new nation moved toward competitive individualism rather than a republic of virtuous citizens upholding the common good (see chapter 1). Anti-slavery demands for immediate abolition helped launch a struggle that won a sort of freedom very different and very much less complete than the abolitionists had envisaged (see chapter 3). When a reporter asked the Socialist Party leader Norman Thomas if Franklin D. Roosevelt's New Deal had carried out the Socialists' program, he replied, "Roosevelt did not carry out the Socialist platform, unless he carried it out on a stretcher."[5]

If, as observers since Alexis de Tocqueville have observed, America has been a nation of acquisitive individualists, it has been the fate of American radicals to offer a counter-tradition. Richard Hofstadter half a century ago said that the nation had been a democracy, but a "democracy in cupidity rather than a democracy of fraternity."[6] Protesters, however, contended that there were American ideals higher than private gain. In the Revolutionary era, Americans widely believed that a self-governing nation (a republic) could not survive without "civic virtue," which demanded a sense of community, solidarity, and self-sacrifice. Radical movements from independence through the nineteenth century drew upon republican strains of common good and equality.

Often, nineteenth-century radicals associated republican virtues with a "producer class," those whose efforts produced the goods that people needed in life. Threatening these values and hence the survival of a self-governing republic were parasites: bankers, lawyers, brokers, and other middlemen who profited from others' productive labor. Producer-class radicalism saw the growing gaps in wealth and power in American life as violations of the Declaration of Independence's promise of equal, natural rights. Unlike Marxists, who believed that the fundamental source of oppression was the class divide between property owners and propertyless workers, producer-class radicals generally accepted the institution of private property as long as it was widely and equitably distributed. Honest labor earned property, and this property, in turn, would preserve the independence and virtue of a republic of workers, small businessmen, and farmers.

Although many nineteenth-century radicals adopted the metaphor of an equal start in the race of life, they consistently held that life was not simply a scramble for material riches. "Man over money" was a Populist catch-phrase that encapsulated much of this sentiment. In the twentieth century, as noted above, the emphasis shifted from equality of opportunity to equality of condition or results. But twentieth-century radicals also expressed an idealism that criticized the materialistic society they perceived and sacrificed personal interests for their vision of the common good. Even Marxists, who generally avoided the language of ethical judgment and instead tried to analyze social change through the tenets of "scientific socialism," displayed a striking willingness to risk *their* lives, their fortunes, and their honor for the causes they believed in (see chapters 7 and 8). The immigrant women workers who went out on strike in Lawrence, Massachusetts in 1912 (see chapter 6) carried banners that read "We want Bread and Roses." The African-American Communists in the South during the Great Depression often linked their cause to the values of an uncorrupted Christianity (see chapter 7).

Radicals in the twentieth century (especially those within the Marxist orbit) also reminded their fellow Americans of the significance of social classes in a society which often seemed willfully determined to deny that classes existed. Contending against business unionism, consumerism, a rhetoric of equality and classlessness from the political mainstream, and the homogenizing effects of popular culture, radicals have usually been the ones to stress that the nation has been divided. Their appeals for the unity of the working class may have been simplistic, unrealistic, or unheard, but when attention to social class divisions is absent from the nation's agenda, political debate is thereby impoverished.

Nevertheless, class divisions often intersected with other fissures in American society, notably racial oppression. Racism has been the Achilles' heel of American radicalism. Racism in white America in general has curtailed the appeal of radical movements. Racism among movement participants has divided groups and transformed demands for equality into calls for preserving whites' privileges. Ethnic divisions among European Americans have also hindered movements for change. Explicit or implicit in almost all of the articles in this collection are accounts of ethnic and racial tensions. Admittedly, as in the case of the strikers in Lawrence whose ethnic backgrounds helped motivate their militancy, ethnicity could be a resource for radical movement building (see chapter 6). However, we will also read (see chapter 3) of the uneasy sense among African Americans that John Brown had substituted his will for their self-activity in planning and executing his raid on Harper's Ferry. The egalitarian and democratic sentiments of the Seneca Falls Declaration (see chapter 2) came to coexist with a strain in the movement for women's suffrage that justified it in counteracting the political influence of African-American and recently-arrived immigrant men. Chapter 5 provides a case study of literally murderous racism at the turn of the twentieth century destroying a coalition of white and black farmers in the rural South. African Americans in the South during the Great Depression (see chapter 7) faced the same kind of racism; the Communist Party was the only predominantly white social movement in the US at the time dedicated to full racial equality. White students in the early 1960s whose discontent blossomed into a "New Left" (see chapter 8) found inspiration and gained experience in the movement for black civil rights and integration. In the mid-sixties, with the shift toward African-American nationalism and the rise of Black Power, interracial movements seemed both less possible and less desirable. Left-wing white students in the late sixties seldom found effective ways to work in conjunction with African Americans or other people of color. In more recent decades new social movements such as environmentalism, feminism, and gay and lesbian liberation have also been challenged to deal with racism within their own ranks (see chapter 9). Meanwhile, since the 1960s, as radicals garnered headlines and television news footage, conservatives, taking advantage of a backlash with a substantial racial component, consolidated political power. We cannot predict with any certainty whether racism will continue to thwart aspirations for change, but we can be sure that overcoming racism, both within social movements and in the society at large, is a great challenge facing American radicals.

Those upholding the established order in the United States have frequently described radicals as un-American. They have portrayed dissent as alien and even subversive. Granted, there is some basis for these accusations. Documents in recently-opened Soviet-era archives and newly-declassified decoded cables demonstrate, for instance, that a handful of American Communists were involved in Soviet espionage in the 1930s and 1940s, and that the party continued to take financial assistance from Moscow through the 1980s.[7] In a less sinister sense, American radicals might be called un-American when they identify with radical movements in other nations. Tom Paine, the radical pamphleteer of the American Revolution, was an intense American nationalist, but he also viewed himself as a citizen of the world and joined radical movements in England and France. Immigrants with strong sentiments about their native lands were often at the forefront of radical causes in this country. From sympathizers with the French Revolution in the 1790s to anti-apartheid activists in the 1980s, solidarity across national boundaries has been an aspect of the radical tradition. Much of American radicalism, then, has been internationalist.

Yet it is equally important to insist that our radical tradition is thoroughly and distinctively American. Radicals reflected the values of the surrounding society even as they criticized them. American radicals drew inspiration, not just opportunistic advantage, from the egalitarian rhetoric of the Declaration of Independence (see chapter 2). Garrisonian abolitionists exalted the individual conscience as much as the most unbridled transcendentalists and the individual will as much as the most determined frontiersmen. When the Communist Party in the late 1930s adopted the slogan "Communism is twentieth-century Americanism," their foes claimed it was phony, but party members themselves believed they were taking the best in the American tradition to its historically determined outcome. The students in Austin, Texas who studied European theologians to find a "breakthrough to new life" also drew upon their own middle-American Protestant upbringing (see chapter 8). The 1960s counter-cultural motto "Do your own thing" was not far removed, as Thomas Frank has recently contended, from the advertising slogans of rebellion and non-conformity through consumption.[8]

Beyond this, radicals in this country had to contend with American realities. They grappled with fundamental issues in this society. For instance, the centrality of slavery, racism, and discrimination could not be ignored. Sometimes American Marxists in the early twentieth century lapsed into formulaic statements that capitalism alone caused the "race problem" and that socialism alone was necessary to end it, but the Communist Party threw itself into the struggle against specifically racial oppression (see chapter 7). The women's movement in the late 1960s and 1970s frequently asserted the unity of all women in the face of common oppression, but, hearing the insistent voice of women of color, now contemplates the significance of difference among women. Another example of American radicalism's encounter with basic phenomena of the culture: American religiosity permeates much of the history of American radicalism. Evangelical Protestantism and the second Great Awakening are inseparable from the great antebellum movements for social change. Nor did this relationship disappear in the Gilded Age and Progressive Era: evangelical themes infused the Knights of Labor, the Farmers' Alliances, and People's Party, and even the Industrial Workers of the World (IWW). In the twentieth century, self-proclaimed atheist Marxists have drawn, consciously or otherwise, on the prophetic strains in the Jewish tradition. And in recent decades radical Catholics have been prominent in movements for peace and social justice.

Therefore, both terms in the phrase "American radicalism" deserve our attention. The radical tradition has also been an American tradition. The history of American radicalism presents an array of colorful, controversial personalities and dramatic scenes. There is much to be gained from studying its strategies and styles, even if you find yourself at odds with its values or angered by its tactics. At the same time, we hope this reader will allow you to use American radicalism as a window on broader issues. Interpretations of American history which read radical traditions out of the story miss important dimensions of our past. To comprehend America, we must also come to grips with the radical dimensions of American history. The articles and documents in this reader are selected to further that understanding.

Notes

1 Of course the subjects included in this reader do not encompass all of American radicalism. The American radical tradition is – as this introduction hopes to demonstrate – broad and diverse.
2 Wini Breines, *Community and Organization in the New Left 1962–1968: The Great Refusal*, 2nd ed. (New Brunswick, NJ: Rutgers University Press, 1989), pp. 6–7.
3 Daniel J. Boorstin, *The Genius of American Politics*, paperback ed. (Chicago: University of Chicago Press, 1953), p. 138.
4 Louis B. Hartz, *The Liberal Tradition in America*, paperback ed. (New York: Harcourt, Brace and World, 1955) is probably the best-known example of this interpretation.
5 Quoted in W. A. Swanberg, *Norman Thomas: The Last Idealist* (New York: Charles Scribner's Sons, 1986), p. 204.
6 Richard Hofstadter, *The American Political Tradition and the Men Who Made It*, paperback ed. (New York: Vintage Books, 1954), p. viii.

7 Evidence of espionage, and the involvement of some American Communists, can be found in John Earl Haynes and Harvey Klehr, *Venona: Decoding Soviet Espionage in America* (New Haven, CT: Yale University Press, 1999) and Harvey Klehr, John Earl Haynes, and Fridrik Igorevich Firsov, *The Secret World of American Communism* (New Haven, CT.: Yale University Press, 1995).

8 Thomas Frank, *The Conquest of Cool* (Chicago: University of Chicago Press, 1997).

1
Riot and Radicalism in the American Revolution

1763 British victory in Seven Years War against France leaves her with control of former French possessions east of the Mississippi River. To pay for the war, Britain turns to taxation of its North American colonies.

1763–75 A series of conflicts with Great Britain over taxes, trade regulation, and colonial administration. Americans resent British policies as economic burdens and as threats to their rights as British subjects.

1765 Stamp Act attempts to tax colonial publications, legal documents, etc. Widespread demonstrations prevent its enforcement and it is repealed in 1766.

1767 Townshend Acts tax colonists for imports of common products and tighten customs enforcement.

1768–70 In response to Townshend Acts, colonists adopt and enforce Non-importation Agreements, boycotting British merchants and their products. These stimulate a spurt of domestic production in the colonies. Agreements collapse after repeal of Townshend Acts (except on tea) in 1770.

1773 Tea Act gives advantages to British East India Company in exporting tea to colonies. In protest against the company's "monopoly," Bostonians dump 342 chests of tea into the harbor in the "Boston Tea Party" (December 16).

1774 Parliament passes Coercive Acts to punish colonists for Tea Party. Americans respond with non-importation agreements again. In September, the first Continental Congress convenes in Philadelphia.

April 19, 1775 Battles of Lexington and Concord mark outbreak of war.

July 4, 1776 Declaration of Independence proclaimed.

1775–9 A period of rapid inflation, widespread shortages, and anger at war profiteering. Crowds protest against unjust business practices and demand community regulation of prices to enforce traditional standards of moral business behavior.

October 4, 1779   "Fort Wilson Riot," a violent incident in Philadelphia. The popular militia marches to the home of Congressman James Wilson, a bitter opponent of price controls, attacks the house and battles with an elite defense group.

1780   Continental Congress and state governments fight inflation by restricting the money supply rather than direct price controls, rejecting the idea that governments should directly enforce ethical standards of economic behavior.

October 17, 1781   British General Lord Cornwallis surrenders at Yorktown, Virginia, effectively marking the end of the war and victory for the independent United States of America.

1783   Peace treaty signed in Paris recognizes American independence.

Introduction to the Article

Was the American Revolution a true revolution, comparable to the great upheavals that later shook France, Russia, and China, among other nations? Or was it primarily a struggle for political independence, to gain the "rights of Englishmen" that the colonists considered their entitlement? Historians have debated this for nearly a century and still disagree. In 1913, Carl Becker declared that the American Revolution was not only a war for "home rule" (i.e. self-government) but a battle over "who should rule at home." Becker and other historians in the "Progressive" tradition usually located the social tensions in geographical divisions between seaboard and inland areas or economic differences between commercial and agricultural interests. "Consensus"-oriented historians at mid-century replied that these conflicts were not fundamental. Prosperous, ethnically homogeneous Americans resented taxation without representation and other recently imposed British policies that curtailed the freedom they had once enjoyed.

Another historical debate focuses on whether ordinary white Americans (the vast majority of them living on farms) were eager or reluctant participants in an expanding transatlantic market. The debate is often phrased as a tension between republicanism and liberalism. Republicanism implies a set of ideals which place the common good above individual gain and impose restrictions on seemingly selfish behavior to advance the public's collective interests. Liberalism, until early in the twentieth century, meant a society that prized individual liberty and personal advancement through a competitive market. Were the colonists committed to an entrepreneurial and expansionary economy based on extensive trade? Or did they value a degree of self-sufficiency and view it as patriotic to resist commercial oppression?

In recent decades, some of the most creative work on the Revolutionary period has dug deeper into America's social structure and has found conflict in areas where Progressive historians seldom looked. "When the pot boils, the scum will rise," commented the Massachusetts politician James Otis. The dispossessed groups he disparaged in fact often played active roles in the revolutionary era's upheavals. In Barbara Clark Smith's article, we see "the common people's politics" carried on, not in the drawing rooms and assembly halls of the elite but in the streets, at the warehouses, on the docks. Wartime inflation, shortages, the selfishness of "monopolizers" and the demand for governmental price controls stimulated a wave of food riots. As the war went on, poor city dwellers were increasingly the participants. Crowds enforced their ideas of a moral economy directly and made it clear that their revolution was not identical to that of those who merely wanted to separate from Great Britain.

As Smith contends, the actions of women were crucial "because women's participation, above all else, marked price rioting as revolutionary." Women protesters did not treat their families' need for food and other staples as private concerns. In fact, the gap between public and private, between male politics and female domesticity, emerged in the nineteenth century, not in the Revolutionary era. The women expressed their own ideas about fairness and rights through their actions. Even as elites showed their fear of crowd action and their hostility to price controls, women continued their protests. There is another gender dimension to the protests as well. Note the sarcasm in the *Pennsylvania Journal*'s satire of those who would not give up their British tea when colonists were boycotting it in 1775. Old women, ugly spinsters, and "*old women* of the *male gender*" were called unwilling to give up their tea. The anonymous author of the piece links patriotism and a kind of masculinity together.

Do the food riots demonstrate the nature of the American Revolution's radicalism? Not entirely: as Smith herself indicates, in the symbols, rituals, and appeals to tradition of the demonstrations, crowds looked backward, not forward. Moreover, she notes, the newly independent United States structured political life in ways that suppressed crowd action, promoted ideals of an unregulated market economy, and separated women from political life. For the distinguished historian Gordon Wood, the radicalism of the American Revolution *was* its role in giving birth to the liberal (and male-dominated) individualism of nineteenth-century America (see his prize-winning book, *The Radicalism of the American Revolution*). The Declaration of Independence, with its claim that "all men are created equal" and its promise of "inalienable rights" gave exploited and marginalized groups a language to demand equal rights for all, not just property-owning white men. This kind of legacy of the Revolution, however radical it proved to be, was not the same as the republican radicalism that the food rioters expressed. Yet the republican and communal elements of Revolutionary-era protest, along with the insistence of women that they too were part of the political community, were radical themes which also have resonated during the centuries since the winning of American independence.

Food Rioters and the American Revolution
Barbara Clark Smith

On more than thirty occasions between 1776 and 1779, American men and women gathered in crowds to confront hoarding merchants, intimidate "unreasonable" storekeepers, and seize scarce commodities ranging from sugar to tea to bread. Such food or price riots occurred in at least five northern states – New York, Pennsylvania, Massachusetts, Rhode Island, and Connecticut – as well as in Maryland and, according to one report, Virginia. Some towns, such as East Hartford, Connecticut, and Beverly, Massachusetts, seem to have witnessed only one incident; others, including Boston and Philadelphia, experienced deep, sustained conflict. A good-sized minority of the crowds we know about consisted largely of women; a few others may have included men and women alike. Whatever their composition, most crowds objected to "exorbitant" prices that shopkeepers demanded for their goods or to merchants' practice of withholding commodities from the market altogether. Each crowd voiced specific local grievances, but it is clear that their participants sometimes knew of actions elsewhere and viewed each episode as part of a wider drama.

These riots took place at the intersection of several streams of historical experience. First, they represent one moment in the long-term development of capitalist social relationships in America, particularly in the northern colonies and states. Promoting the availability of foodstuffs, pressing farmers and merchants to sell rather than withhold their

Reprinted from Barbara Clark Smith, "Food Rioters and the American Revolution," *William and Mary Quarterly*, 3rd ser., 51/1 (January 1994), pp. 3–34.

wares, rioters acted on behalf of a plentiful market, although not, it must be stressed, on behalf of a free one. Their actions map an immediate experience of economic distress and articulate popular ideas about economic exchange, its meaning, and the crucial issues of who might claim jurisdiction over it and through what political forms.

The forms themselves compose a second interpretive context, as elements of "the common people's politics" in England and America. In the prominence of women, rioters' adoption of the symbols of authority, and their efforts to pay victims a "reasonable price," America's Revolutionary price riots followed Old World precedents. These riots, which were far more numerous than historians have realized, testify to colonists' access to the repertoire of the English plebeian public, to lines of information and identity that linked ordinary people on either side of the Atlantic. They therefore challenge interpretations that place eighteenth-century crowds solely in a vertical framework defined by elite ideology and accommodation. By contesting high prices and withholding, Americans of lower and middling status often stood against their better-off neighbors; in doing so they laid claim to the powers and rites of Englishmen.

Third, women's prominence in many crowds of the 1770s illuminates aspects of the eighteenth century's construction of gender. Excluded from the vote, unqualified to serve as jurors at courts of law, free women – together with servants, slaves, children, and propertyless men – were politically disabled by their dependent status. Yet women conducted nearly one-third of the riots. Here, then, were possibilities for political action that resistance and revolution opened for women, not as republican wives or mothers but as social and economic actors within household, neighborhood, and marketplace. Food riots have a history in this context, too – in women's substantive, routine participation, not strictly "private" or "public" in nature, in the life of their communities.

Finally, the Revolutionary War, with its dislocations of supply and redoubling of demand, reliance on depreciating paper currency, and rampant inflation, formed the necessary economic context for these riots' occurrence. Beyond that, crowd members and newspaper writers who noted their activities expressed the conviction that a fundamental relationship existed between these incidents and the patriot cause. In a variety of ways, rioters and their allies claimed that confronting merchants in their shops was a patriotic action, much like facing redcoats on the battlefield. As a result, these riots offer a new and decidedly popular angle of vision on Americans' movement for independence from Great Britain and for liberty at home. This essay suggests a new reading of the resistance movement, tracing its relationship to the local world of exchange and marketplace ethics. Most important, it contends that some patriot men and women's resistance to Britain took shape as they negotiated experiences within local networks of exchange, on the one hand, and within the broad Atlantic market on the other. This account of popular participation in the war effort explores one context within which the ideas disseminated by patriot writers and spokesmen in pamphlets, sermons, and the like were received and interpreted.

Wrapped in blankets "like Indians" and with their faces blacked, men gathered in the streets of Longmeadow, Massachusetts, in July 1776 to express "uneasiness with those that trade in rum, molasses, & Sugar, &c." The crowd delivered a written ultimatum to Jonathan and Hezekiah Hale, retailers who had taken advantage of embargo and warfare to raise prices on their increasingly scarce goods:

> Sirs: it is a matter of great grief that you Should give us cause to call upon you in this uncommon way . . . We find you guilty of very wrong behaviour in selling at extravagant prices, particularly West India goods. This conduct plainly tends to undervalue paper Currency which is very detrimental to the Liberties of America We therefore as your offended Brethren demand satisfaction of you the offender by a confession for your past conduct and a Thorough reformation for time to Come.

To prevent misunderstanding, the crowd specified what it considered appropriate prices for rum and molasses. Given an hour to think matters over, the Hales lowered their prices to the levels decreed.

Less swayed by popular opinion was Samuel Colton, who kept shop in a long ell that ran along the back of his Longmeadow mansion. When Colton refused the crowd's terms, it confiscated his supply of West Indian imports and hid them in a nearby barn. In response, wrote local minister Stephen Williams, "Marchant" Colton "made a prayer in publick" – apparently the sort of confession and pledge to reform that townspeople had demanded from the Hales. Afterwards, Colton's goods were returned to him for retail, but within a few weeks he raised prices again. Impatient with "moderate measures," people broke into Colton's locked store and carried away his rum, sugar, molasses, and salt. Colton later complained that the crowd rampaged through the house as well, "ransacking it from top to bottom," causing "great Fear and Terr'r." Williams, although sympathetic to the merchant, reported no destruction or indiscriminate looting. The crowd delivered the goods to the town clerk, who sold them at "reasonable" prices. Eventually, crowd leaders offered the proceeds of the sales to Colton and, when he refused them, took along witnesses and left the money on a table in his house.

A month later, a different commodity created contention in New York. In Fishkill, a group of women assembled to confront New York City alderman Jacobus Lefferts, who had sent "a large quantity of tea" north to Fishkill, intending, as the *Constitutional Gazette* had it, to "make a prey of the friends of the United States by asking a most exorbitant price for the same." When three gentlemen passed by the house where the women were gathered, some of them went out to ask for assistance in their project. When the men refused, the women took matters into their own hands. They confined the three under guard, chose a "committee of ladies" to lead, and marched to Lefferts's store. The alderman declined to part with tea for 9s. per pound, so the women told him they would pay "the continental price" – 6s. per pound, as recently authorized by the Continental Congress. In the event, they apparently paid Lefferts nothing; instead, they appointed a "clerk" and a "weigher," took tea from two boxes, and measured it out into pounds to sell at 6s. each. The women in charge, reported the newspaper, planned to send the proceeds from their sale to the Revolutionary county committee.

Whether supporting local committeemen, sustaining the buying power of Continental money, or dressing "like Indians" in reminiscence of the crowd that had thrown tea into Boston harbor in 1773, these food rioters situated themselves as participants in the patriot cause. Writers in the public press elaborated on the rioters' point of view and denounced farmers who withheld produce from the market and traders who monopolized available goods and jacked up prices. These were more than common grievances, "A Farmer" explained: "This is the very same oppression that we complain of Great Britain!"[1] Historians have treated price riots and price legislation of the era as responses to wartime conditions, as expedients grasped when new economic strains and opportunities revealed cracks in some people's faith in revolutionary governments and their willingness to forgo private gain for the public good. Deeper analysis traces the riots back into the origins of resistance and finds them embedded in the heart of the patriot cause.

It is far from obvious how a merchant's engrossing of salt, tea, or grain was comparable to Parliament's efforts to levy and enforce customs duties, to tax the colonists, or to quarter troops among them. Yet A Farmer was not alone in his arguments and outlook, and food rioters, writers who applauded their actions, and neighbors who stayed at home but nonetheless approved all testify to a different interpretation. In the eighteenth century, A Farmer reminds us, "oppression" was not merely an economic or a political calamity but inextricably both. In an age when people expected governments to protect the poor from privation and the middling sort from inequity, undue economic burdens signaled government failure if not corruption. Similarly, when theorists presumed that self-interest pressed men to aggrandize political power, no neat line distinguished the economic burdens from the political ones under which the people of England and its colonies had sometimes suffered and arguably might suffer again. In the writings of Real Whigs and others, political oppression and economic oppression each implied the other; few thought it possible to disentangle them.

For many colonists, experiences closer to home confirmed the inter-penetration of economic and political matters. Many in the rural north produced primarily for household and neighborhood, routinely swapped labor, tools, manufactures, and produce, and lived within elaborate net-works of local indebtedness. Such households accordingly understood economic dealings within social and ethical frames. They dealt with brethren, kin, and neighbors – people they might or might not hold particularly dear but with whom they expected to go on dealing over and over again. Exchange in this context was bounded, known, and susceptible to widely shared local ideas about what was customary and fair. Thus it was plausible for moralists to argue that exchange should not bring profit at another's expense but should be, in one minister's phrase, "mutually advantageous."

Violating expectations of mutuality among neighbors may well have appeared oppressive, in part because it required a position of advantage to violate them with impunity. For most inhabitants of a locality, main-taining a reputation for probity and fairness mattered; those who out-raged their neighbors' ideas of equity might face private admonition from clergy or other notables or feel pressure to submit to the judgment of three respected local men. Such institutions helped some Americans translate ideals for fair dealing into assumed and even ordinary practice. One Delaware farmer used a revealing shorthand to denote the numer-ous exchanges carried on between two families: the households "neigh-boured." Narrow economic terms do not adequately describe their transactions.

Yet colonial America boasted bustling seaports, swift-sailing merchant vessels, and fashionable merchandise from London and beyond. City populations thrived on trade and suffered during its periodic stagnation. In the countryside, farmers produced for European or West Indian markets, and many country people welcomed the imported goods that filled storekeepers' shelves. Along with local exchange, most free colon-ists also bought and sold in wider markets, participating to one degree or another in a new calculus that included distant markets and relations of credit, new practices of debt settlement, and changing legal forms. Colonists operated within the market *and* outside it; their economy was, as Allan Kulikoff has stressed, "transitional."[2]

In geographic terms, transition meant the existence of central places in the landscape – from ports rimming the Atlantic, to second-rank com-mercial towns and market centers, to country stores, taverns, fairs, and crossroads meeting places. If we lay such a map over the countryside, we see boldly marked centers with lines radiating outward, paths created by lines of credit and return, by peddlers' circuits, by the flow of cloth, ceramics, and hardware to farm villages and the flow of rye, flaxseed, and lumber back to warehouses and wharves.

Yet this view would be partial and in some respects misleading. Engagement with the Atlantic market proceeded unevenly within any one community. We might imagine American society in transition along socioeconomic lines as well as geographic ones. Thus, in many towns and seaports, however embedded in "the market," common people relied on the assize of bread, depended on official activity to secure foodstuffs in times of dearth, and openly defended traditional regulations. In Boston, the city most vulnerable to grain shortages, common people negotiated with superiors through a series of food riots in the 1710s and 1720s, securing legislation that limited exports and a public granary that would buy and sell at cost. Elsewhere, too, commercialization increased social inequality, strained relations among different ranks, and generated demand for customary regulations. Middling and even well-to-do inhabitants sometimes supported such regulation as essential to social order. Everywhere, some inhabitants welcomed the market's opportunities while others resisted its incursion.

Moreover, changes in market participation affected women and men unevenly. We know relatively little about the effects of competitive commodity and labor markets on women's lives. Some colonial commentators fastened on one conspicuous development: the growing availability of some imported goods reframed women's roles more obviously than men's. First in cities, then on farms, store-bought fabrics relieved women and children from the time-consuming work of spinning wool or linen. In what began to appear as "leisure," some women accordingly took on new tasks: shopping for fabrics, dealing with retailers, and mastering the requirements of fashion and social innovations such as tea parties, at which fashion information might be exchanged. Consumption became associated with females, who were then blamed for household extravagance and debt – hence doubly identified with dependence. Critics believed them more susceptible than men to the allurements of the fashionable marketplace, less capable of the public virtue required for civic action. Such aspersions were not new, but in these respects eighteenth-century changes exacerbated the fault lines of gender.

Finally, the transitional nature of northern society appeared in the consciousness and practices of individuals. A farmer or mechanic might take part in both local and distant exchange, swapping labor for a neighbor's produce or meat, supplying potash or lumber to a nearby storekeeper, and purchasing rum manufactured in the West Indies or cloth imported from England. If we imagine some colonists en route from one to another pattern of thought and activity, others struck a balance, joining market transactions and local ones. As Christopher Clark has noted,[3] new behaviors sometimes facilitated old goals: parents might enter the market to purchase land in order to insulate their children from labor and commodity markets. Moreover, market participation had varying results: after all, a farmer's growing vulnerability to the price mechanism of the Atlantic market might make neighborhood ideals more, not less, precious standards for local dealings. If we are to map the northern colonies, then, we must record the various and often contesting forces that existed within market towns and outlying villages alike and unevenly touched men and women, the poor and the well-to-do. We need to attend not only to the capacity of market centers to disseminate commercial practices and ideas but to the ways commercial growth actively supported the vitality of traditional or customary constraints. Moreover, we must recognize towns distant from such centers as creative sites where practices of local exchange engaged inhabitants of various ranks and interests and generated influential ideals of neighboring.

Intrinsic to this state of contrast and change was a particular wariness about the possibilities of "oppression." More than any other factor, the evident and increasing inequality felt in seaports and countryside fed the alarm that Americans felt at midcentury; tension pervaded the visible juxtaposition of one person's advantages in the market with others' dispossession and occasional acute need. That neighbors might sometimes so differ in their experience of the market – in accessibility and opportunity – strained the bonds of mutuality. As colonists acquired a wider circle of reference, they hedged their accountability to local standards and opinion. Equally, and at the same time, the wherewithal and the forms available to resist oppression also came from this transitional moment. Americans' continued engagement in local networks and the practices of neighboring provided a referential experience against which to define oppression, an alternative ground on which to stand and from which to act.

The vitality of those forms became dramatically apparent in the mid-1760s, when Britain's colonial policies raised vital issues about the fairness of economic exchange. With new regulations and taxes and strict measures for their enforcement, Parliament proposed unilaterally to alter the terms of the Atlantic trade and claimed jurisdiction over a host of colonial market transactions. As a result, colonists encountered stamp officers, customs commissioners, and other royal appointees who patently sought to line their pockets from Americans' market participation. One crowd orator in Connecticut notably condemned stamp officers for "oppress[ing] the poor." They and the Parliamentary regulations they enforced would redouble the disadvantages that many already associated with market participation. British policies underscored colonists' vulnerability to oppression, creating the conviction that indebtedness, even engagement in British trade itself, eroded a precious independence.

To regain that independence, many Americans withdrew from the Atlantic market. Faced with the Sugar Act, Stamp Act, Townshend Acts, and Coercive Acts, colonists joined together in nonimportation, nonconsumption pacts, eschewing imports and banning occasions that required or promoted their use. Discontinuing trade might press Parliament to repeal the offensive measures; at the same time, discontinuing imports would reshape relationships within American society. Colonists would re-engage in local networks of production and exchange and embrace the values that inhered therein. Elite Americans would abandon genteel imports in order to patronize local artisans; countrywomen would stay home from the store to produce homespun for their households and possibly for urban consumers. Everyone would put aside profit in a common sacrifice: neither merchants nor mechanics would raise prices to reap a windfall from the shortages that nonimportation would cause. "Prices" and "patriotism" became linked at this moment, then, in the trade boycotts of 1764 through 1775, in a resistance movement that insisted on the political significance of economic and cultural activity, broadly considered. For patriots these pacts were not mere expedients but "solemn leagues and covenants" or "associations" – ways of relating to neighbors and formulating community. By 1774, when the Continental Congress created its boycott – the Association – patriotism was clearly defined on these premises: a patriot did not import, consume, or raise prices on goods and produce on hand.

Equally important, the resistance movement relied heavily upon the political participation of ordinary men and women. Self-appointed groups and individuals policed early nonconsumption, nonimportation pacts. Patriots admonished and cajoled importers and consumers; crowds threatened and sometimes punished those who imported, retailed, or purchased banned commodities. When locally elected committees took up enforcement, committeemen continued to depend on popular surveillance to detect and suppress violations of boycotts. Not infrequently, crowds attended committee meetings, enforced committee desires, or even usurped committee prerogatives. If one's capacity to fend off oppression derived from a certain independence from the Atlantic market, it therefore entailed dependence on local community forms, within which neighbors were held mutually accountable.

Resistance required people to realign themselves vis-à-vis the Atlantic market, on the one hand, and the world of local exchange on the other.

These being the values and commitments of the resistance movement, it was entirely plausible for contemporaries to believe that food riots held a central place within that movement. Indeed, many Americans readily assumed the acceptability of such actions. At the outset of the war, when prices of West Indian goods rose quickly and when towns and countries throughout the colonies mobilized to enforce the Association, riots took place in both rural and urban settings. Members of the crowd that attacked Colton's store in 1776 hailed from agricultural villages such as Enfield, Connecticut, and Wilbraham and Palmer, Massachusetts, as well as from Longmeadow. Similarly, people "from different parts of the country" created an uproar in Kingston, New York in November of that year, breaking into stores and warehouses and seizing tea. In rural Dutchess County, exiles from occupied New York City forcibly stopped outgoing wagons in search of foodstuffs. On several occasions, farmers from various Maryland countries seized quantities of salt. Disorders threatened in Albany in 1775; riots were feared in Salem and broke out in New York City in 1776; but in these years, at least, they were by no means a strictly urban phenomenon.

Participants in crowds were not limited to a single socioeconomic class. The leaders of the Colton crowd were propertied citizens – a church deacon, a well-off Colton in-law – who held positions of responsibility in Springfield and Longmeadow. Slim surviving evidence about the identity of the rank and file suggests that, in this case, crowd members were actually more likely to possess property than were the average male inhabitants of their towns. Elsewhere, too, it was not solely the impoverished and inarticulate who acted. Among the raiders of Lefferts's Fishkill store, the newspaper reported, were Mrs Lefferts's relatives – not necessarily persons of wealth or prominence but presumably not at the bottom of the social and economic ladder either. Maryland rioters were "men of reputation" as well as of "good moral character." Even those who complained about these crowds rarely denounced the class nature of the endeavor. In an age when it was common to dismiss mobs of which one disapproved as composed of "negroes and boys," no one seems to have reacted to food rioters in that way. In most places, reports leave the social composition of the crowds uncertain. Rioters were simply "inhabitants," or "townspeople," or "the people." Although it is unlikely that members of the elite frequently took part – their presence would surely have drawn comment – middling farmers, artisans, and (on one occasion at least) even storekeepers felt moved to take marketing into their own hands when faced with withholding, price gouging, and similar practices that offended their moral or patriotic sensibilities.

At the same time, there were almost certainly crowds composed largely of the lower sorts. A masked and costumed figure known as "Joyce, Jr." – the symbolic descendant of the Cornet George Joyce who had captured King Charles I – led a crowd in the Boston streets in 1777. The role of Joyce, Jr., was reportedly played by John Winthrop, Boston merchant and member of the town's Committee of Correspondence, Safety, and Inspection, comprising its leading patriots. The "concourse . . . of 500" who accompanied him was most likely drawn from the ranks of the city's petty artisans, apprentices, and laborers, the classes who had appeared with Joyce when he had agitated against "Tories" before the war. More common were lower-class crowds unaccompanied by any representative of the elite. Those who took part in the "quarrel for bread" at bakeries in Salem and Marblehead, Massachusetts, and those who joined the "scramble" for coffee at Salem wharf in 1777 were presumably drawn from lower classes. The 900 who gathered in Boston's North End in late 1777 were most likely artisans, mariners, and laborers who lived in that increasingly impoverished neighborhood, as were the 500 who set out to besiege monopolist merchant Jonathan Amory the next day. Sailors reportedly played a major part in battling French soldiers for bread in Boston in 1778, and many members of the Philadelphia crowds of 1779, described as "the rabble" and "the lower sorts," were unquestionably plebeian.

As this sketch suggests, the nature of crowds changed over time. In the later years of the war, price riots became more urban and, correspondingly, more expressive of the beliefs and grievances of the cities' lower classes. This shift was natural enough. In the early war years, prices for imports rose more quickly than prices for domestic products. Farmers whose products bought less rum or sugar, cloth or hardware than was customary and who suspected rural storekeepers of making matters worse by seeking inordinate profits demonstrated their familiarity with traditional forms of the food riot. By the late 1770s, farm prices outstripped imports, and economic distress and food riots both concentrated more heavily in the cities.

That same shift in location also reflected a narrowing of food rioters' social and political base, while a concomitant shift occurred in the ways crowds related to Revolutionary authorities. What may have been the first intimation of a food riot, in 1775, exposed the possibility of conflict between inhabitants and local Revolutionary officials. Merchants were breaking the price equity provisions of the Association, claimed a petition of Albany inhabitants: "We humbly beg of the Committee for

Redress and insist to have an answer in twenty four Hours; and if not answered in that time we shall look upon it that you will not Consider our oppression; and if we find that you will not Vindicate our doleful Circumstance, we will without doubt be obliged to remove these ruinous Circumstances ourselves." The Longmeadow crowd bypassed the local committee, which had exculpated Colton from an earlier charge of price gouging. The Fishkill women donated money from tea sales to their county committee, but the Kingston committee shortly found itself in a very different relationship to local crowds. Women surrounded the committee chamber, the chairman reported, threatening that, unless the committee give them tea, "their husbands and sons shall fight no more." The New York Provincial Congress acknowledged its helplessness and lamely urged Kingston committeemen to try to keep the peace. Within a few months, however, chairman Johannes Sleight had to appeal to central authorities a second time. Kingston inhabitants were "daily alarmed," he said, "and their streets filled with mobs from different parts of the country, breaking of doors, and committing of outrages," all because of "the misfortune of having that detestable article called *tea*, stored there." Committees could be the beneficiaries of crowds, but when they were laggard in their duties or when they themselves withheld goods from the market for army use, they could find themselves targets instead.

Meanwhile in New York, crowds compelled local committees to intervene in the marketing of tea. In October 1776, the provincial congress considered the problem of withholding by New York City tea dealers, whose "unjustifiable and mercenary practices . . . hath in many instances brought upon them the resentment of the people, and many riotous proceedings have thereby been occasioned." Although the city itself was in British hands, the congress ordered local committees elsewhere to seize stocks of tea over twenty-five pounds and to appoint agents to sell it at a set price, pocket a portion of the proceeds for their trouble, and return the rest to the owners. To ensure adequate distribution of the tea, sellers set limits: only twelve pounds to any one person or family. By mandating committee intervention the congress hoped to put an end to riots as well as to curb merchants' extortion.

By the end of 1776, then, crowds had supported, threatened, and supplanted committees as well as, on occasion, roused lethargic committeemen into action. In food riots, Americans negotiated with local patriot leaders over the enforcement of patriotism. Not surprisingly, members of committees, state governments, and the Continental Congress were not completely happy with such crowds. It was true that rioters often enforced resolves of these official bodies. A Massachusetts crowd, for example, came to "the Assistance and rescue" of the committees of Cambridge, Watertown, and Newton as they struggled to block the exportation of goods. When the Continental Congress and the states issued paper money to finance the war, moreover, those bodies and the war effort itself came to rely on the buying power of the bills. It soon became clear that some tories actively worked to depreciate patriot bills; to many, it followed logically that all depreciators thereby declared themselves enemies of the American cause. Price gougers indisputably sought personal gain at their neighbor's expense, and this at a time when enlisting soldiers and their families were becoming dependent on monetary wages, newly vulnerable to inflation. One Maryland crowd that seized salt included farmers "disaffected" from the cause; another, composed of men of "respectable character" and patriotic zeal, was more typical. In the vast majority of cases, charges of toryism, if any, fell on the monopolizers rather than crowds.

Late in 1776, leaders in the New England states came under stiff pressure from their constituents to enforce the price equity clauses of the Association and support the buying power of paper money. Continental bills were pouring into the region, the site of early warfare. Worried about the effects of depreciation, all four New England states enacted legislation that made paper legal tender in private and public transactions, set price ceilings for a host of domestic and imported goods and labor, and outlawed withholding from the market. With these laws, state leaders acknowledged their continued dependence on a participatory and even intrusive committee politics. They did not call for crowds to take to the streets, stores, marketplaces, or wharves. People were to report violations to committeemen or other civil officers, and even committees were expected to prosecute violators through the courts rather than act through extralegal forms. Still, as Elbridge Gerry recorded, price control policies depended on widespread popular vigilance: "The Execution of such laws are undoubtedly difficult but it being the Interest of such multitudes to assist their operations, the Refractory will undoubtedly be diligently watched."

The success of these laws in controlling inflation and preventing mob action depended on local committees' willingness to use strong measures of enforcement. Despite the laws' references to legal prosecutions, in practice people assumed that committees should continue to publish violators' names and that the public should cut off trade with monopolists and hoarders, just as they had with importers, tea drinkers, and other transgressors. Americans continued to prefer their own stringent standards for equity and their own remedies for inequity rather than to accept standards or punishments set by courts or prosecuting officials. Many apparently doubted that the courts would mete out justice to popular satisfaction.

In Salem, Cotton Tufts reported, committeemen proved most doubters wrong, for they had "thrown open the Mercantile Stores and obliged the owners to an Observance of the Acts." The committee was not strict enough for everyone in the city: in July a mob took to the streets demanding sugar and forcing stores open again, yet for the most part committee vigilance preempted crowd action. In contrast, the merchants who sat on Boston's committee hesitated to move forcefully against offenders; as a result, they found themselves caught between many of their fellows' reluctance to abide by price ceilings voluntarily and the popular distress that followed when country suppliers, unable to purchase rum, sugar, coffee, tea, and other items at a set price, stopped bringing produce to the city. As early as March 1777, the town meeting acknowledged the inactivity of its committee by appointing a supplementary body composed of thirty-six men "not in trade." Bostonians urged those appointed to act against violators not through the courts but through the press and the town meeting. As supplies of grain and produce grew scarce, the town meeting bypassed committeemen altogether, calling town merchants publicly to declare their holdings of flour and to abide by price ceilings and marketing laws. These measures may have brought temporary relief, yet within a month bakers were apportioning bread one loaf to the household. As shortages grew worse, tensions mounted.

On April 19, committeeman John Winthrop made his appearance as Joyce, Jr., and supervised an orderly demonstration by some 500 Bostonians. The crowd seized five monopolizing "Tories," placed them in a cart and, in a symbolic hanging, hauled them out of town past the gallows on Roxbury neck, where they "timpd up" the cart, dumped out the men, and warned them never to return to Boston. That night, handbills signed "Joice Junior" appeared in the streets of Boston advising monopolists to begin selling. Winthrop's crew thus pressured town traders to retail at stipulated prices while channeling popular resentment away from the direct seizure of property and into more symbolic forms of action. As a merchant and patriot committee member, Winthrop may have tried to act as a moderating force, hewing a middle course between the city's lower classes and its merchants.

If Winthrop's crowd deflected others from breaking into stores and directly seizing goods, though, it did so only through an assault, however symbolic, on people. Perhaps it is significant that Winthrop himself acted implicitly but not officially on behalf of the town's committee; indeed, as committeemen had no doubt anticipated, the radicalism of the crowd caused consternation among many Bostonians. Merchant Isaac Smith expressed sympathy for one of the crowd's victims: "To be seized when seting down to breakfast and ludgd, into a Cart with his wife and Children hanging round him, not knowing but what he was a going to the Gallows, must be shocking to any One that has the sparks of humanity in them." What worried Smith was the irregularity of the proceedings, the impudence of the crowd in banishing the men "without even the shadow of an Accu[s]ation." He held no brief for real tories, he assured his correspondent, but crowds bypassing the courts of law were more likely to alienate upstanding citizens from supporting the cause than to encourage solidarity. Other objections to the Joyce, Jr., crowd appeared in the *Continental Journal*, while the *Boston Gazette* published defenses. "Joyce, Jr.," himself took to the press to denounce those "Moderate Men, alias Hypocrits," who urged restraint against monopolists, but despite his bravado, Joyce did not appear again at the head of a Boston mob. Indeed, the crowd had gone substantially farther than temporarily suspending a storekeeper's right to retail as he or she saw fit. As Smith noted, it was radical indeed to encourage ordinary Bostonians, acting in crowds, to take it upon themselves to determine who was patriot and who was tory. People who assumed their own competence at delineating the boundaries of the Boston community might assume the right to define the limits of the Revolution itself.

Popular initiative particularly troubled those patriots who sought a simple transfer of power from British to American hands and who saw crowds and even committees as temporary expedients at best. As price inflation and the incidence of food riots increased, "Moderate Men" questioned the policy of keeping equitable dealing at the center of the Revolution. The identification of monopolizers, withholders, and price gougers as enemies caused growing discomfort for patriot merchants and others. As a result, some patriot leaders proposed financial policies that would dissociate prices from patriotism. As early as February 1777, Congressman Benjamin Rush expressed the conviction that commodity prices had little to do with social ethics. "We estimate our Virtue by a false barometer when we measure it by the price of goods," he argued, and other members of Congress concurred. Rush and his allies favored heavy taxation to drain the economy of paper money and discouraged price legislation.

By midyear, merchants and their allies were pressing state governments to repeal price control laws. Worried by Joyce, Jr.'s crowd, Boston merchants rallied to carry the May town meeting against price controls. The laws caused conflict, the meeting told its representatives, as well as operating "directly opposite to the Idea of Liberty," which idea was explicitly equated with free trade. The town meeting in Providence, Rhode Island, called for an end to price ceilings and antiwithholding statutes, complaining that such laws "render a Man's House and Store liable to be opened and searched in a Manner most ignominious and

unworthy in Freemen." Despite the continued popularity of price control laws in rural areas and among urban consumers, mercantile interests
managed to secure their repeal in New Hampshire and Massachusetts by
fall.

With or without laws on the books, however, Bostonians insisted on
their right to enforce equitable exchange. Abigail Adams reported that
"there has been much rout and Noise in the Town for several weeks."
Crowds broke into merchants' stores, seized coffee and sugar, and dealt
them out in small quantities to townspeople. Boston women took to the
streets over the summer, too. One diarist reported a "Female Riot" in
late July: roughly 100 women accosted merchant Thomas Boylston,
placed him in a cart, seized the keys to his warehouse, and confiscated
coffee that he had refused to sell. Another diary suggests that women
appeared on at least one other occasion in Boston, on Copp's Hill. In
September still another crowd followed the precedent set by Joyce, Jr.,
and carted six men across the neck to Roxbury, this time without the
prompting or direction of committee members. James Warren
applauded the mob: "The patience of the people has been wonderful,
and if they had taken more of them, and some of more importance their
vengeance, or rather resentment, would have been well directed." Still,
Warren admitted, others dissented from his view. The action "seems to
be irregular and affords a subject for Moderate Folks and Tories to
descant largely and wisely against mobs."

In the final months of 1777, crowds engaged in aggressive confrontations with engrossing merchants. About 900 gathered in the North End
in their own rump town meeting. They resolved to offer paper money for
engrossed goods but to take the goods "in some other way" if refused.
On the next day some 500 inhabitants met at the store of Jonathan
Amory, a merchant long known for hoarding. A participant later
recalled, "Mr. Amory, in order to quiet the inhabitants, and prevent
his Sugar being taken from him without pay," sent for three members of
Boston's committee and asked them to interpose on his behalf. In turn,
the crowd delegated representatives to confer with the patriot leaders,
who agreed to disburse the sugar at a price acceptable to both parties.
The triumphant crowd carted Amory's sugar to a nearby store, weighed
it, and left it for storage under the supervision of the three committeemen. To Amory's supply the crowd soon added the sugar held by other
merchants (including patriot Isaac Sears). The three men supervised the
sale of West Indian sugar well into the summer of 1778 and, according to
one of them, "kept down the Price of Wood and Grain for above a
Year, till all the Sugars were Sold." By the end of 1777, then, inhabitants
of Boston had bypassed their town meeting and forced committeemen
to take responsibility for ensuring adequate supply and price equity.

The crowd against Amory even established a committee to negotiate with members of Boston's patriot leadership. In Beverly, Massachusetts, a female crowd took similar measures, breaking into a distill-house, seizing sugar, forcing other merchants to hand over their supplies, and setting up one of their number, a storekeeper, to supervise retail.

In both instances, patriot leaders found themselves negotiating with rather than leading crowds and facing "mobs" that set up their own leaders or committees to deal with town officials. These price rioters departed in significant ways from European or colonial precedents; they gave notice that they meant to take an active part in shaping the Revolution.

Tentatively, then assertively, opponents of price regulation publicly endorsed free trade in the patriot press beginning in 1777. Their arguments slowly gained influence, as the difficulty of enforcing price ceilings without repeated recourse to coercive, divisive, and sometimes lower-class crowds became more and more apparent. Patriot leaders gradually turned away from price laws and from formulations of Revolutionary purpose that tied patriotism to equitable prices and economic morality more broadly defined. Outside Poughkeepsie, New York, storekeeper Peter Messier was visited by two or three crowds, mostly women, who seized and paid their own price for tea and, on their last visit, allegedly gave Messier's servants a beating while searching (possibly vandalizing) his house, all in the name of the local committee. In New Windsor, New York, men and women relieved two Albany traders of the tea they were shipping through town, then sold their booty at a price they saw fit. The provincial congress disapproved strenuously. "In a free country," the congress insisted, "no man ought to be divested of his property, but by his own consent or the law of the land." Repeatedly, Revolutionary authorities called on the people to take their grievances to the courts and to leave the matter of chastising monopolists and tories to proper authority.

Equally important, patriot leaders had to suppress conflict between military and civilian supply. When twenty women in East Hartford seized sugar that had been set aside for army use, the patriot press made clear its disapproval. The possibility that crowds would actually hamper the war effort materialized in Boston in 1778, when townspeople and sailors created an incident that threatened to shake the newly concluded alliance with France. The French set up a bakery in Boston to supply their fleet; when the baker refused to sell to townspeople, fighting broke out in the streets and two French officers who intervened were wounded, one of them fatally. Patriot leaders hastened to pass off the incident as the result of British sympathizers' efforts to sow dissension between the allies. In reality, it illustrated the constant potential for conflict between city residents and government agents for military supply.

Ironically, patriot leaders' gravest challenge came from those who insisted that their actions were fully in keeping with the war. In Philadelphia as in Boston, radical leaders, drawn from the ranks of middling artisans and professionals, mediated between conservative merchants and petty artisans and laborers. As in Boston, too, committeemen struggled to retain control of the process and to preempt mob action, even while wielding the threat of such violence against town traders. Matters came to a head in May 1779, when the price of foodstuffs in the city soared. Fifty-one militiamen addressed the Pennsylvania assembly, lamenting the distress felt by poor and middling alike. The city's radical leaders quickly set a public meeting for May 25. That very morning, however, people gave notice that they would not fully trust matters to committees; men armed with clubs visited shopkeepers to force them to lower prices. The mass meeting that followed resolved that, in the face of monopolizing, hoarding, and price gouging, "the public have a right to enquire into the causes of such extraordinary abuses, and prevent them." The meeting established committees to investigate flour engrossing and to set price ceilings in the upcoming months. After the meeting, thousands were reported clamoring for bread, and crowds escorted a merchant, a butcher, and a speculator accused of raising prices to the city jail. As had happened in Boston two years earlier, crowds did more than temporarily suspend the rights of retailers by taking their goods. Instead, they assumed the power to identify and punish enemies to the patriot cause.

The fall brought one final crowd – not strictly a food riot but nonetheless fully of a piece with previous popular actions against monopolists and tories. On October 4, shortly after Philadelphia committeemen acknowledged their inability to stem inflation, a group of militiamen summarily arrested five "tories." In the afternoon the crowd marched to the house of price control opponent James Wilson, where about twenty political conservatives had gathered. As they reached Wilson's residence, a shot rang out from an upper window; the militiamen attacked the house but were dispersed by the "aristocratic silk-stocking brigade," composed in part of men ranked among the city's radical leadership. In ensuing days, the assembly distributed flour among the poor and restated its opposition to forestalling and monopoly. After a foiled attempt by persons unknown to free arrested militiamen from jail, the state pardoned the rioters. With these concessions authorities hoped to damp conflict and bind up the cross-class coalition on which the Revolution had relied from the outset. Yet the specter of violent confrontation helped persuade leaders to abandon that coalition. By 1780, it had become clear that neither Congress nor the states would pursue price control policies; both, moreover, would discourage popular political forms. By 1780, the Revolution had changed.

The fundamental significance of that change comes clear when we consider women's riots, because women's participation, above all else, marked price rioting as revolutionary and its suppression as counter-revolutionary. True, women had not been altogether absent from earlier eighteenth-century crowds. When Boston soldiers returned from defeat at Port Royal in 1707, women met them with jeers and soaked them with the contents of chamber pots in an act of public judgment. Women may have participated in Boston's 1747 anti-impressment riots, and evidence suggests that in rural areas women were among the "people" or "inhabitants" who defended community interests and enforced community morality. For all that, however, women participated more fully in food riots than they had in earlier riots, as the comments of contemporaries make clear. Abigail Adams referred to a Boston's women's crowd as "a New Set of Mobility," during whose proceedings a number of men "stood amazd silent Spectators." The New Windsor store manager who reported that "the women! in this place" had formed a mob to seize tea clearly felt some surprise about it.

Some people had a hard time accepting the political nature of women's actions. The Boston women who forced Thomas Boylston into a cart, confiscated his warehouse keys, and made away with his supply of coffee provoked revealing comments. Abigail Adams reported the rumor that Boylston had received "a Spanking" from the women and added, "this I believe was not true." Given Adams's sense of its unlikelihood, along with the absence of any report of spanking in other accounts of the incident, what seems interesting is the existence of the titillating rumor. Eighteenth-century people may have found it more plausible to characterize the women's effort to mete out punishment in terms of parental discipline, thus casting the action in terms proper to women's familial role, than to invoke metaphors of public hangings and public justice associated with male crowds that, in like manner, put their victims in a cart. John Adams was both condescending and moralistic toward the Boston women. "You have made me merry with the female Frolic," he wrote Abigail, and appended the pious hope that the women would overcome their love of coffee in the future. The association between women and frivolous consumption apparently prevented John from considering other motivations for and implications of the crowd. Yet the Boston town meeting recognized that city dwellers needed coffee and other imported groceries not only for their own consumption but to exchange with farmers for produce and meat.

Despite the mixed reactions to women's crowds, no one seems to have argued that women overstepped their bounds when they challenged hoarding merchants. The *Connecticut Courant* came close. In August 1777, about twenty women met at the Lyon Tavern and, "with a Flank Guard of three chosen Spirits of the male line," began an orderly one-mile march to "Mr. Pitkin's store" in East Hartford. There is no record of the confrontation with Pitkin or his clerk, but the newspaper reported that the women took 218 pounds of sugar that had been stored there for the army. There was a short scuffle with a man on horseback, whom the women took for the owner of the sugar but who quickly rode away. The *Courant* mocked "so unexampled a Spirit of Heroism" and suggested that the women form a battalion to range the countryside and live off of their "perquisites and plunder." Their standard, said the paper, could be decorated with "an elegant device of a lady inverted," a comment implying that the women had indeed stepped out of their place, turning the world upside down. Even here, however, the *Courant's* real objection was that the sugar was earmarked for the army, not that the rioters were female. Victims of the Salem's women's crowd seem to have taken the women quite as seriously as if they had been men, for the victims entered a prosecution against the rioters for theft of goods. (The women – or someone else – responded in dead earnest by leaving burning coals at their prosecutors' doors.)

Overall, the women acted seriously. The Kingston women who threatened that, without tea, they would prevent their sons and husbands from fighting for the cause drew on their power in the household. Elsewhere, women showed that they felt entitled to use conventions more proper to a public role. True, a number of women's crowds engaged at least a few men in their enterprises. The Fishkill women "entreated" male passersby for aid; the East Hartford crowd enlisted three men to raid Pitkin's store; in Beverly, women took along a few men with axes to chop down distillery gates; and the New York women who confronted Messier had three continental soldiers accompany them, thereby arming themselves with male authority in general and army authority in particular. Similarly, women's crowds invoked committees or the Continental Congress to justify or legitimate their actions. But male presence was apparently unnecessary – some crowds involved no men at all – and even support from committees or other Revolutionary authorities was dispensable.

Eighteenth-century women had little reason to doubt their competence at such matters as equitable pricing and neighborly dealing. In America, as in England and on the continent, women took part in marketing and buying for their households. Women were innkeepers, victualers, green-women (supplying urban markets), and storekeepers, like the one who presided over sales of the crowd's booty in Beverly. Female shopkeepers and innkeepers were accustomed to facing profit-seeking wholesalers. Rural and urban housewives participated with men in the exchanges of labor and goods that marked everyday life. Equally important, women were accustomed to responsibility for the welfare of their neighbors. "Charity" and mutual support in times of difficulty lay within women's as well as men's purview. Neither housewives nor tradeswomen trespassed on male terrain when they worried about the equity of prices, for prices represented relationships between neighbors, a part of community life in which women had long been competent and involved. When the Boston women offered Boylston's tea to the impoverished North End, or when the Fishkill women doled out tea in small quantities, they acted in familiar roles if not strictly in familiar ways.

Despite that, women in Boston, Beverly, East Hartford, New Windsor, Fishkill, and Salem established a public presence in ways that their mothers and grandmothers had not done. It was an extraordinary and radical leap for women to claim authority from the Continental Congress or local Revolutionary committees. When they modeled their actions on the activities of Revolutionary authorities, marched the streets as if in the army, or enacted the rituals of male crowds, these women cast themselves as competent actors in a political context from which they had largely been excluded.

Two conditions allowed that to happen. One was the willingness of patriot leaders to breach the line that had separated governmental affairs from everyday life. Beginning in 1765, members of the colonial elite made common cause with their social inferiors. The nonimportation, nonconsumption agreements central to the patriot movement embraced local networks of exchange and ideas about exchange that inhered in those networks. Moreover, pacts such as the Association linked abstract issues of imperial relations, normally the exclusive preoccupation of the elite, to the daily life of free Americans. Such mundane matters as tea drinking, thread spinning, and buying and selling became crucial political matters; their implications in local, provincial, and imperial patterns of power were laid bare. Not only did ordinary men and women join the elite to defend the rights of colonial assemblies, the elite joined ordinary men and women to endorse local ideals of equitable dealing and encourage popular cultural forms. With fervent injunctions to vigilance, patriot leaders authorized ordinary people, men and women alike, to enforce local notions of fairness and the common good.

Equally important, women themselves brought into the resistance and war sources of legitimacy that were their own and that remained even when patriot leaders' commitment to those values wavered and crumbled. It made a difference that Americans knew that women figured prominently in food riots in England and Europe, and it made a difference that ideals of equity, neighborly dealing, and charity informed American women's daily lives in the colonial period. As a result, with or without price control laws on the books, and with or without the support of men, women acted. And what was starkly the case for women's crowds – that some sources for their legitimacy lay outside the control of the elite – was also the case for men's crowds. In responding to price control riots, patriot leaders had to contend with deep-seated and self-supported beliefs that held it legitimate for people outside the political nation, even women, to act to secure equitable dealings according to local standards for the same.

What is revealed by wartime food riots was the existence of a particular political role in the eighteenth century, the experience of a public formed outside the town meeting and open to participation by some who could not vote as well as by many who could. The political premises that undergirded these popular actions are not adequately described by Real Whig theory, which cast crowds in narrow, oppositional terms and contained them within elite conceptions of oppression and elite prescriptions for what resistance might be and do. Price rioters exhibited the capacity for independent judgment; they assumed the right not to be convinced by elite ideas of justice; they asserted the ability to hold and express their own.

How are we to understand this form of politics and the political identity that it offered and required? What relationship did it bear to the more familiar institutions of citizenship that replaced it? In the first place, it was not a liberal form. In the liberal state, citizens offer their allegiance and the state engages to protect them from interference by others and from the state itself. Relationships among citizens may be economic, social, or cultural in nature, but not political, because the "public" is created preeminently by the individual ballot. Citizenship thus consists of vertical ties connecting each individual with the state. By contrast, eighteenth-century Americans lived within and acknowledged horizontal linkages, notable for their multiplicity and intricacy, created by kinship, fellowship, neighboring, and local exchange, and eroded or at least challenged, on the one hand, by growth of a liberal bureaucratic state and, on the other, by increased engagement within the Atlantic market. Relationships within this public were not equal, but they were reciprocal and at one and the same time economic, social, cultural, and political. Women's participation clarifies and secures this conclusion: their political capacity bespoke an economic and social competence derived from neither the Atlantic market nor liberal theory.

Indeed, women's entitlement to riot was not, as John Bohstedt claims for the English case, a form of "proto-citizenship." Women's actions are less easily understood as a parent to the modes of participation available in the nineteenth and twentieth centuries than as a particular eighteenth-century form that was not encompassed in liberal "citizenship." Their political practices were possible because, as Jan Lewis notes, eighteenth-century thought located family and state on a single continuum of society, rather than separating them into public and private realms. Women's participation was possible, in other words, given a peculiar popular access to public time that nineteenth-century citizenship would not encompass and that liberalism would reformulate and, in some instances, actively counter.[4]

If it was not a liberal public that gathered in Revolutionary food riots, was it a republican one? That is a finer question; the answer depends on our understanding of "republican." The public that engaged in food riots was not unbounded: unfree Americans could not easily form themselves into "inhabitants," "the town," or "the people." Nonetheless, the capacity to act within a local, plebeian public arose not from individual traits that set someone apart and above (as civic virtue) but from embeddedness in a community. Exclusion was therefore less definitive of this popular participation than it was of most "republican" forms.

Yet we should not take lightly the rioters' own assertion that they were part of the wider struggle against Britain and on behalf of American liberty. That claim suggests the persuasiveness of the republican ideology preached by the patriot elite, its power to engage and transform popular consciousness; it also suggests the power of a popular stream of culture that appropriated elite ideas. That popular opinion firmly located wartime price riots in the Revolution testifies to a plebeian version of republicanism deeply informed by long-standing ideals for neighborly dealing as well as by the egalitarianism that often infused plebeian notions of equity. The riots reflect the power of popular ideals of right and good. Those ideals, like the men and women who articulated and enforced them on city streets and country roads, resided in local networks and practices of exchange. Equally, like Real Whig thought, those ideals were something of an import. Carried to the New World by immigrants, Anglo-American sailors, English soldiers, and the popular press, traditions of popular politics were among the anglicizing forces shaping eighteenth-century America.

Seen from this perspective, patriotism took shape at the intersection of elite and popular cultural streams, combining the political forms of governed and governors. It is crucial not only to bear in mind that both streams existed but also to imagine their separation or independence as partial and problematic. After all, the food riots of Revolutionary

America reveal unity as well as disagreement between different classes of Americans. At the outset, members of the Continental Congress, Revolutionary state governments, and local committees agreed with rioters that economic transactions had political significance, that price gougers were tories, and that the Revolution hinged on the creation of new (or re-creation of old) standards of obligation among neighbors. We need to consider and investigate the degree to which elite as well as popular republicanism drew on experiences of local exchange and incorporated ideals of neighboring inherent in the collective social arrangements of much of northern colonial society. It would not be surprising if members of the patriot elite shared ideals with the middling farmers, artisans, laborers, and servants who lived in their counties and towns and, in many cases, after all, in their own households. We know that elite Americans recognized the need to negotiate and to accommodate popular values that they did not share. Political insiders, it is said, read the tracts of eighteenth-century commonwealthmen and found a theory that made sense in light of their political experience in lower houses of assembly, particularly as they negotiated and struggled with royal governors. We now can supplement that view: that theory made sense, even to some elite colonists, in light of their experience within and in relationship to the various local publics of American societies. It made sense not on a presumption of equality, which was limited, but on the basis of the existence and durability of horizontal ties, which created a more compelling ideal. We should see republican ideology not merely as something that was imported and then filtered down or disseminated out, but rather – not unlike commodities from England – as seized, interpreted, and applied in the context of local exchange and local ideas.

The story of wartime food riots involves the gradual abandonment of price control policies by patriot governments and the gradual radicalization of rioters. There were many moments of significance: Bostonians followed John Winthrop in carting tories out of town, then repeated the action without elite direction. A Boston crowd named representatives to negotiate with elected committees over the disposition of expensive sugars. In Boston, those left in charge of sugar sales were "gentlemen" rather than crowd members, whereas a Salem mob left retail of confiscated goods in the hands of one of its own, establishing itself in this way as an ongoing institution. North Enders held their own mass meeting to discuss grievances and determine appropriate action. Crowds appropriated the forms of the patriot movement.

Elite patriots at least foresaw the possibility that crowds would not negotiate with committees but replace them. By late 1779, a solid proportion of the patriot leadership was anxious to calm antitory sentiment. As it abandoned the policy of currency finance, the Continental

Congress withdrew its support from a radical popular politics that required active committees and vigilance by people outside committees. Those who argued, with Benjamin Rush, that prices had nothing to do with virtue were not merely adopting ideas of the Scottish Enlightenment, they were opting for crowd and committee quiescence, for the forging of financial policy by men of reason in the halls of Congress and not by crowds in the city streets.

For some years, popular sentiment proved powerful enough to hold the patriot movement to ideals of social and economic equity. As late as 1779, Massachusetts, Rhode Island, and New Hampshire merchants responded to that power; alarmed by Philadelphia events and fearing "a like conflict," these traders took up voluntary price limits again. Although those agreements prevailed for only a few months, they testify to the tenacity of the popular desire to keep local standards of economic fairness central to the Revolution.

It seems unlikely that most price rioters or their sympathizers discarded their belief in fair dealing, not least because those ideals had become bound up in their sense of what the Revolution was about. Long after the Revolution, many Americans maintained the association of moral values and economic life. As their society underwent broad structural change, many citizens of the early republic persisted in viewing such matters as prices, wages, employment, and debt as social relationships, rightfully vulnerable to community values and oversight, amenable to the competence of ordinary intelligence, and proper to the realm of the commonality.

What *was* lost was the social and political frame that made sense of the food or price riot as a political form. The elite drew back from its endorsement of popular politics in 1780; the Continental Congress discouraged crowds and courted the support of wealthy and conservative men. Of all the changes of the postwar years, several were crucial: the suppression of popular cultural forms; the increasing dissociation (however inaccurate for many) of women and production; the growing association of women with consumption and leisure; the growing articulation of social experience into realms either "public" or "private." These aspects of capitalist development critically delimited political practice. The Revolution itself made an ironic difference in political possibility: the new American governments, after all, claimed the status of "We the People." That revolutionary fact provided a rationale for suppressing crowds, channeling participation into the process of the vote, and closing down available terrain outside that chosen form.

Notes

1 "A Farmer," *Connecticut Courant*, February 16, 1778.
2 Allan Kulikoff, "The Transition to Capitalism in Rural America," *William and Mary Quarterly*, 3rd ser., 46 (1989): 125.
3 Christopher Clark, "Economics and Culture: Opening Up the Rural History of the Early American Northeast," *American Quarterly* 43 (1991): 279–301.
4 John Bohstedt, "The Myth of the Feminine Food Riot: Women as Proto-Citizens in English Community Politics, 1790–1810," in Harriet B. Applewhite and Darline G. Levy (eds.) *Women and Politics in the Age of the Democratic Revolution* (Ann Arbor, Mich., 1990); Jan Lewis, "The Republican Wife: Virtue and Seduction in the Early Republic," *William and Mary Quarterly*, 3rd ser., 44 (1987): 693.

Documents

Introduction to the Documents

The documents in this chapter show popular anger at inflation and profiteering as well as some of the forms of crowd action during the Revolutionary era. In Document One, we see a Maryland farmer, Jeremiah Colston, and his neighbors challenging an "ingrosser" of salt, Mr. Chamberlaine. To engross was to withhold an item from sale until desperate buyers would pay an exorbitant price for it. Salt was a necessity for farm activity, and when Chamberlaine refused to sell to Colston, a crowd headed toward Chamberlaine's plantation. Armed with muskets, they proceeded to take what they needed and paid the price they considered just. Note that in describing this incident, the author portrays the crowd as revolutionary patriots and suggests that the "Gentlemen" who profiteer during wartime are pro-British traitors (often called "Tories" during the Revolutionary War). In Document Two, Abigail Adams, the forthright wife of John Adams, writes to him in April 1777. Adams is in Philadelphia as a member of Congress. Complaining of high prices and merchants who have artificially created shortages, Abigail recounts an episode of protest. "Joice Junior" was the pseudonym of a Bostonian who chaired a "committee on tar and feathering." Significantly, the original Joyce was an officer who in Britain's civil war had allegedly seized and executed King Charles I in 1647. Joice Junior led a crowd which captured offending Tory merchants, carried them out of town, and threatened them with death if they returned.

Document Three, addressed to Philadelphia "Gentlemen and Fellow Citizens" in August 1779, suggests the fury of common people facing rapid inflation and shortages. The city's elite seemed unwilling to punish those who wished to see patriotic citizens "enslaved, ruined and starved." In October, anger boiled over into violence when radicals demanding effective price controls fought with elite troops outside the home of one of the city's political leaders, James Wilson. Document Four suggests the complicated gender politics of resistance to British policies. This commentary in the *Pennsylvania Journal* appeared a few weeks before the outbreak of fighting. It satirizes "old women" who were too weak to give up the British tea their compatriots were boycotting. Note the sneering reference to "old women of the male gender" who were unwilling to sacrifice tea to preserve liberty. Barbara Clark Smith's article shows the central role of women in Revolutionary food riots. However, the satirist here equates resistance to oppression with manly virtue. Would the women Clark Smith describes have found this amusing?

Letter to Maryland Council of Safety about Salt Monopolizers

Letter from John Gibson, reprinted from William Hand Browne (ed.) *Archives of Maryland: Journal and Correspondence of the Council of Safety, January 1–March 20, 1777*, vol. 16 (Baltimore: Maryland Historical Society, 1897), pp. 16–18.

Talbot County 4th January 1777

Council of Safty. Gent.

I immagine ere now you've had an impeachment laid before you by Mr Chamberlaine against Jere. Colston, and others of Caroline County for forcibly taking a quantity of Salt from him. And lest you should not have the matter impartially laid before you Honors, I've thought proper at the request of the parties concerned to give a real and true State of their whole proceedings in going out in serch of salt and their coming in, viz. Colston being in extreem want of salt heard it was most likely to be had in Talbot County, and being well acquainted there, He proceeded through it making the strictest enquiry after salt, but could hear of none except that Mr Chamberlaine had ingrossed. He then went to Mr Chamberlaine with an intent to purchase, and finding him not at home, made his business known to the family, who told him Mr Chamberlaine would certainly sell him none and also heard that he had refused selling to many before. Colston went a second time, when he was disappointed in the same manner. On his return he acquainted many as he pass'd with his business and the real want he was in, for he then had 1500 wt of Pork kill'd in his house, which had laid there some time for want of salt, which he could by no means procure and returned empty home again. He was then mentioning his case to his neighbours, who say'd they was in the like circumstances and knew not what to do. He then let them know he was informed Chamberlaine had a quantity of salt, at a plantation of his, (called Plain Dealing) to the amount of 100 Bushels, but would not part with any of it to any person. Those men then after making the strictest enquiry after salt without success, pressed him to go with them, and seemed determined if Colston would join them, to deal plain with the ingrosser of that scarce article salt. They then proposed going with each of them a musket, and also money to buy as much as they had real present need of, which latter they would first offer to Chamberlaine's Trustee, and if he would not take the money and deliver the salt, they would take it by force, to this proposition Colston agreed, the time was appointed when to set out on their expedition, accordingly they met and went down to Plain Dealing to the amount of 17 men with muskets, (though no ammunition) where they found a number of negroes which they expected belonging to the plantation, and the Trustee from home, however his wife was, to whom they apply'd for salt, tho she as well as the negroes had their lesson, say'd there was none there, Colston told her he was credibly informed there was a considerable quantity there, which had laid some time untouched, there-fore insisted to have the door of the house in which the salt lay opened, or they would break it open, at the same time telling her their necessity and like wise of the money for the quantity they wanted, as they did not mean to rob them of it, but to pay a full price, on which the woman say'd if they would not be too lavish, they might get what they wanted, and opened the door, called a negroe, and they ordered him to measure out carefully $17\frac{1}{2}$ Bushels for which they paid her 35 Dollars. Then went home and wrote Mr Chamberlaine their necessity and what they had done, that if the sum they paid for the salt was not sufficient, they would still pay him the price he asked, tho' on hearing it he pursued them to Caroline County as quick as possible and took a poor lad that was a hireling to a man that sent it with them, who I immagine is still confined: the above is a true state of case, in which I make no doubt your Honrs will judge of us favourable as the case will admit of. I need not remind you of these distressing times, for that reason as no violence has been and hope you'll not think them men of seditious principles, who might be desirous of stirring up partie faction. They are by no means such. I know several of the leading men to be men of reputation, who bears and is deserving of a good a moral character as most men in the country; I could wish our leading Gent. on this side of the Bay was as little inclined to partie designs and self-interest as Colston, who was their leader of that Salt company. They have been sincere in their Country's cause and have acted like men of Spirit and principle ever since these distressing times commenced, which is more than can be said with truth of any engrosser of Salt here.

They have not passed through the country publishing the numberless and great difficulties, that we are at in carrying on the War against G. Britain, neither have they through any dastardly conduct or conversation endeavoured to disunite and weaken our cause; which too many of our first Gentlemen have done and in public acts, and speaks with such timid duplicity, which leaves the ignorant in doubt. Was they real friends to their country as they stile themselves, would they ingross that necessary article salt, and keep it from the necessitous as they do in this county, which seems to be for no other purpose than to distress the needy (for what end?) to make the war in which we are engaged more irksome, occasion the people to mutineer and create divisions among them, these are the ends they answer. May just vengeance fall on the heads of all such traitors. The success of Howe's arms when near Philadelphia has unmasked many of our leaders here, which I'me sorry its in my power with truth to say of them, and could with truth say a great deal more to the discredit of our once leaders, which for the present must decline as time will not permit. To conclude, I've thus far given you a true discription of Colston's case, and some of the conduct of our county men, and by which you may the easier judge of the unhappy situation of the people of this shore, must beg your patience a little further while I inform you, that if you should send summons's for those Caroline men to be brought before you on Mr Chamberlaine's charge against them, I know not where it will end, especially with that Gentleman and his tory assistants, for there are not less than 3 or 400 men who have pledged their faith to each other to go at an hour's warning, and at the risk of their lives and fortunes not only release those men, but be revenged of those who occasioned such injuries to be done them, which I really believe is the truth.

I therefore hope your Honrs of the two evils will choose the least, let it pass over, as no one is injured by this conduct yet, and lest it excite more devisions among us than we already have, which are too much encouraged by crafty, designing men, against whom we ought always to be prepared to defend ourselves, by being as unanimous in all our public undertakings as possible, which is the sincere wish of Gentleman,

Your very humble Servant
John Gibson

N. B. Among other facts in the state of Mr Colston within, its set forth that Mr Chamberlaine's Trustee was not at home, which is wrong. He was at home, but sick, which occasioned his wife to act.

J. T. G.
To The Council of Safety. Annapolis.

Letter from Abigail Adams to John Adams

Reprinted from L. H. Butterfield (ed.) *Adams Family Correspondence* (Cambridge, MA.: Harvard University Press, 1963), pp. 217–18.

April 20, 1777

The post is very Regular and faithfully brings me all your Letters I believe. If I do not write so often as you do be assurd that tis because I have nothing worth your acceptance to write. Whilst the Army lay this way I had constantly something by way of inteligance to write, of late there has been as general a state of Tranquility as if we had no contending Armies. . . .

As to the Town of Boston I cannot give you any very agreable account of it. It seems to be really destitute of the Choice Spirits which once inhabited it. Tho I have not heard any perticuliar charges of Toryism against it, no doubt you had your inteligance from Better authority than I can name. I Have not been into Town since your absence nor do I desire to go till a better Spirit prevails. If tis not Toryism, tis a Spirit of avarice, a Contempt of Authority, an inordinate Love of Gain, that prevails not only in Town, but every where I look or hear from. As to Dissapation, there was always enough of it, in the Town, but I believe not more now than when you left us.

There is a general cry against the Merchants, against monopilizers &c. who tis said have created a partial Scarcity. That a Scarcity prevails of every article not only of Luxery, but even the necessaries of life is a certain fact. Every thing bears an exorbitant price. The act which for a while was in some measure regarded and stemed the torrent of oppression is now no more Heeded than if it had never been made; Indian Corn at 5 shillings, Rye 11 and 12 shilling[s], but none scarcly to be had even at that price, Beaf 8 pence, veal 6 pence and 8 pence, Butter 1 & 6 pence; Mutton none, Lamb none, pork none, Sugar mean Sugar £4 per hundred, Molasses none, cotton wool none, Rum N.E. 8 shilling[s] per Gallon, Coffe 2 & 6 per pound, Chocolate 3 shillings.

What can be done? Will Gold and Silver remedy this Evil? By your accounts of Board, Horse keeping &c. I fancy you are not better of than we are Here. I live in hopes that we see the most difficult time we have to experience. Why is Carolina so much better furnished than any other State? and at so reasonable prices.

I Hate to tell a Story unless I am fully informd of every perticuliar. As it happened <last Night> yesterday, and to day is Sunday have not been so fully informed as I could wish. About 11 o clock yesterday William Jackson, Dick Green, Harry Perkins, and Sergant of Cape Ann and a Carry of Charlstown were carted out of Boston under the direction of Joice junr. who was mounted on Horse back with a Red coat, a white Wig and a drawn Sword, with Drum and fife following; a Concourse of people to the amount of 500 followed. They proceeded as far as Roxbury when he ordered the cart to be [tipped] up, then told them if they were ever catched in Town again it should be at the expence of their lives. He then ordered his Gang to return which they did immediately without any disturbance. Whether they had been guilty of any new offence I cannot learn. Tis said that a week or two ago there was a public auction at Salem when these 5 Tories went down and bid up the articles to an enormous price, in consequence of which they were complaind of by the Salem Committee. Two of them I hear took refuge in this Town last Night.

I believe we shall be the last State to assume Government. Whilst we Harbour such a number of designing Tories amongst us, we shall find goverment disregarded and every measure brought into contempt, by secretly undermineing and openly contemning them. We abound with designing Tories and Ignorant avaricious Whigs.

Broadside, Philadelphia

Reprinted from Steve Russwurm, "Equality and Justice: Documents from Philadelphia's Popular Revolution," *Pennsylvania History* 52/4 (October 1985), pp. 261–2.

Gentlemen and Fellow Citiz[ens]

[August 29, 1779]

The time is now arrived to prove whether the suffering friends of [our] country, are to be enslaved, ruined and starved, by a few over-bearing Merchants, a swarm of Monopolizers and Speculaters, an infernal gang of Tories, &c. &c.

Now is the time to prove, whether we will support our Committee or not, whether we shall tamely sit down and see the resolves of the Town-meeting and Committee, violated every day before our faces, and the Delinquents suffered to go unpunished; the case is just this, your opponents are rich and powerful, and they think by their consequence, to over-awe you into slavery, and to starve you in the bargen. But I say it is a shame and disgrace to the virtuous sons of Liberty, while the

ALMIGHTY is fighting our battles without, to suffer those Devils of all colours within us, to overturn all that God and Man has done to save us. My dear [frien]ds, if our Committee is overturned, our Money is inevitably gone, the British Tyrant will then think his Golden bribe has not been misapplied. But I call upon you all, in name of our Bleeding Country, to rouse up as a Lyon out of his den, and make those Beasts of Pray, to humble, and prove by this days conduct, than any person whatever, though puffed like a Toad, with a sense of his own consequence, shall dare to violate the least Resolve of our Committee, it were better for him, that a Mill-stone was fastened to his neck, and he cast into the depth of the Sea, or that he had never been born, *Rouse! Rouse! Rouse!* and

COME on WARMLY

Satirical "Old Women's Petition" against Tea Boycott

From *Pennsylvania Journal*, March 1, 1775, reprinted from Frank Moore, *The Diary of the Revolution: A Centennial Volume Embracing the Current Events in Our Country's History from 1775 to 1781* (Hartford, Conn.: J. B. Burr Publishing Co., 1876), pp. 30–1.

MARCH 1. [1775] THE following "Petition" came to my hand by accident; whether it is to be presented to the Assembly now sitting at Philadelphia, the next Congress or Committee, I cannot say. But it is certainly going forward, and must convince every thinking person that the measures of the late Congress were very weak wicked, and foolish, and that the opposition to them is much more considerable and respectable than perhaps many have imagined:

The PETITION of divers OLD WOMEN of the city of Philadelphia; humbly sheweth:—That your petitioners, as well spinsters as married, having been long accustomed to the drinking of tea, fear it will be utterly impossible for them to exhibit so much patriotism as wholly to disuse it. Your petitioners beg leave to observe, that, having already done all possible injury to their nerves and health with this delectable herb, they shall think it extremely hard not to enjoy it for the remainder of their lives. Your petitioners would further represent, that coffee and chocolate, or any other substitute hitherto proposed, they humbly apprehend from their heaviness, must destroy that brilliancy of fancy, and fluency of expression, usually found at tea tables, when they are handling the conduct or character of their absent acquaintances. Your petitioners are also informed, there are several old women of the other sex, laboring under the like difficulties, who apprehend the above restriction will be wholly insupportable; and that it is a sacrifice infinitely too great to be made to save the lives, liberties, and privileges of any country whatever. Your petitioners, therefore, humbly pray the premises may be taken into serious consideration, and that they may be excepted from the resolution adopted by the late Congress, wherein your petitioners conceive they were not represented; more especially as your petitioners only pray for an indulgence to those spinsters, whom age or ugliness have rendered desperate in the expectation of husbands; those of the married, where infirmities and ill behavior have made their husbands long since tired of them, and those *old women* of the *male gender* who will most naturally be found in such company. And your petitioners as in duty bound shall ever pray, etc.

Suggested Reading

Eric Foner, *Tom Paine and Revolutionary America*, New York: Oxford University Press, 1976. An innovative discussion of the relations between the foremost propagandist of American self-rule and the social upheavals of the Revolutionary War years.

Ronald Hoffman and Peter J. Albert, *The Transforming Hand of Revolution: Reconsidering the American Revolution as a Social Movement*, Charlottesville, VA: University of Virginia Press, 1996. A collection of essays reappraising the nature and extent of social change in the Revolutionary era.

Linda K. Kerber, *Women of the Republic: Intellect and Ideology in Revolutionary America*, Chapel Hill, NC: University of North Carolina Press, 1980. The author analyzes what changed, and what did not, for women in the revolutionary era.

Gordon Wood, *The Radicalism of the American Revolution*, New York: Knopf, 1992. This Pulitzer Prize-winning study argues that the Revolution broke down hierarchies and traditional restraints and created an open, individualistic society.

Alfred F. Young, *The American Revolution: Explorations in the History of American Radicalism*, De Kalb, IL: Northern Illinois University Press, 1976. Pioneering essays on aspects of radical protest and conflict.

2
Women's Networks and Women's Protest

November 12, 1815 Elizabeth Cady, leading figure in nineteenth-century American women's movement, born in Johnstown, New York.

May 1, 1840 Cady marries Henry B. Stanton, a well-known abolitionist. The two attend the World Anti-Slavery Convention in London, where she meets Lucretia Mott (1793–1880), a leading Quaker abolitionist.

1847 Cady Stanton and her family move to Seneca Falls, New York, a small town between Syracuse and Rochester. The area of New York State is known as the "burned-over district," for the many religious revivals there. It is a center of reform activity including anti-slavery organizing.

July 13, 1848 Cady Stanton, Lucretia Mott, and three other abolitionist women meet and decide to call a convention to discuss women's rights.

July 19–20, 1848 Seneca Falls Convention approves "A Declaration of Rights and Sentiments." Among other points, it calls for women's right to vote.

1848 First New York State Married Women's Property Act protects wives' property from their husbands' creditors.

1869 Cady Stanton and Susan B. Anthony found the National Women's Suffrage Association.

1869 The territory of Wyoming grants women the right to vote, but by the end of the century only four western states (Wyoming, Colorado, Utah, and Idaho) had enacted women's suffrage.

August 26, 1920 Nineteenth Amendment to the US Constitution enacted. Women gain the right to vote throughout the nation.

Introduction to the Article

The generations between the American Revolution and the mid-nineteenth century had seen the democratization of American society for white men. Yet white women, like African Americans free and slave, were largely excluded from the political life of the nation. Dissatisfaction with the circumstances of women's lives and their exclusion from public affairs crystalized in July, 1848 at the first Women's Rights Convention, held at Seneca Falls, New York. The Declaration of Sentiments, signed by one hundred (68 women and 32 men) of the three hundred people in attendance, expressed an agenda that was to dominate the women's movement until the Nineteenth Amendment to the Constitution gave women the right to vote in 1920. Indeed, in many respects, the grievances listed at Seneca Falls remain the unfinished business of our contemporary women's movement.

Judith Wellman's article reconstructs the social networks that brought the reformers together and seeks to recapture the moral and political concerns that motivated their commitment to women's equality. She finds them involved in three activist circles: legal reform, especially married women's property rights; political abolitionism and efforts to build an anti-slavery political party; and Garrisonian abolitionism, committed to ending slavery by "moral suasion." (For the supporters of abolitionist leader William Lloyd Garrison, slavery had to be ended not by force or political maneuvers but by demonstrating its sinfulness and the need to break with it immediately.) Those in this last network were frequently dissenting Quakers who felt that the mainstream of their religious denomination had compromised too much with injustice and had allowed hierarchy and inequality to creep into religious practices.

Other historians have emphasized the central role of Elizabeth Cady Stanton in the Seneca Falls Convention. Wellman agrees, but she stresses that participants were likely to have been committed activists, not merely drawn along by Cady Stanton's eloquence and intellectual brilliance. Nor, she argues, do socioeconomic variables explain involvement at Seneca Falls. Signers of the Declaration ranged widely in age, wealth, and occupation. What did frequently bring them together were family relationships. Not only spouses but also brothers and sisters, or parents and children, were likely to attend and endorse the Declaration together. This reinforces her point that networks based on shared ideals of equality were the elements that united the lives of those at Seneca Falls.

Wellman reinforces the point made by Ellen C. DuBois and other scholars. The demands of the Seneca Falls Convention were profoundly radical. The nineteenth-century women's movement has drawn scholarly criticism for being exclusively middle class and too oriented toward winning the right to vote. But the Seneca Falls Declaration drew directly on the Declaration of Independence, using the language that oppressed groups throughout American history have used to claim equality and human rights. Cady Stanton herself invoked the Revolution throughout her long activist career. She described American women as "the daughters of the revolutionary heroes of 76" and demanded their equality on that basis.

The Seneca Falls signers' unity, Wellman contends, was based on principles, not narrow interests. Moreover, the right to vote itself was the defining feature of citizenship in nineteenth-century American life. Without it, women would be confined to subordinate, private roles. With it, they hoped, women could take their place as equal moral actors in a self-governing society.

The Seneca Falls Women's Rights Convention: A Study of Social Networks

Judith Wellman

Shortly after 11.00 a.m. on the bright, sunlit morning of July 19, 1848, Elizabeth Cady Stanton walked to the front of the Wesleyan Chapel in Seneca Falls, New York. The time had come to take public action, to inaugurate, as Stanton later recalled, "the greatest rebellion the world has ever seen." She was so nervous, she remembered, that she "wanted to abandon all her principles" and run away. But she did not, and the first women's rights convention of modern North America began.

For the next two days, perhaps three hundred people met in the Wesleyan Chapel to discuss not only the "social, civil, and religious condition and rights of woman" but also women's political rights, especially the right to vote. When the meeting was over, one hundred people (sixty-eight women and thirty-two men) had signed the Declaration of Sentiments, which was patterned after the Declaration of Independence, and asserted "that all men and women are created equal; that they are endowed by their Creator with certain inalienable rights; that among these are life, liberty, and the pursuit of happiness...." Just as the colonists had brought charges against King George, so the signers at

---

Reprinted from Judith Wellman, "The Seneca Falls Women's Rights Convention: A Study of Social Networks," *Journal of Women's History* 3/1 (Spring 1991), pp. 9–35. Reprinted by permission of Indiana University Press.

Seneca Falls brought charges against the men of America, against an establishment that legitimized male authority, denied women political rights (including the right to vote), gave husbands the power even to beat their wives, discriminated against women in employment, education, and property ownership, and took from women a sense of self-respect and of confidence in their own abilities.

By using the Declaration of Independence as their model, women's rights advocates at Seneca Falls drew immediate public attention to their cause, and they initiated a new, activist phase of the women's rights movement. As the historian Ellen Carol DuBois has argued, "For many years before 1848, American women had manifested considerable discontent with their lot.... Yet women's discontent remained unexamined, implicit, and above all, disorganized.... The women's rights movement crystallized these sentiments into a feminist politics... [and] began a new phase in the history of feminism." Certainly the fires of women's discontent had long been smoldering. The Seneca Falls convention fanned them into bright flames. More than any other place, Seneca Falls symbolizes the beginning of the modern U.S. movement for women's rights.[1]

This is the story of the one hundred signers of the Declaration of Sentiments. Who were they? And why did they sign a document that they agreed was "of the kind called radical"? Because only eight days elapsed between the first newspaper announcement of the convention and the meeting itself, we might assume that those who attended were not simply isolated individuals. In fact, most of the signers were linked together by preexisting social networks.

In 1888, Frederick Douglass, then editor of the *North Star* in Rochester, New York, and himself one of the signers, provided us a clue about the nature of these networks at the fortieth anniversary of the convention, held by the International Council of Women in Washington, D.C.:

> Then who were we, for I count myself in, who did this thing? We were few in numbers, moderate in resources, and very little known in the world. The most that we had to commend us, was a firm conviction that we were in the right, and a firm faith that the right must ultimately prevail.

For Douglass, it was shared values rather than a shared relationship to material resources that brought these women's rights advocates together at Seneca Falls. One value, that of equality, was central to all of their lives. "All men and women are created equal," they had affirmed. So we might hypothesize that the networks that linked the signers would reflect egalitarian values.

Secondary literature offers us more specific insights about the nature of those networks. Two standard approaches explain why the nineteenth-century U.S. women's movement emerged when and where it did. The first one relates most directly to Seneca Falls. It suggests that the Seneca Falls convention was essentially a part of Elizabeth Cady Stanton's own personal history. In this view, Stanton organized the convention as a political response to her own personal experience of discrimination. As a young girl, she realized that her lawyer father valued sons more than daughters and that women faced obstacles not only within the family but also in the legal and political structures of the larger world. The second explanation relates more broadly to the women's rights movement as a whole. It argues that the movement emerged primarily out of the thwarted efforts of American women to participate in the antislavery movement and that major leaders of the women's rights movement emerged from the radical Garrisonian wing of abolitionism (as opposed to the political wing). Both explanations are valid insofar as they rely primarily on evidence about the main leaders of the women's movement, most of whom forged their commitment to reform in the fires of abolitionism.

But those who signed the Seneca Falls Declaration of Sentiments were not leaders. They were, in fact, very ordinary people. Only five of them – Frederick Douglass, Lucretia and James Mott, Martha Wright, and Stanton herself – ever became figures of national importance. Why did these relatively obscure people take such an early and unequivocal stand for women's rights? Were they swept away by arguments from Stanton's own life? Had they been prior advocates of radical, antipolitical abolitionism? Or did their commitment to women's rights flow from entirely different sources? This essay will give a qualified "yes" to each of these questions.

Beyond the simple act of signing the Declaration of Sentiments itself, few of these signers left any record of what shaped and sustained their egalitarian ideals. They did, however, leave imprints of their basic values on the social institutions in which they lived out their daily lives. Using a variety of sources – including census reports, local histories, genealogies, cemetery records, newspapers, church records, tax assessments, subscription lists, and correspondence – I have begun to identify those institutions and to isolate the most important social networks.

Against a backdrop of an expansive and rapidly changing economic and social milieu, these reformers used their energies to promote egalitarian ideals at the local, state, and national levels. Most important, three major reform organizations linked these signers into value-oriented networks long before they knew about the Seneca Falls convention. These networks were composed of (1) legal reformers, who worked to implement the right of married women to own property and who also raised the question of political rights for women; (2) political abolitionists, who helped form the emerging Free Soil party; and (3) Quaker abolitionists, who supported Garrisonian abolitionism.

The first two of these networks were most important in Seneca Falls. The last linked women's rights advocates in Waterloo with those in other parts of central New York. In the spring and early summer of 1848, none of these networks was quite solidified. Events in Elizabeth Cady Stanton's own life would coincide with the particular organizational needs of these three groups to provide the spark that ignited the women's rights movement.

Three networks, three events, three concerns. How did these develop? How did they coalesce in the summer of 1848 to motivate one hundred people to sign the Seneca Falls Declaration of Sentiments? Before we answer these questions directly, let us briefly explore Elizabeth Cady Stanton's own situation, as well as some of the economic and social factors that provided the background for women's rights activism.

Elizabeth Cady Stanton

Elizabeth Cady Stanton was clearly the main organizer of the convention, and understanding her own story is key to understanding why the convention occurred in the first place. In 1847 and early 1848, events in Seneca Falls brought back painful recollections from her girlhood and made her especially receptive to arguments for change.

Three months before Stanton's eleventh birthday, in August 1826, her oldest brother, Eleazer, came home from Union College to die. Three more brothers died in infancy or early childhood, leaving Stanton's parents – Daniel and Margaret Cady – with six girls but no living sons. Daniel Cady never fully recovered, and he rebuffed Elizabeth's efforts to be as good as the sons he had lost. "I taxed every power," she remembered in her autobiography, "hoping some day to hear my father say: 'Well, a girl is as good as a boy, after all.' But he never said it."[2]

A few months later, Elizabeth's sister, Tryphena, married Edward Bayard, and the newlywedded couple became surrogate parents for the remaining Cady children. Edward and his brother, Henry, studied law with Daniel Cady, Elizabeth's father, and she began to spend much of her time in her father's law office. With the revision of New York State's laws in 1828, the legal position of married women was suddenly clouded with doubt, and Daniel Cady's law students liked to tease Elizabeth about her powerlessness under the law. Contacts she made in her father's office would connect her with a significant network of legal reformers.

As she grew, Stanton began to spend considerable time with her cousin and his wife, Gerrit and Nancy Smith, at their home in Peterboro, New York. There she was introduced to a second network, that of political abolitionists. One of the most famous was Henry B. Stanton, abolitionist orator and organizer. Against her father's wishes, Elizabeth married Henry in May 1840. Through Gerrit Smith and Henry Stanton, Elizabeth made important contacts among a second major network, that of political abolitionists.

On their honeymoon, Elizabeth and Henry attended the World Anti-Slavery convention in London. By refusing to seat women delegates, antislavery males unwittingly transformed this meeting into an episode in the development of the women's rights movement. As Stanton recalled:

> The action of this convention was the topic of discussion, in public and private, for a long time, and . . . gave rise to the movement for women's political equality both in England and the United States. As the convention adjourned, the remark was heard on all sides, "It is about time some demand was made for new liberties for women."[3]

Most important for Stanton was her introduction to Lucretia Mott and the circle of Quaker abolitionist women from Philadelphia. As an older woman, an abolitionist, and an accomplished public speaker, Mott represented "a new world of thought" to Stanton. She also connected Stanton to another wing of the antislavery movement, those who emphasized not political action but moral suasion. Often called Garrisonians after William Lloyd Garrison, perhaps the most vocal proponent of this view, these abolitionists embraced total equality for all people, "the *equal brotherhood* of the entire Human Family, without distinction of color, sex, or clime." It may have been in London that Elizabeth began to call herself a Garrisonian. Shortly afterward, she began to subscribe to the *Liberator*, Garrison's newspaper, and she continued to do so, in her own name, until the paper went out of existence.

In 1840, just before the London meeting, political abolitionists had split with moral suasionist Garrisonians at the annual meeting of the American Anti-Slavery Society. They were never to be reconciled. Stanton, however, would maintain strong ties with both groups – with the political abolitionists through her husband, Henry, and her cousin, Gerrit Smith, and with the moral suasionists through her new mentor, Lucretia Mott.

All three of these networks – the legal reformers Stanton had met through her father's law office, the political abolitionists she knew so well through her husband, and the Garrisonian abolitionists that she herself belonged to and that she had come to know through Mott – came together in Stanton's life in the summer of 1848.

Stanton would be ready to take public action with these three networks in 1848, in part because of deeply disturbing events in her own personal life. Stanton had moved to Seneca Falls from Boston, and the change was both dramatic and depressing. With her husband almost always away from home, she struggled to maintain herself and her three rambunctious sons with little household help. Their house was on the outskirts of the village, in an Irish working-class neighborhood, overlooking the Seneca Turnpike, the Seneca and Cayuga Canal, and the mills along the Seneca River. Her life was made even more difficult when her children and servants all developed malaria. As she recalled, "Cleanliness, order, the love of the beautiful and artistic, all faded away in the struggle to accomplish what was absolutely necessary from hour to hour." Overwhelmed, Stanton fled to her parents' home in Johnstown, New York.

Increasingly frustrated, increasingly angry, Stanton tried to make sense of her feelings. She thought about cooperative housekeeping and about the advantages of Fourierist communities. Although she probably suffered either a miscarriage or a still birth, she did not have the fourth child she might normally have had at this stage. She was a woman in a state of siege. At that critical point in her life, events outside her control would rouse her neighbors to organized action. The passage of the Married Women's Property Act in April 1848, the formation of the Free-Soil party, and the organization of dissident Quakers into the Congregational Friends in June 1848 set the stage to help Stanton transform her personal problems into political action through a convention for the rights of women.

Background Influences

Although national in its impact, the Seneca Falls convention was local in its origins. Of the eighty-three known signers, 69 percent of them came either from Seneca Falls or the neighboring town of Waterloo. So many people attended the convention from Waterloo, in fact, that one newspaper called the meeting the "Waterloo Female Convention." A few people came from other townships in Seneca County, and a few more arrived from as far away as Rochester (forty miles west of Seneca Falls), Wayne County (just north of Seneca Falls), or Syracuse (forty miles east). Only three came from farther distances, and these were all on visits to relatives in central New York.

In the 1840s, upstate New York, like the whole northeastern United States, was changing rapidly. Both Seneca Falls and Waterloo were at the cutting edge of economic and social change. Both lay on the country's major east-west transportation route, developed first as the Seneca Turnpike, then as the Erie Canal (connected to Seneca County by the Seneca and Cayuga Canal), and finally as a major rail route. Local industries epitomized the early industrial revolution. The 43-foot waterfall from which Seneca Falls took its name provided abundant waterpower for mills and factories. Four miles west, Waterloo's woolen factory sustained production from the mid-1830s.

By the 1840s, Seneca Falls found itself economically in transition. Strongly affected by the depression of 1837, the town lost its older economy, which was based on milling local wheat into flour for eastern markets, as wheat production moved farther west. Local entrepreneurs had begun to manufacture both pumps and textiles, but these industries would not provide a dependable economic base until the 1850s.

Economic change eroded stable social institutions and challenged basic values of community cohesion. At the same time, it offered opportunities. On the one hand, signers of the Declaration of Sentiments were secure enough in their basic economic, social, and cultural positions to be willing to take risks. On the other hand, they found themselves on the shifting sands of change, where risk was not only possible but necessary. A complex mix – different for different signers – of personal characteristics, economic status, and family patterns set the stage for the involvement of these individuals in reform. By themselves, these elements do not explain why the signers became women's rights activists. They did, however, provide a context that promoted the growth of women's rights activism.

Gender, for example, was an important variable but not a definitive one. Two-thirds of the signers were women. Whether or not men should sign the Declaration of Sentiments was, in fact, one of only two topics that occasioned disagreement at the convention. (The other was the question of women's right to vote.) With the exception of Stanton herself, people from Seneca Falls generally acted on the belief that men as well as women should sign. Half of the signers from Seneca Falls were male. Signers from Waterloo and central New York, however, were predominately female (68.2 percent of the signers from Waterloo and 65 percent from central New York were women). All but one of the unidentified signers was female.

Age did not link the signers, who ranged from fourteen-year-old Susan Quinn, the youngest signer, to sixty-eight-year-old George W. Pryor, the oldest. Their mean age was 38.7 years old.

Ethnicity, race, and place of birth were also contributing but not defining factors. In race and ethnicity, the majority of signers reflected the majority of the surrounding population: they were native-born

European Americans. Only one known signer, Frederick Douglass, was African American. Only one, Susan Quinn, was of Irish descent. Most had been born in New York State, New England, or Pennsylvania.

Wealth, too, provided a context but not a cause for reform. According to the 1850 census, signers' families did, on average, own more property than did nonsigners' families. Variation among signers' families was so great, however, that wealth alone does not adequately distinguish the signers from the ordinary population. Excluding the four richest signatories from our calculations, the average value of property held by signers' families was $2,051. The average value of property held by nonsigning families in Seneca Falls and Waterloo, in contrast, was $1,117. (Seneca Falls had by far the lowest average amount of property ownership, with $869 per family, compared to $2,915 in Waterloo and $4,220 in central New York generally.)

Occupations also provide clues about the relationship of signers to one another and to a new economic order. Although many of the signers worked in occupations strongly affected by economic change, employment associations did not provide the most important link among the signers. Sorting the occupations of the signers' heads of households into primary (farming, fishing, mining, and lumbering), secondary (manufacturing), and tertiary (trade and service) occupations offers a very rough measure of involvement with economic changes.

Those who worked in manufacturing certainly had to confront directly the possibility of dramatic changes in the way they earned their living. In fact, 39.6 percent of signers lived in households that derived their main income from manufacturing. Only 30.2 percent were involved in farming and 30.2 percent in services or trade. In Seneca Falls, most signers (55.2 percent) lived in manufacturing households. Of these, six (37.5 percent) were clearly part of new, large-scale techniques of production. These included one spinner (Justin Williams, the only signer clearly identified as a textile factory worker rather than an owner), one machinist, one sash manufacturer, one candle-maker, and two pump manufacturers. The other nine manufacturers (56.3 percent) – including one boat-builder, one milliner, one carriage-maker, one tailor, and five coopers – worked in older, craft-style occupations. The coopers, in particular, found themselves in declining demand, as local flour mills closed and as their supply of oak trees dwindled.

Other signers, although they listed their occupations as farmers or as professionals, derived at least part of their income from industrialization. Richard P. Hunt, for example, told the census taker that he was a farmer. He did, indeed, own several farms in Waterloo, but he was also the major investor in the Waterloo woolen factory and one of the owners of Waterloo's main business district. Elisha Foote, a lawyer, specialized in patent law and himself held several patents. And John Jones, a steamboat agent, obviously depended on the use of steam power in transportation to create his employment.

Family networks give us another important clue about the relationship of these signers to other people. Almost half the identifiable signers (and perhaps almost two-thirds of the total) attended the convention with at least one other family member. Wives and husbands came together. Mothers brought their daughters, and fathers brought sons. Sisters and brothers came together, and so, in some cases, did uncles and cousins.

These family patterns can be interpreted in two ways. First, they hint at the strength of family ties. Some families did argue among themselves about women's rights. Henry Stanton, for example, refused to attend the convention at all. But many of the signers (including Stanton herself, who brought Harriet Cady Eaton, her sister, and Daniel Cady Eaton, her nephew) could count on at least one other family member to lend support. Women's rights may have divided some families, but it brought others together in a common cause.

Second, these family patterns lead us to suspect that husbands and wives had important ties not only with each other but with their own parents and siblings. While many husbands and wives signed the Declaration together, many women and men also signed the Declaration with members of their birth families. Sometimes these family relationships became very complicated. Richard P. Hunt, for example, signed not only with his wife, Jane, but with two sisters (Lydia Mount and Hannah Plant) and with Lydia's daughter, Mary E. Vail. Experience Gibbs signed with at least one, and possibly two, of her sisters. Amy Post signed with her sister, Sarah Hallowell and Amy's stepdaughter, Mary Hallowell. Mary Ann and Thomas McClintock signed with two of their daughters, Elizabeth and Mary Ann.

Clearly, these signers valued their ties with sisters, brothers, parents, and children as much as those with husbands and wives. Links with their families of origin balanced marital relationships and provided women with a large network of support of "significant others." In spite of legal theory and emerging popular opinion, wives in this group did not define themselves solely by their relationship to their husbands.

Finally, for many signers, home was not simply a private place. It was also a public place, part of the world of work and of social interaction beyond the nuclear family. Many signers incorporated non-family members into their households, including apprentices, servants, boarders, and children. Most unrelated household members were European American, born either in the United States or in Ireland. But some were African American, such as Mary Jackson, aged seventeen, and S. L. Freeman, eight, who lived with the McClintock family, or Matilda

Rany, seventeen, who lived with Margaret and George Pryor. Through networks of kinship and household, these signers reached out to the community as a whole. The emerging distinction between women (whose place was in the home) and men (who worked outside the home) was blurred for these signers. Families and households were not peripheral to public activity but the very basis of community life itself.

All of these factors – sex, age, race and ethnicity, wealth and work, family and household – set the stage for the involvement of these people in the Seneca Falls convention. But these were contributing factors, not defining ones. I believe that the convention happened when and where it did primarily because these signers were linked together into three value-oriented networks and because Elizabeth Cady Stanton herself mobilized people in all three groups to create the Seneca Falls women's rights convention.

Women and Legal Reform in New York State

The first network emerged from a statewide debate about the legal rights of women in New York State. For almost two decades before the Seneca Falls convention, this debate was so widespread and so intertwined with fundamental questions of American identity that it engaged people at a grass-roots level all across New York State. And it framed the debate about women's rights in the language of the Declaration of Independence. Did the phrase "all men are created equal" include women? Were women, indeed, citizens? In effect, the debate over legal rights for married women provided a dress rehearsal for the Seneca Falls convention itself.

In Seneca Falls, legal reform found its most ardent advocate in Ansel Bascom, lawyer, abolitionist, legal reformer, and temperance man. Bascom did not sign the Declaration of Sentiments. He was a candidate for Congress in 1848 and perhaps did not want to commit himself to such a radical position. He did, however, attend the women's rights meeting, and he took a very active part in the discussion.

Stanton herself formed a second member of this legal reform network. As a child, she had listened to her father and her father's law students debate women's legal rights. She had lobbied in Albany for legal reform in the 1840s. And she contributed in her own special way to the Declaration of Sentiments by emphasizing women's citizenship rights, especially the right of all women – married or single – to vote, which she articulated in terms of the statewide debate about women and the law.

Discussions about women's legal rights undoubtedly affected other signers, too. Elisha Foote, for example, a Seneca Falls lawyer and one of Stanton's father's former law students, quite likely took an active part.

So, probably, did men such as Charles Hoskins and Jacob P. Chamberlain, who were politically aware, interested in questions of equality, financially well off, and worried about the future of their several daughters. At least one other signer, Martha Wright from Auburn, New York, mentioned debates about legal reform in an 1841 letter.

Two questions about legal rights for women roused considerable attention in New York State. The first was the right of married women to own property. The second concerned the right of women as citizens to participate in a democratic government. Particularly, should women be allowed to vote? Under the broad umbrella of republican rhetoric that dominated political discourse from the Revolution to the Civil War, these two questions, of property rights and citizenship rights, although often debated separately, were integrally intertwined. Only those with some material investment in the body politic, some argued, should be given a voice in public affairs. Such investment could be property ownership (which led to the payment of taxes) or militia service. As long as women were subject to neither, the rationale for denying them the vote remained intact. If laws were changed to allow married women to own property in their own names, then the whole legal and philosophical scaffolding of resistance to women's political power collapsed. As George Geddes, one of the supporters of a married women's property act, realized, such legislation raised "the whole question of woman's proper place in society, in the family and everywhere."[4]

New York State's citizens had publicly debated the question of women's rights at least since the 1821 state constitutional convention. There, opponents of universal male suffrage (i.e., of voting rights for all males, regardless of property ownership or race) argued that citizenship rights did not necessarily include voting rights. Over and over again, they used the exclusion of women from voting rights (as well as the exclusion of children, native Americans, foreigners, paupers, and felons) as a rationale for denying suffrage to others, including black males and white males without property. If women could legitimately be disfranchised, why could not others be excluded as well?

In 1828, the question of married women's rights emerged in full force. Under the old law, based on English common law, wealthy New York families could protect property rights for their wives and married daughters by means of legal trusts, administered through equity courts. Many New Yorkers, however, viewed equity courts as fortresses of privilege for the wealthy. After 1828, New York State's Revised Statutes abolished equity courts, and with them went any sure protection for the right of married women to own property.

By the mid-1830s, considerable support existed across the state for a law protecting married women's right to own property. Men from wealthy families pushed for such a law most vigorously. They, after all, had most to lose, either to profligate sons-in-law or to ill-fated business ventures. Women's rights advocates, however, added their own small voice for reform. In 1836, Ernestine Rose, who was Polish American and Jewish, circulated a petition urging the passage of the married women's property act promoted by Thomas Herttell, a Democratic assemblyman from New York City. Although only six women signed this petition, it marked the first time that women themselves had taken public action for legal reform.

Nowhere did the argument for full rights for women emerge more clearly than in a speech given in the late 1830s or early 1840s before the lyceum in Ogdensburg, New York. Arguing strenuously for married women's property rights, the author also raised the prospect both of the right to vote and the right to hold office. The Declaration of Independence provided the key. "THAT ALL ARE CREATED FREE AND EQUAL; THAT THEY ARE ENDOWED BY THEIR CREATOR WITH CERTAIN UNALIENABLE RIGHTS; THAT AMONG THESE ARE LIFE, LIBERTY, AND THE PURSUIT OF HAPPINESS – is acknowledged to be the fundamental doctrine upon which this Republic is founded," the author asserted. Furthermore, this idea "is freedom's golden rule. . . . None should ever be allowed to restrict its universality. Women, as well as men, are entitled to the full enjoyment of its practical blessings." Clearly, women were citizens of this Republic, "amenable to the constitution and laws." Yet,

> would any man be denominated free who was deprived of a representation in the government, under which he lived, who was thus disfranchised and had no voice in the affairs of his country? . . . He would be called a slave. Such, I blush for my country to say it – such is the degraded condition of women, in this boasted land of liberty. . . . Is this slavish condition of women compatible with the doctrine that all are created free and equal?

Obviously, in this author's mind, not.

Extensive delays in passing a married women's property act, however, only broadened public awareness. By the 1840s, Elizabeth Cady Stanton remembered, married women's property had become

> the topic of general interest around many fashionable dinner-tables, and at many humble firesides. In this way all phases of the question were touched upon, involving the relations of the sexes, and gradually widening to all human interests – political, religious, civil and social. The press and the pulpit became suddenly vigilant in marking out woman's sphere, while

woman herself seemed equally vigilant in her efforts to step outside the prescribed limits.

As if to prove her point, the *Seneca Observor*, published in Seneca County, New York, argued in 1843 that "the right of voting should be extended to females in common with males" and that "it is a violation of the great doctrine of equal rights that such is not the case."[5]

Discussion of women's rights – both property rights and political rights – reached a crescendo in 1846, when New York State called a new constitutional convention. The convention opened up once more the question of suffrage. Who should be allowed to vote in the State of New York? Should illiterates? Foreigners? Blacks? Even women? The issue seemed especially pressing because of recent unsuccessful efforts to legalize equal rights to suffrage for blacks in New York State.

For women, however, the right to vote was not at first raised by convention members but by female citizens of the state themselves. At least three petitions (from Albany, Jefferson, and Wyoming counties, New York) asked for women's suffrage. Jefferson County petitioners argued, for example, that

> the present government of this state has widely departed from the true democratic principles upon which all just governments must be based by denying to the female portion of the community the right of suffrage and any participation in forming the government and laws under which they live, and to which they are amenable, and by imposing upon them burdens of taxation, both directly and indirectly, without admitting them the right of representation....

No taxation without representation constituted so powerful an argument that the convention could not entirely ignore it. Yet there was little sentiment in favor of doing anything about it. Instead, the opposition successfully used both ridicule and reason to combat the idea. The convention debated a resolution, for example, that "men are by nature free and independent, and in their social and political relations entitled to equal rights." Levi S. Chatfield, from Otsego County, wanted to add the words "without regard to color." Charles O'Connor, of New York, decided to poke some fun. "Will the gentleman accept an amendment to that or an addition," he asked, "viz: the words 'age or sex!'"

Those attending this New York state constitutional convention may have laughed, but Stanton did not. Neither did Samuel J. May, minister of the Unitarian Church in Syracuse. In November, he castigated opponents of women's suffrage from his pulpit. It was, he argued, "all unequal, all unrighteous – this utter annihilation, politically considered, of more than one half of the whole community. . . . This entire disfranchisement of females is as unjust as the disfranchisement of the males would be . . . ."

In April 1848, the New York State legislature again addressed the problem of married women's property rights. Again, they were prodded by petitions from citizens. One in particular revealed the importance of revolutionary rhetoric and grass-roots commitment in sustaining support for women's rights. In March 1848, forty-four "ladies" (married, as they were clear to assert) petitioned the legislature from the towns of Darien and Covington in Genesee and Wyoming counties, New York. Their petition argued, with potent sarcasm:

That your Declaration of Independence declares, that governments derive their just powers from the consent of the governed. And as women have never consented to, been represented in, or recognized by this government, it is evident that in justice no allegiance can be claimed from them.

Your laws after depriving us of property, of the means of acquiring it, and even of individuality, require the same obedience from us as from free citizens.

We therefore think, common justice and humanity would dictate, that when you class us and our privileges with those of idiots, and lunatics, you should do the same with regard to our responsibilities; and as our husbands assume responsibility for our debts and trespasses, they should also for our misdemeanors and crimes; for justice can never hold lunatics, idiots, infants, or married women (as the law now is) accountable for their conduct.

When women are allowed the privilege of rational and accountable beings, it will be soon enough to expect from them the duties of such.

Our numerous and yearly petitions for this most desirable object having been disregarded, we now ask your august body, to abolish all laws which hold married women more accountable for their acts than infants, idiots, and lunatics.

Perhaps inspired (or shamed) by such rhetoric, the New York State legislature did pass its first married women's property act just one month later, in April 1848. In creating a supportive climate for the Seneca Falls women's rights convention, discussion of the legal rights of women was extremely important. Passage of the Married Women's Property Act helped legitimize more radical action and prompted Stanton herself to promote women's right to vote. As Stanton noted, the Married Women's Property Act "encouraged action on the part of women, as the reflection naturally arose that, if the men who make the laws were ready for some onward step, surely the women themselves should express interest in legislation."[6]

Free-Soil Organization

Passage of the Married Women's Property Act in April 1848 was the first major event in 1848 to set the stage for the Seneca Falls convention. Two more key events followed. Both occurred in June. Both linked local people to larger concerns. Both involved value-oriented networks, and both reflected major disruptions in those networks. One (in Seneca Falls) ripped apart political allegiances. It was the growth, in the late spring and early summer of 1848, of the new Free-Soil party. The other (in Waterloo and beyond) mirrored a profound break in religious ties, when a group of Quaker abolitionists split away from the Genesee Yearly Meeting (Hicksite) to form the nucleus of the new Congregational or Progressive Friends. Both splits led directly to a confrontation over questions about equality in American life.

Both also involved people who were part of Elizabeth Cady Stanton's own personal circle. The Free-Soil movement drew support from men (and the women who had married these men) whom Stanton had met in her father's law office, as well as from political abolitionists she had met through her husband, Henry. The Quaker controversy deeply affected Friends who were linked to Lucretia Mott, Stanton's mentor and friend.

Political institutions in Seneca Falls were profoundly strained by debates surrounding the nomination of presidential candidates in 1848. Discussion centered on one question: Should slavery be allowed in the territories? In New York State, the question hit the Democratic party, already under stress from a decade of bickering, with particular force. At a meeting in Syracuse in September 1847, the radical Barn-burner wing of the party stalked out in anger when the conservative Hunkers refused to support resolutions against the extension of slavery. In May 1848, the national Democratic convention nominated Lewis Cass for president. For the Barnburners, now joined by former president Martin Van Buren, that was the last straw. They called a Barnburner state convention, to meet at Utica on June 22. Joined by antislavery Whigs and by men from the Liberty party, these dissident Democrats formed the nucleus of a new Free-Soil party, which would be organized formally at Buffalo in August. Championing "free soil, free labor, free men," they would rally behind Martin Van Buren for president.

Electors in Seneca Falls found themselves swept into this national confrontation. On June 13, in preparation for the Utica meeting, 196 voters published an invitation in the *Seneca County Courier* to the "freemen of Seneca Falls" to meet in the Wesleyan Chapel to consider "the course of action which existing circumstances require of Northern Freemen." Chaired by Jacob Chamberlain, owner of a local flour mill, the attendees of the June 15 meeting agreed that slavery was "the chiefest curse and foulest disgrace" in America. The author of these stern resolutions? Ansel Bascom.

Henry Stanton, too, leaped into the fight with gusto. He teamed up with Bascom to stump the state for the Free-Soil party. And he was one of 102 local delegates to the Buffalo Free-Soil convention, held in August.

Old party issues were insignificant compared to the pressing need to find a presidential candidate who would restrict slavery. Such sentiments allied Seneca Falls Free-Soilers with the party's abolitionist wing. Nationally, many Free-Soil adherents supported the party not from antislavery principles but as a way to keep the west for whites only. People in Seneca Falls, however, considered slavery a moral evil and hoped the new party would strike a mortal blow against it.

Some of them would go even further. They would take the idea of equality seriously enough to consider not only rights for black and white males but also for women. They would attend the Seneca Falls women's rights convention and would sign its Declaration of Sentiments.

Direct influence of the Free-Soil movement on the women's rights convention is easier to document than is the impact of debates over the Married Women's Property Act. Of the twenty-six separate families of signers of the Declaration of Sentiments identifiable from Seneca Falls, eighteen of them also included a Free-Soil advocate. In Seneca Falls, not all Free-Soilers were women's rights advocates. But 69.2 per cent of the households of women's rights advocates (compared to only 21.2 percent of nonsigners households) were affiliated with the Free-Soilers.

Congregational Friends

Organizing for the Free-Soil party, combined with public discussion over women's legal rights, prepared citizens in Seneca Falls for the women's rights convention. Meanwhile, in Waterloo, four miles west of Seneca Falls, a different kind of excitement prevailed at just the same time. The Junius Monthly Meeting of Friends, a member of the Farmington Quarterly Meeting and of the Genesee Yearly Meeting (Hicksite) had just been shaken to its core by disagreements with other members of the Yearly Meeting at their annual June conference. These Friends – Garrisonian abolitionists as well as Quakers – would form the core of another network, drawing people from outside Seneca Falls to the women's rights convention. Based on religious rather than political ties, this network, too, represented a split in traditional organizations. And, like the Free-Soil party, it emerged fully only in June 1848.

The Genesee Yearly Meeting of Friends, held at Farmington, in Ontario County, opened calmly enough, in spite of the heat. But tense disputes, left over from the year before, soon broke the Sabbath peace. On Sunday, June 11, the meeting house was filled to overflowing. Several speakers, "not very talented," as one observer commented, made the audience restive before Lucretia Mott rose and delivered an impressive sermon.

Angry accusations, left over from the year before, erupted during the next two days. Disagreements were acrimonious and fundamental. Partly they centered on slavery. Conservative Quakers objected to the antislavery activities of many of their fellow Friends. Especially they did not want to open Quaker meeting houses for public discussion of abolitionism. The experience of Frederick Douglass, Charles Lenox Remond, and Daniel Delaney in Mendon, New York, was typical. "The weather was cold and otherwise inclement," they reported in December 1847, "and our meeting was held in the school house – Friends meeting house having been closed against us on the ground that our views differed from theirs." The Massachusetts Anti-Slavery Society had argued in 1843 that the Society of Friends, "as a body, is false to its own standard of duty," and many Quaker abolitionists agreed.

Several influential Friends (including Isaac Hopper and Charles Marriott from New York Yearly Meeting, Joseph Dugdale from Green Plain, Ohio, and Griffith Cooper from Farmington Monthly Meeting) left the Society in the 1840s over questions of abolitionism and individual conscience. Such dramatic disownments and resignations helped make these issues the most important internal concerns among Friends generally in the 1840s.

Partly the disagreements involved the question of proper authority. Did essential authority reside within each individual person and then within each individual meeting? Or did the meeting of ministers and elders, along with quarterly and yearly meetings, have special power to determine the actions of local (i.e., monthly) meetings? This issue, like the question of abolitionism, had been festering for many years. The Michigan Quarterly Meeting, subsidiary to the Genesee Yearly Meeting, had discontinued its separate meeting of ministers and elders in 1843. In 1847, the Genesee Yearly Meeting laid down (i.e., severed ties with) the Michigan Quakers, in spite of the "preponderating voice" of "more than one half of the Meeting" in their favor.

For Genesee Yearly Meeting, both these questions came to a head in June 1848. In spite of repeated requests, clerks from both men's and women's meetings refused to read reports from the ostensibly disowned Michigan Quarterly Meeting. When the clerk of the men's meeting accepted reappointment, everyone understood that this was "equivalent to recording a separation of the Yearly Meeting." About two hundred Friends ("something towards half," according to one observer) walked out, unhappy with what they felt was a manipulative and unfair action.

With strong support from Quakers in Waterloo, Rochester, and Wayne County, these dissidents adjourned to a three-day conference of their own, held June 14–16. In *An Address to Friends of Genesee Yearly Meeting and Elsewhere*, they explained their action. "For a number of years past," they wrote:

> we have failed to realize that unity, the existence of which was indispens-
> able to enable us, as a body, to advance the great principles of righteous-
> ness embraced in some of the most needful reforms of this age....
> Evidence has been lamentably furnished, of the existence and growth
> among us of a spirit of proscription and intolerance. A Spirit which has
> been unwilling to concede to every equal brother and sister those rights
> which it claimed for itself – the rights of conscience, and action in con-
> formity to apprehended immediate Divine requiring.

Daniel Anthony, one of the few contemporaries to leave a detailed comment on the split, wrote to his daughter, Susan, that those who had left the "shriveled up nutshell" of the Genesee Yearly Meeting were those "who take the liberty of holding up to view the wickedness of War – Slavery – Intemperance – Hanging & c" and "who are of the opinion that each individual should have a right to even think as well as act for himself & in his own way to assist in rooling [sic] on the wheel of reform."

Daniel Anthony reported, a month after the meeting, that "in Rochester they have commenced a new Meeting under the dictation of neither Priest deacon nor Elder." We can assume that dissident Friends in the Waterloo area, affiliated with the Junius Monthly Meeting (after the original name of the township that once included Waterloo), did the same, for in Waterloo lived one of the main organizers of the walkout, a worthy Friend, Thomas McClintock.

Thomas McClintock had been a Quaker leader in Philadelphia in 1828 when the Quakers had split into two wings. Orthodox Friends emphasized such Christian ideas as the Trinity. Hicksite Friends, how-ever (named after the Quaker Elias Hicks), focused on the more tradi-tional Quaker belief in the inner light and its power to give continuing revelation. Thomas McClintock had been not only a biblical scholar of some renown and a founder of the Free-Produce Society, but also a Hicksite leader, and, by 1835, a Quaker minister.

The McClintock family (Thomas and Mary Ann and their four children) had come to Waterloo by canal in 1837. Thomas ran a drugstore on Main Street, where, in a business block constructed by his brother-in-law, Richard P. Hunt, McClintock sold goods "free from the labor of slaves." Hunt also rented the family a comfortable brick house just behind the store.

In Waterloo, the McClintock family continued their religious and reform work. As Quakers and as abolitionists, they took leadership roles in their own meeting. Thomas acted as minister for the Junius Monthly Meeting. From 1839 to 1843, he was also clerk of the Genesee Yearly Meeting. Mary Ann was assistant clerk of the Women's Yearly Meeting. The whole family signed abolitionist petitions, helped organize antislavery fairs, and hosted antislavery lecturers.

When the split in the Genesee Yearly Meeting came in June 1848, Thomas was one of those who walked out. In the fall, this group would meet again. They would call themselves the Congregational Friends, and they would adopt a new form of organization. Men and women would meet together, not separately, as in traditional Quaker meetings. No person was to be subordinate to another. There were to be no ministers and no hierarchy of meetings. They were not to be tied to creeds or rituals, and they need not agree with one another on points of doctrine. They would focus instead on practical philanthropy, on "unity of heart and oneness of purpose in respect to the great practical duties of life." The document that outlined this new organization was called *The Basis of Religious Association,* and it was written, at least in part, by Thomas McClintock.

Lucretia Mott, ever in the forefront of Quaker developments, clearly sympathized with these egalitarian abolitionists. Separate meetings for ministers and elders were a major source of the problem, she believed. "After nearly thirty years' experience and observation of the results of this establishment [she noted in 1846], we have come to the conclusion that nearly all the divisions among us have their origin in these meetings." Mott was equally sure that cooperation with non-Quaker abolitionists was a legitimate part of the Quaker tradition. "Our Friends .... know full well," she asserted, "that such a position is neither contrary to our Discipline, to Scripture, ... nor to common sense." Finally, Mott linked these issues to the question of equality for men and women. She charged in 1846 that "the assumed authority of men's meetings, and the admitted subordination of women's is another cause of complaint."

In mid-July, these Friends would become the single largest group to sign the Seneca Falls Declaration of Sentiments. At least twenty-three signers were affiliated with this wing of Friends. Most of them (nineteen) came from Junius Monthly Meeting at Waterloo. One signer, Rhoda Palmer, remembered, in fact, that "every member" of that meeting attended the women's rights convention.

Just as the Free-Soilers of Seneca Falls had broken out of traditional political parties, so had the Waterloo Quakers broken away from their traditional religious affiliation. Both had split away over issues of equality. Both did so in dramatic and emotionally wrenching ways.

In late June and early July, both groups were in the process of self-definition. They had many questions: Who were their members? What did they believe? In particular, how far did they want to carry this idea of equality?

The Results of Local Agitation

At this critical juncture, in the midst of excitement caused by the Free-Soilers and the Congregational Friends, Lucretia Mott came with her sister, Martha Wright, to meet with Quaker women at the home of Jane and Richard Hunt. Elizabeth Cady Stanton was also invited. There, Stanton "poured out," as she remembered, "the torrent of my long-accumulating discontent, with such vehemence and indignation that I stirred myself, as well as the rest of the party, to do and dare anything." That evening, they wrote the call for a woman's rights convention and published it on Tuesday, July 11, in the *Seneca County Courier.* Area newspapers (the *North Star* and the *Ovid Bee,* for example) printed the call in their own editions on Friday, July 14.

Local people, concerned about women's legal rights, agitated about deep changes in their own institutional affiliations, and willing in this time of trial and transformation to expand their own boundaries, considered the purposes of the women's rights convention to be, as Stanton later remembered, "timely, rational and sacred." A core group of legal reformers, Free-Soilers, and Congregational Friends found the Declaration of Sentiments sensible, a logical extension of their own beliefs in ideals of liberty, equality, and independence.

But what about Elizabeth Cady Stanton? Can she still be called the convention's main organizer? Indeed she can. The convention would not have happened at all without her. Before the women's rights convention, Free-Soilers and advocates of legal reform in Seneca Falls had few identifiable contacts with the Congregational Friends of Waterloo and central New York. Stanton, however, knew leaders in all three movements. She knew Ansel Bascom, champion of legal reform. Among the

Free-Soilers, she could count as friends not only Jacob Chamberlain (president of the June 13 Free-Soil meeting and Stanton's neighbor), and Charles Hoskins (secretary of that meeting and fellow attender of the Episcopal Church), but also her own husband, Henry. Finally, Stanton gained credibility among the Quakers of Waterloo, first, by her long-standing friendship with Lucretia Mott and, second, by her introduction to the McClintocks, who wholeheartedly endorsed her convention plans. Stanton persuaded these leaders to come to the convention. They, in turn, would attract their followers. She would become what network theorists call a broker, bringing together three networks at a critical juncture in their own development.

Stanton willingly played this position, not because she wanted primarily to promote the Free-Soil party or Congregational Friends, nor even because she wanted to take up the challenge posed to women by passage of the Married Women's Property Act, to act on their own behalf. Instead, Stanton's most powerful motivation emerged from the stresses of her own personal life in 1848. The move to Seneca Falls, Henry's frequent absences, the lack of trained household help, and her family's sickness threatened to overwhelm her. Other women might have become depressed. Not Elizabeth Cady Stanton. Instead, she used her energy to enlist legal reformers, Free-Soilers, and Congregational Friends into a battle against social structures that oppressed women, rather than against individual oppressors.

People across the country reacted to the Seneca Falls convention. Many observers ridiculed the whole idea. The New York *Evening Post* squealed incredulously that the convention "had seriously resolved that all men and women are created equal!" Women's rights, said the *Mechanic's Advocate*, were "impracticable, uncalled for, and unnecessary," "a monstrous injury to all mankind," while *The Religious Recorder* of Syracuse simply dismissed it as "excessively silly."

A few, however, endorsed women's rights with enthusiasm. "Success to the cause in which they have enlisted," cheered O. C. W. in the Herkimer *Freeman*. "Railroad speed to the ends they would accomplish!" The Rochester *National Reformer* encouraged continued agitation. "To the ladies we say," wrote editor George W. Cooper, "act – agitate – bid high, you will not get, in this age, more than you demand."

It had been the genius of the convention's organizers, however, to couch their demands in terms of the Declaration of Independence. Americans found it difficult to repudiate the document upon which their nation had been founded. Many, therefore, would have agreed with Horace Greeley, the influential editor of the *New York Tribune*. Greeley, always logical, had to admit the justice of the cause, for when a sincere republican is asked to say in sober earnest, what adequate reason he can give for refusing the demand of women to an equal particip- ation with men in political rights, he must answer, None at all ... However unwise and mistaken the demand, it is but the assertion of a natural right, and as such must be conceded.

By using the language of the Declaration of Independence, the Seneca Falls Declaration of Sentiments reached deep into the culture and con- science of many Americans. Although it may have been a historical accident that Stanton found herself in Seneca Falls in 1848, she seized the moment of agitation over married women's property rights, of polit- ical turmoil among the Free-Soilers, and of religious divisions among the Quakers to turn her personal vision into what would become a major political movement.

Notes

1 Ellen DuBois, *Feminism and Suffrage: The Emergence of an Independent Women's Movement in America, 1848–1869* (Ithaca: Cornell University Press, 1978), p. 21.
2 Elizabeth Cady Stanton, *Eighty Years and More*, reprint (New York: Schocken Books, 1971), ch. 2.
3 Ibid., p. 82.
4 Geddes to Matilda Joslyn Gage, November 25, 1880, in Stanton, Anthony, and Gage (eds.) *History of Woman Suffrage* (New York: Fowler and Wells, 1881), I, p. 65.
5 Stanton and Gage, *History of Woman Suffrage*, pp. 51–2.
6 Theodore Stanton and Harriet Stanton Blatch (eds.) *Elizabeth Cady Stanton as Revealed in Her Letters, Diary and Reminiscences*, 2 vols. (New York: Harper & Bros., 1922), I, p. 149.

Documents

Introduction to the Documents

Judith Wellman's article traces the social networks that converged in the first women's rights convention at Seneca Falls in 1848. Document One, the Seneca Falls "Declaration of Sentiments," indicts "man" for his mistreatment of women and demands equality in the spheres of law, politics, religion, and economics. The parallel with the Declaration of Independence is clear, and Seneca Falls demonstrates how powerful Jefferson's language was for nineteenth-century groups claiming equal rights. Note also the depth of the criticism of male domination and the breadth of the demands in the resolutions.

Document Two, reminiscences of a rural woman inspired by Seneca Falls, demonstrates that for these women "the personal was political," to borrow a slogan of the women's liberation movement of the late twentieth century. Collins sees oppressions of private life, the demands of child care and housework and the danger of domestic violence, as reasons to organize for social change.

Frederick Douglass, the escaped slave who became the leading African-American public figure of his era, lived in nearby Rochester, New York and attended the Seneca Falls Convention. In his newspaper, *The North Star*, he strongly supported the Declaration of Sentiments. At the same time, he chastised more conservative abolitionists who had withdrawn from the American Anti-Slavery Society in opposition to women's equal participation in the movement.

The final extract, Document Four, is Elizabeth Cady Stanton's 1892 speech, "The Solitude of Self." Cady Stanton, the intellectual leader at Seneca Falls, remained the most profound thinker in the women's movement throughout the rest of her long life. She was open to new ideas and experiences, but this speech shows that her commitment to natural rights for women remained unaltered. This is an eloquent statement, but consider how different groups of women – immigrants, women of color, working-class women – might respond to her insistence on strictly individual rights and responsibilities. They might find cooperation and solidarity more important and more effective than the solitude she embraced.

Seneca Falls "Declaration of Sentiments"

Reprinted from Philip S. Foner (ed.) *We, the Other People* (Urbana: University of Illinois Press, 1976), pp. 78–83.

When, in the course of human events, it becomes necessary for one portion of the family of man to assume among the people of the earth a position different from that which they have hitherto occupied, but one to which the laws of nature and of nature's God entitle them, a decent respect to the opinions of mankind requires that they should declare the causes that impel them to such a course.

We hold these truths to be self-evident: that all men and women are created equal; that they are endowed by their Creator with certain inalienable rights; that among these are life, liberty, and the pursuit of happiness; that to secure these rights governments are instituted, deriving their just powers from the consent of the governed. Whenever any form of government becomes destructive of these ends, it is the right of those who suffer from it to refuse allegiance to it, and to insist upon the institution of a new government, laying its foundation on such principles, and organizing its powers in such form, as to them shall seem most likely to effect their safety and happiness. Prudence, indeed, will dictate that governments long established should not be changed for light and transient causes; and accordingly all experience hath shown that mankind are more disposed to suffer, while evils are sufferable, than to right themselves by abolishing the forms to which they were accustomed. But when a long train of abuses and usurpations, pursuing invariably the same object evinces a design to reduce them under absolute despotism, it is their duty to throw off such government, and to provide new guards for their future security. Such has been the patient sufferance of the women under this government, and such is now the necessity which constrains them to demand the equal station to which they are entitled.

The history of mankind is a history of repeated injuries and usurpations on the part of man toward woman, having in direct object the establishment of an absolute tyranny over her. To prove this, let facts be submitted to a candid world.

He has never permitted her to exercise her inalienable right to the elective franchise.

He has compelled her to submit to laws, in the formation of which she had no voice.

He has withheld from her rights which are given to the most ignorant and degraded men – both natives and foreigners.

Having deprived her of this first right of a citizen, the elective franchise, thereby leaving her without representation in the halls of legislation, he has oppressed her on all sides.

He has made her, if married, in the eye of the law, civilly dead.

He has taken from her all right in property, even to the wages she earns.

He has made her, morally, an irresponsible being, as she can commit many crimes with impunity, provided they be done in the presence of her husband. In the covenant of marriage, she is compelled to promise obedience to her husband, he becoming, to all intents and purposes, her master – the law giving him power to deprive her of her liberty, and to administer chastisement.

He has so framed the laws of divorce, as to what shall be the proper causes, and in case of separation, to whom the guardianship of the children shall be given, as to be wholly regardless of the happiness of women – the law, in all cases, going upon a false supposition of the supremacy of man, and giving all power into his hands.

After depriving her of all rights as a married woman, if single, and the owner of property, he has taxed her to support a government which recognizes her only when her property can be made profitable to it.

He has monopolized nearly all the profitable employments, and from those she is permitted to follow, she receives but a scanty remuneration. He closes against her all the avenues to wealth and distinction which he considers most honorable to himself. As a teacher of theology, medicine, or law, she is not known.

He has denied her the facilities for obtaining a thorough education, all colleges being closed against her.

He allows her in Church, as well as State, but a subordinate position, claiming Apostolic authority for her exclusion from the ministry, and, with some exceptions, from any public participation in the affairs of the Church.

He has created a false public sentiment by giving to the world a different code of morals for men and women, by which moral delinquencies which exclude women from society, are not only tolerated, but deemed of little account in man.

He has usurped the prerogative of Jehovah himself, claiming it as his right to assign for her a sphere of action, when that belongs to her conscience and to her God.

He has endeavored, in every way that he could, to destroy her confidence in her own powers, to lessen her self-respect, and to make her willing to lead a dependent and abject life.

Now, in view of this entire disfranchisement of one-half the people of this country, their social and religious degradation – in view of the unjust laws above mentioned, and because women do feel themselves aggrieved, oppressed, and fraudulently deprived of their most sacred rights, we insist that they have immediate admission to all the rights and privileges which belong to them as citizens of the United States.

In entering upon the great work before us, we anticipate no small amount of misconception, misrepresentation, and ridicule; but we shall use every instrumentality within our power to effect our object. We shall employ agents, circulate tracts, petition the State and National legislatures, and endeavor to enlist the pulpit and the press in our behalf. We hope this Convention will be followed by a series of Conventions embracing every part of the country.

Resolutions

Whereas, The great precept of nature is conceded to be, that "man shall pursue his own true and substantial happiness." Blackstone in his Commentaries remarks, that this law of Nature being coeval with mankind, and dictated by God himself, is of course superior in obligation to any other. It is binding over all the globe, in all countries and at all times; no human laws are of any validity if contrary to this, and such of them as are valid, derive all their force, and all their validity, and all their authority, mediately and immediately, from this original; therefore,

Resolved, That such laws as conflict, in any way, with the true and substantial happiness of woman, are contrary to the great precept of nature and of no validity, for this is "superior in obligation to any other."

Resolved, That all laws which prevent woman from occupying such a station in society as her conscience shall dictate, or which place her in a position inferior to that of man, are contrary to the great precept of nature, and therefore of no force or authority.

Resolved, That woman is man's equal – was intended to be so by the Creator, and the highest good of the race demands that she should be recognized as such.

Resolved, That the women of this country ought to be enlightened in regard to the laws under which they live, that they may no longer publish their degradation by declaring themselves satisfied with their present position, nor their ignorance, by asserting that they have all the rights they want.

Resolved, That inasmuch as man, while claiming for himself intellectual superiority, does accord to woman moral superiority, it is preeminently his duty to encourage her to speak and teach, as she has an opportunity, in all religious assemblies.

Resolved, That the same amount of virtue, delicacy, and refinement of behavior that is required of woman in the social state, should also be required of man, and the same transgressions should be visited with equal severity on both man and woman.

Resolved, That the objection of indelicacy and impropriety, which is so often brought against woman when she addresses a public audience, comes with a very ill-grace from those who encourage, by their attendance, her appearance on the stage, in the concert, or in feats of the circus.

Resolved, That woman has too long rested satisfied in the circumscribed limits which corrupt customs and a perverted application of the Scriptures have marked out for her, and that it is time she should move in the enlarged sphere which her great Creator has assigned her.

Resolved, That it is the duty of the women of this country to secure to themselves their sacred right to the elective franchise.

Resolved, That the equality of human rights results necessarily from the fact of the identity of the race in capabilities and responsibilities.

Resolved, therefore, That, being invested by the Creator with the same capabilities, and the same consciousness of responsibility for their exercise, it is demonstrably the right and duty of woman, equally with man, to promote every righteous cause by every righteous means; and especially in regard to the great subjects of morals and religion, it is self-evidently her right to participate with her brother in teaching them, both in private and in public, by writing and by speaking, by any instrumentalities proper to be used, and in any assemblies proper to be held; and this being a self-evident truth growing out of the divinely implanted principles of human nature, any custom or authority adverse to it, whether modern or wearing the hoary sanction of antiquity, is to be regarded as a self-evident falsehood, and at war with mankind.

Emily Collins, "Reminiscences"

Reprinted from Elizabeth Cady Stanton, Susan B. Anthony, and Matilda Joslyn Gage (eds.) *History of Woman Suffrage,* vol. 1, 2nd. ed. (Rochester, NY: Charles Mann, 1889), pp. 88–92.

I was born and lived almost forty years in South Bristol, Ontario County – one of the most secluded spots in Western New York; but from the earliest dawn of reason I pined for that freedom of thought and action that was then denied to all womankind. I revolted in spirit against the customs of society and the laws of the State that crushed my aspirations and debarred me from the pursuit of almost every object worthy of an intelligent, rational mind. But not until that meeting at Seneca Falls in 1848, of the pioneers in the cause, gave this feeling of unrest form and voice, did I take action. Then I summoned a few women in our neighborhood together and formed an Equal Suffrage Society, and sent petitions to our Legislature; but our efforts were little known beyond our circle, as we were in communication with no person or newspaper. Yet there was enough of wrong in our narrow horizon to rouse some thought in the minds of all.

In those early days a husband's supremacy was often enforced in the rural districts by corporeal chastisement, and it was considered by most people as quite right and proper – as much so as the correction of refractory children in like manner. I remember in my own neighborhood a man who was a Methodist class-leader and exhorter, and one who was esteemed a worthy citizen, who, every few weeks, gave his wife a beating with his horsewhip. He said it was necessary, in order to keep her in subjection, and because she scolded so much. Now this wife, surrounded by six or seven little children, whom she must wash, dress, feed, and attend to day and night, was obliged to spin and weave cloth for all the garments of the family. She had to milk the cows, make butter and cheese, do all the cooking, washing, making, and mending for the family, and, with the pains of maternity forced upon her every eighteen months, was whipped by her pious husband, "because she scolded." And pray, why should he not have chastised her? The laws made it his privilege – and the Bible, as interpreted, made it his duty. It is true, women repined at their hard lot; but it was thought to be fixed by a divine decree, for "The man shall rule over thee," and "Wives, be subject to your husbands," and "Wives, submit yourselves unto your husbands as unto the Lord," caused them to consider their fate inevitable, and to feel that it would be contravening God's law to resist it. It is ever thus; where Theology enchains the soul, the Tyrant enslaves the body. But can any one, who has any knowledge of the laws that govern our being – of heredity and pre-natal influences – be astonished that our jails and prisons are filled with criminals, and our hospitals with sickly specimens of humanity? As long as the mothers of the race are subject to such unhappy conditions, it can never be materially improved. Men exhibit some common sense in breeding all animals except those of their own species.

All through the Anti-Slavery struggle, every word of denunciation of the wrongs of the Southern slave, was, I felt, equally applicable to the wrongs of my own sex. Every argument for the emancipation of the colored man, was equally one for that of woman; and I was surprised that all Abolitionists did not see the similarity in the condition of the two classes. I read, with intense interest, everything that indicated an awakening of public or private thought to the idea that woman did not occupy her rightful position in the organization of society; and, when I read the lectures of Ernestine L. Rose and the writings of Margaret Fuller, and found that other women entertained the same thoughts that had been seething in my own brain, and realized that I stood not alone, how my heart bounded with joy! . . .

But, it was the proceedings of the Convention, in 1848, at Seneca Falls, that first gave a direction to the efforts of the many women, who began to feel the degradation of their subject condition, and its baneful effects upon the human race. They then saw the necessity for associated action, in order to obtain the elective franchise, the only key that would unlock the doors of their prison...

Our Society was composed of some fifteen or twenty ladies, and we met once in two weeks, in each other's parlors, alternately, for discussion and interchange of ideas. I was chosen President; Mrs. Sophia Allen, Vice-President; Mrs. Horace Pennell, Treasurer; and one of several young ladies who were members was Secretary. Horace Pennell, Esq., and his wife were two of our most earnest helpers. We drafted a petition to the Legislature to grant women the right of suffrage, and obtained the names of sixty-two of the most intelligent people, male and female, in our own and adjoining towns, and sent it to our Representative in Albany. It was received by the Legislature as something absurdly ridiculous, and laid upon the table. We introduced the question into the Debating Clubs, that were in those days such popular institutions in the rural districts, and in every way sought to agitate the subject. . . .

Frederick Douglass, "The Rights of Women"

Reprinted from Elizabeth Cady Stanton, Susan B. Anthony, and Matilda Joslyn Gage (eds.) *History of Woman Suffrage*, vol. 1, 2nd ed. (Rochester, NY: Charles Mann, 1889), pp. 74–5.

One of the most interesting events of the past week, was the holding of what is technically styled a Woman's Rights Convention at Seneca Falls. The speaking, addresses, and resolutions of this extraordinary meeting were almost wholly conducted by women; and although they evidently felt themselves in a novel position, it is but simple justice to say that their whole proceedings were characterized by marked ability and dignity. No one present, we think, however much he might be disposed to differ from the views advanced by the leading speakers on that occasion, will fail to give them credit for brilliant talents and excellent dispositions. In this meeting, as in other deliberative assemblies, there were frequent differences of opinion and animated discussion; but in no case was there the slightest absence of good feeling and decorum. Several interesting documents setting forth the rights as well as grievances of women were read. Among these was a Declaration of Sentiments, to be regarded as the basis of a grand movement for attaining the civil, social, political, and religious rights of women. We should not do justice to our own convictions, or to the excellent persons connected with this infant movement, if we did not in this connection offer a few remarks on the general subject which the Convention met to consider and the objects they seek to attain. In doing so, we are not insensible that the bare mention of this truly important subject in any other than terms of contemptuous ridicule and scornful disfavor, is likely to excite against us the fury of bigotry and the folly of prejudice. A discussion of the rights of animals would be regarded with far more complacency by many of what are called the *wise* and the *good* of our land, than would be a discussion of the rights of women. It is, in their estimation, to be guilty of evil thoughts, to think that woman is entitled to equal rights with man. Many who have at last made the discovery that the negroes have some rights as well as other members of the human family, have yet to be convinced that women are entitled to any. Eight years ago a number of persons of this description actually abandoned the anti-slavery cause, lest by giving their influence in that direction they might possibly be giving countenance to the dangerous heresy that woman, in respect to rights, stands on an equal footing with man. In the judgment of such persons the American slave system, with all its concomitant horrors, is less to be deplored than this *wicked* idea. It is perhaps needless to say, that we cherish little sympathy for such sentiments or respect for such prejudices. Standing as we do upon the watch-tower of human freedom, we can not be deterred from an expression of our approbation of any movement, however humble, to improve and elevate the character of any members of the human family. While it is impossible for us to go into this subject at length, and dispose of the various objections which are often urged against such a doctrine as that of female equality, we are free to say that in respect to political rights, we hold woman to be justly entitled to all we claim for man. We go farther, and express our conviction that all political rights which it is expedient for man to exercise, it is equally so for woman. All that distinguishes man as an intelligent and accountable being, is equally true of woman; and if that government only is just which governs by the free consent of the governed, there can be no reason in the world for denying to woman the exercise of the elective franchise, or a hand in making and administering the laws of the land. Our doctrine is that "right is of no sex." We therefore bid the women engaged in this movement our humble Godspeed.

Elizabeth Cady Stanton, "The Solitude of Self"

Excerpts from a speech originally delivered before the Committee of the Judiciary of the United States Congress, January 18, 1892, reprinted from Library of Congress American Memory Website, "Votes for Women" Collection, http://memory.loc.gov/ammem/naw/nawshome.html

The point I wish plainly to bring before you on this occasion is the individuality of each human soul; our Protestant idea, the right of individual conscience and judgment – our republican idea, individual citizenship. In discussing the rights of woman, we are to consider, first, what belongs to her as an individual, in a world of her own, the arbiter of her own destiny, an imaginary Robinson Crusoe with her woman Friday on a solitary island. Her rights under such circumstances are to use all her faculties for her own safety and happiness.

Secondly, if we consider her as a citizen, as a member of a great nation, she must have the same rights as all other members, according to the fundamental principles of our Government.

Thirdly, viewed as a woman, an equal factor in civilization, her rights and duties are still the same – individual happiness and development.

Fourthly, it is only the incidental relations of life, such as mother, wife, sister, daughter, that may involve some special duties and training.... In discussing the sphere of man we do not decide his rights as an individual, as a citizen, as a man by his duties as a father, a husband, a brother, or a son, relations some of which he may never fill. Moreover he would be better fitted for these very relations and whatever special work he might choose to do to earn his bread by the complete development of all his faculties as an individual.

Just so with woman. The education that will fit her to discharge the duties in the largest sphere of human usefulness will best fit her for whatever special work she may be compelled to do.

The isolation of every human soul and the necessity of self-dependence must give each individual the right, to choose his own surroundings.

The strongest reason for giving woman all the opportunities for higher education, for the full development of her faculties, forces of mind and body; for giving her the most enlarged freedom of thought and action; a complete emancipation from all forms of bondage, of custom, dependence, superstition; from all the crippling influences of fear, is the solitude and personal responsibility of her own individual life. The strongest reason why we ask for woman a voice in the government under which she lives; in the religion she is asked to believe; equality in social life, where she is the chief factor; a place in the trades and professions, where she may earn her bread, is because of her birthright to self-sovereignty; because, as an individual, she must rely on herself. No matter how much women prefer to lean, to be protected and supported, nor how much men desire to have them do so, they must make the voyage of life alone, and for safety in an emergency they must know something of the laws of navigation. To guide our own craft, we must be captain, pilot, engineer; with chart and compass to stand at the wheel; to match the wind and waves and know when to take in the sail, and to read the signs in the firmament over all. It matters not whether the solitary voyager is man or woman.

Nature having endowed them equally, leaves them to their own skill and judgment in the hour of danger, and, if not equal to the occasion, alike they perish.

To appreciate the importance of fitting every human soul for independent action, think for a moment of the immeasurable solitude of self. We come into the world alone, unlike all who have gone before us; we leave it alone under circumstances peculiar to ourselves. No mortal ever has been, no mortal ever will be like the soul just launched on the sea of life. There can never again be just such environments as make up the infancy, youth and manhood of this one. Nature never repeats herself, and the possibilities of one human soul will never be found in another. No one has ever found two blades of ribbon grass alike, and no one will never find two human beings alike. Seeing, then, what must be the infinite diversity in human character, we can in a measure appreciate the loss to a nation when any large class of the people is uneducated and unrepresented in the government. We ask for the complete development of every individual, first, for his own benefit and happiness. In fitting out an army we give each soldier his own knapsack, arms, powder, his blanket, cup, knife, fork and spoon. We provide alike for all their individual necessities, then each man bears his own burden.

Again we ask complete individual development for the general good; for the consensus of the competent on the whole round of human interest; on all questions of national life, and here each man must bear his share of the general burden. It is sad to see how soon friendless children are left to bear their own burdens before they can analyze their feelings; before they can even tell their joys and sorrows, they are thrown on their own resources. The great lesson that nature seems to teach us at all ages is self-dependence, self-protection, self-support...

In youth our most bitter disappointments, our brightest hopes and ambitions are known only to ourselves, even our friendship and love we never fully share with another; there is something of every passion in every situation we conceal. Even so in our triumphs and our defeats.

The successful candidate for Presidency and his opponent each have a solitude peculiarly his own, and good form forbids either [to] speak of his pleasure or regret. The solitude of the king on his throne and the prisoner in his cell differs in character and degree, but it is solitude nevertheless.

We ask no sympathy from others in the anxiety and agony of a broken friendship or shattered love. When death sunders our nearest ties, alone we sit in the shadows of our affliction. Alike mid the greatest triumphs and darkest tragedies of life we walk alone. On the divine heights of human attainments, eulogized and worshiped as a hero or saint, we stand alone. In ignorance, poverty, and vice, as a pauper or criminal, alone we starve or steal; alone we suffer the sneers and rebuffs of our fellows; alone we are hunted and hounded thro dark courts and alleys, in by-ways and highways; alone we stand in the judgment seat; alone in the prison cell we lament our crimes and misfortunes; alone we expiate them on the gallows. In hours like these we realize the awful solitude of individual life, its pains, its penalties, its responsibilities; hours in which the youngest and most helpless are thrown on their own resources for guidance and consolation. Seeing then that life must ever be a march and a battle, that each soldier must be equipped for his own protection, it is the height of cruelty to rob the individual of a single natural right.

To throw obstacle in the way of a complete education is like putting out the eyes; to deny the rights of property, like cutting off the hands. To deny political equality is to rob the ostracized of all self-respect; of credit in the market place; of recompense in the world of work; of a voice among those who make and administer the law; a choice in the jury before whom they are tried, and in the judge who decides their punishment....

An uneducated woman, trained to dependence, with no resources in herself must make a failure of any position in life. But society says women do not need a knowledge of the world, the liberal training that experience in public life must give, all the advantages of collegiate education; but when for the lack of all this, the woman's happiness is wrecked, alone she bears her humiliation; and the solitude of the weak and the ignorant is indeed pitiable. In the wild chase for the prizes of life they are ground to powder.

In age, when the pleasures of youth are passed, children grown up, married and gone, the hurry and hustle of life in a measure over, when the hands are weary of active service, when the old armchair and the fireside are the chosen resorts, then men and women alike must fall back on their own resources. If they cannot find companionship in books, if they have no interest in the vital questions of the hour, no interest in watching the consummation of reforms, with which they might have been identified, they soon pass into their dotage. The more fully the faculties of the mind are developed and kept in use, the longer the period of vigor and active interest in all around us continues. If from a lifelong participation in public affairs a woman feels responsible for the laws regulating our system of education, the discipline of our jails and prisons, the sanitary conditions of our private homes, public buildings, and thoroughfares, an interest in commerce, finance, our foreign relations, in any or all of these questions, her solitude will at least be respectable, and she will not be driven to gossip or scandal for entertainment.

The chief reason for opening to every soul the doors to the whole round of human duties and pleasures is the individual development thus attained, the resources thus provided under all circumstances to mitigate the solitude that at times must come to everyone. . . .

Nothing strengthens the judgment and quickens the conscience like individual responsibility. Nothing adds such dignity to character as the recognition of one's self-sovereignty; the right to an equal place, everywhere conceded; a place earned by personal merit, not an artificial attainment, by inheritance, wealth, family, and position. Seeing, then that the responsibilities of life rest equally on man and woman, that their destiny is the same, they need the same preparation for time and eternity. The talk of sheltering woman from the fierce storms of life is the sheerest mockery, for they beat on her from every point of the compass, just as they do on man, and with more fatal results, for he has been trained to protect himself, to resist, to conquer. Such are the facts in human experience, the responsibilities of individual. Rich and poor, intelligent and ignorant, wise and foolish, virtuous and vicious, man and woman, it is ever the same, each soul must depend wholly on itself.

Whatever the theories may be of woman's dependence on man, in the supreme moments of her life he can not bear her burdens. Alone she goes to the gates of death to give life to every man that is born into the world. No one can share her fears, no one mitigate her pangs; and if her sorrow is greater than she can bear, alone she passes beyond the gates into the vast unknown. . . .

We see reason sufficient in the outer conditions of human being for individual liberty and development, but when we consider the self dependence of every human soul we see the need of courage, judgment, and the exercise of every faculty of mind and body, strengthened and developed by use, in woman as well as man.

Whatever may be said of man's protecting power in ordinary conditions, mid all the terrible disasters by land and sea, in the supreme moments of danger, alone, woman must ever meet the horrors of the situation; the Angel of Death even makes no royal pathway for her. Man's love and sympathy enter only into the sunshine of our lives. In that solemn solitude of self, that links us with the immeasurable and the eternal, each soul lives alone forever. A recent writer says:

I remember once, in crossing the Atlantic, to have gone upon the deck of the ship at midnight, when a dense black cloud enveloped the sky, and the great deep was roaring madly under the lashes of demoniac winds. My feelings was not of danger or fear (which is a base surrender of the immortal soul), but of utter desolation and loneliness; a little speck of life shut in by a tremendous darkness. Again I remember to have climbed the slopes of the Swiss Alps, up beyond the point where vegetation ceases, and the stunted conifers no longer struggle against the unfeeling blasts. Around me lay a huge confusion of rocks, out of which the gigantic ice peaks shot into the measureless blue of the heavens, and again my only feeling was the awful solitude.

And yet, there is a solitude, which each and every one of us has always carried with him, more inaccessible than the ice-cold mountains, more profound than the midnight sea; the solitude of self. Our inner being, which we call ourself, no eye nor touch of man or angel has ever pierced. It is more hidden than the caves of the gnome; the sacred adytum of the oracle; the hidden chamber of eleusinian mystery, for to it only omniscience is permitted to enter.

Such is individual life. Who, I ask you, can take, dare take, on himself the rights, the duties, the responsibilities of another human soul?

Suggested Reading

Lois W. Banner, *Elizabeth Cady Stanton: A Radical for Women's Rights*, New York: Little, Brown, 1980. A brief, lively modern biography of the intellectual and activist leader of the Seneca Falls Convention and of the nineteenth-century women's movement.

Ellen Carol DuBois, *Feminism and Suffrage: The Emergence of an Independent Women's Movement in America 1848–1869*, Ithaca, NY and London: Cornell University Press, 1978. An influential work which demonstrates the radicalism of the demand for women's suffrage in the context of the times, as well as the complex challenges facing the movement.

Elisabeth Griffith, *In Her Own Right: The Life of Elizabeth Cady Stanton*, New York: Oxford University Press, 1984. Another modern treatment of Cady

Stanton's life, using psychological "social learning theory" to illuminate aspects of her personality.

Steven Mintz, *Moralists and Modernizers: America's Pre-Civil War Reformers*, Baltimore: Johns Hopkins University Press, 1995. A brief, up-to-date overview of the spectrum of reform activities in antebellum America.

Mary P. Ryan, *Women in Public: Between Banners and Ballots, 1825–1880*, Baltimore: Johns Hopkins University Press, 1990. Despite ideologies that held that women's sphere should be domestic and private, nineteenth-century American women did play important public roles, as Ryan indicates.

A website on the history of the women's suffrage movement contains several of the major documents relating to the Seneca Falls Convention. See

http://www.rochester.edu/SBA/history.html

(Note that URLs on the Web are often subject to change. This link was valid in August 2000.)

3

Violence and Manliness in the Struggle against Slavery

May 9, 1800   John Brown born in West Torrington, Connecticut.

1818   Frederick Douglass born a slave on the eastern shore of Maryland. He escapes to the North in 1838 and becomes a leading figure in the anti-slavery movement.

1776–1860   Although northern states enact measure for gradual emancipation, the slave population of the United States grows rapidly, from about half a million to over 4 million.

1831   William Lloyd Garrison begins publishing *The Liberator*, marking the rise of "immediatism" in the anti-slavery movement. Garrisonian abolitionists, who form the American Anti-Slavery Society (AASS) in 1833, insist that non-violent "moral suasion" is the only way to end slavery.

1840   AASS divides over questions of political action and women's rights.

1840s and 1850s   Growth of anti-slavery politics. By mid-1850s, the Republican Party has emerged as a major party. Although it is not abolitionist, it calls for an end to the spread of slavery and measures to limit the political power of slaveholders.

1850   A new Fugitive Slave Law leads to confrontations over slaveholders' attempts to capture escaped slaves in northern states.

1854–8   "Bleeding Kansas": Conflict over slavery in the territory leads to virtual civil war.

October 16, 1859   John Brown and associates launch raid on Harper's Ferry, Virginia government arsenal. Brown is captured, tried and, on December 2, 1859, hanged.

November 6, 1860   Abraham Lincoln, Illinois Republican, is elected President.

April 12, 1861   Southern forces fire on Fort Sumter, South Carolina. Civil War begins.

January 1, 1863   President Lincoln issues Emancipation Proclamation.

December 18, 1865   The Thirteenth Amendment to the United States Constitution outlaws slavery in the United States.

Introduction to the Article

On October 16, 1859, John Brown and twenty-one supporters (five of them black) launched a raid on the government arsenal at Harper's Ferry, Virginia. Brown, a white farmer and abolitionist, hoped to stimulate a broad uprising to overthrow American slavery. The strategy failed badly. The US Army and the Virginia militia quickly recaptured the arsenal and killed ten of Brown's men. Captured and awaiting execution, Brown cast himself in the role of heroic martyr for the cause and won the admiration of white and black foes of slavery. His execution on December 2, 1859 brought forth a wave of eulogies.

The response of free African Americans in the North to John Brown's raid and his execution tells us much about black opposition to slavery and strategies for resisting and overturning it. The struggle against slavery had been closely linked to nonviolence, either as a moral principle or a strategic necessity. The best-known white abolitionist, William Lloyd Garrison, and his followers, had long contended that only "moral suasion" could end slavery and urged an extreme pacifism, "nonresistance." Although white abolitionists agreed that blacks were human beings with equal moral capacity, entitled to equal rights, the doctrine of nonresistance seemed to suggest that slaves were not supposed to act on their consciences to resist oppression but to wait for the ethical awakening of white America. But black abolitionists had seldom rejected violent means of overthrowing slavery as immoral. By the 1850s, political polarization and increasingly aggressive assertions of the power of slave owners were causing even many white abolitionists to rethink the issue of resistance.

The response also teaches us about the nature of the racial stereotypes that African Americans faced from white America and their responses to those stereotypes. As historian Daniel Littlefield explains, white male Americans tended to equate blacks with females as intuitive and emotional, deficient in intellect, reasoning, and courage. Slaveholders used this to justify enslaving African Americans, but even some white abolitionists portrayed black virtues as essentially "female." Black responses to John Brown were designed not only to honor the man and his deeds but to uphold a "masculine" ideal of African Americans as forceful, determined, and brave.

As Littlefield shows, African Americans expressed warm admiration for Brown, but there were elements of the situation that were troubling. Brown himself had seemed to doubt black leadership capabilities – at least to lead in the directions he desired – and held some rather patronizing racial views. The raid itself had been a military fiasco. The first person the raiders killed was black, as was the first of the raiders to die. And only a few slaves rallied to join the uprising Brown had hoped to provoke. Thus, eulogies were mixed with questions and judgments. Over the years, John Brown and Harper's Ferry have held mixed meanings for African Americans.

This article reminds us of several key themes in the history of American radicalism. Ambivalence about the role of violence has characterized movements for social change in a society where defenders of the status quo have seldom hesitated to use it. Even in the movement to end slavery and establish racial equality in the United States, racism (or, as Littlefield suggests in this instance, racialism) divided participants and gave African Americans and whites differing perspectives. Perceptions of gender (e.g. that white men were the bearers of highly desirable "manly" traits) also influence the behavior and style of radical movements. The article also implicitly warns us not to treat oppressed groups solely as suffering victims, thus ignoring their role in making their own history. The fact that slaves did not respond in large numbers to John Brown was not evidence of their passivity or their contentment under slavery. The power and violence of the slave system erected formidable barriers to its own overthrow, barriers that were surmounted only through a massive Civil War in which African-American participation was crucial.

Blacks, John Brown, and a Theory of Manhood

Daniel C. Littlefield

"No event of a similar nature for many years had produced a more marked sensation," the *Weekly Anglo-African* reported concerning the December 2, 1859, response of Boston blacks to the execution of John Brown. "Most of the colored men closed their places of business, and many wore crape on their arms, rosettes in mourning, &c. It was also observed as a day of fasting, prayer and religious worship." The Twelfth Baptist Church on Southac Street had three services that day, in the morning, afternoon, and evening. Blacks in Pittsburgh, closing their businesses between ten and three, convened for worship at eleven o'clock at the African Methodist Episcopal Church. They met again that evening. The fiery and controversial Reverend Henry Highland Garnet, described by one newspaper as having done more than anyone else "to excite the colored people at the North," presided over services in New York's Shiloh Church. He decreed that henceforth "the Second day

Reprinted from Daniel C. Littlefield, "Blacks, John Brown, and a Theory of Manhood," in Paul Finkelman (ed.) *His Soul Goes Marching On: Responses to John Brown and the Harper's Ferry Raid* (Charlottesville and London: University of Virginia Press, 1995), pp. 67–97.

of December will be called 'MARTYR'S DAY,'" a suggestion other congregations embraced.

There were also public, interracial gatherings. An evening meeting at
Tremont Temple attracted hundreds and "was probably the largest
gathering of the kind ever held in Boston." Cleveland's Melodeon Hall
hosted its own commemoration, attracting an audience "considerably
checkered – alternate black and white, like the finger-board upon a
piano." And solemn congregations in Poughkeepsie's two black
churches did not prevent "a large number of colored persons" from
also attending a meeting at Concert Hall. Hartford, Connecticut,
sponsored no public ceremonies, though the dull, hazy morning
accurately captured the gloomy sentiments of most of the seven
hundred blacks there. A black man hired to drape City Hall's figure of
justice in mourning during the night was discovered and the black suit
removed.

John Brown's attack on Harpers Ferry galvanized the nation and
captured the particular imagination of blacks. Beyond its immediate
significance, however, this bold act capped nearly three decades of tensions between black and white abolitionists, and within the black community itself, about widely held views of race and slavery and about the
relationship between manhood and violence. If, as Merton Dillon
argues, abolitionists, who had once pictured blacks as "fierce, wronged
warriors about to break their bonds," transformed them in the years after
1830 into "pathetic, helpless victims" in need of white benevolence, it
was an image clearly at odds with the prospect of their assuming the
"manly" duties and obligations of citizenship.[1]

Brown's raid took place in a culture that equated boldness and heroic
violence with masculinity. It was a culture, moreover, that had a racial
bias. It claimed as racial traits the qualities of boldness, violence, and
masculinity, and the capacity for self-government necessary to citizenship. The Unitarian minister and militant abolitionist Theodore Parker
expressed this conceptual nexus in prideful speeches and sermons
throughout his career. The Anglo-Saxon, Parker wrote in 1854, was
noted for "his restless disposition to invade and conquer other lands;
his haughty contempt of humbler tribes which leads him to subvert,
enslave, kill, and exterminate; his fondness for material things, preferring
these to beauty; his love of personal liberty, yet coupled with most
profound respect for peaceful and established law; his inborn skill to
organize things to a mill, men to a company, a community, tribes to a
confederated state; and his slow, solemn, inflexible, industrious, and
unconquerable will." These characteristics were not all laudable but,
withal, he thought, Anglo-Saxons were "the best specimen of mankind . . . in the world."

In contrast, most white Americans, including abolitionists, viewed the black, in George M. Fredrickson's words, as an "inept creature who was a slave to his emotions, incapable of progressive development and self-government" and lacking "the white man's enterprise and intellect." The preeminence of emotion over intellect was not necessarily bad, however. Nineteenth-century romantic racialists believed that each of the various ethnicities, nationalities, or racial groups – they seldom distinguished among these concepts precisely – had its own peculiar gift to contribute to the human family: its own "genius" or national character. That of blacks was sensuality, sensitivity, gentleness, deep feeling, and an extraordinary capacity for forgiveness and long-suffering. "Even [in his] wild state," Parker assured the Massachusetts Anti-Slavery Society in 1858, the African was "not much addicted to revenge." This characterization, as Dillon suggests, was at odds with an earlier, eighteenth-century view of blacks as potentially violent savages, quick to take offense, and prone to pitiless retaliation. In some ways and places this view still abided in the nineteenth century, some-times dormant, lurking below the surface but liable to resurrection when it suited the needs or fears of slavery's supporters or opponents. Its survival created an underlying tension in the thinking of white people toward blacks (and, indeed, in attitudes of blacks about themselves), thereby complicating an already confused mix of ideas. But the prevail-ing conviction regarding black docility, ironically appropriated partly from proslavery literature in the service of antislavery, fit the require-ments of a romantic age that, in contrast to eighteenth-century ration-alism, elevated heart over head.

The attributes assigned to blacks were also applied to women, and blacks and women were thus equated. "In all the intellectual activities which take their strange quickening from the moral faculties – which we call instincts, intuitions," one booster commented, "the negro is super-ior to the white man – equal to the white woman. It is sometimes said – that the negro race is the feminine race of the world." Under the best of circumstances, some thought (Parker among them), blacks' essentially soft, feminine characteristics might counter the hard, masculine traits of Anglo-Saxons in America. In particular, blacks, like women, were con-sidered more susceptible to Christianity, a great virtue among reformers who based their appeal on Christian morality. But abolitionists were not consistent. While they argued that blacks and whites diverged in sens-ibilities, it was essential to their cause that they also portray blacks as no different from white people – in aims, aspirations, emotions, perhaps even capabilities – if they were to evoke among whites adequate sym-pathy for the plight of the slave. Thus, when a black abolitionist accused Parker of accepting the stereotype of the meek black, Parker responded with an expression of faith: he fondly hoped that blacks would rise and achieve "their freedom by the only method which the world thoroughly and heartily accepts, and that is, by drawing the sword and cleaving the oppressor from his crown to his groin, until one half falls to the right, and the other half falls to the left." "I have said many times," Parker concluded, "I thought the African would not be content to be a slave always; I wish he would not a single day more."

Because Brown's raid dealt with slavery, and involved African Americans as well as whites, it inevitably served as a lens through which whites and blacks alike would perceive black masculinity. It was, however, an imperfect lens: rather than clarify views of black manhood, the raid revealed fissures both in the ideology of race and masculinity and in alliances between black and white abolitionists. Indeed, the admiration some blacks had for Brown may well have masked, or mystified, the involvement of their own race in the raid and the availability of other models of black masculinity, ranging from romantic racialist ones of Jesus-like forbearance, at one extreme, to the vengeful image of Nat Turner at the other.

From the Atlantic to the Pacific, blacks held meetings in Brown's honor. They compared him to the great captains of history, like Oliver Cromwell, and to revolutionary patriots, like George Washington. For some who knew him he was an angel "entertained unawares"; for others he was a John the Baptist or a Jesus Christ; and for some he was a model without peer or precedent. When blacks compared him to men of the revolutionary generation, however, they often introduced a racial dimension. Brown stood out because the others fought for white men, while he, a white man, had fought for blacks.

The revolutionary comparison also introduced the issue of violence itself, for many abolitionists, white and black, were nonresistants – Christian anarchists and pacifists who believed any force, even that exercised by governments, to be immoral. One might argue that this ideological outlook was stronger among whites than among blacks. But for those who followed the most prominent white abolitionist of the age, William Lloyd Garrison – whose devotion to the cause blacks had little reason to doubt – it was an anchor of the philosophical platform that governed their activities, and the abolitionist movement was one of the few contexts in which blacks and whites could normally cooperate. Baptist minister and former fugitive J. Sella Martin therefore cautiously broached an opinion in Boston, Garrison's stronghold, and in Garrison's presence, that could have sparked controversy. Denying any senseless feeling of rage, he nevertheless declared that, with respect to Harpers Ferry, he was "prepared, in the light of all human history, to approve of the *means*" as "in the light of all Christian principle, to approve of the *end*." In his view, Fourth-of-July orators sanctioned both. Moreover, he found "an endorsement of John Brown's course in the large assembly" who had gathered to lament his execution. "I look at this question as a peace man. I say, in accordance with the principles of peace, that I do not believe the sword should be unsheathed, I do not believe the dagger should be drawn, until there is in the system to be assailed such terrible evidences of its corruption, that it becomes the *dernier resort*. And, my friends, we are not to blame the application of the instrument, we are to blame the disease itself. . . . So John Brown chose the least of two evils. To save the country, he went down to cut off the Virginia cancer." Applauded, Martin evoked no dispute. Garrison responded by distancing himself from some of Brown's sentiments and by arguing that Brown intended a peaceful mission to Virginia. He alluded perhaps to Brown's last speech before the court, in which Brown alleged that he had never intended insurrection or to arm slaves against their masters. He had intended, Brown said, merely to run slaves off to freedom in Canada as he had done in Kansas – a statement he later repudiated. Yet, Garrison concluded, "If a tax on tea justified revolution, did not the souls of men and women?" Garrison was a man of peace and a nonresistant; still, he was "emboldened to say success to every insurrection against slavery, here and elsewhere."

Ironically, the militant Henry Highland Garnet, whose 1843 call upon the slaves to rise had split the Colored Convention in Buffalo, New York (and, incidentally, had also influenced John Brown), adopted a more moderate tone at the Shiloh Church in 1859. He was "not a man of blood," held "human life to be sacred, and would spare even a man-stealer, if he stood not in the bondman's path to freedom." But his hope that slavery would end peacefully was "clouded," and he was full of praise for John Brown. Blacks in Providence, Rhode Island, resolved on similar praise.

Yet some expressed greater ambivalence. Albany's blacks admitted disagreement as to the wisdom of Brown's actions while lauding his intentions. In New Bedford, Massachusetts, one minister supported resolutions endorsing Brown but demurred from his "fanaticism." The following speaker, however, pointedly "ignored the idea that John Brown was a fanatic, and compared him with the martyrs, who in ancient times had laid down their lives for Christ's sake." But at Garnet's meeting in New York the disagreement was less subtle:

Rev. Wm. Goodell was introduced, and expressed himself encouraged by the signs of the times – lauded John Brown's zeal, but deprecated physical force. This exception called to his feet Rev. J. N. Gloucester, who eloquently endorsed Mr. Brown's course. Mr. Goodell replied, "Our weapons are not carnal – our means are moral, ecclesiastical and religious." Rev. Sampson White asked, "Why do we venerate the name of George Washington? In the struggle of release from what was termed English oppression, did the advocates of American liberty take the position, 'our weapons are not carnal'? Not at all – but 'Resistance to tyrants is obedience to God' was their motto. I have an arm – God has given me power, and whenever and wherever my God given rights are invaded, I shall feel it my duty to use it."

In grappling with the necessity of using violence to end slavery, blacks were going against two distinct strains of American political and social thought prominent among their allies and others: the Garrisonian idea that moral suasion alone was sufficient to bring slavery to its knees, making bloodshed not only objectionable but unnecessary; and the romantic, racialist notion that blacks by temperament and outlook were docile and unsuited to violent protest. Blacks were probably less inclined to accept the latter belief anyway, but they were attracted to the militant abolitionism of the 1830s because it furnished one of the few avenues through which their frustrations with American society could be channeled. It also provided a context within which they could cooperate with white supporters who believed that both slavery and black citizenship were moral issues on which the nation ought not to compromise.

But the alliance was not without conflict. In making slavery a moral issue, white abolitionists often adopted an idealism that made them less practical than their black counterparts. White abolitionists tended to be concerned with ethical concepts, whereas black abolitionists wanted concrete progress. Consequently, blacks were more willing to take pragmatic steps toward achieving their goals rather than (to mix a metaphor) insisting on the whole loaf or nothing. Some of the differences derived from divergent views of slavery and freedom. For whites, slavery and freedom were opposites to which they attached absolute value judgments: the one was bad; the other good. For blacks, however, slavery and freedom were relative concepts. Their American experience had conditioned them to perceive a continuum between the two: degrees of freedom and degrees of slavery. A favored slave might have a great deal of liberty within the institution of slavery, while, because of discrimination, most free blacks still suffered many of the ill effects of slavery even in freedom. Whites focused their attack on slavery; blacks desired an assault on prejudice and discrimination as well. In theory, white abolitionists agreed, but since prejudice and discrimination existed in their own ranks – sometimes recognized, sometimes not – they could not entirely see eye to eye with blacks. Many whites viewed abolition either as the culmination of their fight, thus ignoring slavery's complexities and underestimating its ramifications, or as part of a grander struggle for freedom, including temperance and gender discrimination, thereby deemphasizing its importance. "One group saw slavery too narrowly," Ronald G. Walters comments; "the other almost missed seeing it for looking too widely." More intimately involved with the institution, blacks had greater singleness of purpose, and they saw a connection between slavery and prejudice. Most blacks regarded abolition as only the beginning of struggle, so long as their social proscription continued. White abolitionists often seemed more worried about their own souls than about the slave, a luxury that black abolitionists could not afford. For whites slavery was an abstraction; for blacks it was a reality.

White abolitionists also tended toward arrogance and paternalism. They told blacks to adopt the puritan ethic, to work hard, to be industrious and accumulate property, but then condemned black attempts to reap the rewards of hard work. Any concern that blacks had for material well-being white abolitionists criticized as cheap, tawdry, and self-seeking. Thus, for example, when white abolitionist Sarah Grimké visited black abolitionist Samuel Cornish, who had a respectable middle-class home, she condemned it as "like the abode of sanctimonious pride and pharisaical aristocracy." Another white abolitionist who visited Cornish came away with the same opinion. These and other incidents revealed the extent to which many white abolitionists objectified blacks, rather than treating them as ordinary human beings with interests similar to those of white people. Increasingly, therefore, blacks began to form their own separate institutions or organizations to deal with issues that peculiarly affected them. Indeed, anticipating the course of black militants in the late 1960s, Cornish suggested that whites work within the abolitionist movement to abolish slavery while blacks worked in their own societies to end discrimination. Blacks sought to secure economic opportunity, promote social mobility, acquire the franchise, and ensure civil rights, as well as to establish black identity. They rejected white abolitionists' condemnation of independent black activity as racist, although the issue caused dissension among blacks, too.

Black separatism, of course, did not necessarily mean lack of respect for white efforts. Blacks' perspectives embraced variant visions for black liberation, particularly if the stance was aggressive, and such stances were few and far between. Thus black intellectual John S. Rock announced: "The only events in the history of this country which I think deserve to be commemorated are the organization of the Anti-Slavery Society and the insurrections of Nat Turner and John Brown." Consequently, even when they disagreed with him, blacks endorsed Garrison and his brand of abolitionism. They applauded his condemnation of colonization. They supported his newspaper. Blacks in Philadelphia praised Garrison in 1851 for having "pointed out to us the hope of immediate and unconditional liberty." Likewise, blacks in Boston and New York held memorial services to eulogize white, antislavery editor Elijah P. Lovejoy after an antiabolitionist mob killed him in Alton, Illinois, in 1837. Blacks lauded white abolitionists who spoke before a Massachusetts legislative committee opposing slavery in the District of Columbia. And Samuel Cornish addressed delegates to a meeting of the American Anti-Slavery Society in 1838 as "wise men of the nation . . . great and good men . . . the salt of the earth, the leaven which preserves our nation, morally and politically, and which will wipe off America's reproach and eventually be America's glory."

But blacks were caught between conflicting loyalties when, in the 1840s, white abolitionists split among themselves. Garrison and his supporters wanted radical reforms that went well beyond the simple abolition of slavery: they desired fundamental changes in society and government. They rejected political action, disdained organized religion, and sought to depend solely on moral suasion to bring about a series of interrelated reforms, including temperance and women's rights. Garrison's opponents, centering around the wealthy Tappan brothers (Arthur and Lewis) of New York, were more conservative. They adopted a more pragmatic approach, fearing that agitation for women's rights and other such issues would deflect the movement from its primary goal. They also made use of established religious organizations and the existing political system. The dispute was as much about factional influence as about strategic ordering or fidelity to principle, however, each side accusing the other of similar misdeeds.

As conflict between the two factions became more vicious, blacks increasingly saw the arguments as needlessly splitting the group on which they had placed their best hopes. In their view, the dispute was beside the point. As John Lewis, of New Hampshire, wrote his local Garrisonian society in 1840, "As a colored man, and a representative of my people, I feel it a duty to make the advocacy of the [antislavery] cause the paramount question." He indicated that he would no longer attend meetings to debate divisive issues, though he would still be available for antislavery lectures. But Garrisonians, failing to recognize the point, criticized him as hungry for publicity.

In the 1840s, then, many blacks adopted a more militant and separatist bent; and the Fugitive Slave Act and Dred Scott Decision of the 1850s – the one facilitating slave recapture and the other declaring that blacks were not United States citizens – caused despair and disillusionment among even the most optimistic. Despite their general regard for Garrison, many deserted his standard. Several went so far as to consider emigration – for reasons other than the legislative compromise that caused many fugitives to flee the threat of reenslavement. Legislation passed during the 1850s reinforced the perception of many of the need for a distinct black nationality. Even Frederick Douglass, who stood against the tide of radicalism in the 1840s, broke with Garrison at the end of the decade. A staunch integrationist, Douglass himself flirted ever so briefly with emigration in 1861. The mood of impatience among blacks was something that John Brown perceived. After all, he had black friends and associates, and he read and contributed to black newspapers.

Oswald Garrison Villard, grandson of the abolitionist and Brown's first serious biographer, argued that Brown "was by nature unable to sympathize with the Garrisonian doctrine of non-resistance to force" and by the 1850s was "all impatience with men who only talked and would not shoot." Nor was Brown the only white man to be pushed toward action in the decade of conflict before the Civil War. The strife in Kansas during the middle of the decade caused restlessness even among some who retained a theoretical commitment to nonviolence. Political conditions drove romantic racialists among the "Secret Six" who supported Brown's activist stance to forsake their avowed devotion to pacificism. They were willing to test the efficacy of violence among blacks as a way to resolve their conflicting views to the effect that force was not a natural part of blacks' makeup but that they would not be worthy of citizenship without this capacity. Blacks themselves occasionally accepted elements of romantic racialist thought, a black correspondent referring to one of Brown's colored companions, for example, as "a fine looking dark mulatto, six feet high and well proportioned, with superb African features and a considerable admixture of European boldness and intellectuality." But they seldom took seriously these notions of their innate passivity. Nevertheless, they were equally anxious to prove themselves by heroic postures, and not merely verbal ones.

John Brown argued that America would respect the blacks' willingness to fight. Indeed, it might be the only way to prove their manhood or humanity. Moreover, there was a need to demonstrate that several aspects of romantic racialism were wrong. Blacks were neither docile innocents nor pliable dolts. Black activist Charles H. Langston interpreted Brown's raid in just that fashion: as a vindication of blacks' humanity. Brown went South to "put to death . . . those who steal men and sell them, and in whose hands stolen men are found." There was one problem with that argument, however. John Brown was a white man and, contrary to his expectations, blacks had not flocked to support him. J. Sella Martin, at pains to explain this black reluctance, found it in Brown's conservatism: he had been unwilling to follow the logic of his movement and shed sufficient blood, and he therefore "left slaves uncertain how to act." Condemned in the North as cowardly, slaves "were not cowards, but great diplomats. When they saw their masters in the possession of John Brown, in bonds like themselves, they would have been perfect fools had they demonstrated any willingness to join him. They have got sense enough to know, that until there is a perfect demonstration that the white man is their friend – a demonstration bathed in blood – it is all foolishness to co-operate with them." The black man's record in America's past wars was ample evidence of his capacity and willingness to fight, provided he had something for which to fight.

Yet almost a quarter of the raiders were black, and the ease with which the black presence at Harpers Ferry was often overlooked was a source of irritation, then and later. Henry Ward Beecher, two months after the event, and while John Brown still lived, had already written blacks out of the record. In a remarkable sermon at Plymouth Church, Brooklyn, on October 30 – a sermon later revised for publication and therefore the subject of some reflection – he charged the affair to seventeen white men who went South without blacks' asking and found among them an unwelcome reception. Nevertheless, they had terrified Virginia. "Seventeen white men surrounded two thousand, and held them in duress." For blacks, Beecher's emphasis was misplaced. It was the black men who accompanied John Brown, and the black men in their midst, who caused Virginians to quake. "Mr. Beecher must have read the papers," complained a black editorial, "must have read that there were twenty-two invaders, seventeen white and five black. Why does he omit all mention of the latter? Were they not men?"

In the view of many white people, of course, consistent with the implications of romantic racialism and also suggested by the arguments of John Brown, they were not. They had been too few and they had acted, if at all, under white direction. They could therefore be safely, or should be wisely, discounted. Beecher, along with most of the class he represented, including supporters of John Brown, had serious doubts about black character and capability. "It is the low animal condition of the African that enslaves him," Beecher reasoned; to gain their freedom blacks had to acquire "truth, honor, fidelity, manhood." But they were not ready yet:

> Now, if the Africans in our land were intelligent; if they understood themselves; if they had self-governing power; if they were able first to throw off the yoke of laws and constitutions, and afterwards to defend and build themselves up in a civil state; then they would have just the same right to assume their independence that any nation has.

But does any man believe that this is the case? Does any man believe that this vast horde of undisciplined Africans, if set free, would have cohesive power enough to organize themselves into a government, and maintain their independence? If there be men who believe this, I am not among them.

Consistent with his racial outlook, Beecher interpreted incidents of mental acuity, the yearning for liberty, and skillful flight from slavery to achieve it (which is to say, any evidence of manhood) as resulting from racial admixture. Consequently, had he acknowledged their presence at all, the fact that most of the blacks who accompanied John Brown had white genes would scarcely have caused him to modify his general opinion about black incapacity.

Still, Beecher obviously respected action and, although they shifted the emphasis, so did many blacks. Some, however, rejected the notion that violent upheaval, especially in face of superior forces, was the best evidence of manhood. One black commentator wondered, for example, whether Henry Ward Beecher would have viewed Brown's course as so hopelessly misguided had it been directed in the cause of whites. Blacks deserved white support because they were human beings denied the common rights of man, whether they plotted against their masters or not. Humanity, the commentator thought, was indivisible, and the idea of separate criteria based on blood, color, class, or nationality was objectionable. Blacks need not vindicate their humanity by bloodshed. H. Ford Douglas even played on the romantic racialist stereotype. "If muscle is evidence of the highest manhood," he perorated, "you will find any of the 'short boys' of New York, any of the 'plug-uglies' and ugly plugs of Tammany Hall, better qualified to be President" than one of the current aspirants in 1860. Blacks exhibited the *highest* elements of manhood, Christian patience and long-suffering tolerance. For others, however, it was "high time, when white men fight and die for our rights, we should learn to act for ourselves."

The twin concerns about "discipline" and "cohesive power" that preoccupied Henry Beecher also engaged John Brown. In Brown's satirical "Sambo's Mistakes" – constructive criticism offered to blacks through one of their newspapers, the *Ram's Horn* in 1848 or 1849 – he complained, among other things, about their lack of unity, their unwillingness to resolve minor differences for the sake of concerted action. He also ridiculed their submissiveness and ability to suffer insults, finding therein no grace or virtue, no nobility – no manhood. He moved to correct these defects when he formed the United States League of Gileadites in Springfield, Massachusetts, in 1851. A self-defense organization, designed to help blacks protect themselves against slave catchers authorized by the Fugitive Slave Act, Brown began his "Words of Advice" for the group with the motto "Union is Strength." "Nothing so charms the American people," he declared, "as personal bravery." Moreover, in typical nineteenth-century fashion, he interpreted that quality in male terms. (Recalling Shirley Chisolm's comment in 1972, however, addressed to the Congressional Black Caucus of primarily male politicians, that she was the only one among them who had "balls" enough to run for president, it might be wrong to confine that attitude to the nineteenth century.) Harriet Tubman, one of the blacks who adhered to his cause and whose intrepidity Brown respected, Brown referred to as a male: "*He Hariet* is the most of a *man* naturally; that *I ever* met with.*" Until blacks were willing to stand up for their rights, though, they clearly deserved no respect – but he was ready to show them the way.

While blacks, including historians W. E. B. Du Bois and Benjamin Quarles, stressed Brown's belief in racial equality, his attention to "discipline" had some of the same racial content of Beecher's and at Harpers Ferry amounted to anxiety. This solicitude, argues historian Craig Simpson, explains his "mysterious indecisiveness" after he captured the arsenal. If he recalled advice at all, Brown might have been guided by that of black clergyman James N. Gloucester, who told him that "the colored people are *impulsive* . . . they need sagacity . . . to distinguish their proper course." Religious and self-righteous, Brown knew he had the proper wisdom. Simpson contends that Brown did not think a slave revolt could succeed without white leadership, that such an attitude is implicit in "Sambo's Mistakes" and "Words of Advice," and that it is supported by comments of his daughter Annie. Of course, Brown's reflections in "Sambo's Mistakes" merely echoed the self-criticism in black newspapers and other publications, with some of which at least he ought to have been familiar. (He subscribed to Frederick Douglass's paper, for example.) Whether he thought a similar statement from him would have more effect is moot. The case is stronger for "Words of Advice" because he assumed leadership in forming the Gileadites. Whether or not blacks needed *white* leadership (his study of the Haitian rebellion would not have supported *that* conclusion), they certainly needed leadership.

On various occasions Brown offered leadership positions to blacks, though they did not always accept. No blacks would accept the presidency of his provisional government formed at Chatham, Ontario, even though some were nominated. Osborne Anderson stated that Brown also offered command positions at Harpers Ferry to blacks, who declined for lack of experience. It is true, however, that Brown was somewhat distrustful and, while willing to have black leaders as figureheads, he wanted to exercise firm control. The reason was not so much that he doubted the success of a black revolution without white leadership, all else being equal. Rather, he feared the direction such a revolution might take. Brown acted out of a firm commitment to American political values and Christian morality. The first caused him to view the Chatham document not as a rejection of the American political system but as its purification. He did not see himself as committing treason: he maintained a firm devotion to the flag, the government, and a particular historical tradition of the United States. He merely wanted to purge American society of slavery – an ill inconsistent with what he considered the country's highest ideals. Consequently, he rejected an attempt of Chatham delegates to remove Article 46 of the provisional constitution, which reaffirmed his allegiance to the American flag. He could not participate on any other grounds. Furthermore, he dismissed with disdain a suggestion that the conspirators wait until the country was involved in a foreign war before they acted. The Stars and Stripes had served patriots in their struggle to win freedom for white men; he intended the same standard to "do duty" for blacks.

But black objections to service under the American flag could only fan Brown's suspicions of black autonomy and emphasize his perception of the need for rigid direction. Opposition rapidly collapsed when he threatened to wash his hands of the whole project. His leadership style of coercive, psychological manipulation basically had nothing to do with racial considerations, for he used the same ploy at the Kennedy farm in Maryland when the raiders objected to his plan to seize the federal arsenal. Still, the short disjuncture at Chatham indicated divergent viewpoints between blacks and Brown and thus underlines the degree to which his thinking and theirs did not totally coincide. Some Canadian blacks, for example, had begun to feel that they should regard themselves as British subjects rather than American refugees, and while they maintained a commitment to the slave, they did not necessarily desire the same tie to the government they had fled. Blacks in the United States were equally disenchanted with their national government, particularly after the Dred Scott Decision robbed them of citizenship, and some felt absolved of allegiance. But Brown intended to impose, not convoke, a consensus. Changed conditions might change outlooks, as the Civil War revealed. Nevertheless, it is notable that Brown's proposals did not cause Martin Delany, a participant at the convention, to forsake his emigrationism. Blacks had their agendas; Brown had his own.

In terms of Brown's commitment to Christian morality, his daughter Annie's comments regarding his attitude toward blacks are instructive: "He expected . . . that if they had intelligent white leaders that they would be prevailed on to rise and secure their freedom without revenging their wrongs, and with very little bloodshed." Brown could not have studied Haiti without being aware of the terrible atrocities there, which he obviously wanted to avoid. The reaction to his Kansas massacre may have reaffirmed his intention. In short, he was caught on the horns of a dilemma between his belief that blacks ought to demonstrate their manhood by physical resistance and his fears about the possible consequences of their passions unleashed. He was not sure he could control them. Thus his plea to Frederick Douglass: "I want you for a special purpose. When I strike, the bees will begin to swarm, and I shall want you to help hive them."

In view of his indecision at the Ferry, it is doubtful he would have known what to do had large numbers of slaves come forward. It would have taken a Frederick Douglass or a Harriet Tubman to take control: both would have recognized the need for either a bloody, violent action to galvanize the slaves, or swift, elusive action to encourage them. Brown would do neither, though, in addition to which many blacks already disapproved of his plan. Douglass did not think it was workable, and Tubman, reputedly sick, may not have thought so either, as it ultimately developed. She is said to have been recruiting support for the raid while Brown was in Maryland making final preparations; she assumed the plan was to run off slaves and did not know of his final dispositions. It is difficult to imagine her sitting waiting to be surrounded, even if she had agreed to take the arsenal in the first place. Henry Highland Garnet reportedly also opposed as much of the plan as he learned about. J. Sella Martin, speaking at a commemorative service in London in 1863, remarked that none of the blacks who had heard of the project had thought it a good one or likely to succeed, however much they appreciated Brown's willingness to sacrifice.

By comparison with Brown's self-sacrifice, blacks also felt lacking. A member of the Chatham convention who wrote to say that he would not come to Harpers Ferry indicated that he was disgusted with himself "and with the whole negro set, God damn em!" Douglass engaged in equal self-flagellation. Defending himself against a charge that he had broken a pledge to appear, he said that he had "not one word to say" in extenuation of his "character for courage." He had "always been more distinguished for running than fighting – and, tried by the Harper's Ferry insurrection test," was "miserably deficient in courage." But he had never promised to be there.

Blacks recognized that Brown was right in his assertion that Americans respected courage, even the foolhardy kind, and while blacks rejected, they could not avoid the connection made between forthright (to the point of physical) opposition to oppression and the perception of manhood or humanity. In the aftermath of the affair, therefore, some took pains to highlight black involvement. For historians this sometimes took the form of counterfactual arguments focusing on the failure of the raid to attract more blacks. Quarles and Du Bois both blamed this shortcoming (and Du Bois emphasized if he did not exaggerate the number of active black participants) on the raid's postponement in 1858. Adherents at Chatham were discouraged, and scattered to other interests. Quarles mentions, for example, that Martin Delany, a Chatham delegate in 1858, was away in Africa in 1859. But Delany appears never to have committed himself to the raid, and plans for his African trip were already well underway at the earlier date. These black historians also suggest, as Osborne Anderson reported, that even in 1859 Brown moved sooner than anticipated, before others who were expected could arrive.

But this suggests that a few more men would have made a significant difference. No one implies that he awaited hundreds; nor could hundreds have come undetected. It might be argued that even a few more men would have made a greater impression of strength and caused slaves to join him. But this does not appear likely. The townspeople already overestimated Brown's numbers, if they bothered to figure at all. Fearing a slave insurrection, they fled to the surrounding heights, seeming "not to notice a few of the very Negroes they dreaded cowering in their midst, as terrified as any of the whites." Or, it might be argued, with a larger force Brown would have been able to fight his way out of his entrapment. But he still would have needed to act more quickly than he was apparently inclined to do.

For many white people, Brown was simply insane, a consideration that easily explained his foibles. But blacks (and Brown himself) rejected that explanation out of hand. "The newspapers and able editors may talk as they will about the insanity of Capt. Brown," one black snorted, "but to us there is something sacred in the madness of this old man." J. Sella Martin agreed. "If he was mad," Martin declaimed, "his madness not only had a great deal of 'method' in it, but a great deal of philosophy and religion." Blacks (and whites, too, who rejected the insanity plea) were consequently at pains to find some rationale for his actions.

The initial attack, of course, went more or less according to plan. It was on the following day, however, in face of growing opposition and lagging support, that Brown refused to act, allowing himself to be surrounded and trapped. Black survivor Osborne Anderson said that Brown "appeared to be somewhat puzzled" and that his "tardiness" in leaving town as previously agreed "was sensibly felt to be an omen of evil by some of us" and led to the raiders' defeat. Historians have therefore focused on what Oates calls Brown's "mysterious" delay. Du Bois argued that Brown was not indecisive at the Ferry; rather, he was waiting the delivery of guns supposed to be brought by Charles P. Tidd, who dallied, which prevented a retreat into the mountains as originally planned to draw off slaves. Brown never expected to begin the foray with many blacks, knowing that he must first gain their confidence by a "successful stroke." The idea was that only after an initial success would blacks come in droves.

In Du Bois's demonology, the soldier of fortune Hugh Forbes figures in the 1858 failure; Charles Tidd in that of 1859. Quarles suggests that Brown tarried at the Ferry for expected reinforcements from the local populace: much antislavery sentiment existed in western Virginia, and Brown expected to gather slaves and antislavery whites to his standard. While he waited, however, he miscalculated the speed with which the militia reacted, disregarded advice from his subordinates about the need to depart, and finally could not extricate himself from the encirclement. But Simpson, while agreeing that Brown hoped to be joined by slaves and antislavery whites, argues that he proved nevertheless psychologically unable to act. This irresolution proceeded from a failure of nerve concerning the possible cost in blood of the type he had condoned at Pottawatomie if the slaves actually rose. Brown said when he took the town that if the citizens resisted he was prepared to burn the place and "have blood." But, actually facing the prospect, he quailed and spent more time trying to gain the understanding of his slaveholding prisoners than threatening to destroy them for their transgressions. In preference to sacrificing others, he ultimately preferred to sacrifice himself. This much blacks appreciated. An interest in the number of blacks involved, therefore, had much to do with the issue of sacrifice – in the commitment of blacks to their own freedom.

Anderson, the only black raider to survive, reported that "many colored men gathered to the scene of action" and that "a number were armed for the work" and fought at various locations. Frederick Douglass, who was not there, says fifty slaves collected. But historian Quarles, who has no reason to minimize black participation, confirms the presence of only twelve slaves, captured and taken to the armory by Brown. Du Bois, basing himself largely on Anderson, stated that about fifty people participated, of whom at least seventeen were black. It is not entirely clear whom he was counting, but presumably he meant fifty people in addition to the raiders. (He also said that between twenty-five and fifty slaves at the arsenal were armed.) If the twelve slaves taken to the armory are added to the five black raiders (Du Bois argued that six or seven of the raiders were black), that adds up to seventeen. Of the twelve slaves, however, only two seem to have made any voluntary contribution; the rest followed orders without apparent enthusiasm and deserted at the first opportunity. However many slaves there were, and however brave or timid, they were not stupid. They could count, and what they saw did not add up to victory. Contemporary Virginia whites, pleased at the poor black turnout, charged it either to prevailing goodwill and mutual affection between master and slave, to the ease with which restless slaves could abscond to freedom already, or, in the most racist explanation, to congenital black docility. Blacks were a "good-humored, good-for-nothing, half-monkey race," as one expressed it. They certainly could not be expected to fight.

When the dust had settled and all the available facts were out, what had happened at the Ferry was in some ways what blacks would have expected to happen, even if the events were adventitious. The first person killed by the raiders was black; the first person killed among the raiders was black. Hayward Shepard, a free black porter and baggage handler at the railroad station, was shot as he turned away when ordered to halt. It was dark and the raiders did not know his color. But the sniper who shot Dangerfield Newby the next day (with a six-inch spike rather than a ball or bullet) as he and two other raiders retreated from a bridge almost certainly did know his color, and his white companions were not hit. That is to say, he was targeted and they were not. Newby had come down simply to free his wife, whose master had broken a promise to sell her to him, and he carried her letter in his pocket. Instead, his body ended up brutalized, his ears were cut off as trophies, and his wife and family were sold farther south.

Blacks knew that they could not rise without forethought and careful planning, and Brown provided neither. Moreover, what ideas he had he was reluctant to share with those he expected to aid him. He disregarded the opinions of Northern blacks when they contradicted his own, and if he anticipated help from nonslaveholding whites he did not tell them so. Simpson argues, Du Bois assumes, and Anderson states that some slaves did know of Brown's plans, but they could not have known the details, for these were denied even the raiders until they gathered at the Kennedy farm – and they caused dissension when they were revealed. When the raid was carried out, few people, whether black or white, knew what to expect. Contemporary blacks therefore concentrated on the inadequacies of the plan and on the heroism of those blacks who did participate. "There has been a systematic attempt to underrate the bravery of the colored men who fought with Brown at Harper's Ferry," a Canadian black complained. Northern whites were blind to everyone except "Brown and seventeen [sic] white men." One black admirer went so far as to reverse the usual order of things and state that "black men fought at Harper's Ferry, and John Brown aided them." He did not intend to diminish the leading figure, however, for blacks were more than willing to give Brown his due.

Indeed, even among blacks the preoccupation with Brown was such that his colored companions were sometimes slighted. One observer noted that in the widespread proposals to succor Brown's family, the plight of his black followers was seldom mentioned, although, as he suggested, at least one, Lewis Leary, had a family in need. A black self-critic used comments similar to Brown's in "Sambo's Mistakes" to contrast unfavorably the frivolous young men "with gold chains, perfumed hair, and gloved hands, and young women with that upon their heads which is alike unbecoming to their complexions and unworthy of their adornment" as Christians with the devotion and dedication of John Brown. "Would to God we could find under the dark skin the heroic energy, the unselfish love, the glowing spirit of martyrdom that consumed that loving and unselfish spirit!" In fact, the quiet self-sacrifice of Shields Green equaled that of John Brown. After listening, in August 1859, to Brown and Frederick Douglass debate the issue of the proposed raid at Chambersburg, Pennsylvania, and in the face of Douglass's refusal to go along, Green decided to put aside his doubts and go with the "ole man." At the Ferry when, in the midst of an obvious disaster, he was offered the chance to escape, he again chose to stick with Brown.

These details were perhaps not common knowledge at the time, but blacks did attempt to publicize the fortitude and calm deportment of both Green and John Copeland as each met his death on the scaffold. Copeland's letters from jail, with their tone of brave resignation, equation of his own action with that of George Washington, pointed recollection of Crispus Attucks's death in the Boston Massacre, and earnest expression of confidence in the justice of his cause, were printed, as was his comment on the way to the gallows that he would rather die than be a slave. Neither he nor Green would speak at the trial, their silence standing in eloquent contrast to the self-serving statements made by their codefendants. Copeland impressed even the judge and prosecutor, the latter commenting that if it had been possible to recommend a pardon for anyone, he would have chosen Copeland. Ironically, Copeland's death was the most excruciating (he strangled slowly), and the ropes were lengthened thereafter. At least a few blacks resolved to set aside October 16, the first day of the raid, and December 16, the day Green and Copeland died, as well as December 2 (the date of John Brown's execution), as days of remembrance.

On short notice, three thousand people attended a funeral in Oberlin, Ohio, for John Copeland, although his body remained in Virginia to be dissected by medical students. At the same time, they began planning a monument to Green, Copeland, and Leary, the latter two, having lived in the area, being celebrated as townsmen. Because the three martyrs were "*representative men*, of whom every colored person in the land" had reason to be proud, the people of Oberlin were prepared to share the burden of fund-raising with others, and blacks in Boston and elsewhere took up the challenge. William C. Nell, for example, sought to respond to colored American interest in their racial kinsmen and simultaneously to help surviving relatives and the monument fund by publishing histories of the three who were to be honored. He did not complete the project but published at least one of a proposed series of newspaper "sub-sketches" – one on Shields Green that was particularly moving. Never a resident of Oberlin and originally included mistakenly by the monument committee, Green was retained because of his manly conduct. He was the first black recruited for the Ferry, and, Nell noted, "fully redeemed the characteristic pledge upon his business card [as a clothes cleaner in Rochester, N.Y.]: 'I make no promise that I am unable to perform.'" Fund-raising did not meet expectations and the scale of the memorial had to be reduced, but Oberlin did succeed in erecting one.

In 1881 Frederick Douglass, perhaps unaware of the cenotaph at Oberlin, or feeling it inadequate, or simply to make a point, suggested that if a statue were erected to John Brown, Shields Green should have a prominent place upon it. He meant thereby to honor the loyalty and courage of his old friend and to equate Green's deeds to Brown's. Eight years later, though, when Douglass's son proposed that blacks erect a monument to John Brown, he ran afoul of the militant, race-conscious editor T. Thomas Fortune, who thought that Nat Turner was more worthy of black men's pennies. Given that white men already had monuments to John Brown, in parchment if not stone, he was unlikely to be forgotten. Moreover, much as he respected John Brown, Fortune thought that blacks should honor blacks. A black editor had counterpoised Nat Turner to John Brown earlier (in 1859) when he offered their approaches as contrasting choices in the road to slavery's inevitable destruction: the bloody course of Turner or the relatively bloodless path of Brown.

The two editorials, separated by thirty years of varying circumstances, captured essential aspects of the conundrum Brown posed for blacks. A man of conviction who gave his life for a vision of freedom and equality, he had nevertheless ultimately subordinated the liberty of blacks to the lives of whites. "Had Captain Brown's sympathies not been aroused in favor of the families of his prisoners," bemoaned Osborne Anderson, "a very different result would have been seen." Turner, the black revolutionary, had no such qualms: he would slay all who stood in the way of freedom. This attitude doubtless informed the fury of those blacks who objected so vehemently to William Styron's 1960s' portrait of Nat Turner as a man undone by affection for a young white girl. It might indeed be true that the image they received was not the one Styron intended; that he viewed Turner as not undone but transcendent in his rage and humanity. (Rage aside, however, that is the way Harriet Beecher Stowe viewed Uncle Tom – nonetheless a well-known term of opprobrium in the 1960s.) For some blacks, Styron's representation was unmanly; it was counterrevolutionary; it negated the call for "any means necessary."

Yet Brown's vision of ultimate interracial harmony, as the 1859 editorial made clear, was the more appealing to black Americans. Nat Turner, the editor suggested, posed the spectre of black domination and racial strife. Of course, racial strife already existed, and black domination, a bugaboo justifying black oppression, was neither practicable nor, the editor implied, desirable, even among blacks. What blacks appreciated in Turner was the willingness to fight and die for his own and to provide, in the process, a model of emulation unalloyed by ambiguity. Blacks could have no doubt about his relevance to their history or his place in their pantheon of heroes. It might be true, as Frederick Douglass, Jr., argued, that "character and good acts" were worthy of recognition and perpetuation regardless of a person's color. It might even be true, which Douglass did not say, that because Brown had a choice and chose for blacks, he had greater call on their esteem. Nor could his sensitivity to the feelings of women and children be held against him. But there was also a good case for Fortune's response that "the absence of race pride and race unity" made "white men despise black men all the world over." Black worship of John Brown, however worthy he might be, did nothing to answer that concern.

Indeed, Martin Delany's cooperation with Brown came back to haunt him in his own attempt to build a race movement under black leadership. When he formed the Niger Valley Exploring Party to seek out an African homeland in 1858, he became caught up in rivalries among blacks and whites over who should control this emigration scheme. The conflict was exacerbated by his difficulties in securing economic backing for his planned African expeditions. A secular black nationalist, Delany was forced to seek aid from the American Colonization Society, whose aims and white leadership he deplored and whose African stepchild, Liberia, he had attacked as a tool of whites. Moreover, he rejected their concern with Christianization, feeling that religion sapped black independence. Whites in the ACS, recognizing a long-standing black opposition to their organization, sought to achieve their aims of "civilization and Christianization" in Africa through the expatriation of black colonists (and the removal of blacks from America) by forming the African Civilization Society. (Some whites were members of both groups.) The new organization used black figureheads like Henry

Highland Garnet, who was president of the society; it also sought to subsume the Niger Valley Exploring Party. Trying to maintain as much independence of action as possible and denied formal ACS backing, Delany nevertheless sailed to Africa on their economic resources. In England, after his return from Africa, he subsequently competed for financial backing of an African settlement with white representatives of the African Civilization Society who attempted to claim his organization as theirs. Although English sympathizers eventually decided that a black man claiming to represent black interests had more credibility than white men who did the same, the experience intensified Delany's belief that blacks should lead blacks. In addition, it became painfully clear that too close a tie to white people could weaken a call for black unity and black leaders.

When Delany and others tried to make this point against Garnet in connection with a Haitian emigration scheme, however, the incisive minister responded:

> The fault that you have charged me with is that I have accepted an appointment of agent of Haytian emigration from . . . a *white man* . . . You are indignant at the acknowledgment of the leadership of a *white man* in any work that particularly concerns *black men*. Now, sir, . . . I see by the newspapers that in the convention held in 1848 [*sic*] at Chatham, C.W., one *John Brown* was appointed leader – commander-in-chief – of the Harper's Ferry invasion. There were several black men there, able and brave; and yet John Brown was appointed leader. The unfortunate Stevens moved for the appointment, and *one Dr. Martin R. Delany seconded the motion*. Now, sir, tell me where I shall find your consistency, as John Brown was a *very* white man – his face and glorious hairs were all white.

Garnet's comment was inaccurate in detail but effective in direction. He had appropriated for blacks a white man's vision, knowing that the aim was shared if the method was not, and knowing, too, the sensitivities and ambiguities the name John Brown evoked among blacks.

Even black radicals in the 1960s maintained a traditional black appreciation for the martyr, H. Rap Brown writing that "John Brown was the only white man I could respect and he is dead." But for some blacks no white man, no matter how committed, could view their plight like another black, no matter how flawed. Even though John Brown came closer to the mark than most, he could still be found wanting. It does not matter that many who would criticize had not the gall to go as far as he had gone. Frederick Douglass commented that colored people more than others criticized him for not joining Brown's quest, and yet, more often than not, these were the very ones who had remained respectfully remote while Brown lived. But all the more need for a black man to go the distance. Shields Green might be said to equal John Brown. Nat Turner had gone beyond him.

John Brown's image nonetheless endures among blacks, and not only in the United States. When Haitian soldiers set up roadblocks to search for handguns in Port-au-Prince in May 1992, they placed one at the corner of John Brown and Martin Luther King Avenues. In America, meanwhile, Denmark Vesey's portrait was installed in Charleston's Gaillard Municipal Auditorium, marking the recognition of his unrealized insurrection as a part of local lore – a herald of Martin Luther King's dream of a day when men would be judged by character rather than color, or an acknowledgment of modern political realities, or both. It caused controversy, periodically renewed, but Vesey's was a plot that died aborning. Some even argue that there was no plot at all – but either way it was relatively safe. Not even a black governor, however, has ventured to name a Virginia street after Nat Turner (though there may be one somewhere) or to put his portrait in any Virginia public place. Turner, like Brown, failed, but he did move from thought to action, and the implications of his action remain frightening. Turner's image as avenging angel clearly is more palatable to blacks than to whites. When white opponents talked of John Brown inciting the murder of women and children, black supporters in particular retorted that that is what slavery did. It might be nice to end slavery peacefully. It might be necessary to end it violently. Philosophically, Brown embraced either tenet, although emotionally, after Kansas, he leaned toward the first. Nat Turner had no such ambivalence; indeed he had no such choice.

Brown, like abolitionists generally, struggled against his history and culture. He was an extreme personification of the abolitionist impulse, embodying the conflicting strands of their contradictory beliefs, including a principled commitment to the ideal of human equality, together with a strong suspicion, if not an outright conviction, of black inferiority. For those who, like Theodore Parker, assumed that Anglo-Saxons were "the best specimen of mankind" that had "ever attained great power in the world," blacks could not help but suffer by comparison. Even if one argued for their superior virtue, or that a composite of the two groups would make a better person still, blacks remained somehow lacking. Of course, the Irish received nearly equal deprecation; and when Parker spoke about warfare necessitating enlistment of "Americans, Negroes, Irishmen," he distinguished the last two from the first. But neither the exclusion nor the company provided blacks much comfort. His doubts about black equality notwithstanding, Parker spoke as feelingly against the discrimination faced by Northern blacks as he condemned the servitude of Southern blacks. In his own terms, he made perfect sense.

By our lights, most abolitionists were racists, particularly if we accept Joel Kovel's definition. "Far from being the simple delusion of a bigoted and ignorant minority," he says, racism "is a set of beliefs whose structure arises from the deepest levels of our lives – from the fabric of assumptions we make about the world, ourselves, and others, and from the patterns of our fundamental social activities."[2] Yet, if we distinguish between those who added hate, aspersions, and despicable acts to their core beliefs and those who questioned their ideological environment, *racist* is much too inclusive and simplistic a term. Perhaps *racialist* is better. Life in a racially based culture determined that Americans of whatever disposition would be confronted with a certain set of assumptions, even if they didn't all think the same way; that they would have certain common points of reference, Brown no less than others. Blacks were both docile and bloodthirsty, and despite Brown's desire to disprove the first premise he was ultimately hampered by his fear of the second. He tried to dissolve his doubts in the ferocity of his actions; yet, in the end, they rose to plague him. He was a man who started a fight then stopped to think about it: his biggest battle was an internal one, and that he could not win. But his struggle with himself and with his culture commended him to blacks. It was ennobling.

The struggle of blacks was different. They were part of the same culture, but viewed it from a variant perspective. As Christians, they could appreciate the value of a moral stance that prized restraint; as realists, they saw the overwhelming obstacles to successful insurrection; as human beings, they were not always willing to lay down their lives for simple pride or self-esteem to no practical effect, though many did so, and many others applauded such acts. Ultimately, though, they were "damned if they did" and "damned if they didn't." In case of violent upheaval they were aggressive and unprincipled savages; in case of acquiescence they were meek and ignorant savages. White Americans might appreciate heroic violence, but in their adversaries, particularly of "lesser breeds," they admired it best after its failure. Noble savages are nearly always dead ones. They are at least devoid of power and safely under control.

But the predisposition to privilege heroic action was as much a part of black as of white American character, and blacks had more at stake in its exhibition. Boston abolitionist Samuel Gridley Howe, engaged in self-recrimination for not having acted forcefully enough to prevent the 1854 rendition to Virginia of fugitive slave Anthony Burns, noticed " 'a comely colored girl of eighteen' who happened to be standing near him as Anthony Burns passed. She stood watching the column with 'clenched fists . . . flashing eyes and tears streaming down her cheeks, the picture of indignant despair.' When he noticed how upset the girl was, Howe tried to comfort her. He told her not to cry; Burns wouldn't be hurt. Immediately, the black girl turned to him and screamed: 'Hurt! I cry for shame he will not kill himself. Oh why is he not man enough to kill himself!' "

Nat Turner, like Malcolm X at a later date, represented black manhood – the evidence that blacks, like others, were prepared to die for their freedom (and thus merited honor, respect, and the rights of citizenship). It would be better, of course, for them and their children if they could *live in* freedom. Martin Luther King perhaps represented that hope; moreover, he illustrated that peaceful protest could also be militant; that nonviolence did not mean docility. Nineteenth-century blacks knew this too, but they did not have the means to build a mass movement based upon this idea – certainly not in the South, where King eventually worked, and where nonviolent protest, no less than violent, could be suicidal. For violence to be other than futile there must be a chance for success. At the very least it has to be admonitory, instilling fear or caution so that its objects will hesitate to tempt fate in the same way again. Brown, to many blacks, represented hope but also futility – a futility, moreover, rooted in fear of blacks. For his part, Turner represented hope and a warning.

Notes

1 Merton L. Dillon, *Slavery Attacked: Southern Slaves and Their Allies, 1619–1865* (Baton Rouge, 1990), p. 174.
2 Joel Kovel, *White Racism: A Psychohistory* (New York, 1984), p. 3.

Documents

Introduction to the Documents

Free people of color in the years before the Civil War were in the vanguard of anti-slavery activity. Unlike many of their white abolitionist counterparts, however, they seldom were committed in principle to ending slavery through "moral suasion" alone even if they accepted the need for nonviolence as a practical reality. As early as 1843, Henry Highland Garnet, addressing a national convention of African Americans in Buffalo, New York, endorsed violent slave resistance (Document One). Indeed "voluntary submission" to slavery was itself sinful in Garnet's eyes. Garnet appealed to African traditions, past heroes, and an ethos of manliness to justify his position. In Document

Two, Frederick Douglass, the leading black abolitionist of his era and himself an escaped slave, recommended "a good revolver" as the response to the Fugitive Slave Act of 1850. Note Douglass's praise for the "Heroes of the American Revolution." Those heroes had won independence for a slaveholding nation but had at the same time advanced doctrines of equality and natural rights that African Americans could use in their struggles for liberation. Documents Three and Four are two responses to John Brown's martyrdom, the first a letter from a group of African-American women to Brown's wife Mary, the second a tribute from a group in Detroit on the day of his execution. How did women deal with the equation of manhood and courage that Littlefield discusses? Consider the lessons that each group drew from John Brown's raid and his fate.

Henry Highland Garnet, Speech Appealing for Violent Resistance

---

Henry Highland Garnet's speech at the 1843 Black National Convention, reprinted from C. Peter Ripley, Roy E. Finkenbine, Michael F. Hembree, and Donald Yacovone (eds.) *Witness for Freedom: African American Voices on Race, Slavery, and Emancipation* (Chapel Hill: University of North Carolina Press, 1993), pp. 165–6, 168–9.

Address to the Slaves of the United States of America

Brethren and Fellow Citizens:

Your brethren of the north, east, and west have been accustomed to meet together in National Conventions, to sympathize with each other, and to weep over your unhappy condition. In these meetings we have addressed all classes of the free, but we have never until this time, sent a word of consolation and advice to you. We have been contented in sitting still and mourning over your sorrows, earnestly hoping that before this day, your sacred Liberties would have been restored. But, we have hoped in vain. Years have rolled on, and tens of thousands have been borne on streams of blood, and tears, to the shores of eternity. While you have been oppressed, we have also been partakers with you; nor can we be free while you are enslaved. We therefore write to you as being bound with you.

Many of you are bound to us, not only by the ties of common humanity, but we are connected by the more tender relations of parents, wives, husbands, children, brothers, and sisters, and friends. As such we most affectionately address you. . . .

SLAVERY! How much misery is comprehended in that single word. . . . TO SUCH DEGRADATION IT IS SINFUL IN THE EXTREME FOR YOU TO MAKE VOLUNTARY SUBMISSION. The divine commandments, you are in duty bound to reverence, and obey. . . . Your condition does not absolve you from your moral obligation. The diabolical injustice by which your Liberties are cloven down, NEITHER GOD, NOR ANGELS, OR JUST MEN COMMAND YOU TO SUFFER FOR A SINGLE MOMENT. THEREFORE IT IS YOUR SOLEMN AND IMPERATIVE DUTY TO USE EVERY MEANS, BOTH MORAL, INTELLECTUAL, AND PHYSICAL, THAT PROMISE SUCCESS. . . .

Brethren, it is as wrong for your lordly oppressors to keep you in slavery, as it was for the man thief to steal our ancestors from the coast of Africa. You should therefore now use the same manner of resistance, as would have been just in our ancestors, when the bloody footprints of the first remorseless soul thief was placed upon the shores of our father-land. The humblest peasant is as free in the sight of God, as the proudest monarch that ever swayed a scepter. Liberty is a spirit sent out from God, and like its great Author is no respecter of persons.

. . . Look around you, and behold the bosoms of your loving wives, heaving with untold agonies! Hear the cries of your poor children! Remember the stripes your fathers bore. Think of the torture and dis-grace of your noble mothers. Think of your wretched sisters, loving virtue and purity, as they are driven into concubinage, and are exposed to the unbridled lusts of incarnate devils. Think of the undying glory that hangs around the ancient name of Africa – and forget not that you are native-born American citizens, and as such, you are justly entitled to all the rights that are granted to the freest. Think how many tears you have poured out upon the soil which you have cultivated with unrequited toil, and enriched with your blood; and then go to your lordly enslavers, and tell them plainly, that YOU ARE DETERMINED TO BE FREE. . . . Tell them in language which they cannot misunderstand, of the exceeding sinfulness of slavery, and of a future judgement, and of the righteous retributions of an indignant God. Inform them that all you desire, is FREEDOM, and that nothing else will suffice. Do this, and forever after cease to toil for the heartless tyrants, who give you no other reward but stripes and abuse. If they then commence the work of death, they, and not you, will be responsible for the consequences. You had far better all die – *die imme-diately*, than live slaves, and entail your wretchedness upon your poster-ity. If you would be free in this generation, here is your only hope. However much you and all of us may desire it, there is not much hope of Redemption without the shedding of blood. If you must bleed, let it all come at once – rather, *die freemen, than live to be slaves*. It is impossible, like the children of Israel, to make a grand Exodus from the land of bondage....

Fellow men! patient sufferers! behold your dearest rights crushed to the earth! See your sons murdered, and your wives, mothers, and sisters, doomed to prostitution! In the name of the merciful God! and by all that life is worth, let it no longer be a debateable question, whether it is better to choose LIBERTY or DEATH!

In 1822, Denmark Vesey, of South Carolina, formed a plan for the liberation of his fellow men. In the whole history of human efforts to overthrow slavery, a more complicated and tremendous plan was never formed. He was betrayed by the treachery of his own people, and died a martyr to freedom....

The patriotic Nathaniel Turner followed Denmark Vesey. He was goaded to desperation by wrong and injustice. By Despotism, his name has been recorded on the list of infamy, but future generations will number him upon the noble and brave.

Next arose the immortal Joseph Cinqué, the hero of the *Amistad*. He was a native African, and by the help of God he emancipated a whole ship-load of his fellow men on the high seas. And he now sings of Liberty on the sunny hills of Africa, and beneath his native palm trees, where he hears the lion roar, and feels himself as free as that king of the forest. Next arose Madison Washington, that bright star of freedom, and took his station in the constellation of freedom. He was a slave on board the brig *Creole*, of Richmond, bound to New Orleans, that great slave mart, with a hundred and four others. Nineteen struck for Liberty or death....

We do not advise you to attempt a revolution with the sword, because it would be INEXPEDIENT. Your numbers are too small, and moreover the rising spirit of the age, and the spirit of the gospel, are opposed to war and bloodshed. But from this moment cease to labor for tyrants who will not remunerate you. Let every slave throughout the land do this, and the days of slavery are numbered. You cannot be more oppressed than you have been – you cannot suffer greater cruelties than you have already. RATHER DIE FREEMEN, THAN LIVE TO BE SLAVES. Remember that you are THREE MILLIONS.

It is in your power so to torment the God-cursed slaveholders, that they will be glad to let you go free. If the scale was turned and black men were the masters, and white men the slaves, every destructive agent and element would be employed to lay the oppressor low. Danger and death would hang over their heads day and night. Yes, the tyrants would meet with plagues more terrible than those of Pharaoh. But you are a patient people. You act as though you were made for the special use of these devils. You act as though your daughters were born to pamper the lusts of your masters and overseers. And worse than all, you tamely submit, while your lords tear your wives from your embraces, and defile them before your eyes. In the name of God we ask, are you men? Where is the blood of your fathers? Has it all run out of your veins? Awake, awake; millions of voices are calling you! Your dead fathers speak to you from their graves. Heaven, as with a voice of thunder, calls on you to arise from the dust.

Let your motto be RESISTANCE! RESISTANCE! RESISTANCE! No oppressed people have ever secured their Liberty without resistance. What kind of resistance you had better make, you must decide by the circumstances that surround you, and according to the suggestion of expediency. Brethren, adieu. Trust in the living God. Labor for the peace of the human race, and remember that you are three millions.

Frederick Douglass, "The True Remedy for the Fugitive Slave Bill"

Editorial from *Frederick Douglass' Paper*, June 9, 1854, reprinted from C. Peter Ripley, Roy E. Finkenbine, Michael F. Hembree, and Donald Yacovone (eds.) *Witness for Freedom: African American Voices on Race, Slavery, and Emancipation* (Chapel Hill: University of North Carolina Press, 1993), pp. 183–4.

A good revolver, a steady hand, and a determination to shoot down any man attempting to kidnap. Let every colored man make up his mind to this, and live by it, and if needs be, die by it. This will put an end to kidnapping and to slaveholding, too. We blush to our very soul when we are told that a negro is so mean and cowardly that he prefers to live under the slave driver's whip – to the loss of life for liberty. Oh! that we had a little more of the manly indifference to death, which characterized the Heroes of the American Revolution.

African-American Women's Letter to Mary Brown

Letter to John Brown's wife, from *Weekly Anglo-African*, December 17, 1859, reprinted from Benjamin Quarles, *Blacks on John Brown* (Urbana: University of Illinois Press, 1972), pp. 16–19.

No. 62 East Sixteenth St., N.Y.

November 23, 1859

Dear Mrs. Brown: A few weeks since some colored ladies of this city met at the house of the Rev. Henry Highland Garnet, an old and, I doubt not, highly valued friend of your husband's, to supplicate our common Father in behalf of one whom they felt had offered up his life, and the lives of those dearer to him than his own, in the effort to obtain for their oppressed race their "God given rights." It was a time of strong supplication, of weeping, and of wrestlings with God, and some of us felt we had, through Him, who had been our beloved brother's Exampler, obtained an answer of peace, and I think I may say, from our united experience, "Be comforted."

Till that meeting for prayer I, and I know many of them, had labored, as it were, under a horror of great darkness. Before the gray dawn had broken over a sleeping world, through the busy hours of the day, at evening tide, and in the mid-watches of the night, the cry had gone up unceasingly from our sorrowful and burdened spirits: "Lord, send deliverance to our brother from the hands of fierce and cruel men who seek his blood!" We could get no rest – we could give but little comfort to each other; but since then the burden has been taken from my heart individually, and strange to say, *I cannot feel* troubled about him. Ah, you weepingly say, "he is not their husband." Yet, dear friend, he is our honored and dearly-loved brother, and we are satisfied that there is One who cares for him more tenderly than we, or than even his sorrowing and desolate companion. We know he is dear to our God as the apple of his eye. Do you doubt it? We do not, and we are sure you do not. Can not our Heavenly Father quickly send ten legions of Angels to strike terror into the hearts of these men? Can he not send *one* bright visitant, as in the days of old, when his faithful servant, chained and manacled, lay sleeping between his keepers, and yet at that light touch, and in obedience to that angel voice, arose and went forth, not knowing but "that it was a vision?" Yes, surely. Our God changes not; and if your husband be delivered, to sorrow a few more years those scenes of cruelty which have so wrung his noble spirit for more than thirty years; and if it be his Master's will to whisper now to him, "Come up higher!" would you hold back the chariot wheels, though they be wheels of fire. No, my dear sorrowing sister – we are assured, from what we gather of your like-mindedness with your noble champion, your motto is: "It is my God – my covenant God – who doeth all things well." Well, we wanted to tell you how we have met again and again in prayer for you, and those who are still in bonds, and how, in offering this word of sympathy to you now we desire to express our deep, undying gratitude to him who has given his life so freely to obtain for us our defrauded rights, and whose bereaved ones we accept, according to his suggestion in "The Tribune" of November 12, as a solemn legacy at his hands – if indeed it be our Master's will to give him now the Crown of Glory, which awaits all those to whom it will be said at that day: "Inasmuch as ye have done it unto the least of these ye have done it unto me."

Tell your dear husband then, that henceforth you shall be our own! We are a poor and despised people – almost forbidden, by the oppressive restrictions of the Free States, to rise to the higher walks of lucrative employments, toiling early and late for our daily bread; but we hope – and we intend, by God's help – to organize in every Free State, and in every colored church, a band of sisters, to collect our weekly pence, and pour it lovingly into your lap. God will help us, for he is the Judge of the widow and the Father of the fatherless. And you have all been made widows, and your children fatherless, because your husbands, and your children's fathers, counted not their lives as dear, so that they might fulfill this command of our God's: "Therefore I say unto you, whatsoever ye would that others should do unto you, do ye even so unto them, for this is the law and the prophets." (The Mosaic as well as the Christian dispensation.)

Fear not, beloved sister. Trust in the God of Jacob. He who of old sent his prophet forth with this word to the tyrant who oppresses, and woe, woe, woe, is theirs if, instead of honoring the word of the Lord, they slay the prophet. Trust then in this same God, and if you will cast your fatherless ones upon Him, and if you and they will, as your beloved husband has done, deal justly, love mercy, and walk humbly with your God, and it shall be well with you in time and in eternity.

We hope soon to send you the first fruits of our offering of love. Many will doubtless minister to you; but in our ministration we trust to make a fund to minister to you and yours till you shall say it is enough, and until you yourselves shall say to us: "Clothe the naked, feed the hungry, shelter the homeless ones, who are daily fleeing from the oppressor."

We do not ask you to write now. We know, we cannot be unmindful of the loneliness, and we fear the agony of these solemn days. The one who is privileged to write these words for her sisters unto you, knows well the heart of the widow and all its desolations; but we pray that He whose you are, whom you serve, who has said that not a cup of cold water shall be given to a disciple in His name, without receiving a disciple's reward, will cause His face to shine upon you, will speak peace to your troubled spirit, will send the strong consolations of the Gospel, which have the voices in his counsel and the guide of the life of your husband and our brother into your heart. May a Triune Jehovah shed life, light and peace around your dwelling,

Pray your loving sisters.

African-American Tribute to John Brown

Tribute to John Brown, Detroit, December 2, 1859, from Weekly Anglo-African, December 17, 1859, reprinted in C. Peter Ripley, Roy E. Finkenbine, Michael F. Hembree, and Donald Yacovane (eds.) Witness for Freedom: African American Voices on Race, Slavery, and Emancipation (Chapel Hill: University of North Carolina Press, 1993), pp. 207–9.

Whereas, We, the oppressed portion of this community, many of whom have worn the galling chain and felt the smarting lash of slavery, and know by sad experience its brutalizing effects upon both the body and the mind, and its damaging influence upon the soul of its victim; and

Whereas, We, by the help of Almighty God and the secret abolition movements that are now beginning to develop themselves in the southern part of this country, have been enabled to escape from the prison house of slavery, and partially to obtain our liberty; and having become personally acquainted with the life and character of our much beloved and highly esteemed friend, Old Capt. John Brown, and his band of valiant men, who, at Harpers Ferry, on the 16th day of October, 1859, demonstrated to the world his sympathy and fidelity to the cause of the suffering slaves of this country, by bearding the hydra-headed monster, Tyranny, in his den, and by his bold, effective, timely blow is now causing the whole South to tremble with a moral earthquake, as he boldly and freely delivered up his life today as a ransom for our enslaved race and thereby, "solitarily and alone," he has put a liberty ball in motion which shall continue to roll and gather strength until the last vestige of human slavery within this nation shall have been crushed beneath its ponderous weight. Therefore,

Resolved, That we hold the name of Old Capt. John Brown in the most sacred remembrance, as the first disinterested martyr for our liberty, who, upon the true Christian principle of his Divine Lord and Master, has freely delivered up his life for the liberty of our race in this country. Therefore will we ever vindicate his character throughout all coming time, as our temporal redeemer, whose name shall never die.

Resolved, That, as the long lost rights and liberties of an oppressed people are only gained in proportion as they act in their own cause, therefore are we now loudly called upon to arouse to our own interest, and to concentrate our efforts in keeping the Old Brown liberty ball in motion and thereby continue to kindle the fires of liberty upon the altar of every determined heart among us, and continue to fan the same until the proper time, when a revolutionary blast from liberty's trump shall summon them simultaneously to unite for victorious and triumphant battle.

Resolved, That we tender our deepest and most heartfelt sympathy to the family of Capt. John Brown in their sad bereavement, and pledge to them that they shall ever be held by us as our special friends, in whose welfare we hope ever to manifest a special interest.

Suggested Reading

Paul Finkelman (ed.) *His Soul Goes Marching On: Responses to John Brown and the Harper's Ferry Raid*, Charlottesville, VA: University of Virginia Press, 1995. A wide-ranging collection of essays on varied aspects of Brown and the Harper's Ferry raid. Daniel Littlefield's essay in the current volume is drawn from this collection.

Stephen B. Oates, *To Purge this Land with Blood: A Biography of John Brown*, 2nd ed., Amherst, MA: University of Massachusetts Press, 1984. A vivid biography of Brown that argues he was not insane and that his raid was a crucial step on the path to a Civil War that ended slavery in the United States.

David Potter, *The Impending Crisis 1848–1861*, completed and edited by Don E. Fehrenbacher, New York: Harper & Row, 1976. A sweeping and thorough narrative of the period preceding the Civil War by a leading American historian.

Benjamin Quarles (ed.) *Blacks on John Brown*, Urbana, IL: University of Illinois Press, 1972. A broad compilation of documents about African-American responses to John Brown and his raid on Harper's Ferry. The book includes both reactions at the time and later commentaries.

C. Peter Ripley, Roy E. Finkenbine, Michael F. Hembree, and Donald Yacovone (eds.) *Witness for Freedom: African American Voices on Race, Slavery and Emancipation*, Chapel Hill, NC: University of North Carolina Press, 1993. A collection of documents in which African Americans comment on slavery, race, and resistance. The volume shows the growing militancy among free blacks working to end slavery.

An excellent introduction to John Brown, the Harper's Ferry raid, and its impact on the coming of the Civil War is at:

http://jefferson.village.virginia.edu/jbrown/master.html

This is part of a major web project examining the coming of the Civil War through studies of two communities, North and South. Professor Edward L. Ayers of the University of Virginia is the creator of the Valley of the Shadow web project.

Another valuable website on Harper's Ferry is part of the Library of Congress's American Memory series at

http://lcweb2.loc.gov/ammem/today/oct16.html

(Note that URLs on the Web are often subject to change. These links were valid in August 2000.)

4
Chicago's Anarchists and the Haymarket Bombing

1877 The "Great Strike" against railroads stops work across the country. President Rutherford B. Hayes calls out the army to suppress a "national insurrection." In Chicago, dozens of protesters are killed and hundreds wounded in battles with police and soldiers.

1883 International Working People's Association (IWPA) joins together several anarchist and socialist factions. The group issues its "Pittsburgh Manifesto" calling for social revolution.

1884 With strong anarchist influence, Chicago's Central Labor Union (CLU) forms, dedicated to direct action and opposed to compromise with employers. The CLU challenges the unions of skilled workers in the Trades and Labor Assembly and the reform-oriented Knights of Labor.

1885–6 A mass movement for an eight-hour work day brings explosive growth in the labor movement.

May 1, 1886 Led by anarchists Albert and Lucy Parsons, 80,000 workers parade up Michigan Avenue, Chicago. Forty thousand go out on strike for the eight-hour day.

May 3, 1886 In a clash with police near the McCormick Reaper Works at least two workers are killed.

May 4, 1886 Bomb explodes at an anarchist rally at Haymarket Square. Police fire into crowd. Seven policemen and about the same number of protesters are killed.

August 1886 Eight anarchists are convicted of murder although there is no evidence linking them directly to the bombing. Seven are sentenced to death, and one to 15 years' imprisonment.

November 11, 1887 Four of the "Haymarket Martyrs" are hanged; one commits suicide shortly before the execution. Sentences of two others had previously been commuted to life in prison.

June 26, 1893 Illinois Governor John Peter Altgeld grants unconditional pardons to the three imprisoned martyrs.

Introduction to the Article

About 10:30 on the night of May 4, 1886 somebody hurled a bomb at a squad of policemen who were moving in to disperse a labor rally at Haymarket Square, Chicago. The officers then fired into the crowd. Seven policemen died from the bomb's blast and the subsequent gunfire. About sixty of them were wounded. Civilian casualties probably numbered seven or eight dead and thirty to forty injured. Most if not all of the gunshot wounds on both sides came from police weapons, since few if any of the workers had fired.

Chicago was already the scene of violent labor strife. Radical anarchists dominated the city's Central Labor Union. Some 80,000 workers had marched up Michigan Avenue on May 1 (May Day), and tens of thousands had gone out on strike demanding an eight-hour work day. Two days later, police attacked demonstrators near the McCormick Reaper factory, killing at least two. Anarchists summoned a rally at Haymarket Square on May 4. Some of the announcements urged workers to "arm yourselves and appear in full force!" but the crowd numbered only two or three thousand. The bomb and the gunfire erupted as the meeting was disbanding peacefully.

In the aftermath of Haymarket, Chicago and the nation as a whole experienced a "red scare," a period of vehement and often violent repression of radicals. Although there was no valid evidence linking them to the bomb, eight Chicago anarchists were arrested and put on trial for murder. Judge Joseph Gary instructed the jury that if the defendants had advised or encouraged the commission of murder, they were as guilty as if they had carried out the killings themselves. All were convicted. Of the eight, four were hanged, one committed suicide in prison, and three remained in jail. In 1893, Governor John Peter Altgeld, a pro-labor reformer, issued a pardon for the three imprisoned anarchists. More than a century later, the bomb thrower's identity is still unknown, although a leading historian of Haymarket, Paul Avrich, claimed some years ago that a German anarchist named George Meng, probably acting on his own, was the likely perpetrator.

Bruce Nelson, in these excerpts from his book *Beyond the Martyrs: A Social History of Chicago's Anarchists, 1870–1900*, analyzes both the radicals and the workers' movement they strived to lead. Scattered groups of anarchists had convened in Pittsburgh in 1883, founding a group known as the International Working People's Association (IWPA). They issued a declaration of principles calling both for the "destruction of the existing class rule by all means" and "a free society based upon co-operative organization of production." As Nelson indicates, their enemies had labeled the radicals anarchists, and they had taken the name as a badge of pride. Strictly speaking, they did not reject all government. Equality and an active citizenry were their political ideals. Economically, they were socialists; the anarchists' understanding of capitalism was based on the ideas of Karl Marx. Distrusting the ballot and existing political parties, they were committed to violent revolution, although they were often vague on how this would take place. Finally, Nelson points out, they were freethinkers and atheists who thought organized religion oppressed workers.

The Haymarket affair was a dramatic moment in American labor history. Several of its aspects indicate broader themes in the nation's radical past. First, as Nelson indicates, both the anarchists themselves and the workers of Chicago were ethnically diverse. Germans, Bohemians, and Scandinavians predominated in the anarchist-influenced Central Labor Union. Members of other Chicago labor groups – the Knights of Labor and the Trades and Labor Assembly – were more likely to be of Irish or British descent. Not only ideology but ethnic, religious, and cultural differences have often hindered cooperation among reform and radical groups. Second, the anarchists' role in the Central Labor Union indicates that a relatively small number of self-consciously revolutionary activists could influence a much wider constituency. In doing so, anarchists found themselves fighting not for social revolution but for an immediate reform – the eight-hour day – which a generation later became the norm in American business. What was the relationship between the reforms workers demanded and the revolutionary aspirations of radical groups? Finally, Haymarket reminds us that the history of American radicalism is often violent and that the violence, more often than not, is repressive, not revolutionary. Movements for radical or revolutionary change have repeatedly had to assess the prospects of peaceful transformation and the potential of violent means. Convinced that the system could not be overthrown without bloody struggle, Chicago's anarchists preached violence, though they seldom practiced it. Their fate in the aftermath of Haymarket indicates that radicals themselves often became the victims of government-sanctioned violence.

From *Beyond the Martyrs: A Social History of Chicago's Anarchists*

Bruce C. Nelson

Four Threads in the Cloth of Ideology

> I follow four commandments. Thou shalt deny God and love Truth; therefore I am an atheist. Thou shalt oppose tyranny and seek liberty; therefore I am a republican. Thou shalt repudiate property and champion equality; therefore I am a communist. Thou shalt hate oppression and foment revolution; therefore I am a revolutionary. Long live the social revolution!
>
> Johann Most, *Die Freiheit*, 15 July 1882

It is difficult to assess Johann Most's impact on Chicago's anarchists. For Chester Destler, Most's arrival "galvanized" an otherwise moribund movement in the United States.[1] *The Alarm, Die Arbeiter-Zeitung,* and *Die Anarchist* reprinted articles from his *Die Freiheit*, and he visited the city on three agitational tours. If Most did not have the influence Destler claimed, his creed serves now as a convenient catalog of four threads in the cloth of anarchist ideology: atheism, republicanism, communism, and revolution, although I want to consider those elements in a slightly different order. And to anticipate, the argument here is that Chicago's anarchists can be best understood as revolutionary socialists, the self-conscious heirs of the failed bourgeois revolutions of 1848.

The anarchists were political republicans

The year 1848 had been "the springtime of the peoples": an awakening of republicanism and hope. When they failed, Chicago received many of "the refugees of revolution," not just Germans, but also Czechs and Scandinavians. The *Illinois Staats-Zeitung* denounced those Forty Eighters who "came over here to America, their heads filled with

Reprinted from Bruce C. Nelson, "Bakunin Never Slept in Chicago" and "Eight Hours, Riot, and Repression," in *Beyond the Martyrs: A Social History of Chicago's Anarchists, 1870–1900* (New Brunswick, NJ: Rutgers University Press, 1988) pp. 156–65, 170–3, 177–200. Copyright © 1988 by Rutgers, The State University. Reprinted by permission of Rutgers University Press.

world messianic dreams," explaining that too many had become "enthusiastic and reckless representatives of socialism."

The IWPA mingled two republicanisms: an indigenous, Anglo-American one, the other immigrant, almost "alien," and European. This mixture may have sacrificed coherence for cogency. Born in different places, under different conditions, the two were not identical; yet they shared similar notions, heroes, conceptions, and vocabulary. Both Anglo-American and European republicans believed in limited government, with a mixed and balanced structure, and in the sovereignty of the people. Both native and immigrant republicans embraced as first principles the notions that property ought to be widely dispersed, that anti-monopoly vigilance was imperative, and that luxury was not just a sign of wealth but of the corruption of the republic. Both shared what Eric Foner has described as "a passionate attachment to equality (defined not as leveling of all distinctions, but as the absence of inequalities of wealth and influence), a belief that independence – the ability to resist personal or economic coercion – was an essential attribute of the republican citizenry, and a commitment to the labor theory of value, along with its corollary, that labor should receive the full value of its product."[2]

Republicanism pervaded the movement's thought but was most visible in its conception of civil society and of citizenship. In 1878 *The Socialist* argued: "With us there is no necessity for an appeal to arms involving a bloody revolution. We have a Declaration of Independence and a Constitution, and under them we have the right, now enjoyed for a century, of promolgating [sic] our ideas and of establishing a party in support of them." The socialists presented the Lehr- und Wehr-Verein as a civic organization. In defending the verein, *Die Arbeiter-Zeitung* quoted from its charter: "The Society's duty is to develop mental and physical qualifications of their members, and thus enable them to exercise their duty as good citizens, that the member should get acquainted with the law, and political economy and practice military and gymnastic drilling." Citizenship carried with it obligations, "the duty" of "good citizens." The verein presented itself as a popular militia, composed of workers and organized as their defense against the "servile militia" of the bourgeoisie. As Conrad Conzett explained, "It is our duty to train ourselves in order to be able to lead the coming uprising of the people in such a way that the victory of the oppressed cannot fail." With its roots in 1848, the verein could still claim the legacy of 1776. In parades, some of its members dressed "in Continental style" and carried placards emblazoned "Give Me Liberty or Give Me Death"; its wagons bore the placard "1876."

Both socialists and anarchists believed that workers were citizens; in turn, their notion of citizenship underpinned their conception of the republic. In 1879 and 1880, at election time, *Die Arbeiter-Zeitung* argued that any worker who failed to vote was unworthy of that privilege. Yet citizenship was never conceived in nationalist or chauvinist terms. Indeed, the children of IWPA members were welcomed as "neue Welt-burgern," citizens of the world. In the wake of electoral failure and fraud, many abandoned their faith in the ballot as *Der Vorbote* contrasted "Reformschwindel und Revolution." A year later Lizzie Swank considered "Election Day":

> The American citizen has walked boldly up to the polls, deposited a piece of paper in a box, gone back to 12 hours work, a shanty and a crust of bread, and thus demonstrated to the world his glorious freedom and independence! Perhaps his vote counted, perhaps not, for all he had to vote about, it does not matter. He was offered a choice between two sets of men, of whom he knows nothing, nominated he does not know how, or why, or by whom, and actuated by one and the same principle – to get there.

The anarchists argued that the aristocrats and monopolists had perverted the political process with their greed. They rejected "what may be termed the American theory of government": "the theory that each voter is a sovereign of the Republic; that on election day at the ballot-box the rich and the poor, the wage-class and the capitalistic class are upon a level of equality; [and] that the ballot of the propertyless is as potential for enacting law as is that of the property-holding classes." In 1879, socialists protesting the new Militia Bill passed out leaflets as they marched. One of them was headed, "Eternal vigilance is the price of liberty! Citizens, stand by the Constitution of your country! The militia bill is the product of a conspiracy to overthrow the republic, that has been cemented by the blood of our forefathers, and to dragoon the working people of Illinois into abject submission." The last banner in the procession repeated the warning "Citizens, Wake Up to the Situation and Save the Republic." Two years later John Blake told the Chicago Labor Union, "We have political freedom, but now we will assert our industrial freedom by a central council of amalgamated trade and labor unions that will place us in a position to offer a united front to the business community." By 1884, John Keegan, a young Irishman active in the IWPA's American Group, argued at the Lakefront "This is not a republic and never will be until the present industrial system should be abolished."

The anarchists were economic socialists

One of the speakers at the celebration of Turn-Verein Vorwaerts's fifteenth anniversary complained: "Although we are living under a republican form of government (a government by the people!) much is left to be fought for. Merely existing is not satisfying, we are desirous of higher ideals. We strive for a socialist state based on righteousness, truth and humanity." Because the conflict between virtue and commerce had corrupted the American republic, these Chicagoans broke with Anglo-American republicans and bourgeois political economy. The system of private property had destroyed the republican promise and brought with it wage slavery. "Those who believe they have equal rights," advised *The Socialist*, "should walk, after work, through the fashionable avenues," whose residents had bought the workingman's rights because they owned both his labor and their capital. When Frank Stauber was denied a seat in the City Council, *Der Vorbote* charged "that the holiest institution of the American people, the right to vote, had been desecrated" and became "a miserable farce and lie." "'Practical politics'," concluded *The Alarm*, "means the control of the propertied class. Politics and poverty, like oil and water, won't mix."

Svornost's editor argued in 1880 that socialism would counteract the political power of "the capitalists, railroad kings, industrialists, land speculators, and monopolists." Capitalism was worse than slavery, charged Frantisek Zdrûbek, for "the slaveowner had to provide for the welfare of his slave.... The employer, however, had no regard for his employee and was not concerned about the wages he paid him." The solution, believed Zdrûbek, could not come through cooperation with the existing parties, but through "labor cooperatives and direct social change..., for socialism promised prosperity to all who wanted to work."

Anarchist oratory and editorials were replete with phrases like "the abolition of slavery" and the "emancipation of the working class." In his first Chicago speech, Paul Grottkau linked the two: "whereas the Americans had evinced a spirit of liberty in ransoming the Negro," Grottkau could barely "entertain a hope that eventually the rights of the white laboring men would also be respected." Five years later, Albert Parsons almost presented the IWPA as a vanguard party, arguing: "The International is a labor organization composed of people who are devoting their time, their energy, their money and their lives to bring about the abolition of economic slavery and the complete emancipation of the working class from the tyranny of capital." "State Socialism," he argued "is the natural production of the age. It is the end of republican government. It is the complete union of all in one, and one for all alike."

What kind of socialism? In short, all kinds....

Others remained ignorant of socialism until they got to America, and Chicago in particular. Thus August Spies wrote in his "Autobiography" that "when I arrived in this country I knew nothing of Socialism, except what I had seen in the newspapers." Although he arrived in Chicago in 1873, "I think it was in 1875, at the time the 'Workingmen's Party of Illinois' was organized [that] upon the invitation of a friend, I visited the first meeting in which a lecture on Socialism was delivered." For George Engel "Chicago is the first place where I heard something of socialism for the first time in my life." In 1874 a socialist "showed me a news-paper, *Der Vorbote....* I found the paper very interesting and saw that it contained great truths. I was delighted. In it was an advertisement of a meeting held by the "International Workingmen's Association."...I went to the meeting." Oskar Neebe heard his "first communistic speech and that all men are equal" at New York's Commune in 1872, but did not join the communists in Chicago until 1877. Socialism meant the abolition of both private property and the wage system, and its replace-ment by a system of cooperative production and distribution. If the movement debated the finer points of theory at all, it shared a passionate opposition to the capitalistic system.

The invitation to the Pittsburgh Congress that founded the IWPA in 1883 had advertised it as a "Congress of North American Socialists," and left the definition of "socialist" to the reader. Throughout its history the IWPA sought to be an inclusive, rather than exclusive, associa-tion....

The anarchists were social-revolutionaries

...The necessity for and inevitability of a social revolution became a third article of faith. In 1884, the Progressive Cigarmakers, Die Metall-Arbeiter Union, and the Central Labor Union proclaimed their belief "that the only means whereby the emancipation of mankind can be brought about is the open rebellion of the robbed class in all parts of the country against the existing economic and political institutions." There was, as Henry David noted, an "annoying vagueness" about the anarchists' notion of revolution. For Parsons, it meant "the time when the wage-laborers of this and other countries will assert their rights – natural rights – and maintain them by force of arms. The social revolu-tion means the expropriation of the means of production and the resources of life." And as David noted, "it rarely occurred to the leaders of the movement to clarify the meaning of the term 'social revolution' for the benefit of themselves and their followers."

There was no ambiguity about the weaponry to be used. Articles headed "Dynamite," "Assassination," "Explosives," "Bombs!" "War with All Means," "Streetfighting," and "How to Meet the Enemy," which appeared in *The Alarm, Die Arbeiter-Zeitung,* and *Der Vorbote* from 1884 through 1886, are infamous. Many reappeared, first as evidence in the Haymarket Trial, then in contemporary and sensational histories of anarchism, still later in scholarly accounts. Their uncritical repetition has become a hallmark of anarchist scholarship and exaggerated the "cult of dynamite." According to *The Alarm*, "one dynamite bomb, properly placed, will destroy a regiment of soldiers." Wage slaves were urged "to start a manufactory of hand grenades"; "Instructions Regarding its Use and Operations, precautions in handling and storage" were available at *Die Arbeiter-Zeitung*'s offices.

The cult centered around *Die Anarchist*, Engel, Fischer, Lingg, and Gruppe Nordwestseite, who had condemned *Die Arbeiter-Zeitung* as insufficiently radical. Twenty years after his pardon Oskar Neebe was still "indignant at the 'defense' literature that made the victims bleating lambs. They were emphatically brave soldiers, and Engel was an out-and-out militarist." Johann Most's meticulously researched pamphlet *Revolutionare Kriegswissenschaft* became their bible. The English translation of its title page accurately describes its contents: *The Science of Revolutionary War: A Manual of Instruction in the Use and Preparation of Nitroglycerine and Dynamite, Gun-Cotton, Fulminating Mercury, Bombs, Fuses, Poisons, etc.*

The "Intransigents," as Paul Avrich has labelled them, came to embrace the propaganda of the deed and to use it as a theory of radicalization. The *attentater* was to be a revolutionary sacrifice; his *tat* would revenge the working class, frighten the bourgeoisie, result in his own martyrdom, and then serve as propaganda for the movement. The propaganda of the deed was conceived as a sympathetic and symbolic act of violence. By attacking a representative of the oppressors, the intransigents expected to focus the nation's attention on oppression and then trigger a series of *attentats* that would inevitably culminate in revolution.[3]

Most of this was talk, "bomb-talking," as Floyd Dell perceptively called it. "Why then did these men talk dynamite?" Dell asked as he caught one side of the phenomenon: "It was done partly to attract attention to their real beliefs – it was a way of shocking the public into attention. So desperate a means of securing an audience is only taken by a small faction – it is a sign of weakness." George Schilling thought it more dangerous than desperation and weakness. In a remarkable letter to Lucy Parsons in 1893 he argued

the open espousal of physical force – especially when advocated by foreigners – as a remedy for social maladjustments can only lead to greater despotism. When you terrorize the public mind and threaten the stability of society with violence, you create the conditions which place the

Bonfields and Garys' in the saddle... Fear is not the mother of progress and liberty but oft times of reaction and aggression.

Speaking of the martyrs, and to Parsons' widow, Schilling maintained "They worshipped at the shrine of force; wrote and preached it; until finally they were overpowered by their own Gods and slain in their own temple."[4]

While Chicago's anarchists revelled in bomb talking, the propaganda of the deed remained a recessive characteristic within the anarchist movement. If two of Chicago's IWPA groups published *Die Anarchist*, twenty-four supported *Die Arbeiter-Zeitung*. The majority of the movement never embraced the *attentat*, nor did they ever denounce those who had. The best explanation for that failure must lie in their recognition that force would be required in the future. Instead the movement pointed to five revolutions, three within their lifetimes, as social revolutions. They were farthest removed from the American Revolution, but they celebrated Tom Paine's birthday annually, and venerated George Washington enough to place his portrait next to Ferdinand Lassalle's at other celebrations. They quoted Jefferson and the Declaration of Independence in the Pittsburgh Manifesto. The French Revolution of 1789 was almost as distant, and the anarchists chose to remember Gracchus Babeuf and "Die Baboeufisten" as heroes....[5]

Finally, there was more than a streak of revolutionary romanticism in all their discussions of revolution and armed struggle. During a violent strike in 1875, John Simmens prophesied a "proletarian revolution within a few decades." The waiting period seemed brief, the glorious revolution just around the corner, needing but a single spark. The capitalist system was in crisis and on the verge of collapse. Many had convinced themselves of "an already approaching revolution," which "promises to be much grander than that at the close of the last century"; and Parsons spoke fondly, "We see it coming. We predict it, we hail with joy!" "Tremble, oppressors of the world!" proclaimed the Pittsburgh Manifesto. "Not far beyond your purblind sight there dawns the scarlet and sable lights of the Judgement Day." For some revolution meant the millennium.

The anarchists were atheists and freethinkers

Most anarchists expected it would be a godless millennium. E. A. Stevens, the president of the Chicago Liberal League and an active member of both the SLP and the Knights, wrote to the Detroit *Labor Leaf* a week after the Riot: "The authorities are making a point against them that they do not believe in God. The police are principally Irish Catholics, and were glad to have a pretext to make the attack."

At a time when the rhetoric of the American labor movement was couched in evangelical Protestantism, and the Knights of Labor in Chicago enjoyed close ties to the Roman Catholic church, the anarchists rejected both the symbols and content of Christianity. This rejection alienated not only the police and clergy, but also many in the labor movement, especially the Knights. We should not be confused that "conservative trade unionists and radical anarchists and socialists... often appealed to Christianity for its sanction." On the other hand it is clear, as David Montgomery has argued, that "the deepest line of division within the working class... was that of religion." Yet both insights underestimate the complexity of the situation in Gilded Age Chicago where Protestants and Catholics confronted a third group of atheists and freethinkers found in Scandinavian, Bohemian, German, and even native-born neighborhoods. Not only were these ethnic freethinking groups aware of one another's presence, but they frequently cooperated....[6]

Atheism and free thought intertwined in the nineteenth century, especially in the eyes of the faithful. Not all freethinkers were socialists, but most socialists were freethinkers. Atheism and free thought cut two ways in the Gilded Age. On the one hand, freethinking organizations (like the Skandinavisk Fritaenkere Forening or the Bohemian Svoboda obec Chicagu) were breeding grounds for socialism; in Richard Schneirov's words, they "provided a congenial environment for socialism to thrive and develop." Reverend Adams, a contemporary, put it succinctly: "The result of atheism always must be anarchism." On the other hand, atheism divided the city's labor movement by separating socialists from other immigrants, and from the native-born. Protestants and Catholics, pietists and ritualists, may well have divided at election time, but they shared an intense hatred of the godless.

Adams was not alone in seeing that connection. In 1844, Marx asserted that the "criticism of religion [was] the premise of all criticism." Beyond the organizational nexus, atheism was already political when it immigrated to America. Free thought became political in Europe when it confronted the established church. For Marcus Thrane in Norway and Lev Palda or Ladimir Klacel in Bohemia, anticlericalism served as a preliminary critique of not just the church but also the state. It was antihierarchical; it was egalitarian because it refused to recognize any Supreme Being, focusing instead on man. Moreover, free thought was materialist; by refusing to yield to another world, it concentrated on this world. Its ethics and morality flowed from that materialist egalitarianism. And while Americans enjoyed a constitutional separation of church and state, and many immigrants clung to their ethnic parishes, these radical immigrants brought a political antagonism to religion and to the state into a society and culture where that antagonism was utterly inappropriate.

Bakunin Never Slept in Chicago

... in this country, above all countries in the world, is Anarchy possible.... In those strong European governments ... they strangle Anarchism or ship it here. Everybody comes to our climate; everybody reaches our shores; our freedom is great – and it should never be abridged – and here with that freedom, with that great enjoyment of liberty to all men, they seek to obtain their end by Anarchy, which in other countries is impossible. As I said, there is one step from republicanism to Anarchy.

There were at least three other threads in the cloth of this movement's ideology. One was a precocious feminism evident in Lizzie Swank's articles on "Factory Girls" and the prominence of women in the American Groups. The IWPA remained uninterested in women's suffrage, indeed the anarchists "offered no path to combat their oppression – except the social revolution, which would somehow solve all problems." An ambiguous position on racism formed a second. While Chicago's anarchists applauded Riel's Rebellion in Canada and supported the American Indian, their positions on anti-Chinese activity and towards American blacks remained ambiguous – "at best fuzzy about the very existence of racism" in Paul Le Blanc's judgment. A third thread denounced chauvinism, as *The Alarm* maintained that "Real internationalists despise and loathe the name and spirit of Nationalism." And yet four major threads can be easily discerned within the fabric of anarchist ideology: republicanism, socialism, revolution, and atheism.

If the two Russians Mikhail Bakunin and Peter Kropotkin epitomized nineteenth-century anarchism, then Chicago's IWPA was not anarchist. Indeed the only Chicagoan in any way affiliated with the IWPA who had met Bakunin was Dr. Ernst Schmidt. They met, only briefly, in St. Louis in March 1861, the month before the start of the Civil War. Beyond the continuities of membership and organization lay an ideological evolution, one best understood as a transcendence of nineteenth-century republicanism. This was not an evolution from socialism to anarchism but from republicanism, through electoral socialism, to revolutionary socialism. However unscrupulous he may have been, State's Attorney Julius Grinnell understood that there was but "one step from republicanism to Anarchy."

Republican images pervaded socialist and anarchist rhetoric. The republic depended upon the independence of the citizenry and its active involvement in society. Capitalist development, as some of Chicago's radicals saw it, had destroyed independence and liberty and the concentration of wealth had corrupted the republic. Greed had perverted the political process and concentrated power in the hands of the few. "He who must sell his labor power or starve will sell his vote when the same alternative is presented. Our political institutions are but the reflex of the economic, and our political reformers should learn that the workers are not poor because they vote wrong, on the contrary, they vote wrong because they are poor." Despite rampant vote fraud, these anarchists did not completely reject the electoral process until 1882.

They had already broken with republican political economy when they identified private property as the cause of corruption, economic depression, and social revolution. "Private property in the resources of life – the means of existence – is sanctified by the Church, made legal by the Constitution, enforced by the law, backed up and maintained by the army, navy, and police of the bourgeoisie." That identification was an irreconcilable breach with the republican notion that liberty and property were entwined. Anarchists argued that the concentration of private property had corrupted the republic, and that a free society must be based on the cooperative organization of production.

And they broke with republican notions of the state and social evolution by embracing revolution. As socialists they had viewed the state as socially neutral and politics as mere electioneering. For anarchists, the state was not neutral and politics extended far beyond elections into the workshop and factory. Social revolution, on the model of the Paris Commune, promised to reestablish the republic. The Pittsburgh Manifesto thundered that "the political institutions of our time are the agencies of the propertied class" and that "their mission is the upholding of the privileges of their masters." The ultraradicals, those Paul Avrich has labelled the "Intransigents," rejected the legitimacy of any form of government. The majority within the movement seemed unconvinced by such arguments. Both envisioned the "destruction of the existing class rule, . . . [and] the establishment of a free society." Convinced that the ruling class would "never resign their privilege voluntarily . . . there remains but one recourse – FORCE! Our forefathers have not only told us . . . that force is justifiable . . . but they themselves have set the immemorial example."

Irreligion served as a fourth thread in their ideology. English-speaking marchers carried banners emblazoned with "No God, No Master," Germans carried "Neider mit Thron, Altar und Geldsack," the Czechs "Zadný bůh Zadný pan." Few attended any church, even fewer believed; most subscribed to Bakunin's denunciation of God and State. Free thought and atheism contributed to anarchist conceptions of liberty, equality, and fraternity, and to the assault of both property and authority. Their lack of faith might have been tolerable, except that the Knights of Labor were deeply pious, the city's working class was still engaged by Protestant revivals, and the anarchists delighted in both blasphemy and sacrilege.

Finally, the movement's ideology, like its culture, reflected the dynamic interaction of ideologues and membership, and must be understood as part of a larger cultural system. The active membership hired its editors and between 1874 and 1886 fired at least ten of them. If the Martyrs moved ideologically from socialism to anarchism, the active membership seems to have moved from republicanism, through parliamentary socialism, to revolutionary socialism. And the movement expressed that ideology culturally. While our understanding of their ideology has relied on editorials and manifestoes, each of these four threads was woven figuratively into the banners carried by the rank and file. Socialist singing societies, theater groups, dances, picnics, parades, and festivals tried to promote a sense of solidarity and mission within the active membership, which then offered its abilities and services to the sympathetic following within the city's working class.

Eight Hours, Riot, and Repression

The size, growth, composition, organization, culture, and ideology of the anarchist movement form the background for understanding the Haymarket Affair. That movement was both large and growing at the time of the riot and had organized around a vital, militant socialist press; an active, democratic club life; and an ominous federation of "progressive" unions. Movement culture expressed an ideology that transcended artisan republicanism by becoming collectivist, solidaristic, and communitarian as it embraced revolutionary socialism. In sum, the anarchist movement threatened to assume the leadership of the city's working class.

This [section] focuses on the riot's immediate foreground, the organization and agitation of the Great Upheaval of 1885–86, in which the IWPA and the Central Labor Union played the central role. We need to look first at the unprecedented mass movement to establish the eight-hour working day. Then, we can briefly review the riot in Haymarket Square the night of 4 May 1886. Finally, we need to understand the trial and the executions of the Martyrs as part of a much wider program of repression, one which began before and continued beyond the legal proceedings, beyond the executions, and well into the 1890s.

This is familiar ground, and it is not my intention to reconstruct either riot or trial at any length; that project has already been done by competent historians. The point instead must be to understand that the Haymarket Affair offered an opportunity to try eight prominent anarchists as criminal conspirators, and to bring the full weight of civil authority against the most radical organization within the city's working class. Finally, we need to assess the impact of repression on the movement as a whole.

The Eight Hour Movement

The year of 1886 was a year of great activity in the labor movement. The Knights of Labor had had a previous convention and resolved to engage in an effort to establish the eight-hour day. In May, 1886, and some months before, they had entered into an agitation to accomplish their purpose. There was no knowledge of that movement in our group at all; information about it was distributed through the American and German press, but since we could read neither German nor English, ... we knew nothing of that movement; but it was in the atmosphere and it seemed to have crossed the border of our settlement, because in the months of February and March there was quite a lot of dissatisfaction among our people about the prices paid for work.

That description comes from Abraham Bisno, a twenty-year-old Russian-born Jewish sewing-machine operator, who had arrived in Chicago in 1882 and joined the Eight Hour Movement four years later. The earliest meetings of the Jewish garment workers were "very cleverly" arranged by someone unknown to them. "There was a great tumult[,] everybody was talking and nobody knew quite what this thing was about." A Knight appeared at a second meeting and signed the workers up. According to Bisno, "All I then knew of the principles of the Knights of Labor was that the[ir] motto ... was, 'One for All, and All for One.' I think they did require us to pay in a dollar per man ... and [then] we were all initiated with great ceremony."

Bisno was mistaken. The Knights were not the driving force behind the eight-hour day, nor was the Trades Assembly, nor the Central Labor Union. Two years earlier, in 1884, at a convention in Chicago, the Federation of Organized Trades and Labor Assemblies had ordained 1 May 1886 for the inauguration of the eight-hour day. Both ordination and inauguration died for lack of interest. In the fall of 1885, however, the movement was reborn by the unskilled and unorganized. Their "dissatisfaction," in Bisno's words, deepened and organization spontaneously appeared. Indeed, the organized and skilled found themselves drawn into a movement they had not started and long disdained.

Although it had hosted the federation's convention, Chicago's Trades Assembly neither endorsed the eight-hour demand nor established an eight-hour committee until October 1885. Two months later, and six months before May Day, only eleven of the Assembly's twenty-five member unions had endorsed the movement for shorter hours. The assembly was more concerned with fighting the introduction of new machinery, and with fighting the dilution of craft skills by female, child, unskilled, and prison labor. However beleaguered, Chicago's skilled and organized workers could not get enthusiastic over shortened hours. Because they treated the relations between labor and capital "from a conservative point of view," and because they recognized the reality of intercity competition, the assembly held that eight hours was unwinnable.

While the anarchists and socialists scurried from meeting to meeting, *The Alarm* complained in January that "the Trade and Labor Assembly has done but little or nothing."

> Thus far the only large mass-meetings in behalf of the "Eight Hour Movement," have been held by those who have been accused of being opposed to the movement – The revolutionary Socialists, Anarchists, Internationalists, or whatever you may call the "ignorant foreigners" who follow the red flag and proclaim that wage-slavery is the curse of this age.

Two weeks later Albert Parsons explained: "The Trades Assembly has so much to do in other directions that they don't get time to bother with such little things as the Eight Hour Movement." The Knights of Labor were similarly unenthusiastic. In March, the Order's Grand Master Workman released his "secret circular" which disavowed the eight-hour strikes, refused to charter new assemblies for forty days, and counseled against both strikes and boycotts.

Until Haymarket, the anarchists remained ambivalent towards the Knights. When Powderly appeared to concede to Jay Gould on the Southwest strikes in March 1886, *Der Vorbote* labelled him a "monarchical, outdated labor leader" who "might have been of use a thousand years ago." "The Knight of the rueful countenance" became "Pope Powderly I," the head of "the established Catholic Church of modern times," – "an arrogant, ambitious ignoramus." The Knights became "muddleheads and men of simple belief who do not understand their position in society and don't know anything about economic laws." In April, *Der Vorbote* cautioned a new union against "the haphazard step" of joining the Knights, recommending instead an "independent" course.

While the German newspapers attacked, the American Groups and their paper cooperated with the Knights. In March, *The Alarm* reported that an attempt "to create ill-feeling between the Socialists and the Knights" had "proved a dismal failure." During a meeting of the American Group "a laborer in the audience rose and inquired if he could join the Knights of Labor as he had come to the meeting for that purpose." The chairman, according to *The Alarm*, "informed him that the Knights of Labor was a secret organization and that the International was not, and he would have to go to some Knight . . . Assembly in order to join it." Instead of denouncing the Noble Order, the chairman merely directed the man down the street. *Der Vorbote* hoped the Eight Hour Movement would "lead the Knights in the right direction toward radicalism." Despite their vicious criticism of the local and national leadership, Spies and Schwab argued "their demonstration of power is a very favorable development." Although Spies had approached Bisno and the Jewish tailors, the anarchists were not disturbed when they joined the Knights. Oskar Neebe remained adamant that "hundreds of our speakers [spoke] to workingmen to organize themselves, no matter in what form as unions or Knights [arguing] that in organization lay their strength." As the anarchists organized, they "did not assail" the Knights, "on the contrary, [they] applauded them."

Neither the IWPA nor the CLU was initially enthusiastic about shorter hours. "We do not antagonize the eight hour movement," *The Alarm* explained, "viewing it from the standpoint that it is a social struggle – we simply predict it is a lost battle." Asked why the IWPA did not support the Eight Hour Movement, *The Alarm* answered, "Because we will not compromise." Other anarchists were less adamant. At a CLU meeting in the Bohemian Turner Hall in December Josef Pecka judged the movement a good one "as it afforded an opportunity to spread revolutionary ideas." Confronting the groundswell of a mass movement, the anarchists moved to join it that fall.

On the eve of the Great Upheaval, Chicago's labor movement contained three different organizations, with different memberships and organizations. That fragmentation was typified by the 1,381 production workers in McCormick's reaper works. The Knights claimed 750 members among them, the Metall-Arbeiter Union (which belonged to the CLU) 250, and the Molder's Union (which belonged to the Trades Assembly) 10; the remaining 300 were nonunion men. The Trades Assembly remained a conservative body composed of skilled and organized Anglo-Americans. The Knights were organizing both skilled and unskilled, male and female, under an Irish-American leadership. The CLU had been organized by skilled European immigrants, but in the heat of the movement for shorter hours, would push hardest for the organization of the unskilled and previously unorganized.

As the winter of 1885–86 set in, the CLU found itself caught up in the Great Upheaval, and the IWPA followed. Before the end of the year the two organizations scheduled weekly, then almost daily meetings. From the Deering reaper works on the far North side, to a hall outside of Pullman on the far South side, its speakers addressed workingmen and - women in German, English, Czech, Norwegian, Danish, and Polish. Their agitation penetrated at least one community, the Polish, which had been ignored by previous organizing campaigns. As late as January 1886, the *Times* reported, "The Poles and Bohemians are absolutely without any organization; except so far as their inborn sympathy with socialistic ideas has impelled them to join army military companies." Led by the CLU, "the Polish and Bohemians have finally begun to organize."

The pace became even more frenetic in the last months before May 1. Established unions within the CLU, like the International Carpenters and Joiners, composed of Germans and Bohemians, continued to grow. In April, Die Möbel-Arbeiter Union claimed 1,600 members in its four branches. Existing unterstützsungvereine, like those among the German and Bohemian bakers, led by Mathias Schmeidinger, and among the German butchers, led by Thomas Florus, became unions and joined the CLU. Under the eight-hour banner, other wholly new unions organized. In March, the brewers, with 400 members, joined the CLU. In April, the IWPA and the CLU called a mass meeting to create an Unskilled Laborers Eight-Hour League and about thirty men signed up at the first meeting. The Butcher Clerks' Union took the lead among the grocery clerks, organizing 250 members almost immediately. And on the night of May 4, Samuel Fielden, Lucy and Albert Parsons were late to the protest meeting in Haymarket Square because the American Group had been working, like the Working Women's Union seven years earlier, to bring organization to the city's sewing girls.

Die Lumberyard Arbeiter Union was one of the newest unions. The Irish dockworkers in the lumber district had organized in the 1870s, but the Bohemian yardworkers, who had struck in 1876 and were prominent in the 1877 Upheaval, had never enjoyed any permanent organization. It came only with the Eight Hour Movement, and, like the Jewish tailors, only in the last weeks before May 1. The *Tribune* reported that "the majority of the men who are employed in the lumberyards [are] repres-entatives of the rabid branch of the Anarchists and Socialists." Of ten officers elected by the new union, five were members of the IWPA, including the vice-president, the Bohemian-language secretary, and all three delegates to the CLU. The union's growth was meteoric: "About

60 new members joined the union, which now contains about 3,000 in the German branch and 2,500 in the Bohemian. Night before last 400 joined." The *Tribune* ominously noted: "The Lumber-Workers['] union is not a branch of the Knights of Labor[,] but of the notorious Central Labor Union."

The unionization campaign that accompanied the Eight Hour Movement was frenzied. Under the heading "Stadt Chicago," *Der Vorbote*'s last page was filled with the announcements and reports of union meetings. The 21 April 1886 issue, for example, reported meetings of Die Möbel-Arbeiter Union; a mass meeting just outside Pullman where the Metall-Arbeiter Union gained fifty new members and Die Möbel-Arbeiter Union No. 3 initiated seventy-five; the Linseed Oil Arbeiters; die Maurer [masons]; tanners, butchers (with forty-five new members); carpenters (fifty-four new members in two locals); saddlers ("fifty neue Mitglieder"); and Die Metall-Arbeiter Union, which gained ninety-six new members for a total "uber 900." According to the *Tribune*, the Passementerie Workers' Union added "25 new members, mostly girls," the shop tailors were organizing and about seventy joined, and the wagonmakers union had decided to affiliate with the CLU.

Each of the city's three labor organizations grew in the Great Upheaval. The Trades Assembly reported some twenty-five member unions in October 1885; five months later there were fifty. The CLU had eight founding unions in February 1884; two years later it had twenty-four, including the eleven largest unions in the city. One month before the riot, *Der Vorbote* estimated the Assembly at 20,000 members; a week before the bomb it claimed 28,000 for the CLU. Despite long-standing fears of "mushroom growth" and Powderly's secret circular, the membership of the Noble and Holy Order continued to grow. Indeed if District Assembly 24 obeyed the circular, DA 57 did not. At the end of March 1886, the *Tribune* counted about twenty-six local assemblies and 5,000 Knights attached to DA 57, and "about the same membership" in DA 24, for a total of 10,000. In June 1886, the Illinois Bureau of Labor Statistics reported about 18,000 Knights in Cook County; in July the Knights's *General Assembly Proceedings* reported a total of 22,592 affiliated with the city's three DAs.

The contrasts could not have been plainer than in the juxtaposition of Chicago's two Eight Hour demonstrations in April 1886. The first was scheduled by the Knights and the Trades Assembly and held in the Cavalry Armory on a Saturday night. Of thirty people who can be identified in the platform party, 60 percent had Irish surnames; another 26 percent came from Britain; no more than 14 percent were immigrants from continental Europe. The Knights claimed sixteen representatives,

the Assembly eleven. All of the evening's speakers, including the
Protestant ministers and the head of Chicago's Clan-na-Gael, spoke in
English. Their speeches were fervent but cautious, almost conciliatory.
According to the *Tribune*:

> Workingmen were called upon to organize and to join the Knights of
> Labor; to abstain from whiskey-drinking and prepare themselves for the
> 1st of May... [when] the clink of the hammer and the turn of the wheel
> should stop and the fires be drawn resolutely.... They were to ask for eight
> hours of work and eight hours' pay;... and the justice of their demand
> would assure its realization.

Two weeks later the CLU and the IWPA arranged a second eight-hour
demonstration that the *Tribune* dismissed as "Mainly Communistic." It
drew from 10,000 to 15,000 marchers, male and female, who gathered
in Market Square and then wound through the Loop led by seven bands.
A great crowd accompanied the marchers, who divided towards two
speaker stands, one for English and Germans, the other for English
and Czechs. This second demonstration was multilingual, as were the
speakers. The ministers were absent, for the procession and rally had
been scheduled on Easter Sunday. The red flag far outnumbered the
Stars and Stripes; where the Knights and unionists sang "My Country
'Tis of Thee," the anarchists and their followers sang the "Marseillaise."
While those in the Armory petitioned for an eight-hour day, those in the
streets demanded shorter hours with no reduction.

There was a strident difference between the two organizing slogans,
the Knights and unionists calling for eight-hours' work at eight-hours'
pay, the anarchists and CLU demanding eight-hours' work for ten-
hours' pay. The first was presented respectfully, almost deferentially;
the second was brazenly, defiantly, demanded. The first conceded to the
reigning notions of political economy; the second utterly rejected them.
If the anarchists had initially disdained the Eight Hour Movement,
historians, not contemporaries, faulted and discounted them. As they
organized during 1885–86, Chicago's workers enjoyed the luxury of
choosing from among the established trade unions, the reformist
Knights, and the revolutionary CLU, all of which offered organizers.
That many chose to follow the anarchists and the CLU does not mean
they chose anarchy or revolution. By May 1, 47,500 workers had already
won shorter hours, many at a higher wage; on May Day an additional
62,500 struck, including the building trades, cigar-makers, freight handlers, lumber shovers, furniture and garment workers. According to the
state Bureau of Labor Statistics, 16,000 of the 19,000 workers surveyed
had demanded eight-hours' work at ten-hours' pay.

On May Day, the *Tribune* published an interview with an otherwise unidentified anarchist who compared the organizing campaigns of the two major competitors:

> The German and Bohemian workmen are thoroughly organized and armed and will fight to achieve their end. The brewers, malters, butchers, and bakers have already achieved their eight hour day. The Knights of Labor are principally American and Irish; they don't train with the Germans and Bohemians. And we can't get them to do aggressive work in the movement[:] they hang back and take what they can get, while the Germans and Bohemians go out and get what they want.

Beyond their organizational and agitational skills, the anarchists and the Central Labor Union brought a sense of militancy to Chicago's Eight Hour Movement, giving it a confrontational edge.

The Haymarket riot, trial, and executions

That edge reinforced the shadow of 1877. Nine years before Haymarket, Federal troops who had campaigned with General Custer fought Bohemian and Irish workers in "The Battle of the Halsted Street Viaduct." That afternoon police had charged into the Westside Turner Hall and, in the course of breaking up a negotiating session of furniture workers and their bosses, killed one worker and wounded others. After being fired from the *Times*, Parsons went to speak in Market Square that night and remembered in his autobiography "over 100 policemen charged upon this peaceable mass-meeting, firing their pistols and clubbing left and right." For three days that July men, women, and children had taken the streets, closed the city's factories and workshops, and fought not only police but state militia and two Army regiments. About thirty workingmen had been killed, another 200 wounded. The police were undermanned, practically unarmed, and so ill equipped that Marshall Field, a leading merchant, lent the department his delivery wagons for transportation. Led by the Board of Trade, the city's business elite had formed a Veteran's Corps and a Citizen's Patrol. The police proved so ineffective that the militia and cavalry had to be summoned.

The socialists had long been identified as troublemakers. During the 1877 strike, the mayor and a group of businessmen threatened Parsons in the police chief's office, advising him to leave the city. In March 1879, the militia had been garrisoned next to the Commune festival in the Exposition Building; a month later the state legislature outlawed the Lehr- und Wehr-Verein and revitalized the state militia. As recently as July 1884, nineteen-year-old Wilhelm Spies, the youngest of August

Spies's brothers, had been fatally gut-shot by an Irish cop while defending a drunken friend from arrest. If plainclothes detectives had shadowed socialists since 1877, the first Pinkerton agent did not infiltrate the anarchist movement until December 1884. He was not alone: John Dusey recognized and "scolded" four Pinkertons at a lakefront meeting in July 1885.

There were more recent incidents of what had become routine police violence. The most brutal came in the first week of July 1885 during a citywide streetcar strike. Led by an as yet unknown lieutenant, John Bonfield, twenty-five officers mounted a train's first car and towed a second for prisoners and a third for their reinforcements along the Madison Street line. Anyone who blocked or passed the train was clubbed, anyone who shouted "scab" or "rat" was similarly treated, and Bonfield earned the nickname "Blackjack." The track was slowly cleared and more than 150 arrested, including sixty-five strikers and two groups of jeering bystanders. Such brutality was unprovoked and widely denounced by all sections of the community; yet it was also effective and the strike collapsed. The Trades Assembly called for Bonfield's job, but Mayor Harrison deferred. Most importantly the strike marked a new, and unauthorized, aggression by the police.

As May 1 approached, the forces of order prepared with the Police Department as the first line of defense. Between 1880 and 1883 it had grown from 473 to 637 men; by 1886 it had been expanded to just over 1,000. While they were not officially armed, a few relied on their nightsticks. The department recruited the native-born, British, and Irish, and did not hire its first Bohemian, for example, until 1882. The department was not fully trusted by the city's manufacturers. In 1882 it had failed to intercede during a streetcar strike; in 1884 the firm of Cribben and Sexton had been forced to hire Pinkertons when the department failed to control strikers. The most recent scandal had revealed that an officer had refused to order his men to break up a strike by boxmakers in the winter of 1885–86. Behind the force stood a larger group of police "extras" and "specials," reinforced in turn by an expanding militia. If the Lehr- und Wehr-Verein was training in the basements of their meeting halls, another rumor had Marshall Field's clerks armed and drilling in his company's warehouses. The Citizen's Association supported the expansion of both the police and the militia; the Commercial, Union League, and Chicago clubs preferred a nearby garrison of Federal troops but continued to patronize the National Guard's officers and armories.

The Haymarket riot can best be understood then in a context of suspicion, hostility, and fear, for the Eight Hour Movement reawakened the terror of 1877. For a decade and a half, Chicago's communists had annually celebrated, even invoked, the specter of the Paris Commune. In

January 1885, during another of the city's recurrent red scares, the state militia put "a voluntary guard" on the First Regiment's Armory to protect it from a possible attack by the Lehr- und Wehr-Verein. When the attack never materialized, the *Inter Ocean* interviewed several members of the LWV and of the Jaeger Verein; two weeks after those rumors first appeared, the *Daily News* headlined "No Cause for Alarm."

Those fears multiplied in the Great Upheaval. The First Infantry Regiment "satisfactorily performed" its street-riot drill on Thanksgiving Day 1885. The next month "an infernal machine" was found on a judge's doorstep, obviously placed there by "an insane freak of some socialistic crank." In January 1886, stories, emanating from New York, reappeared "regarding a socialistic outbreak in Chicago." The *Tribune* responded with an editorial calling for "A Regular Army Garrison in Chicago" which could quell "the dangers of riot and insurrection." In March, Charles Bodendeick, a member of the American Group, frightened another judge "by calling at his house late at night and demanding $25;" bound by a $1,500 bond, "the defendant exclaimed: 'I am a socialist, and am proud of being one.'"

The forces of order expected the worst as they planned for the inauguration of the eight-hour day. Two days before the CLU's procession and Lakefront demonstration, the First Cavalry Regiment performed another exhibition drill and dress parade for the Commercial Club. Three days later the First Infantry Regiment held its annual inspection and the same club, led by Philip Armour, subscribed more than $2,000 "to furnish the regiment with a good machine gun, to be used by them in case of trouble." The anarchists did nothing to calm the city. From February 1885 through March 1886, *Die Arbeiter-Zeitung* reportedly advertised free rifle instruction to workers at Smrz's Hall on Clybourn Avenue; the IWPA's English and German organs had issued directions for making and using dynamite; *The Alarm* published diagrams on street fighting and how to attack a Gatling gun. Military rhetoric permeated every discussion of the labor movement and class relations. On May Day, *Die Arbeiter-Zeitung* called:

> Bravely forward! The conflict has begun. An army of wage-laborers are idle. Capitalism conceals its tiger claws behind the ramparts of order. Workmen, let your watchword be: No compromise! Cowards to the rear! Men to the front! The die is cast. The first of May, whose historic significance will be understood and appreciated only in later years, has come.

May 1 came and nothing untoward happened. Expecting, even predicting "trouble" and "violence," the bourgeois press waited. When an anarchist let slip that "Herr Most" was expected that afternoon, the *Tribune* sent its reporter to police and military headquarters. Police Chief Frederick Ebersold had "no intimation that there is to be any great amount of trouble" and dismissed "all this talk of police reserves, police preparations and special orders" as "nonsense." On the other hand, "the arms and ammunition of the regiment were in readiness for immediate use" at D Battery's armory. At the First Infantry Regiment's new armory and headquarters, "extra men were in charge" but there were "no extraordinary precautions." If the police remained resolute, and the militia stood ready, the *Tribune* reassured its readers that a Gatling gun had been bought and would arrive that very night. Chief Ebersold, Inspector Bonfield, and the precinct captains quietly met "in consultation" the second day, but all the press could report was that "the police will be disposed about the city . . . and others will be held to act at a moment's notice. The entire force will be on active duty." The Knights, the Trades Assembly, and the CLU met, separately of course, and went over strike reports. That night the Assembly held a "slimly attended" Eight-Hour Ball at Battery D's armory.

The Trades Assembly held another "protracted" meeting on Monday, May 3. A resolution from the floor recommended "the formation of an Executive Board, composed of representatives of all trades," which would have meant not just recognition of the CLU, but outright cooperation at least for the Eight Hour Movement. R. C. Owens, from the carpenters' union and LA 1307, seconded the resolution, arguing that such cooperation was both timely and essential to success. The vulnerable Andrew Cameron, former editor of the *Workingman's Advocate* and one of the oldest of Chicago's labor reformers, took the floor to denounce any notion of cooperation:

> I am one of those who do not think it a crime to be an American, or worse than murder to speak the English language. I am opposed to any movement toward joining with those who carry the red flag of Socialism [from] Europe to the democratic-republicanism of America. The Trade Assembly will be certainly smirched if it takes on such a responsibility.

Additional denunciations followed, echoing Cameron's lead, and the resolution was allowed to drop.

That same afternoon the lumber shovers invited August Spies to address a strike meeting. Attended by more than 5,000 from the union, the meeting was held a block from McCormick's plant, and attracted about 500 of the strikers there. At shift's end, the strikebreakers started to file out, and Spies's audience left to jeer the scabs. A police detail arrived unexpectedly, fired on the strikers, and then charged; at least two strikers were killed, five or six wounded, and others injured. Spies rushed back to his office, dashed off the "Revenge Circular," and handed it to the composing room foreman.

Only 200 or 300 of the 20,000 handbills carried the word "Revenge" as they announced a mass meeting that evening to protest the latest police outrage. And however durable, the label "the Haymarket Riot" is wrong on two counts. Based on the CLU's turnout a week before, the meeting's planners expected a crowd of 25,000 and originally chose Market Square. When someone objected that it was "a mousetrap" with few exits, the site was changed to the Haymarket Square. When the crowd never materialized, the event did not take place in Haymarket Square, but in an alley off the square. Second, it was the police, not the crowd, who rioted. The meeting was called for 8:30 p.m. but none of the speakers was present and runners were sent to find them. Mayor Harrison stopped by to measure the crowd, judged it "tame," concluded that "nothing had occurred yet, or looked likely to occur to require interference," and suggested that the reserves at the Desplaines Street Police Station be sent home.

Spies spoke first, then deferred when Parsons, his wife, children, and Fielden finally arrived. Parsons spoke for almost an hour, then introduced Fielden who spoke for about ten minutes. Threatened by rain, the meeting was about to break up when the police arrived. "In the name of the people of the state of Illinois," Captain Ward intoned, "I command this meeting immediately and peaceably to disperse." When Ward repeated the order Fielden replied, "We are peaceable." A moment later the bomb exploded. Chaos ensued; then the police reformed, opened fire, reloaded, and fired again. There may have been some return fire from the fleeing crowd, then all was quiet.

Who was in the square that night? We can identify only eighty-two in a crowd estimated between 600 and 3,000. This is not, however, a random sample and there is little reason to believe it representative. About a third of the sample were marked by the riot: sixteen were shot that night, four more got clubbed, four arrested, four died. We know the ages of only seventeen, with a mean of thirty-five years old; we know that twelve in the crowd had been city residents for an average of eleven years. One victim was visiting from Indianapolis, but the majority had addresses within eight blocks of the square. All three of the speeches that night were in English, but 60 percent of the crowd had German surnames; about 10 percent English; another 10 percent native-born; the remaining 20 percent were split among Bohemians, Poles, Swedes, and French. Drawn from the surrounding neighborhood, the crowd was composed of "workingmen of all beliefs and views," just as Spies described them; and shoemakers comprised the single largest occupational group.

We have much more accurate information on the police contingent commanded by Lieutenants Ward and Bonfield. They were "all select men, the flower of the Central Detail", "a company of giants," according to the department's official historian, and each carried two loaded revolvers. Mathias Degan died instantly; officers Mueller, Barrett, Flavin, Sheehan, Redden, and Hansen died later; up to seventy others were injured, most by police bullets, most shot in the back. The detachment had a mean age of 33.5 years. Four of the officers had been with the department for only fourteen days; two had served seventeen years; overall they had a mean of five years of service. A microcosm of the department, Captain Ward's squad was an Irish-American unit: fully 40 percent had been born in Ireland, 24 percent were native-born, 22 percent in Britain, and the only Pole, Charles Dombrowski, "disgraced his uniform by fleeing."

The bomb thrower's identity remains a mystery. The grand jury indicted Rudolph Schnaubelt, who figured as the bomber throughout the trial, but the evidence remains inconclusive. There are two schools for speculation. One holds that the bomber was an agent provocateur. Parsons maintained that the bomb was thrown "to break up the eight-hour movement, thrust the active men into prison, and scare and terrify the workingmen into submission." Eight months later the *Arbeiter-Zeitung* still had "every reason" to believe that the bomb was thrown by a police agent. If Henry David failed to identify the bomb thrower after weighing the evidence against eight suspects, Paul Avrich has argued more recently that it was thrown by someone inside the movement. In 1984, Avrich's best guess identified George Schwab (no relation to Michael), "a German shoemaker and ultramilitant." In 1986, he proposed a new candidate, George Meng, "a German anarchist, a 'self-determined' militant in the Chicago groups, a known figure in the movement." Without some startling new evidence the mystery will apparently endure.

Repression

On Wednesday, 5 May 1866, the day after the riot, the police regrouped and struck back. Armed, but without a warrant, they charged into *Die Arbeiter-Zeitung*'s offices and arrested everyone they found: August Spies, Michael Schwab, Adolph Fischer, and the entire staff of reporters, compositors, even the printer's devil. The police returned, arresting a few more, confiscating manuscripts, type, galley proofs, the library's books, the paper's records and such. That afternoon Blackjack Bonfield led the detachments that closed both Zepf's and Greif's halls on Lake Street. The next day, May 6, the police raided and closed *Lampcka* and

Budoucnost's offices, where they again confiscated manuscripts, back issues, records, and a dozen banners. They also netted three anarchists (Jakub Mikolanda and Vaclav and Hynek Djmek) and a list of the paper's subscribers. The Djmek brothers were promised money and jobs to turn state's evidence; both refused and were eventually released. Within two weeks the police had raided each of the IWPA's known and suspected meeting places, more than fifty in all.

Throughout their investigations the police followed State's Attorney Julius Grinnell's advice to "Make the raids first and look up the law afterwards!" More than 200 men and women were arrested in their homes, at work, and in the streets. The police arrested Henry Spies because of his last name, and William Boege when he bragged about the riot in a saloon. Martel Obermann was pinched carrying a half-empty revolver, and George Dietz, a cabinetmaker, had a breechloader, cartridges, bullet molds, bulk lead, and several hundred copies of the *Arbeiter-Zeitung*. Captain Schaack proudly published his versions of the interrogations of about seventy prisoners, revealing in the process that many were denied counsel, food, water, and medical treatment.

The program of repression was never selective. The day after the riot, Inspector Bonfield met with a group of freight handlers "and advised them to avoid assembling in crowds upon the streets, and especially not to march in procession. He gave them a lot of good advice about avoiding even the appearance of evil, and withdrew." Some never heard the advice. The same morning 600 Jewish tailors marched from their ghetto towards the garment district; "patrol wagons came in on us from all sides...hundreds, probably thousands of policemen were unloaded in very short order...every policeman had a billy and they began to chase us and beat us unmercifully." Yet, as Abraham Bisno remembered, "None of us were arrested, none of us had time to do anything that would warrant an arrest."

> After May 1st, 1886 [sic, May 4th] picketing became absolutely impossible. The police arrested all pickets, even two or three. The attitude on the part of the police was practically the same as though the city was under martial law. Labor unions were raided, broken up, their property confiscated, the police used their clubs freely. Arrests were made without any cause, and the life of a working man was not quite safe when out on strike.

Some, of course, fled immediately. *Lampcka*'s editor and publisher, Anton Hradecny, left Chicago Tuesday or Wednesday night but returned to give himself up on the Tenth. John Henry ran to St. Louis; Balthaser Rau ran to friends in Omaha, Neb., only to be arrested (without a warrant) and returned to Chicago. After being twice arrested,

Rudolph Schnaubelt shaved off his beard, and chose flight, telling Sigmund Zeisler: "I believe it would be better for me to get out of Chicago for a time." He never returned. Albert Parsons, the most famous fugitive, fled first to William and Lizzie Holmes's house in Geneva, Ill., and then hid out in Waukesha, Wis. Others went underground within the city. William Seliger ran to a comrades' home in Lakeview but was later turned in by his own wife. The Seligers' boarder, Louis Lingg, hid out with two friends on the South side only to be tracked down when he sent for his tools. As late as August, the *Tribune* reported that Hendrich Sever, Solene Henri, and Justus Mont, all "parties to the Haymarket tragedy," had been traced to Ottawa (Illinois or Canada?) and that extradition was being arranged.

On May 5 the coroner's jury ruled that Officer Degan's death had been murder and charged all those then in custody with its responsibility. A grand jury was empaneled on May 17, conducted its investigation without a trace of secrecy, and dutifully presented an indictment on June 5 which concluded by thanking "the police force [whose] heroic bravery [had] saved this city from a scene of bloodshed and devastation equal to or perhaps greater than that witnessed by the Commune of Paris." The indictment named thirty-one men: the eight Martyrs, Schnaubelt, and twenty-two others who never stood trial. All but Schnaubelt and Parsons were already in custody.

Their trial became the most prominent manifestation of repression. We need not dwell on it at any length, yet some points deserve our attention. It was a long trial, lasting two months from jury selection to verdict; the transcript ran to 8,000 typed pages. Fully 981 talesmen were examined for the jury, and as the bailiff guaranteed, the defense exhausted its peremptory challenges. In the end, the prosecution managed to pack the jury with men who freely admitted their prejudice. The presiding judge, Joseph Gary, was grossly biased and consistently ruled against the defense. The defense team was inexperienced: Moses Salomon and Sigmund Zeisler were immigrant labor lawyers, only recently admitted to the bar; they were joined by Captain William Black, a corporation lawyer.

Led by State's Attorney Julius Grinnell, the prosecution charged the defendants as accessories to Officer Degan's murder, having incited "a person or persons unknown" to commit the act. In exchange for immunity, Gottfried Waller and Bernard Schrade testified that Engel and Fischer planned the bombing in Zepf's Hall. William Seliger testified about Lingg's bomb making, and Engel's peculiar furnace was introduced along with the chemical analysis of the bomb fragments. Two reporters, Harry Gilmer and M. M. Thompson, swore they saw Schnaubelt throw the bomb. Additional testimony placed Fielden, Spies, and

Parsons in the square that night. The evidence against Neebe remained especially thin: he owned stock in the *Arbeiter-Zeitung* and had been arrested in its offices, he read the "Revenge Circular," was a member of the IWPA, and owned a pistol, sword, breech-loading rifle, and red flag. Perhaps the most damaging testimony was read to the jury from *Die Arbeiter-Zeitung* and *The Alarm* in order to illustrate their revolutionary content, inflammatory rhetoric, and criminal intent. The core of the prosecution's case lay in conspiracy, not murder.

Led by Captain Black, the defense probably erred by basing its case on the evidence and the charges. The eyewitnesses contradicted themselves and each other. Neither Gilmer nor Thompson was particularly reliable; Seliger, Waller, and Schrade admitted they had received money, jobs, and immunity for their testimony. The state had offered no proof that any of the defendants had thrown the bomb, indeed the state failed to connect its general conspiracy theory with the meeting in Zepf's Hall. The defense hammered at testimony and evidence, discounting the conspiracy, convictability, and manifest guilt of the defendants. In his closing remarks Grinnell explained the obvious: "Law is on trial. Anarchy is on trial. These men have been selected, picked out by the grand jury and indicted because they were leaders. They are no more guilty than the thousands who follow them. Gentlemen of the jury; convict these men, make examples of them, hang them and you save our institutions, our society."

On August 20 the jury announced that all of the defendants were guilty as charged. With the exception of Neebe, who received fifteen years, all were sentenced to death. Captain Black appealed to the Illinois Supreme Court for a writ of error and the executions were postponed. A year passed before the final appeal to the United States Supreme Court failed and the date of execution set. On 10 November 1887, Governor Oglesby commuted Fielden and Schwab's sentences to life imprisonment. At nine o'clock the next morning the law was avenged: Lingg committed suicide; an hour and a half later Engel, Fischer, Parsons, and Spies were hanged.

The red scare continued unabated outside the courtroom. Captain Schaack supplied the commercial press with a steady diet of raids, arrests, and interviews. Secret "anarchist arsenals" were still being discovered, in basements, and under sidewalks, throughout July and August. More than a week after the trial had ended, the police were reportedly prepared to move on the Bohemian anarchists who haunted the Sixth Ward. A second round of grand-jury indictments was repeatedly threatened but never produced. Suppressing anarchy became a big business. By May 18, responsible citizens had contributed $67,445 to a fund for the families of officers killed or injured in the square. Schaack used a different, larger fund to hire Pinkerton detectives, and Melville Stone, editor of the *Daily News*, paid for still others. One contemporary questioned Schaack's zeal:

> He saw more anarchists than vast hell could hold. Bombs, dynamite, daggers, and pistols seemed ever before him; in the end, there was no society, however innocent or even laudable, among the foreign-born population that was not to his mind engaged in deviltry. The labor unions, he knew were composed solely of anarchists, the Turner societies met to plan treason, stratagems, and spoils; the literary guilds contrived murder; the Sunday schools taught destruction. Every man that spoke broken English and went out o'nights was a fearsome creature whose secret purpose was to blow up the Board of Trade or loot Marshall Field's store.

Police Chief Ebersold, who proved unwilling to restrain him at the time, tried much later to disown his subordinate.

> Captain Schaack wanted to keep things stirring. He wanted bombs to be found here, there, all around, everywhere. I thought people would... sleep better if they were not afraid their homes would be blown to pieces any minute. But this man, Schaack,... wanted none of that policy.... After we got the anarchist societies broken up, Schaack wanted to send out men to organize new societies right away.... He wanted to keep the thing boiling, [to] keep himself prominent before the public.

The police had help investigating anarchy. According to George McLean, "the most sensational evidence" to come out of the trial "was that of Detective Andrew C. Johnson, of the Pinkerton Agency,... who was detailed in December, 1884 by his agency, which had been employed by the First National Bank to furnish details of the secret meetings which it was known were being held by revolutionary plotters at various places throughout the city." Masquerading as a cabinetmaker, Johnson had infiltrated the American Group in February 1885 and joined its armed group. Although William Holmes later insisted that the "spies" were "generally known," both Parsons and Charles Bodendeick had vouched for Johnson. Johnson's testimony was sensational, if not wholly manufactured, but Holmes mentioned "spies," for Johnson was not alone. As soon as he got the case Captain Schaack

> at once employed a number of outside men, choosing especially those who were familiar with the Anarchists and their haunts. The funds for this purpose were supplied to me by public-spirited citizens who wished the law vindicated and order preserved in Chicago. I received reports from the men thus employed from the beginning of the case up to November 20,

1887. There are 253 of the reports in all, and a most interesting history of Chicago Anarchy do they make in themselves.

For eighteen months after the riot, Schaack "had at least one man present" whenever the dreaded anarchists met: "Before midnight I would know all that had transpired at meetings of any importance." Once Schaack ordered his officers to listen through a hole cut in the floorboards; another time they hid under the floor of the stage in Thalia Hall. Some of this could be amusing: two spies, both in Schaack's employ, denounced each other to the Captain. Yet undercover work also proved dangerous: one agent barely avoided disclosure by denouncing a legitimate member; Schaack also reported that another of his detectives was "betrayed by beauty" and mysteriously drowned by a female anarchist.

Cheered on by an adoring press, the police continued both surveillance and repression long after the trial and executions. In September 1886, State's Attorney Grinnell announced he was ready to prosecute the Bohemian anarchists who had been arrested in May and still sat in jail. Although all were convicted, their trials were reported as the beginning of a detailed investigation of anarchism in the heathen Czech community. The day before the executions a judge restored the indictments of nineteen anarchists and issued the appropriate warrants "as a precautionary measure." None, however, was ever used.

The city's reaction to the entire affair split along complex lines. The English-language press universally denounced the riot, the conspirators, the defense, the appeals, and the foreign-born in general. The *Staats-Zeitung* labeled the anarchists as "the worst enemies of the Germans" but noted the "deplorable fact that most of them bear German names [and] that many talk no other language but German." Led by *Svornost*'s editor, "reputable Bohemians" disclaimed any connection with or sympathy for the dreaded anarchists. The *Times* quoted a similar resolution issued by a meeting of "reputable Polish residents: "Our nationality is moved by motives only of good citizenship ... [we] have always denounced[,] in no measured terms[,] communism, socialism, and anarchism."

Yet others, less respectable perhaps, rallied to support the accused, the convicted, and the condemned. A committee, drawn from the CLU, but headed by Dr. Ernst Schmidt, collected funds for the defense and appeals. Most contributions were under a dollar, yet the committee raised more than $40,000. After the trial, and when the appeals failed, the defense committee became an Amnesty Association and expanded its base. The movement tried to provide for the Martyrs' families. When Oskar Neebe's wife died in March 1887, the movement arranged both wake and funeral. A month before, *Der Vorbote* had published the initial call and the constitution of the Pioneer Aid and Support Association, which would care for the martyrs' widows and orphans. The association arranged frequent benefits to raise money. One, in January 1889, was described by the *Staats-Zeitung:* fully 7,000 people came to a concert sponsored by twenty clubs, "mostly singing and athletic." It was "a cheerful gathering and ... all enjoyed the skillful performances" of 200 singers and fifty-odd gymnasts. Beyond honoring the Martyrs, such family support had long been a feature within the movement.

The forces of order chose to see any defense activity as proof of anarchism. Noting that both Christian and August Spies "had been members for years," the Aurora Turn-Verein contributed $100 to the defense fund in July; their continued support later rebounded. Two years later the Sozialer Turn-Verein had to deny, in the pages of the rabid *Saats-Zeitung*, that it had glorified anarchy or insulted the American flag. The national Turn-Verein, which had removed the word "sozialistische" from its name in 1856, broke its affiliation with the Chicago Turngemeinde in June 1887 over its repeated requests to support the Martyrs. The red flag remained an issue. During the November 11 memorial meeting in Vorwaerts TurnHall in 1891 "Lt. Gibbons, followed by a squad of policemen in civil clothing" mounted the speakers' platform to demand that the American flag be raised among the red ones. Then in May 1892, Julius Vahlteich was expelled from the Turngemeinde "for anarchistic speeches" in its halls.

Organized repression continued long after the executions. In July 1888, the police trotted out still another conspiracy when three Czech anarchists, John Hronek, Frank Chleboun, and Frank Capek, were arrested and charged with plotting to assassinate State's Attorney Grinnell. Hronek was convicted and sentenced to twelve years in prison on Chleboun's bargained testimony. Two months after their trial, Charles Bodendeick was arrested and held incommunicado for twelve days, charged with "manufacturing dangerous explosives and conspiracy to destroy city hall." He never went to trial, but Captain Bonfield reportedly told him "to immediately leave the country as he was liable to arrest in every city and town in the United States."

A year after the executions some of the more naive anarchists reorganized as the Arbeiterbund and foolishly published their constitution in *Der Vorbote*. The police quickly raided their earliest meetings and Mayor Roche argued that the city's ordinances gave him the authority to suppress any meeting that he considered revolutionary or otherwise illegal. Arguing free speech and assembly, the anarchists took the case to court, managing to get it before a judge who had originally been elected by the SLP (in 1879) and more recently reelected by the United Labor Party (in 1886). He ruled in their favor, arguing: "Anarchists have the same rights as other citizens to assemble peaceably for the discussion of their views;... in no other city of the United States except Chicago have the police officials attempted to prevent the right of free speech on such unwarranted pretenses and assumptions of power, and... it is time to call a halt." Although the *Tribune* published the Bund's constitution and listed the names of its "secret agitation committee," *Die Arbeiter-Zeitung* still rejoiced in the decision with a story headlined "Chicago Vanquished!"

In September 1888, *Die Fackel* charged Schaack with nepotism, moonlighting, and possession of a $75,000 fortune. Considering the source, nothing came of the story. Then, sixteen months later, during a messy divorce case, the wife of one of Schaack's detectives charged that her husband and his boss had robbed prisoners, received stolen goods, and committed extortion. When *Die Arbeiter-Zeitung* published the story, its editor found himself arrested and charged with criminal libel, despite the fact that he had only commented on an article that originally appeared in the *Times*.

The police continued to harass the annual commemorations of November 11 and to raid anarchist haunts. As the marchers came back from the cemetery in 1888, they were accosted and ordered to remove their red lapel ribbons. That year the bakers' union chose to hold a secret memorial, but the *Staats-Zeitung* still reported it. The harassment and surveillance did not stop when Schaack and Bonfield were suspended and later dismissed from the force in 1889. A prominent site for both the SLP and IWPA, Thomas Greif's Hall at 54 W. Lake Street remained a meeting place for anarchists, socialists, and unions past the turn of the century. The police raided it several times in the weeks after the riot and irregularly thereafter. The last two raids apparently came in April and November 1891, the latter occasioned by the semiannual business meeting of the Arbeiter-Zeitung Publishing Company's stockholders.

In January 1892, the *Herald* charged that the most recent raid on Greif's Hall "was simply a scheme to show men who had been putting up money to keep down anarchist movements that the followers of Parsons and Spies were not yet dead." An anonymous group of businessmen had reportedly raised an annual fund of more than $115,000, instructing the police: "Use this money as you may find best, the object being to crush out anarchy." In October 1891, they closed their books; $487,000 had been spent since May 1886, and although $57,670 remained on hand, nothing had been spent in the past year. The *Herald* charged that the last raid had been staged to reopen the fund. The surviving elements of the anarchist movement still had police shadows as late as September 1895. When 3,000 of them assembled at Hahn's

Garden there were fifty plainclothes policemen on the grounds and another fifty in uniform held in reserve a block away. "All these numerous peace guardians gave the harmless picnic more the appearance of a serious affair of state," yet according to *Die Abendpost*, a bourgeois German paper, the "picnic was absolutely peaceful."

In addition to surveillance by Pinkertons, the department's own detectives, and Schaack's "privates," Chicago's anarchists were watched by Imperial German police agents. "According to the press in Berlin at the beginning of 1890 a man named Heinrich Danmeyer or Dammeyer, who had been regarded as a wide-eyed socialist or anarchist, was revealed to be a police agent in Chicago. He was considered to be one of the most 'raging' of the anarchists,... the most outstanding of the leaders of the [Arbeiterbund],... of the Freethinkers' Association and... of the Karl Marx Assembly. Danmeyer had been in the pay of the police since at least 1886 and had called for the assassination of [the] police, state['s] attorney and judge connected with the Haymarket Trial."

Surveillance of German emigré radicals began in 1878 after an assassination attempt on Kaiser Wilhelm I. An adjunct to Bismarck's anti-socialist laws, it aimed at preventing emigrés and their literature from returning to the Reich. And an editorial in the *Inter Ocean* ten days after the riot reported a communication from Baron Schaeffer, an Austrian minister, to the American secretary of state asking his help in stopping the return of exiled Czech radicals. German surveillance continued until World War I. In Chicago, two agents submitted their reports to the consular staff, and two more agents were hired through the Pinkerton Agency. In 1902, those agents prepared a list of Chicago's "anarchists" for the Reichschancellor. Of the 145 names listed, forty appear to have been active in the IWPA before the Haymarket riot. The majority of the people only became "dangerous" after the riot, but 27 percent of the total were long-time activists.

Although we can chronicle the program of repression organized by the civil authorities, we know little of the private sector's program. Immediately after the riot, the *Times* had screamed that "public justice" demanded "that no citizen shall employ or keep in his service any person who is a member of such...[an]...association of conspirators and assassins." Just as quickly, the Chicago Furniture Manufacturers' Association pledged not to employ "any communist, anarchist, nihilist, or socialist, or any other person denying the right of private property." *Die Möbel-Arbeiter Journal* reported that those resolutions made it "impossible for members of the union to find employment." Surely there were other resolutions, and with the names, addresses, and descriptions of alleged, accused, and suspected anarchists widely circulating, the program must have been effective.

The city's business community supported the forces of order and the program of repression. They raised one fund for the families of the police officers who died or were injured in the square. Even before the trial verdict a citizen suggested that another fund reward the jurors. Still another, raised and directed by the Citizens' Association, not only paid for Pinkerton detectives but also supplemented police salaries. In 1889, the Commercial Club bought land thirty miles north of Chicago and donated it to the federal government for a garrison because Marshall Field felt safer with the troops at Fort Sheridan "instead of a thousand miles away, like Fort Laramie or Fort Riley." If the whole program remained uncoordinated, with detectives, "privates," Pinkertons, and German agents crossing each other and reporting to different superiors, it was nonetheless effective.

Repression affected all three levels within the anarchist movement. The trial decimated the leadership by convicting the combined editorial staffs of *The Alarm*, the Socialist Publishing Society's three papers, and *Der Anarchist*. Although he escaped the first indictment, a second trial subsequently convicted Jacob Mikolanda, from *Budoucnost*; and Anton Hradecny closed down *Lampcka*. The raids, arrests, and harassment similarly affected the active membership. Expelled from the Knights of Labor, many were also fired from their jobs and found it difficult to get employment. Reputations and friendships gained before the riot haunted many for years. And repression hit at the movement's sympathetic following. The raids on Greif's Hall and *Budoucnost's* office confiscated two different subscription lists and the police assured the commercial press that every name would receive special attention.

The anarchist revolutionaries reacted to such harassment in a most peculiar and ironic way. Arguing freedom of speech and assembly, some turned to the law and the courts for protection. The core of the Haymarket defense committee did not rest with the convictions, the appeals, the executions, or the pardons. On the contrary, they kept busy well into the 1890s. In the last half of 1888, *Die Arbeiter-Zeitung* regularly reported the activities of "The Chicago Workers' Legal Aid Society," which had been formed to defend Hronek, Chleboun, and Capek. The profits of an evening entertainment in October were "to be used for the defense of those Bohemian workers who were spotted by Bonfield, the bloody Haymarket slayer, as his latest sacrifices." The society became more than an ad hoc organization, for its services enjoyed a frequent, if not constant, demand. In 1896, the Chicago Socialist Trade and Labor Alliance announced the founding of the Alliance Bureau of Law. Staffed by T. J. Morgan and Paul Ehmann, among others, the bureau was "designed to furnish a convenient and reliable institution to which working people may safely apply for free advice and assistance in all legal and business matters."

The breadth and duration of repression affected the movement in two different ways. According to Henry David, "In the decade after 1887, Chicago witnessed a more active, widespread, and intelligent discussion of revolutionary doctrines and labor theories than ever before." On the other hand, repression fundamentally subverted the movement's energies and organization away from revolution and the working class and towards its own survival. The activities of the defense committee, Amnesty Association, Arbeiter Rechtsschutz-Verein, Personal Rights League, and the Alliance Bureau of Law were altogether different than the activities of the IWPA. Although the new organizations still depended on festivals, picnics, and dances to raise funds and solidify their members, mere survival replaced agitation.

Notes

1 Chester Destler, *American Radicalism, 1860–1901* (New London, Conn.: Connecticut State College, 1946), p. 79.
2 Eric Foner, "Abolitionism and the Labor Movement in Ante-bellum America," in Foner, *Politics and Ideology in the Age of the Civil War* (New York: Oxford University Press, 1980), pp. 58–9.
3 Paul Avrich, *The Haymarket Tragedy* (Princeton, NJ: Princeton University Press, 1984), pp. 150–9; Bruce Nelson, "Das Attentat: The Propaganda of the Deed in the American Anarchist Movement" (Bachelor's seminar paper, Northern Illinois University, 1972), pp. 41–7, 70–3.
4 Floyd Dell, "Socialism and Anarchism in Chicago," in J. Seymour Currey (ed.) *Chicago: Its History and Its Builders*, 5 vols. (Chicago: S. J. Clarke, 1912) 2, pp. 361–405, 391.
5 Henry David, *The History of the Haymarket Affair* [1936] rev. edn. (New York: Russell and Russell, 1958), pp. 124–5.
6 David Montgomery, *Beyond Equality: Labor and the Radical Republicans, 1862–1872* (New York: Knopf, 1967), p. 42.

Documents

Introduction to the Documents

As Bruce Nelson points out in this chapter's chosen piece, Chicago's anarchists in the 1880s were both anti-government and anti-capitalist. During their imprisonment, those convicted of the Haymarket bombing had opportunities to expound their philosphies and proclaim their innocence. In Document One, Albert R. Parsons, the only defendant born in the United States, equates anarchism and socialism and emphasizes the oppressiveness of industrial capitalism. In this, Parsons is securely within the Marxist tradition. Yet he also states, "Anarchy is liberty." Complete personal freedom is the goal he holds up as anarchism's ideal.

Document Two, George Engel's speech to the court which sentenced him to death provides an autobiographical account of his progression toward anarchism. Like Parsons, he has faith in a scientific socialism and believes that the laws of nature are propelling society toward a socialist future. At the same time, the anarchists preach the need for workers to organize to overthrow capitalism by force. This tension – between the inevitability of capitalism's downfall and the call to bring it about through class warfare – is one that runs through the history of Marxist movements.

Document Three displays the polarization between radical labor and the authorities. The "Revenge!" circular, in English and German, calls for workers to avenge the killing of protesters outside the McCormick factory. (Note that the circular claims six had died; this probably exaggerated the fatalities. Only two are known to have been killed.) The engraving of the Haymarket bomb also distorts the situation. Published in the genteel middle-class magazine *Harper's Weekly*, it shows an angry bearded orator apparently urging on the demonstrators, some of whom seem to be taking careful aim at the police as the bomb explodes. But the crowd was dispersing when the bomb was thrown, and the majority of officers wounded by gunshot were hit by guns fired by their fellow officers.

Document Four shows Captain Schaack's characterization of anarchist goals and tactics. Like the radicals he hated and hounded, he used the terms "anarchism" and "socialism" interchangeably, and quickly dismissed those socialists who favored peaceful means of change as insignificant. The excerpt shows that the police were using spies to infiltrate anarchist gatherings. After the bombing, Schaack aggressively pursued anarchist suspects. He equated anarchism with violence and disorder. To the anarchists, their philosophy meant harmony and liberty. During the Haymarket trial, one of the defendants turned the tables on him, calling his police force a gang, "one of the worst in the city." He continued, "You are an Anarchist, as you understand it."

"Parsons' Plea for Anarchy"

First published in *New York Herald*, August 30, 1886, reprinted from A. R. Parsons, *Anarchism: Its Philosophy and Scientific Basis* (Chicago: Mrs. A. R. Parsons, Publisher, 1887), pp. 107–9.

So much is written and said nowadays about socialism or anarchism, that a few words on this subject from one who holds to these doctrines may be of interest to the readers of your great newspaper.

Anarchy is the perfection of personal liberty or self-government. It is the free play of nature's law, the abrogation of the statute. It is the negation of force or the domination of man by man. In the place of the law maker it puts the law discoverer and for the driver, or dictator, or ruler, it gives free play to the natural leader. It leaves man free to be happy or miserable, to be rich or poor, to be mean or good. The natural law is self-operating, self-enacting, and cannot be repealed, amended or evaded without incurring a self-imposed penalty. The statute law is license. Anarchy is liberty. The socialistic or anarchistic programme leaves the people perfectly free to unite or disunite for the purpose of production and consumption. It gives absolute freedom of contract by and between individuals or associations, and places the means of life – capital – at the disposal of the people. To those persons who may regard these aspirations as merely sentimental or utopian, I invite their attention to the operation of our capitalistic system, as outlined by Marx and others.

The capitalist system originated in the forcible seizure of natural opportunities and rights by a few, and converting these things into special privileges, which have since become vested rights formally entrenched behind the bulwarks of statute law and government. Capital could not exist unless there also existed a class, a majority class, who are property-less – that is, without capital. A class whose only mode of existence is by selling their labor to capitalists. Capitalists maintained, fostered and perpetuated by law. In fact, capital is law, statute law, and law is capital.

Labor is a commodity, and wages is the price paid for it. The owner of the commodity, labor, sells it (himself) to the owner of capital in order to live. Labor is the expression of the energy or power of the laborer's life. This energy or power he must sell to another person in order to live. It is his only means of existence. He works to live. But his work is not simply a part of his life. On the contrary, it is the sacrifice of it. It is a commodity which under the guise of "free labor" he is forced by necessity to hand over to another party. The aim of the wage laborer's activity is not the product of his labor. Far from it. The silk he weaves, the palace he builds, the ores he digs from out the mine are not for him. The only thing he produces for himself is his wage, and silk, ores and palace are merely transformed for him into a certain quantity of means of existence – viz: a cotton shirt, a few pennies and the mere tenancy of a lodging house.

And what of the laborer who for twelve or more hours weaves, spins bores, turns, builds, shovels, breaks stones, carries loads, and so on? Does his twelve hours weaving, spinning, boring, turning, building, shoveling, etc., represent the active expression or energy of his life? On the contrary, life begins for him exactly where this activity, this labor of his ceases – viz: at his meals, in his tenement house, in his bed. His twelve hours work represents for him as a weaver, builder, spinner, etc., only so much earnings as will furnish him his meals, clothes and rent. Capital ever grows with what it feeds on – viz: the life, the very existence, the flesh and blood of the men, women and children of toil. The wage slaves are "free" to compete with each other for the opportunity to serve capital and capitalists to compete with each other in monopolizing the laborer's products. This law of "free" competition establishes the iron law of subsistence wages. Thus in every country the average wage of the working people is regulated by what it takes to maintain a bare subsistence and perpetuate their class.

The increase of capital grows with every stroke of the laborers. So does his dependence. To-day there are but two classes in the world – to wit: the capitalist class and the wage class; the latter a hereditary serving class, dependent upon the former for work and bread; the former a dictating class, dominating and exploiting the latter.

The struggle of classes, the conflict between capital and labor is for possession of the labor product of the laborers. As profits rise wages fall, and as wages rise profits fall. As the share of the capitalist (his profit) increases, the share of the laborer (his wages) diminishes, and the interest of the capitalist class is in direct antagonism to the interests of the wage class. Profit and wages for every class are in inverse proportion. Wage laborers are doomed by the capitalist system to forge for themselves the golden chains which bind them more securely in industrial slavery. Thus the industrial war wages – to wit: the captains and generals of industry contest with each other as to who can dispense with the greatest number of industrial soldiers. This brings on a rapid subdivision and simplification of the productive process, the employment of women and children, and the introduction of labor-saving machinery. Result, surplus laborers.

The United States Commissioner of Labor Statistics tells us in last year's report that over one million able-bodied men were in compulsory idleness, and that the general average of wages for the whole wage class was estimated at fifty-five cents per day. As the struggle for existence intensifies among the laborers the struggle among capitalists for profits intensifies also. The crisis? What is it? When the dead level of cost of production is reached, which is near if not already at hand – the capitalist system – being no longer able to preserve the lives of its slaves – the wage workers – will collapse, will fall of its own weight, and fail because of its own weakness. Modern enterprise and commercialism is the old-time piracy of our fathers legalized, made respectable and safe. The homeless, the destitute, hungry and ragged, and ignorant and miserable, are the victims, the creatures, the offspring, the product of our modern system of legalized piracy. The capitalist system has its morality – a plastic, convenient morality – which it puts on or off like a coat.

The golden rule of the carpenter's son is made subservient to the laws of trade, whose morality and religion are expounded in the churches (temples of Mammon) where the clergy propagate that good philosophy which teaches man (poor man) that he is here to suffer, denouncing as atheistic and anarchistic that other philosophy which says to man: "Go! the earth is the gift of God to the whole human race. Discover nature's laws, apply them and be happy."

To quarrel with socialism is silly and vain. To do so is to quarrel with history; to denounce the logic of events; to smother the aspirations of liberty. Mental freedom, political freedom, industrial freedom – do not these follow in the line of progress? Are they not the association of the inevitable?

George Engel, Speech to the Trial Court

Reprinted from "George Engell [sic] on Anarchism," in A. R. Parsons, *Anarchism: Its Philosophy and Scientific Basis* (Chicago: Mrs. A. R. Parsons, Publisher, 1887), pp. 86–7.

This is the first occasion of my standing before an American court, and on this occasion it is murder of which I am accused. And for what reasons do I stand here? For what reasons am I accused of murder? The same that caused me to leave Germany – the poverty – the misery of the working classes.

And here, too, in this "free republic," in the richest country of the world, there are numerous proletarians for whom no table is set; who, as outcasts of society, stray joylessly through life. I have seen human beings gather their daily food from the garbage heaps of the streets, to quiet therewith their knawing hunger....

When in 1878, I came here from Philadelphia, I strove to better my condition, believing it would be less difficult to establish a means of livelihood here than in Philadelphia, where I had tried in vain to make a living. But here, too, I found myself disappointed. I began to understand that it made no difference to the proletarian, whether he lived in New York, Philadelphia, or Chicago. In the factory in which I worked I became acquainted with a man who pointed out to me the causes that brought about the difficult and fruitless battles of the workingmen for the means of existence. He explained to me, by the logic of scientific socialism, how mistaken I was in believing that I could make an independent living by the toil of my hands, so long as machinery, raw material, etc., were guaranteed to the capitalists as private property by the State. That I might further enlighten my mind in regard to these facts, I purchased with money earned by myself and family, sociological works, among them those of LaSalle, Marx, and Henry George. After the study of these books, it became clear to me why a workingman could not decently exist in this rich country. I now began to think of ways and means to remedy this. I hit upon the ballot box; for it had been told me so often that this was the means by which workingmen could better their condition.

I took part in politics with the earnestness of a good citizen; but I was soon to find that the teachings of a "free ballot box" are a myth, and that I had again been duped. I came to the opinion that as long as workingmen are economically enslaved they cannot be politically free. It became clear to me that the working classes would never bring about a form of society guaranteeing work, bread, and a happy life by means of the ballot....

Soon enough I found that political corruption had burrowed through the ranks of the social-democrats. I left this party and joined the International Working People's Association, that was just being organized. The members of that body have the firm conviction that the workingman can free himself from the tyranny of capitalism only through force; just as all advances of which history speaks, have been brought about through force alone. We see from the history of this country that the first colonists won their liberty only through force; that through force slavery was abolished, and just as the man who agitated against slavery in this country, had to ascend the gallows, so also must we. He who speaks for the workingman to-day must hang. And why? Because this republic is not governed by people who have obtained their office honestly.

Who are the leaders at Washington that are to guard the interests of this nation? Have they been elected by the people, or by the aid of their money? They have no right to make laws for us, because they were not elected by the people. These are the reasons why I have lost all respect for American laws.

The fact that through the improvement of machinery so many men are thrown out of employment, or at best, working but half the time, brings them to reflection. They have leisure, and they consider how their conditions can be changed. Reading matter that has been written in their interest gets into their hands, and faulty though their education may be, they can nevertheless cull the truths contained in those writings. This, of course, is not pleasant for the capitalistic class, but they cannot prevent it. And it is my firm conviction that in a comparatively short time the great mass of proletarians will understand that they can be freed from their bonds only through socialism.

Haymarket *"Revenge!"* Circular and Harper's Weekly *Engraving*

"Revenge!" circular of May 3, 1886, and engraving of the Haymarket bombing from *Harper's Weekly*, May 15, 1886, reproduced from Paul Avrich, *The Haymarket Tragedy* (Princeton, NJ: Princeton University Press, 1984).

REVENGE!

Workingmen, to Arms!!!

Your masters sent out their bloodhounds — the police —; they killed six of your brothers at McCormicks this afternoon. They killed the poor wretches, because they, like you, had the courage to disobey the supreme will of your bosses. They killed them, because they dared ask for the shortening of the hours of toil. They killed them to show you, "Free American Citizens", that you must be satisfied and contended with whatever your bosses condescend to allow you, or you will get killed!

You have for years endured the most abject humiliations; you have for years suffered unmeasurable iniquities; you have worked yourself to death; you have endured the pangs of want and hunger; your Children you have sacrificed to the factory-lords — in short: You have been miserable and obedient slave all these years: Why? To satisfy the insatiable greed, to fill the coffers of your lazy thieving master? When you ask them now to lessen your burden, he sends his bloodhounds out to shoot you, kill you!

If you are men, if you are the sons of your grand sires, who have shed their blood to free you, then you will rise in your might, Hercules, and destroy the hideous monster that seeks to destroy you. To arms we call you, to arms!

Your Brothers.

Rache! Rache!

Arbeiter, zu den Waffen!

Arbeitendes Volk, heute Nachmittag morbeten die Bluthunde Eurer Ausbeuter 6 Eurer Brüder draußen bei McCormick's. Warum morbeten fie diefelben? Weil fie den Muth hatten, mit dem Loos unzufrieden zu fein, welches Eure Ausbeuter ihnen befcheben haben. Sie forderten Brod, man antwortete ihnen mit Blei, eingedenk der Thatfache, daß man damit das Volk am wirkfamften zum Schweigen bringen kann! Viele, viele Jahre habt Ihr alle Demüthigungen ohne Widerfpruch ertragen, habt Euch vom frühen Morgen bis zum fpäten Abend gefchunden, habt Entbehrungen jeder Art ertragen, habt Eure Kinder felbft geopfert — Alles, um die Schatzkammern Eurer Herren zu füllen, Alles für fie! Und jetzt, wo Ihr vor fie hintretet, und fie erfucht, Eure Bürde etwas zu erleichtern, da hetzen fie zum Dank für Eure Opfer ihre Bluthunde, die Polizei, auf Euch, um Euch mit Bleikugeln von der Unzufriedenheit zu kuriren Sklaven, wir fragen und befchwören Euch bei Allem, was Euch heilig und werth ift, rächt diefen fchändlichen Mord, den man heute an Euren Brüdern beging, und vielleicht morgen fchon an Euch begehen wird. Arbeitendes Volk, Herkules, Du bift am Scheideweg angelangt. Wofür entfcheideft Du Dich? Für Sklaverei und Hunger, oder für Freiheit und Brod? Entfcheideft Du Dich für das Letztere, dann fäume keinen Augenblick; denn, Volk, zu den Waffen! Vernichtung den menfchlichen Beftien, die fich Deine Herrfcher nennen! Rückfichtlofe Vernichtung ihnen — das muß Deine Lofung fein! Denk' der Helden, deren Blut den Weg zum Fortfchritte, zur Freiheit und zur Menfchlichkeit gebahnt — und ftrebe, ihrer würdig zu werden!

Eure Brüder.

Michael J. Schaack, from Anarchy and Anarchists

Reprinted from Michael J. Schaack, *Anarchy and Anarchists* (Chicago: F. J. Schulte, 1889), pp. 74–6.

The Constitution of the United States guarantees the right of free speech, free discussion and free assemblage. These are the cardinal doctrines of our free institutions. But when liberty is trenched upon to the extent of advocacy of revolutionary methods, subversion of law and order and the displacement of existing society, Socialism places itself beyond the pale of moral forces and arrays itself on the side of the freebooter, the bandit, the cut-throat and the traitor. Public measures and public men are open to the widest criticism consistent with truth, decency and justice, but differences of opinion are no more to be brought into harmony through blood than the settlement of private disputes is to be effected by means of the bludgeon, the knife or the bullet. The freedom of speech which is valuable either to the individual or to humanity is that which builds up, not destroys, society.

Now, what does Socialism, or Anarchy, precisely teach, and at what does it aim? It is true, there are two schools of Socialism – one conservative and the other radical to a sanguinary degree; one seeking a change in existing society and government through enlightenment, and the other the attainment of the same principles through force. But the conservatives form so small a portion of the Socialistic body that they cut no figure in the general direction and management of the organization; and so far as relates to the visible manifestations of that body, Socialism in the United States may be regarded as synonymous with Anarchy.

As I have shown, the ostensible object of the organization in Chicago, as elsewhere, at the outset, was peaceful, but the ulterior aim – the establishment of Socialism through force, when sufficiently powerful in numbers – has in later years clearly developed. The early Socialist orators only hinted at force as a possible factor in the social revolution they advocated, and it was reserved for the active agitators of the past ten years to boldly and openly proclaim for the methods of the Paris Commune.

Before proceeding to particulars as to the utterances of Anarchist leaders, the sources of their inspiration and their definition of Socialism, it may be well to advert to some incidents in connection with their movements as a revolutionary party. One incident specially worthy of mention was a meeting held at Mueller's Hall, corner of Sedgwick Street and North Avenue, on the evening of January 12, 1885. It was a secret gathering, but, despite Socialistic vigilance, Officer Michael Hoffman managed to remain and quietly note the drift of the speeches. Parsons first took the floor, and said:

> Gentlemen, before we call this meeting to order, I want you to be sure that we are all right and all one. I want you to see if there are any reporters or policemen present. See if you can discover any spies. If you find any one here, you can do with him as you please, but my advice to you is, take him and strangle him and then throw him out of the window; then let the people think that the fellow fell out. And if you should give one of them a chance for his life, tell him, if he has any more notions to come to our meetings, he should first go to St. Michael's Church, see the priest and prepare himself for death, say farewell to all his friends and family – and then let him enter. I want all these people to know that I am not afraid of them; I don't like them, and let them stay away from me.

After precautions had been taken to exclude objectionable persons, the proceedings began. Four speeches were delivered, two in English and two in German. Parsons confined his remarks to the capitalists. All present were poor, he said, and they only had themselves to blame. One-half of all the wealth in the country belonged to the poor people, but the capitalists had robbed them of it. The poor offered no resistance, and yet the capitalist was doing the same thing day after day. He was getting richer, and the poor poorer, because the working people lay down and permitted themselves to be robbed. He recounted some of Most's experiences, and insisted that capitalists must submit to workingmen. They must be shown that their lives are worth no more than the lives of the working people.

He next touched upon the merits of a new invention by which, he said, many hundreds of houses could be set on fire, and exhibited a small tin box or can with a capacity of four ounces. This can, he remarked, could be filled with some chemical stuff to serve as an explosive. A great many of these cans could be carried in a basket, and, travelling around as match peddlers or under some other guise, his hearers could secure entrance to the houses of capitalists. All they would then be obliged to do was to either place or drop one of "those darlings" in a secure place and go about their business. It would do its work, without any one's presence to attend to it, in less time than an hour. If they would get the boxes ready, he would tell them where to get the "stuff." This plan of operations would keep the fire and police departments quite busy. If they organized and went to work with a resolute spirit, they could have things all their own way throughout the city and obtain possession of what remained after their work of destruction. He also urged all his comrades to become familiar with dynamite and said that for the necessary instructions they could come to a building on Fifth Avenue (107, the offices of the *Arbeiter-Zeitung* and *Alarm*), where he and others could be found to help them. There was no other way now left, he continued, except for the laborers to use the sword, the bullet and dynamite, and, closing sententiously, he said:

> I probably will be hung as soon as I get out on the street, but if they do hang me, boys, don't forget what I have been telling you about the little can and the dear stuff, dynamite, because this is the only way I and you can get our rights.

It goes without saying that Parsons was applauded to the echo.

Suggested Reading

Paul Avrich, *The Haymarket Tragedy*, Princeton, NJ: Princeton University Press, 1984. A comprehensive account of Haymarket by a leading expert on the history of anarchism.

Paul Buhle, *Marxism in the United States: Remapping the History of the American Left*, London and New York: Verso, 1991. A broad history of American radicalism that gives appropriate attention to its anarchist strains.

Henry David, *The History of the Haymarket Affair: A Study in the American Social Revolutionary and Labor Movements*, 2nd ed., New York: Russell & Russell, 1958. Because of David's impressive, detailed scholarship this work, originally published in 1936, remains an important account of Haymarket.

Melvyn Dubofsky, *Industrialism and the American Worker 1865–1920*, 3rd ed., Wheeling, IL: Harlan Davidson, 1996. A brief but scholarly history of American labor that discusses labor's responses to the dramatic social and economic changes of the era.

Bruce Nelson, *Beyond the Martyrs: A Social History of Chicago's Anarchists*, New Brunswick, NJ: Rutgers University Press, 1988. The source of this chapter's extract on Haymarket, this is a social and cultural history of the anarchist community in late nineteenth-century Chicago.

Dave Roediger and Franklin Rosemont (eds.) *Haymarket Scrapbook*, Chicago: C. H. Kerr, 1986. A compendium of primary source material relating to the Chicago anarchists and Haymarket.

Professor Dana Ward at Pitzer College has a comprehensive "Anarchy Archives" website which contains a section on Haymarket at
http://dwardmac.pitzer.edu/ Anarchist_Archives/haymarket/ Haymarket.html
(Note that URLs on the Web are often subject to change. This link was valid in August 2000.)

5

Southern Populism, Interracial Alliances, and Racist Violence

1865 End of Civil War and emancipation of slaves. Sharecropping becomes the predominant form of agricultural labor for African Americans in the decades after the war. Many white southerners also became tenant farmers during these years.

1873–96 Long period of deflation (falling prices) causes economic difficulties for farmers. Farmers' debts become increasingly burdensome as dollars become scarcer and more valuable.

1877 Farmers' Alliance forms in Lampasas County, Texas. The Alliance becomes known as the Southern Alliance and spreads throughout much of the South and parts of the West. Parallel organizations, the Northern Alliance and the Colored Farmers' Alliance, also grow in the 1880s and early 1890s.

1889 Alliance leader C. W. Macune proposes the "subtreasury plan" to provide federal loans to farmers. The plan would allow farmers to market their crops at advantageous times.

1890 Georgia Allianceman Tom Watson elected to Congress. Watson calls on black and white farmers to recognize their common enemies and work together for an interracial movement of poor people.

1890–1 Farmers' Alliance members come together for political action and form the People's Party (also known as the Populist Party).

July 4, 1892 At Omaha, Nebraska Convention, Populists endorse the radical "Omaha Platform," which demands major reforms to control big business and aid farmers and workers.

1892 Populist Presidential ticket wins 8.5 percent of the popular vote and 22 Electoral College votes.

1893–6 Severe economic depression deepens farm problems.

1896 A divided Populist Party backs Democratic Presidential nominee William Jennings Bryan in presidential election. Bryan endorses one popular Populist issue, the free coinage of silver, but not the radical demands of the Omaha Platform. Republican William McKinley's victory effectively ends the national influence of the Populists.

Mid-1890s–early 1900s Widespread measures to deny African Americans in the South the right to vote. "Jim Crow" legislation extended to increase racial segregation.

1900 In Grimes County, Texas, Populist black–white coalition which had controlled the county government for nearly two decades is defeated by violence and intimidation. "White Man's Union" seizes power; the county's African-American population declines by 30 percent or more.

Introduction to the Article

The Populist movement of the late nineteenth century seems to some a futile, backward-looking effort to preserve a society based on small family farmers in an era of urbanization and industrialization. To others, especially the distinguished historian Lawrence Goodwyn, Populism represented the nation's last, best hope for true grass-roots democracy and effective restraints on corporate power.

The People's Party, which grew out of the Farmers' Alliances of the 1870s and 1880s, was one of the nation's most successful third-party efforts. In the South and the Great Plains, farmers had joined together to push for higher prices for their crops, better treatment from railroad companies and other middlemen, and greater public control over the money supply and the banking system. By the early 1890s, most Alliance members concluded that a new political party was the best way to achieve their goals, which they enumerated in their most radical document, the Omaha Platform of 1892. In elections that year, the Populist Presidential candidate, James B. Weaver, drew over 8 percent of the popular vote; Kansas and Colorado elected Populist governors. In 1896, however, the party faced a difficult choice: to run its own candidate or to endorse the Democrats' nominee, Nebraska's William Jennings Bryan. Bryan, a great orator, adopted the style of the Populists but not their comprehensive program for change. Instead, the Bryan campaign emphasized the single issue of "free silver," a limited reform of monetary policy. The Populists chose "fusion" with the Democrats, but Bryan lost badly and the Populists fell apart as a national political force.

Goodwyn points out, however, that farmer radicalism did not die at the grass roots after the 1896 vote. In Grimes County, Texas, a coalition of white and black rural radicals kept control of the county's politics. In 1899, Democrats began a campaign to split the races in the half-black county through terror and intimidation. The article graphically describes the results. In seeking explanations for the failures of radical movements in the United States, it is important to understand the role that violent repression has played. It alone cannot account for radical weaknesses, but dominant groups have rarely hesitated to suppress dissent forcibly. In Grimes County, the "White Man's Union" maintained its grip on the county government for half a century.

For modern commentators, the most exciting aspect of Populism in the South was its appeal for cooperation between poor whites and poor blacks. To base a political movement on an interracial alliance of the poor was a daring act a hundred years ago, the peak era for lynchings, a time when "scientific" racism pronounced African Americans inferior, and an era when blacks throughout the deep South lost even the right to vote. However, white Populists were not free of racism. They distinguished between cooperation and "social equality," which they almost all rejected. The Georgia Populist leader Tom Watson was far ahead of moderate and conservative politicians when he urged white and black farmers to unite against their common enemies. But in the new century Watson emerged as a rabid advocate of white supremacy and segregation. Racism was the Achilles' heel of Southern Populism and a destructive force throughout the history of American radicalism. In the case of Grimes County, Texas, racist violence imposed a system of white domination and black exclusion that lasted for more than half a century, a system that mirrored patterns throughout the South until the rise of the civil rights movement.

Goodwyn's article tells a dramatic story while raising important interpretive issues. Can radicals hope to win and maintain power in a "third party" when the two-party system is so ingrained in American politics? Can an interracial coalition work without a full commitment to equality? How can the poor and the powerless resist the repressive forces of the dominant order? Goodwyn's article, with its use of oral history techniques to recall memories of the Populist era, also provokes a question about the uses of history. Activists may ask how historical memory of past radical movements may encourage and enlighten efforts for fundamental change in the present.

Populist Dreams and Negro Rights: East Texas as a Case Study

Lawrence C. Goodwyn

Nearly a century later the Populist decade lingers in historical memory as an increasingly dim abstraction. The very word "Populism" no longer carries specific political meaning. It is now invoked to explain George Wallace, as it was used to explain Lyndon Johnson in the sixties, Joe McCarthy in the fifties, and Claude Pepper in the forties. Though afflicting principally the popular mind, this confusion is at least partly traceable to those historians who have insisted on concentrating on Populism as exhortation, so that Ignatius Donnelly's utopian novels or Mary Lease's pronouncements on the respective uses of corn and hell become the explanatory keys to agrarian radicalism. For scholars who mine political movements with a view to extracting cultural nuggets, the focus has been chiefly upon the word, not the deed; in the process the agrarian crusade has become increasingly obscure.

Much of the difficulty centers on the subject of race. There is essential agreement that, on economic issues, Populists were men of the Left, primitive to some, prophetic to others, but leftists to all. But did their banner indicate a highly selective nativist radicalism for whites only, or did they grapple with the inherited legacies of the caste system as part of an effort to create what they considered a more rational social and economic order? The analysis of Populist rhetoric has left us with contradictory answers.

While party platforms can be useful tools in determining professed attitudes, the gap between asserted ideals and performance is sufficiently large to defeat any analysis resting on the implicit assumption that political manifestos have an intrinsic value apart from the milieu in which they existed. In America the distance between assertion and performance is especially evident in matters of race; as a result, on this issue above all, the context of public assertions is central to the task of their political evaluation. An inquiry into the murkiest corner of Populism, interracial politics, should begin not merely with what Populists said but what they did in the course of bidding for power at the local level. What was the stuff of daily life under Populist rule in the rural

Reprinted from Lawrence C. Goodwyn, "Populist Dreams and Negro Rights: East Texas as a Case Study," *American Historical Review* 76 (December 1971), pp. 1435–56.

enclaves where the third party came to exercise all the authority of public office, including police authority? What can we learn not only about Populist insurgency but also about the orthodoxy the third party opposed?

Grimes County, Texas, was one of many counties scattered across the South and West where the People's party achieved a continuing political presence in the latter part of the nineteenth century. Located some sixty miles north of Houston in the heart of what the natives call the Old South part of Texas, Grimes County displayed the cotton-centered economy typical of rural East Texas in 1880. Its largest town, Navasota, contained 1,800 persons in 1890 and its second largest town, Anderson, the county seat, only 574 persons as late as 1900. Farms in Grimes County ranged from plantation size in the rich bottomland country of the Brazos River on the county's western border to small, single-family agricultural units on the poorer land of the northern part of the county. The 1890 census revealed a county population of 21,312, of which 11,664 were black.

Populism in Grimes County is the story of a black–white coalition that had its genesis in Reconstruction and endured for more than a generation. In time this coalition came to be symbolized by its most enduring elected public official, Garrett Scott. The Scotts had roots in Grimes County dating back before the Civil War. Their sons fought for the Confederacy and returned to face a postwar reality by no means unique in the South; possessing moderately large holdings of land but lacking necessary capital to make it productive, the Scotts did not achieve great affluence. During the hard times that continued to afflict undercapitalized Southern agriculture through the 1870s Garrett Scott became a soft-money agrarian radical. His stance was significant in the political climate of Grimes County in the early 1880s. During Reconstruction Negroes in the county had achieved a remarkably stable local Republican organization, headed by a number of resourceful black leaders. When Reconstruction ended and white Democrats regained control of the state governmental machinery in Texas, Grimes County blacks retained local power and sent a succession of black legislators to Austin for the next decade. The local effort to end this Republican rule took the usual postwar Southern form of a political movement of white solidarity under the label of the Democratic party. In supporting the Greenback party Garrett Scott not only was disassociating himself from the politics of white racial solidarity, he was undermining it.

In 1882 a mass meeting of various non-Democratic elements in Grimes County nominated a variegated slate for county offices. Among the candidates were black Republicans, "lily-white"

Republicans, and Independent Greenbackers. Garrett Scott was on the ticket as the Independent Greenback candidate for sheriff. Not much is known about the racial climate in Grimes County in 1882, but it must not have been wholly serene, because the "lily-white" nominee for county judge, Lock MacDaniel, withdrew from the ticket rather than publicly associate with black candidates. Garrett Scott did not withdraw, and in November he was elected. Also elected, as district clerk, was a black man who became a lifelong political ally of Scott, Jim Kennard. Thus began an interracial coalition that endured through the years of propagandizing in Texas by the increasingly radical Farmers Alliance and through the ensuing period of the People's party. The success of the coalition varied with the degree of white participation. After the collapse of the Greenback party in the mid-eighties visible white opposition to the Democratic party declined for several years before Grimes County farmers, organized by the Alliance, broke with the Democracy to form the nucleus of the local People's party in 1892. Scott and Kennard were the most visible symbols of the revitalized coalition, but there were others as well. Among them were Morris Carrington, a Negro school principal, and Jack Haynes, both staunch advocates of Populism in the black community, as well as J. W. H. Davis and J. H. Teague, white Populist leaders. These men led the People's party to victory in the county elections of 1896 and again in 1898.

A subtle duality creeps into the narrative of events at this point. To the world outside Grimes County in the 1890s, to both Populists and Democrats, Garrett Scott was simply another Populist officeholder, distinguished for his antimonopoly views and his generally radical approach to monetary policy. To his white supporters within Grimes County he was doubtless respected for the same reasons. But to the Democrats of Grimes County the sheriff symbolized all that was un-Southern and unpatriotic about the third party. Under Populist rule, it was charged, Negro school teachers were paid too much money; furthermore, in Scott's hands the sheriff's office hired Negro deputies. The two Democratic newspapers in Navasota were fond of equating Populist rule with Negro rule and of attributing both evils to Scott. The Navasota *Daily Examiner* asserted that "the Negro has been looking too much to political agitation and legislative enactment.... So long as he looks to political agitation for relief, so long will he be simply the means of other men's ambition." To the Navasota *Tablet* Scott was simply "the originator of all the political trouble in Grimes County for years." Both these explanations oversimplify Grimes County politics. The political presence and goals of blacks were definite elements of local Populism, as was, presumably, the personal ambition of Garrett Scott. But the Populists' proposed economic remedies had gained a significant following among the county's white farmers, and this was of crucial importance in inducing white Populists to break with Democrats and ally themselves with blacks. Garrett Scott was a living embodiment of white radicalism; he did not cause it. Beyond this the political cohesion of blacks was a local phenomenon that had preceded Scott's entry into Grimes County politics and had remained relatively stable since the end of the war. The ease with which Democratic partisans saw the fine hand of Garrett Scott in Negro voting was more a reflection of their own racial presumptions than an accurate description of the political dynamics at work in the county.

Through the election of 1898 Democrats in Grimes County had labored in vain to cope with the disease of Populism among the county's white farmers. Finally, in the spring of 1899, the Democrats moved in a new direction. The defeated Democratic candidate for county judge, J. G. McDonald, organized a clandestine meeting with other prominent local citizens and defeated Democratic office seekers. At this meeting a new and – for the time being – covert political institution was created: the White Man's Union. A charter was drawn providing machinery through which the Union could nominate candidates for county offices in elections in which only White Man's Union members could vote. No person could be nominated who was not a member; no person could be a member who did not subscribe to these exclusionary bylaws; in effect, to participate in the organization's activities, so adequately expressed in its formal title, one had to support, as a policy matter, black disfranchisement. Throughout the summer and fall of 1899 the White Man's Union quietly organized.

Writing years later McDonald explained that care was taken not to launch the organization publicly "until the public attitude could be sounded." By January 1900 the covert organizing had been deemed sufficiently successful to permit the public unveiling of the White Man's Union through a long story in the *Examiner*. During the spring the *Examiner*'s political reporting began to reflect a significant change of tone. In April, for example, the *Examiner*'s report of a "quiet election" in nearby Bryan noted that friends of the two mayoral candidates "made a display of force and permitted no Negroes to vote. All white citizens went to the polls, quietly deposited their ballots for whom they pleased and went on about their business." The *Examiner* had progressed from vague suggestions for disfranchisement to approval of its forcible imposition without cover of law.

The first public meetings of the White Man's Union, duly announced in the local press, occupied the spring months of 1900 and were soon augmented by some not-quite-so-public night riding. The chronology of these events may be traced through the denials in the local Democratic press of their occurrence. In July the *Examiner* angrily defended the county's honor against charges by the Negro Baptist State Sunday School Conference that the county had become unsafe for Negroes. The Austin *Herald* reported from the state's capital that the Sunday School Board, "after mature thought and philosophical deliberation," had decided to cancel its annual meeting scheduled for Navasota. The *Examiner* cited as "irresponsible slush" the charge that Negroes were being threatened and told to leave the county, but within weeks reports of just such events began cropping up in the *Examiner* itself. One example of terrorism left no one in doubt, for it occurred in broad daylight on the main street of the county seat: in July Jim Kennard was shot and killed within one hundred yards of the courthouse. His assailant was alleged to be J. G. McDonald.

Intimidation and murder constituted an even more decisive assault on the People's party than had the ominous bylaws of the White Man's Union. The Populist leadership recognized this clearly enough, and Scott went so far as to attempt to persuade Southern white farmers to shoulder arms in defense of the right of Negroes to vote. Beyond this we know little of the measures attempted by the local Populist constabulary to contain the spreading terrorism. A well-informed member of the Scott family wrote a detailed account of these turbulent months, but the manuscript was subsequently destroyed. In the early autumn of 1900 members of the White Man's Union felt sufficiently strong to initiate visits to white farmers with a known allegiance to the People's party. Under such duress some of these farmers joined the White Man's Union.

In August the Union, aided by a not inconsiderable amount of free publicity in the local press, announced "the Grandest Barbecue of the Year," at which the "workings of the White Man's Union" would be explained to all. The leadership of the People's party objected to announced plans to include the local state guard unit, the Shaw Rifles, in the program. After some discussion the Texas adjutant general, Thomas Scurry, placed at the discretion of the local commander the question of the attendance of the Shaw Rifles in a body. The commander, Captain Hammond Norwood, a leading Navasota Democrat and a member of the White Man's Union, exercised his option, and the Shaw Rifles appeared en masse at the function. Populist objections were brushed aside.

Shortly after this well-attended barbecue had revealed the growing prestige of the White Man's Union as well as the inability of the People's party to cope with the changing power relationships within the county, a black exodus began. People left by train, by horse and cart, by day and by night. The *Examiner*, with obvious respect for the new political climate its own columns had helped engender, suggested elliptically that the exodus could produce complications. Some citizens, said the *Examiner*, "are beginning to feel a little nervous as the thing progresses, and lean to the idea that the action will bring on detrimental complications in the labor market."

The next day, however, the paper printed a public address that it said had been "ordered published by the executive committee of the White Man's Union in order to combat the many reports that are calculated to injure the Union." After reaffirming the Union's intent to end "Negro rule" in the county, the report concluded with a message "to the Negroes":

> Being the weaker race, it is our desire to protect you from the schemes of those men who are now seeking to place you before them. . . . Therefore, the White Man's Union kindly and earnestly requests you to keep hands off in the coming struggle. Do not let impudent men influence you in that pathway which certainly leads to trouble. . . . In the future, permit us to show you, and convince you by our action, that we are truly your best friends.

Fourteen days later a black Populist leader, Jack Haynes, was riddled with a shotgun blast by unknown assailants. He died instantly in the fields of his cotton farm.

The White Man's Union held a rally in Navasota two nights later that featured a reading of original poetry by one of the Union's candidates, L. M. Bragg. The verse concluded:

> Twas nature's laws that drew the lines
> Between the Anglo-Saxon and African races,
> And we, the Anglo-Saxons of Grand Old Grimes,
> Must force the African to keep his place.

Another White Man's Union rally held in Plantersville the same week displayed other Union candidates whose conduct won the *Examiner*'s editorial approval: "They are a solid looking body of men and mean business straight from the shoulder." Apparently this characterization of the Plantersville speakers was not restricted to approving Democrats; Populists, too, responded to events initiated by the men who "meant business." In October the Plantersville school superintendent reported that only five white families remained in his school district and that all the Negroes were gone. The superintendent stated that twelve white families had left that week, and "the end is not in sight."

Amid this wave of mounting terror the People's party attempted to go about its business, announcing its nominating conventions in the local press and moving forward with the business of naming election judges and poll watchers. But there were already signs of a fatal crack in Populist morale. The People's party nominee for county commissioner suddenly withdrew from the race. His withdrawal was announced in the *Examiner*, and no explanation was offered.

Throughout the late summer and autumn of 1900 the demonstrated power of the White Man's Union had protected McDonald from prosecution in the Kennard slaying. Nothing short of a war between the Populist police authority and the White Man's Union could break that extralegal shield. An exasperated and perhaps desperate Garrett Scott angrily challenged a White Man's Union official in October to "go and get your Union force, every damn one of them, put them behind rock fences and trees and I'll fight the whole damn set of cowards." That Scott had to use the first person singular to describe the visible opposition to the Union underscores the extent to which terror had triumphed over the institutions of law in Grimes County. By election eve it was clear that the Populist ticket faced certain defeat. The third party had failed to protect its constituency. White Populists as well as black were intimidated. Many would not vote; indeed, many were no longer in the county.

Over 4,500 votes had been cast in Grimes in 1898. On November 6, 1900, only 1,800 persons ventured to the polls. The People's party received exactly 366 votes. The Populist vote in Plantersville fell from 256 in 1898 to 5 in 1900. In the racially mixed, lower-income precinct of south Navasota the Populist vote declined from 636 to 23. The sole exception to this pattern came in a geographically isolated, lower-income precinct in the extreme northern part of the county that contained few Negroes and thus, presumably, fewer acts of terrorism. The Populist vote in this precinct actually increased from 108 to 122 and accounted for one-third of the countywide vote of 366. In north Navasota, also almost all white but not geographically isolated from the terror, the Populist vote declined from 120 to 3. An additional element, nonstatistical in nature, stamped the election as unusual. The underlying philosophy of the South's dominant political institution, the Democratic party, has perhaps never been expressed more nakedly than it was in Grimes County in 1900 when "the party of white supremacy," as C. Vann Woodward has called the Southern Democracy, appeared on the official ballot as the White Man's Union.

On the way to its landslide victory the Union had grown more self-confident in its willingness to carry out acts of intimidation and terrorism in defiance of the local Populist police authority. Now that that authority had been deposed and a sheriff friendly to the White Man's Union had been elected, would terrorism become even more public?

On November 7, 1900, the morning after the election, a strange tableau unfolded on the streets of Anderson, the tiny county seat.

Horsemen began arriving in town from every section of the county, tied their horses all along the main street, and occupied the second floor of the courthouse. In a nearby house Garrett Scott's sister, Cornelia, and her husband, John Kelly, watched the buildup of Union supporters on the courthouse square, not fifty yards from the sheriff's official residence on the second floor of the county jail. They decided the situation was too dangerous to permit an adult Populist to venture forth, so the Kellys sent their nine-year-old son with a note to warn Scott not to appear on the street.

At about the same time that this mission was carried out Garrett Scott's younger brother, Emmett Scott, came into town from the family farm, rode past the growing clusters of armed men, and reined up in front of the store belonging to John Bradley, his closest friend in town. Bradley was a Populist but, as befitting a man of trade, a quiet one. His store was adjacent to the courthouse.

Cornelia Kelly's son found the sheriff at Abercrombie's store across the street from the jail and delivered the warning note. As Scott read it an outbreak of gunfire sounded from the direction of Bradley's store. Scott stepped to the street and peered in the direction of the fusillade. Rifle fire from the second floor of the courthouse immediately cut him down. Upon hearing the gunfire Cornelia Kelly ran out of her house and down the long street toward the courthouse. The gunsights of scores of men tracked her progress. Seeing her brother's body in the street she turned and confronted his attackers. "Why don't you shoot me, too," she yelled, "I'm a Scott." She ran to her brother and, with the assistance of her son, dragged him across the street to the county jail. He was, she found, not dead, though he did have an ugly wound in his hip. Inside Bradley's store, however, three men were dead – Emmett Scott, Bradley, and Will McDonald, the son of a Presbyterian minister and a prominent member of the White Man's Union. McDonald had shot Scott shortly after the latter had entered the store: the two men grappled for the gun, and the fatally wounded Scott fired one shot, killing McDonald. Bradley was killed either by a shot fired from outside the store where Union forces had gathered near the courthouse or by a stray bullet during the struggle inside.

The siege of Anderson continued for five days, with the wounded sheriff and his deputies – black and white – in the jail and the White Man's Union forces in the courthouse. Shots crossed the fifty yards between the two buildings intermittently over the next several days. On the evening of the fatal shooting another member of the Scott clan, Mrs. W. T. Neblett, had left Navasota for Austin to plead with the governor, Joseph D. Sayers, for troops. On Friday she returned, accompanied by the adjutant general of the State of Texas, Thomas

Scurry – the same official who had earlier acquiesced in the participation of the state guard in the White Man's Union barbecue. After conferring with the contending forces Scurry pondered various methods to get the wounded Scott out of town and into a hospital; gangrene had set in. For protection, Scurry suggested that he be authorized to select a group of twenty prominent citizens of Navasota to escort the sheriff from the jail to the railroad station. Since most of the "prominent citizens" of Navasota were members of the White Man's Union, it is perhaps understandable that Scott declined this offer. The adjutant general then suggested that the Shaw Rifles be employed as an escort. This idea was respectfully declined for the same reason. Asked what he would consider a trustworthy escort, the wounded sheriff suggested a state guard unit from outside the county.

On Saturday, four days after the shooting, a company of Houston light infantry of the Texas Volunteer State Guard detrained at Navasota and marched the eleven miles to Anderson. On Sunday morning Garrett Scott was placed on a mattress, the mattress put in a wagon, and the procession began. In the wagon train were most of the members of the large Scott clan—Emmett Scott's widow and children, the Kelly family, and the Nebletts, all with their household belongings piled in wagons. A file of infantrymen marched on either side as the procession formed in front of the jail, moved past hundreds of armed men at the courthouse and onto the highway to Navasota, and then boarded a special train bound for Houston.

Thus did Populism leave Grimes County. From that day in 1900 until well after mid-century Negroes were not a factor in Grimes County politics. J. G. McDonald regained his judgeship and served for many years. The White Man's Union continued into the 1950s as the dominant political institution in the county. None of its nominees, selected in advance of the Democratic primary, was ever defeated. The census of 1910 revealed the extent of the Negro exodus. It showed that Grimes County's Negro population had declined by almost thirty per cent from the 1900 total. School census figures for 1901 suggest an even greater exodus.

To this day the White Man's Union, as a memory if no longer as an institution, enjoys an uncontested reputation among Grimes County whites as a civic enterprise for governmental reform. In this white oral tradition the general events of 1900 are vividly recounted. Specific events are, however, remembered selectively. The exodus of Negroes from the county is not part of this oral tradition, nor is the night riding of the White Man's Union or the assassination of the Negro Populist leaders.

As for Garrett Scott, he endured a long convalescence in a San Antonio hospital, regained his health, married his nurse, and moved to a farm near Houston. He retired from politics and died in his bed. He is remembered in the oral tradition of the black community as the "best sheriff the county ever had." Kennard and Haynes were killed because they "vouched" for Scott among Negroes. In this black oral tradition the Negro exodus plays a central role. It is perhaps an accurate measure of the distance between the races in Grimes County today that two such contradictory versions of famous events could exist side by side without cross-influence.

To these two oral traditions a third must be added – the Scott tradition. The Scotts were, and are, a proud family. One by one, as they died, they were brought home to be buried in the family plot in the Anderson cemetery, little more than a mile from the site of the bloody events of 1900. Tombstones of female members of the clan bear the Scott middle name, defiantly emblazoned in marble. Edith Hamilton of Richards, Grimes County, was ten years old in November 1900 and remembers vividly the day her nine-year-old brother carried her mother's message to Garrett Scott. She remembers the defiance of her mother, the political commitment of her father, the acts of intimidation by the White Man's Union, the Negro exodus, and what she calls the "intelligence of Uncle Garrett." "They said that Uncle Garrett was a nigger-lover," recalls Mrs. Hamilton. "He wasn't a nigger-lover, or a white-lover, he just believed in being fair to all, in justice."

The Scott oral tradition – similar to the black oral tradition and at odds with the white tradition – is virtually the only legacy of the long years of interracial cooperation in Grimes County. Beyond this the substance of political life that came to an end in Grimes County in 1900 cannot be measured precisely from the available evidence. Very little survives to provide insight into the nature of the personal relationship that existed between Garrett Scott and Jim Kennard, between any of the other Populist leaders of both races, or between their respective constituencies. Scott and his third-party colleagues may have been motivated solely by personal ambition, as the White Man's Union charged; on the other hand, the impulses that made them Populists in the first place may have led them toward public coalition with blacks. It is clear that such stridently white supremacist voices as the Navasota *Tablet* were unable to project any reason other than personal ambition to explain the phenomenon of white men willingly associating themselves politically with black men. To what extent this attitude reflected Populist presumptions is another question. White Populists and black Republicans shared an animosity toward the Southern Democracy that grew in intensity during the bitter election campaigns of the 1890s. Democratic persistence in raising the cry of "Negro domination" to lure Populist-leaning voters back to the "party of the fathers" was effective enough to keep white Populists on the defensive about the race issue throughout the agrarian revolt in the South. The circumstance of a common political foe nevertheless provided Populists and Republicans with a basis for political coalition that was consummated in a bewildering variety of ways – and sometimes not consummated at all. The stability of local black organizations and their demonstrated capacity to withstand Democratic blandishments or acts of intimidation were only two of the factors governing the complex equation of post-Reconstruction inter-racial politics. A stable, local black political institution existed in Grimes County, and its enduring qualities obviously simplified the organizational task confronting Garrett Scott. What might be regarded as "normal" Bourbon efforts to split blacks from the Populist coalition – mild intimidation, petty bribery, campaign assertions that the Democrats were the Negroes' "best friends," or a combination of all three – failed to achieve the desired results in Grimes County in the 1890s. The precise reasons are not easily specified. The Navasota *Tablet*, seeing the world through lenses tinted with its own racial presumptions, ascribed the credit for Negro political cohesion solely to the white sheriff. In the face of all Democratic stratagems, the third party's continuing appeal to Negroes was, in the *Tablet*'s view, a thing of "magic." A white supremacist view does not automatically exclude its holder from rendering correct political analyses on occasion, and it is possible that the *Tablet*'s assessment of the cause of Negro political solidarity was correct; however, such an analysis does not explain how the Negro Republican organization was able to send a succession of black legislators to Austin in the 1870s and 1880s, before Garrett Scott became politically active. It seems relevant that when Grimes County Democrats decided upon an overt campaign of terrorism, the men they went after first were the leading black spokesmen of Populism in the county rather than the third party's white leadership. To this extent the actions of Democratic leaders contradicted their public analysis of the causal relationships inherent in the continuing Populist majorities.

Before they indulged in terrorism the Democrats already possessed another method of splitting the Populist coalition: regaining the loyalty of white Populists. Against the historic Democratic campaign cry of white supremacy, the People's party had as its most effective defense the economic appeal of its own platform. The persuasiveness of Populism to white farmers in Grimes County was confirmed by newspaper accounts of the public reaction to the Populist–Democratic debates that occurred during the years of the agrarian uprising. While the reports in the *Examiner* were uniformly partisan and invariably concluded that

Democratic spokesmen "won" such debates hands down, the papers conceded that Populist speakers also drew enthusiastic responses from white residents. The absence of reliable racial data by precincts renders a statistical analysis of the Populist vote in Grimes County impossible; however, the fragmentary available evidence suggests that the People's party was generally able to hold a minimum of approximately thirty per cent of the county's white voters in the four elections from 1892 to 1898 while at the same time polling approximately eighty to ninety per cent of the Negro electorate. The inability of the Democratic party to "bloc vote" the county's white citizenry, coupled with the party's failure to win black voters by various means or, alternatively, to diminish the size of the Negro electorate, combined to ensure Democratic defeat at the polls. The fact merits emphasis: both the cohesion of black support for the People's party and the maintenance of substantial white support were essential to the local ascendancy of Populism.

This largely deductive analysis, however, reveals little about the internal environment within the third-party coalition during the bitter struggle for power that characterized the decade of Populist-Democratic rivalry. However scrutinized, the bare bones of voting totals do not flesh out the human relationships through which black and white men came together politically in this rural Southern county. In the absence of such crucial evidence, it seems prudent to measure the meaning of 1900 in the most conservative possible terms. Even by this standard, however, a simple recitation of those elements of Grimes County politics that are beyond dispute isolates significant and lasting ramifications.

An indigenous black political structure persisted in Grimes County for thirty-five years following the Civil War. Out of his own needs as a political insurgent against the dominant Southern Democratic party, Garrett Scott decided in 1882 to identify his Greenback cause with the existing local Republican constituency. Once in office as sheriff he found, among other possible motives, that it was in his own self-interest to preserve the coalition that elected him. It is clear that the style of law enforcement in Grimes County under Scott became a persuasive ingredient in the preservation of black support for the People's party. The presence of black deputy sheriffs and Scott's reputation within the black community seem adequate confirmation of both the existence of this style and its practical effect. The salaries paid Negro school teachers constituted another element of third-party appeal. Comparisons with white salaries are not available, but whatever black teachers received, partisans of the White Man's Union publicly denounced it as "too much." It is evident that Grimes County Negroes supported the People's party for reasons that were grounded in legitimate self-interest – an incontestable basis for political conduct. The point is not so much that the county's Negroes had certain needs, but that they possessed the political means to address at least a part of those needs.

From this perspective the decisive political event of 1900 in Grimes County was not the overwhelming defeat of the local People's party but the political elimination of that part of its constituency that was black. Scott was valuable to Negroes in short-run terms because he helped to translate a minority black vote into a majority coalition that possessed the administrative authority to improve the way black people lived in Grimes County. In the long run, however, it was the presence of this black constituency – not the conduct of a single white sheriff nor even the professed principles of his political party – that provided the Negroes of the county with what protection they had from a resurgent caste system. As long as Negroes retained the right to cast ballots in proportion to their numbers they possessed bargaining power that became particularly meaningful on all occasions when whites divided their votes over economic issues. Disfranchisement destroyed the bargaining power essential to this elementary level of protection. Arrayed against these overriding imperatives for Negroes such questions as the sincerity of Garrett Scott's motives fade in importance. Whatever the sheriff's motives, both the political realities that undergirded the majority coalition and Scott's ability to respond to those realities shaped a course of government conduct under the People's party that was demonstrably of more benefit to Negroes than was the conduct of other administrations before or since. The permanent alteration of those realities through black disfranchisement ensured that no other white administration, whether radical, moderate, or opportunistic, would be able to achieve the patterns in education and law enforcement that had come to exist in the county under Populism. Stated as starkly as possible, after 1900 it was no longer in the interest of white politicians to provide minimal guarantees for people who could not help elect them.

Beyond this crucial significance for the county's black people, disfranchisement also institutionalized a fundamental change in the political environment of whites. More than a third party passed from Grimes County in 1900; in real political terms an idea died. Though a new political idea invariably materializes in democratic societies as an expression of the self-interest of a portion of the electorate, the party that adopts the idea in the course of appealing for the votes of that sector of the electorate inevitably is placed in the position of having to rationalize, defend, explain, and eventually promote the idea. If the concept has substance, this process eventually results in the insinuation of the idea into the culture itself. In this sense it is not necessary to know the precise depth of the commitment to Negro rights of the Grimes County People's party to know that the *idea* of Negro rights had a potential constituency among white people in the county as long as black people were able to project its presence through their votes. Given the endurance of this real and potential constituency, one could reasonably intuit that twentieth-century politics in Grimes County would have contained one, or a dozen, or a thousand Garrett Scotts – each more, or less, "sincere" or "ambitious" than the Populist sheriff. Disfranchisement destroyed the political base of this probability. A political party can survive electoral defeat, even continuing defeat, and remain a conveyor of ideas from one generation to the next. But it cannot survive the destruction of its constituency, for the party itself then dies, taking with it the possibility of transmitting its political concepts to those as yet unborn. It is therefore no longer possible to speak of two white political traditions in Grimes County, for the White Man's Union succeeded in establishing a most effective philosophical suzerainty. Seventy years after disfranchisement Mrs. Hamilton can recall the racial unorthodoxy of Uncle Garrett; she cannot participate in such activity herself. "The Negro people here don't want this school integration any more than the whites do," she now says. "They're not ready for it. They don't feel comfortable in the school with white children. I've talked to my maid. I know."

While Garrett Scott's memory has been preserved, the local presence of the creed of his political party died with the destruction of that party. There has been literally no political place to go for subsequent generations of Scotts and Teagues, or Kennards and Carringtons. This absence of an alternative political institution to the Democratic party, the party of white supremacy, has been a continuing and unique factor in Southern politics. The circumstance is based on the race issue, but in its long-term political and social implications it actually transcends that issue.

The Populist era raises a number of questions about the interaction of the two races in the South, both within the third party and in the larger society. It is widely believed, by no means merely by laymen, that after the failure of Reconstruction meaningful experiments with the social order were finished in the South and that the aspirations of blacks were decisively thwarted. The example of Grimes County suggests, however, the existence of a period of time – a decade perhaps, or a generation – when nascent forms of indigenous interracial activity struggled for life in at least parts of the old Confederacy. Was some opportunity missed and, if so, how? How widespread through the South, and the nation, was this opportunity?

The White Man's Union was organized and led by men who considered themselves the "best people" of the South. If this attitude was typical, major adjustments must be made in our understanding of precisely how, and for what reasons, the antebellum caste system, in altered form, was reinstitutionalized in Southern society a generation after the formal ending of slavery. Was the "red-neck" the source of atrocity, or was he swept along by other stronger currents? And what of the Populist role? To what extent was agrarian racial liberalism in Texas traceable to an overall philosophy within the third-party leadership? Through what intuition of self-interest did the radical organizers of the Farmers Alliance, the parent institution of the People's party, accept the political risks of public coalition with blacks? What were their hopes and fears, and where did they falter? And, finally, what does the substance of their effort tell us about the Democrats in the South and the Republicans in the North who opposed them?

Answers to these questions rest, in part, on detailed knowledge of such events as those in Grimes County, but they require more than compilations of local histories, just as they assuredly require more than cultural assessments based on novels, speeches, and party manifestoes considered apart from their organic milieu. These answers will not provide much of a synthesis – Populism was too diverse, too congregational, and too ideologically thin – but they should tell us more about the larger society that, along with the Populists, failed to erect the foundations for a multiracial society in the nineteenth century. As the inquiry proceeds, it should be remembered that Populism perished before developing a mature philosophy – on race, on money, or on socialism. One must generalize, therefore, not only from contradictory evidence but, more important, from incomplete evidence. An analogy, doubtless unfair, could be made with the plight that would face modern historians of Marxism had that movement been abruptly truncated at the time, say, of the Brussels Conference in 1903. Who could have predicted on the evidence available to that date the Stalinist reign of terror that evolved from the mature, victorious revolutionary party of 1917? By the same token sweeping generalizations about what Populist radicalism could have become are not only romantic but historically unsound.

It should be sufficient to observe that in the long post-Reconstruction period – a period not yet ended – during which the social order has been organized hierarchically along racial lines, Populism intruded as a brief, flickering light in parts of the South. For a time some white Southerners threw off the romanticism that has historically been a cover for the region's pessimism and ventured a larger, more hopeful view about the possibilities of man in a free society. Under duress and intimidation this public hope failed of persuasion at the ballot box; under terrorism it vanished completely.

The Grimes County story dramatically illustrates this failure, but in the insight it provides into the underlying politics of black disfranchisement and the achievement of a monolithic one-party political environment in the American South it is not unique. Other Populists in East Texas and across the South – white as well as black – died during the terrorism that preceded formal disfranchisement. In Texas the extraparliamentary institutions formed by white Democrats to help create the political climate for disfranchisement bore a variety of local names: the Citizens White Primary of Marion County; the Tax-Payers Union of Brazoria County; the Jaybird Democratic Association of Fort Bend County; and the White Man's Union of Wharton, Washington, Austin, Matagorda, Grimes, and other counties. The available historical material concerning each of these organizations comes largely from the founders themselves, or their descendants, reflecting an incipient or a mature oral tradition – one oral tradition. The secondary literature based on these accounts, including scholarly works used in graduate schools as well as primary and secondary textbooks, is correspondingly inadequate.

A surprising amount of uninterpreted material from violently partisan white supremacist sources has found its way into scholarly literature. One example from the Grimes experience pertains directly to the scholarly characterization of Negro political meetings during the Populist era. It is worth attention as an illustration of the impact of white supremacist modes of thought on modern scholarship. The sunup-to-sundown work routine of Southern farm labor obviously precluded daytime political meetings. Accordingly, Kennard, Haynes, and Carrington campaigned among their black constituents by holding political meetings in each of the towns and hamlets of the county at night. Democratic partisans termed these rallies "Owl Meetings" and characterized black Populist leaders as "'fluence men." Drawing upon their own party's time-honored campaign technique with Negroes, Democrats further asserted that owl meetings were more concerned with sumptuous banquets and whisky than with politics. If partisans of white supremacy had difficulty finding reasons for white acceptance of political coalition with blacks, they were culturally incapable of ascribing reasons for Negro support of the third party to causes other than short-run benefits in terms of money and alcohol. The point is not that Democrats were always insincere in their descriptions (as white supremacists they were quite sincere), but that scholars have subsequently accepted such violently partisan accounts at face value. The darkly sinister picture of "'fluence men" corrupting innocent blacks with whisky at surreptitious owl meetings served to justify, at least to outsiders, the use of terrorism as the ultimate campaign technique of Democratic interracial politics. This sequential recording of events has found its way into scholarly monographs that otherwise demonstrate no inherent hostility to the Populistic inclinations of Southern farmers, black or white. In *The People's Party in Texas* Roscoe Martin precedes his brief allusion to the White Man's Union with a resumé of owl meetings and "'fluence men" that reflects in detail the bias of white supremacist sources. Other scholars writing broadly about Gilded Age politics have routinely drawn upon such monographs as Martin's, and by this process "'fluence men" have materialized as an explanation of Negro political insurgency in the nineties. In the heat of local political combat, however, Democratic leaders often were able to face a wholly different set of facts in the course of persuading their followers, and the citizenry as a whole, to adjust to the necessity of terrorism. As the time approached for actual precinct campaigning in Grimes County in the autumn of 1900, the executive board of the White Man's Union published a notice of the Union's intentions, climaxed by a "fair distinct warning" to the county's Negro leadership. The statement is revealing – not only of the transformation visited upon normal campaign practices when they were viewed through the cultural presumptions of white supremacy but also of the dangers of uncritical acceptance of such perspectives by scholars relying upon monoracial sources. The notice read in part:

> The Union is largely composed of the best citizens of the county. . . . They are the tax payers, representing the worth, the patriotism, the intelligence, and the virtues of the county. . . . We are not fighting any political party or individuals, but only those who band together under any name, who seek to perpetuate negro rule in Grimes County. [Good citizens] are astounded at the manner in which the children's money has been expended. Colored teachers with fat salaries and totally incompetent have been appointed for political "fluence." Our white teachers, male and female, enjoy no such fat salaries as these colored politicians or these sweet colored girls. . . . One of the most corrupting practices in the past has been the system of Owl Meetings which has been in vogue for years. . . . This is the school and hot bed where the negro politician received his inspiration, and riding from one end of the county to the other as an apostle of his race, corrupting his own people who may be in the honest pathway of duty. We give fair warning that any effort to continue these Owl Meetings – by the appointment of special deputies sheriffs to organize and carry them on – will be prevented. No threat of shotguns will deter us from the discharge of this duty.

Even without recourse to other perspectives this view of the existing political situation in Grimes County contains serious internal contradictions. Black Populist leaders were "incompetent" but as "apostles of their race" they had been so effective that their efforts needed to be stopped. Black teachers were paid "fat salaries" solely for political reasons, but among those receiving such gross patronage were "sweet colored girls," who obviously were not conducting owl meetings. The assertion that black teachers were actually paid more than white teachers must be rejected out of hand. In addition to the compelling fact that such an arrangement would have constituted poor political behavior on the part of a third party strenuously endeavoring to hold a substantial portion of the white vote and the further reality that such expenditures were unnecessary since parity for blacks in itself would have represented a notable accomplishment in the eyes of Negro leaders, Democrats had access to the records of all county expenditures and no such charge was ever leveled, much less documented, at any other time during the Populist decade. Whites complained that Negro teachers received "too much," not that they received more than white teachers. In any case, it seems necessary only to observe that American political parties have routinely utilized night gatherings without having their opponents characterize them as owl meetings and that persons who benefited from incumbency were not presumed to be acting in sinister ways when they campaigned for their party's re-election. The only thing "special" about Garrett Scott's deputies was that some of them were black. Viewed as some sort of black abstraction Jim Kennard might appear convincing as a shadowy "'fluence man," but as an intelligent and determined voice of the aspirations of Negro people he merits scholarly attention from perspectives not bounded by the horizons of those who murdered him. To an extent that is perhaps not fully appreciated, decades of monoracial scholarship in the South have left a number of Jim Kennards buried under stereotypes of one kind or another. They sometimes intrude anonymously as "'fluence men," but they simply do not appear as people in books on Southern politics.

This circumstance suggests that not only the broad topic of interracial life and tension but the entire Southern experience culminated by disfranchisement needs to be tested by a methodology that brings both black and white sources to bear on the admittedly intricate problem of interpreting a free society that was not free. At all events, evidence continues to mount that monoracial scholarship, Northern and Southern, has exhausted whatever merit it possessed as an instrument of investigating the variegated past of the American people. The obvious rejoinder – that written black sources do not exist in meaningful quantity – cannot, of course, be explained away; at the same time, this condition suggests the utility of fresh attempts to devise investigatory techniques that offer the possibility of extracting usable historical material from oral sources. The example of the erroneous report in the Navasota *Examiner* of Morris Carrington's death illustrates, perhaps as well as any single piece of evidence, not only the dangers inherent in relying on such "primary sources" for details of interracial tension in the post-Reconstruction South but also the value of received oral traditions in correcting contemporary accounts. Nevertheless, the problem of evaluating such source material remains; white and black versions of the details of racial conflicts are wildly contradictory. When they are measured against other contemporary evidence, however, the interpretive problem becomes considerably less formidable; indeed, the task of penetrating the substance behind partisan contemporary accounts may be lessened through recourse to available oral sources, as I have attempted to demonstrate.

Since much of the *Realpolitik* of the South, from Reconstruction through the modern civil rights movement, rests on legal institutions that, in turn, rest on extralegal methods of intimidation, the sources of political reality may be found less in public debate than in the various forms of intimidation that matured in the region. However determined a historian may be to penetrate the legal forms to reach this extralegal underside of the political culture of the South he is, in our contemporary climate, blocked off from part of his sources by his skin color. For black scholars there are limits to the availability both of courthouse records in the rural South and of responsive white oral sources. There are corresponding limits to the information white scholars can gain from interviews in black communities. Here, then, is fertile ground for scholarly cooperation. Methods of achieving this cooperation need to be explored. In its fullest utilization the subject is not black history or Southern history but American history.

Documents

Introduction to the Documents

As Lawrence Goodwyn's article demonstrates, the bravest accomplishments and the Achilles' heel of Southern Populism both came in the area of race relations. The documents in this section suggest both the hope of interracial cooperation and the tragedy of racism's impact. In Document One, the Georgia Populist leader Tom Watson argues for an alliance of poor whites and blacks against "financial despotism which enslaves you both." Note, however, the racist implications of Watson's dismissal of "social equality" and "Negro domination." By early in the twentieth century, Watson had become a vociferous advocate of white supremacy, black disenfranchisement, and strict segregation. Document Two, a letter to an Alabama Populist newspaper, demonstrates that at least some African Americans agreed with the

Populist prescription. The Colored Farmers' Alliance had enrolled hundreds of thousands of black farmers across the South and took part in the founding of the People's Party. Document Three provides two brief accounts of the group, including a fragmentary report on a cotton pickers' strike in 1891 in Texas. That most white members of the Southern Farmers' Alliance were landowners and most blacks in the Colored Alliance were tenants was bound to be a source of conflict. Finally, Document Four indicates what the Populist movement was up against. "Pitchfork Ben" Tillman, a South Carolina senator, had initially been elected with Farmers' Alliance backing, but he cast his lot with the Democratic Party. In 1900, he spoke on the US Senate floor to justify the 1895 measure that effectively denied blacks the right to vote in his state. In his address, he also gave his support to "the shotgun" used to keep blacks from political power.

Tom Watson, "The Negro Question in the South"

Reprinted from *The Arena* 6 (October 1892), pp. 540–3, 546–50.

The Negro Question in the South has been for nearly thirty years a source of danger, discord, and bloodshed. It is an ever-present irritant and menace.

Several millions of slaves were told that they were the prime cause of the civil war; that their emancipation was the result of the triumph of the North over the South; that the ballot was placed in their hands as a weapon of defence against their former masters; that the war-won political equality of the black man with the white, must be asserted promptly and aggressively, under the leadership of adventurers who had swooped down upon the conquered section in the wake of the Union armies.

No one, who wishes to be fair, can fail to see that, in such a condition of things, strife between the freedman and his former owner was inevitable. In the clashing of interests and of feelings, bitterness was born. The black man was kept in a continual fever of suspicion that we meant to put him back into slavery. In the assertion of his recently acquired privileges, he was led to believe that the best proof of his being on the right side of any issue was that his old master was on the other. When this was the case, he felt easy in his mind. But if, by any chance, he found that he was voting the same ticket with his former owner, he at once became reflective and suspicious. In the irritable temper of the times, a whispered warning from a Northern "carpet-bagger," having no justification in rhyme or reason, outweighed with him a carload of sound argument and earnest expostulation from the man whom he had known all his life; who had hunted with him through every swamp and wooded upland for miles around; who had wrestled and run foot-races with him in the "Negro quarters" on many a Saturday afternoon; who had fished with him at every "hole" in the creek; and who had played a thousand games of "marble" with him under the cool shade of the giant oaks which, in those days, sheltered a home they had both loved.

In brief, the end of the war brought changed relations and changed feelings. Heated antagonisms produced mutual distrust and dislike – ready, at any accident of unusual provocation on either side, to break out into passionate and bloody conflict. . . .

Now consider: here were two distinct races dwelling together, with political equality established between them by law. They lived in the same section; won their livelihood by the same pursuits; cultivated adjoining fields on the same terms; enjoyed together the bounties of a generous climate; suffered together the rigors of cruelly unjust laws; spoke the same language; bought and sold in the same markets; classified themselves into churches under the same denominational teachings; neither race antagonizing the other in any branch of industry; each absolutely dependent on the other in all the avenues of labor and employment; and yet, instead of being allies, as every dictate of reason and prudence and self-interest and justice said they should be, they were kept apart, in dangerous hostility, that the sordid aims of partisan politics might be served!

So completely has this scheme succeeded that the Southern black man almost instinctively supports any measure the Southern white man condemns, while the latter almost universally antagonizes any proposition suggested by a Northern Republican. We have, then, a solid South as opposed to a solid North; and in the South itself, a solid black vote against the solid white.

That such a condition is most ominous to both sections and both races, is apparent to all.

If we were dealing with a few tribes of red men or a few sporadic Chinese, the question would be easily disposed of. The Anglo-Saxon would probably do just as he pleased, whether right or wrong, and the weaker man would go under.

But the Negroes number 8,000,000. They are interwoven with our business, political, and labor systems. They assimilate with our customs, our religion, our civilization. They meet us at every turn, – in the fields, the shops, the mines. They are a part of our system, and they are here to stay. . . .

Suppose two tenants on my farm; one of them white, the other black. They cultivate their crops under precisely the same conditions. Their labors, discouragements, burdens, grievances, are the same.

The white tenant is driven by cruel necessity to examine into the causes of his continued destitution. He reaches certain conclusions which are not complimentary to either of the old parties. He leaves the Democracy in angry disgust. He joins the People's Party. Why? Simply because its platform recognizes that he is badly treated and proposes to fight his battle. Necessity drives him from the old party, and hope leads him into the new. In plain English, he joins the organization whose declaration of principles is in accord with his conception of what he needs and justly deserves.

Now go back to the colored tenant. His surroundings being the same and his interests the same, why is it impossible for him to reach the same conclusions? Why is it unnatural for him to go into the new party at the same time and with the same motives?

Cannot these two men act together in peace when the ballot of the one is a vital benefit to the other? Will not political friendship be born of the necessity and the hope which is common to both? Will not race bitterness disappear before this common suffering and this mutual desire to escape it? Will not each of these citizens feel more kindly for the other when the vote of each defends the home of both? If the white man becomes convinced that the Democratic Party has played upon his prejudices, and has used his quiescence to the benefit of interests adverse to his own, will he not despise the leaders who seek to perpetuate the system?

The People's Party will settle the race question. First, by enacting the Australian ballot system. Second, by offering to white and black a rallying point which is free from the odium of former discords and strifes. Third, by presenting a platform immensely beneficial to both races and injurious to neither. Fourth, by making it to the *interest* of both races to act together for the success of the platform. Fifth, by making it to the *interest* of the colored man to have the same patriotic zeal for the welfare of the South that the whites possess....

The white tenant lives adjoining the colored tenant. Their houses are almost equally destitute of comforts. Their living is confined to bare necessities. They are equally burdened with heavy taxes. They pay the same high rent for gullied and impoverished land.

They pay the same enormous prices for farm supplies. Christmas finds them both without any satisfactory return for a year's toil. Dull and heavy and unhappy, they both start the plows again when "New Year's" passes.

Now the People's Party says to these two men, "You are kept apart that you may be separately fleeced of your earnings. You are made to hate each other because upon that hatred is rested the keystone of the arch of financial despotism which enslaves you both. You are deceived and blinded that you may not see how this race antagonism perpetuates a monetary system which beggars both."

This is so obviously true it is no wonder both these unhappy laborers stop to listen. No wonder they begin to realize that no change of law can benefit the white tenant which does not benefit the black one likewise; that no system which now does injustice to one of them can fail to injure both. Their every material interest is identical. The moment this becomes a conviction, mere selfishness, the mere desire to better their conditions, escape onerous taxes, avoid usurious charges, lighten their rents, or change their precarious tenements into smiling, happy homes, will drive these two men together, just as their mutually inflamed prejudices now drive them apart.

Suppose these two men now to have become fully imbued with the idea that their material welfare depends upon the reforms we demand. Then they act together to secure them. Every white reformer finds it to the vital interest of his home, his family, his fortune, to see to it that the vote of the colored reformer is freely cast and fairly counted.

Then what? Every colored voter will be thereafter a subject of industrial education and political teaching.

Concede that in the final event, a colored man will vote where his material interests dictate that he should vote; concede that in the South the accident of color can make no possible difference in the interests of farmers, croppers, and laborers; concede that under full and fair discussion the people can be depended upon to ascertain where their interests lie – and we reach the conclusion that the Southern race question can be solved by the People's Party on the simple proposition that each race will be led by self-interest to support that which benefits it, when so presented that neither is hindered by the bitter party antagonisms of the past.

Let the colored laborer realize that our platform gives him a better guaranty for political independence; for a fair return for his work; a better chance to buy a home and keep it; a better chance to educate his children and see them profitably employed; a better chance to have public life freed from race collisions; a better chance for every citizen to be considered as a *citizen* regardless of color in the making and enforcing of laws, – let all this be fully realized, and the race question at the South will have settled itself through the evolution of a political movement in which both whites and blacks recognize their surest way out of wretchedness into comfort and independence. . . .

To the emasculated individual who cries "Negro supremacy!" there is little to be said. His cowardice shows him to be a degeneration from the race which has never yet feared any other race. Existing under such conditions as they now do in this country, there is no earthly chance for Negro domination, unless we are ready to admit that the colored man is our superior in will power, courage, and intellect.

Not being prepared to make any such admission in favor of any race the sun ever shone on, I have no words which can portray my contempt for the white men, Anglo-Saxons, who can knock their knees together, and through their chattering teeth and pale lips admit that they are afraid the Negroes will "dominate us."

The question of social equality does not enter into the calculation at all. That is a thing each citizen decides for himself. No statute ever yet drew the latch of the humblest home – or ever will. Each citizen regulates his own visiting list – and always will.

An African-American Populist's Letter to the People's Weekly Tribune

William Drewry Jackson, letter to *People's Weekly Tribune* (Birmingham, Alabama), March 19, 1896, reprinted from Norman Pollack (ed.) *The Populist Mind* (Indianapolis: Bobbs- Merrill, 1967), pp. 393–4.

In my opinion, it would be the heighth of wisdom and of superlative importance were the Afro Americans to repudiate both the old parties, and renounce all of their allegiance and fidelity thereto, and switch in and ally themselves with the rank and file of those who are endeavoring, bona fide, to devise some plans by which to substantiate a popular government, a government of the people, for the people and by the people.

... I hope the day is not far distant when the common masses of the common people, including the laborers of towns and cities, as well as the great body of yeomanry, will wake up to a sense of duty, come together and vote in a common cause to throw off and exonerate themselves from the yoke that has been pinching their necks for the last decade, for in reality they are only serfs and vassals used by the demagogues to fill the coffers of the magnates and money kings.

Two Reports on the Colored Farmers' Alliance in Texas

Reprinted from Herbert Aptheker (ed.) *A Documentary History of the Negro People in the United States*, vol. I (New York: Citadel Press, 1951), pp. 806–7, 810.

From the Secretary of the Texas Colored Farmers' Alliance, 1890

He spoke of other organizations among the colored people. How, from time to time, efforts had been made to draw them together and unite them in one solid body, but those efforts all had failed and all former organizations had utterly broken down. On the contrary, the National Alliance Movement had now been in existence for about three years. It had gathered strength every hour of that time. It was peculiarly a movement of the people, by the people and for the people. The colored race had been educated and elevated; they had saved millions in money, and had been trained to look forward to homes of their own and independence and happiness around their own firesides; and these were some of the causes why the National Alliance had prospered and would continue to prosper, and would finally bring the entire colored race together as a unit.

The Cotton Pickers' Strike, 1891

The colored cotton pickers in Texas have agreed not to pick cotton after September 20 for less than $1 per hundred pounds and board. This organization of cotton pickers has been perfected through the Colored Alliance, and now numbers more than half a million, with thousands being added every day throughout the Southern states. Col. R. A. Humphrey, general superintendent of the Colored Alliance, with headquarters at Galveston, admitted the existence of the organization, saying it had been induced by organizations some time ago, of planters and merchants in certain sections, notably Memphis and Charleston – to reduce the price for picking to a very low standard, and that the colored pickers had combined to protect themselves from this dictation, and he thought they would be able to do so. It is learned that a circular has been mailed at Houston, Tex., to every colored sub-alliance throughout the country, fixing the date when the strike of the pickers will be simultaneously inaugurated, and how it shall be conducted.

Senator Benjamin R. Tillman, Speech to the Senate

Speech of March 23, 1900, reprinted from *Congressional Record*, 56th Congress, 1st Session, pp. 3223–4.

As to the rights of the negroes in the South, of which he now claims to be the champion –

MR. SPOONER. No.

MR. TILLMAN. Well, I do not understand the Senator. I am very unfortunate in being unable to gather his meaning. He speaks clearly, and I usually have the means of interpreting language that is plain and unmistakable; but he did say something about the rights of those people.

MR. SPOONER. I did.

MR. TILLMAN. And he said we had taken their rights away from them. He asked me was it right to murder them in order to carry the elections. I never saw one murdered. I never saw one shot at an election. It was the riots before the election, precipitated by their own hot-headedness in attempting to hold the government, that brought on conflicts between the races and caused the shotgun to be used. That is what I meant by saying we used the shotgun.

I want to call the Senator's attention to one fact. He said that the Republican party gave the negroes the ballot in order to protect themselves against the indignities and wrongs that were attempted to be heaped upon them by the enactment of the black code. I say it was because the Republicans of that day, led by Thad Stevens, wanted to put white necks under black heels and to get revenge. There is a difference of opinion. You have your opinion about it, and I have mine, and we can never agree. . . .

Mr. President, I have not the facts and figures here, but I want the country to get the full view of the Southern side of this question and the justification for anything we did. We were sorry we had the necessity forced upon us, but we could not help it, and as white men we are not sorry for it, and we do not propose to apologize for anything we have done in connection with it. We took the government away from them in 1876. We did take it. If no other Senator has come here previous to this time who would acknowledge it, more is the pity. We have had no fraud in our elections in South Carolina since 1884. There has been no organized Republican party in the State.

We did not disfranchise the negroes until 1895. Then we had a constitutional convention convened which took the matter up calmly, deliberately, and avowedly with the purpose of disfranchising as many of them as we could under the fourteenth and fifteenth amendments. We adopted the educational qualification as the only means left to us, and the negro is as contented and as prosperous and as well protected in South Carolina to-day as in any State of the Union south of the Potomac. He is not meddling with politics, for he found that the more he meddled with them the worse off he got. As to his "rights" – I will not discuss them now. We of the South have never recognized the right of the negro to govern white men, and we never will. We have never believed him to be equal to the white man, and we will not submit to his gratifying his lust on our wives and daughters without lynching him. I would to God the last one of them was in Africa and that none of them had ever been brought to our shores. But I will not pursue the subject further.

Suggested Reading

Lawrence Goodwyn, *Democratic Promise: The Populist Moment in America*, New York: Oxford University Press, 1976. A monumental work by the author of the study of Grimes County. Goodwyn emphasizes the grass-roots nature of the movement and its challenge to corporate dominance. An abridged version is *The Populist Moment: A Short History of the Agrarian Revolt in America*, New York: Oxford University Press, 1978.

Richard Hofstadter, *The Age of Reform: From Bryan to F.D.R.*, New York: Knopf, 1955. A Pulitzer Prize-winning interpretation, highly influential but very controversial. Hofstadter maintains that Populism was in many ways a backward-looking and bigoted social movement.

Michael Kazin, *The Populist Persuasion: An American History*, rev. ed., Ithaca, NY: Cornell University Press, 1998. A survey of Populism broadly defined, as movements opposed to elite-driven social change. Kazin finds that the political right has been more successful than the left in using Populist appeals in recent decades.

Leon Litwack, *Trouble in Mind: Black Southerners in the Age of Jim Crow*, New York: Knopf, 1998. A broad history of African-American lives in the South between the end of Reconstruction and the First World War.

Robert McMath, *American Populism: A Social History 1877–1898*, New York: Hill & Wang, 1993. A judicious brief account and interpretation of the farmers' revolt of the late nineteenth century.

C. Vann Woodward, *Tom Watson: Agrarian Rebel*, New York: Rinehart & Co., 1938. A classic biography of the Georgia Populist leader who called for interracial cooperation but later turned to racism.

6

Women's Work, Community, and Radical Labor

1886 American Federation of Labor formed. Under the leadership of Samuel Gompers, the AFL remains predominantly a federation of skilled workers' crafts unions, focused on "business unionism" instead of radical change.

1905 Industrial Workers of the World (IWW, also known colloquially as the "Wobblies") holds founding convention in Chicago. The IWW emphasizes "One Big Union" of all workers and direct action on the job rather than electoral politics. In the preamble to its constitution the IWW states, "The working class and the employing class have nothing in common."

1905–9 IWW organizing successes are concentrated in the West, where they appeal to miners, timber workers, agricultural laborers, and others who have been generally ignored by American Federation of Labor crafts unions.

1909–13 IWW leads a series of strikes in Eastern industries. Workers of many different ethnic and racial groups take part.

January 1912 Women workers in the Lawrence, Massachusetts textile mills lead a strike to protest a pay cut. Almost 30,000 women, men, and children take part. By late March, the workers had won their main demands and returned to the mills.

1913–17 The IWW returns to organizing in the West.

April 1917 The United States enters World War I. Fierce repression of IWW continues throughout the war and the ensuing "red scare" period of 1919–20. By the 1920s the IWW has been severely weakened.

Introduction to the Article

By 1912 the men, women, and children of three generations had come to Lawrence, Massachusetts to work in the textile mills. Immigrants to America and their children accounted for about 85 percent of the grimy city's population of 85,000. The majority of the textile workers labored 56 hours a week and earned an average of less than nine dollars. They crowded into wooden tenements and boardinghouses where respiratory diseases such as tuberculosis and pneumonia were common and infant mortality rates high.

Only a small fraction of the Lawrence textile workers benefited from union membership. The nation's dominant labor organization, the American Federation of Labor (AFL), considered skilled crafts workers, usually native-born white men, their constituency. They generally shunned organizing unskilled laborers or machine-tenders. Unions that comprised the AFL usually practiced "business unionism," which was designed to advance the immediate material interests of their members, not to confront the capitalist system. Beginning in 1905, however, the Industrial Workers of the World (IWW, also known colloquially as the "Wobblies") challenged the skilled trades' unions. It sought to bring all workers, regardless of race, gender, or ethnicity, into "One Big Union" and to wage an uncompromising struggle against the bosses. "The working class and the employing class have nothing in common," stated the IWW constitution. In its first years, the IWW appealed primarily to workers in extractive industries in the West: miners, timber workers, oilfield workers, agricultural laborers. From 1909 to 1913, it scored some major successes in eastern manufacturing centers, including Lawrence.

As Ardis Cameron notes, the 1912 strike in Lawrence began when women mill workers found that the mill owners had cut their pay in proportion to a slight reduction in their working hours that the state of Massachusetts had legislated. Over 30,000 workers struck. Highly dramatic episodes punctuated the two-month strike. Strike opponents planted a dynamite cache, but the press concocted claims of a strikers' plot to blow up the city. During a confrontation with police, a young Italian-American woman striker was shot and killed. With no evidence, authorities charged two of the IWW's organizers with inciting murder. To conserve relief funds and to symbolize the strikers' plight, the IWW arranged to send hundreds of young children to live with sympathizers in other cities while the struggle continued. Infuriated by the favorable publicity the strikers were gaining, the local police marched in and beat a group of adults and children as the children attempted to board a train to Philadelphia. Repression failed to break the strike, and by mid-March the owners granted all of the workers' main demands.

Beneath the drama, we can identify some important themes in the history of American labor militance. First, there was the challenge of the IWW to crafts union conservatism. The Lawrence strike showed that the Wobblies' radicalism appealed to many unskilled workers and that they were capable of conducting a prolonged strike with great energy and courage. The rapid weakening of the IWW presence in Lawrence after the strike settlement, however, showed the problem of translating initial victories into permanent radical organizing.

Second, Lawrence showed that ethnic differences within the working class were not insurmountable barriers. Leaders from among the different nationalities stepped forward during the strike and encouraged their compatriots. The IWW sent organizers who were fluent in several languages. As Ardis Cameron points out, women's neighborhood experiences gave them networks that joined members of different ethnic groups together. This in turn suggests a third historical lesson of Lawrence. In a way reminiscent of the women food rioters of the American Revolution described by Barbara Clark Smith (see chapter 1), the working-class women of Lawrence lived with few boundaries between "private" and "public" life. During the strike, "shopping visits, social gatherings, communal meals and frequent street assemblies continued to be used as organizational meetings." Activist women directly invoked democratic symbols and ideals. They did not view politics as a male preserve. Thus working-class radicalism blended in the Lawrence strike with a radical challenge to dominant notions about women's nature and women's roles.

Bread and Roses Revisited

Ardis Cameron

On January 11, 1912, a group of about a hundred women waited in the weave room of the Everett Mill to see if their pay envelopes had been cut. A recent Massachusetts law had reduced the maximum hours of work for women and children from 56 to 54 hours per week and the mills had

Reprinted from Ardis Cameron, "Bread and Roses Revisited: Women's Culture and Working-class Activism in the Lawrence Strike of 1912," in Ruth Milkman (ed.) *Women Work and Protest: A Century of US Women's Labor History* (Boston: Routledge & Kegan Paul, 1985), pp. 42–58.

hinted that the subsequent loss in production would be made up in lower wages. Loomfixers, highly skilled male workers, had responded by setting up committees in all mills that employed fixers and planned to strike as a group, but to stagger their protest from mill to mill so that "all members could cooperate but remain working until their turn came." Local 20 of the IWW had made similar plans. On January 5, the IWW had written to William Wood, president of the American Woolen Company, requesting a meeting to discuss the entire question. On January 9, 200 black boys had walked out, but they quickly returned when the traditionally rebellious mule spinners, who depended on the quick hands and feet of the boys to operate their machines, rounded them up and angrily pointed out that it wasn't the right time of year for a strike. "Besides," shouted one spinner, "we are married men and do not take kindly to the action of boys."

These independent strategies, however, were quickly forgotten when the female operatives at the Everett discovered their pay was short. Throwing down their aprons and grabbing picket sticks, the women marched out of the mill and called for others to follow them. They stood on one another's shoulders to shout orders, and sent "flying squadrons" of men and women through all the other mills to recruit supporters and shut down machines. Carrying American and Italian flags, 3,500 marchers linked arms and stormed the city's major mills, slashing power belts, smashing windows, and breaking down mill gates to release other workers. By January 13, 25,000 operatives had gone out. The "Bread and Roses" strike of 1912 was under way.

Coming on the heels of the 1909 strike at McKees Rocks and the "Uprising of the 20,000" shirtwaist-makers in the Lower East Side, the strike at Lawrence climaxed a series of proletarian revolts. Its success gave renewed legitimacy to the class-conscious factions in the labor movement, and demonstrated an alternative to the craft-union strategy of the American Federation of Labor. As David Montgomery has suggested, these mass industrial strikes made skilled workers, increasingly under attack from scientific management and technological change, more willing to align themselves with the unskilled, providing a strong fillip for the "new unionism" which characterized the years between 1909 and 1922.[1]

The Lawrence strike was extraordinary both in its tactics and in the quantity and diversity of the participants. Almost 30,000 men, women and children struck, and forty nationalities were represented in their ranks. Contemporaries wrote extensively about the "Revolutionary Strike," the "Industrial War," the "Revolt of the Masses" and the "Boiling Over of the Melting Pot." Almost without exception, they describe a city in revolt, and they repeatedly express horror, delight or confusion over the vast numbers of striking women who, as one judge noted, "have lots of cunning and also lots of bad temper." "They're everywhere," complained another town official, "and it seems to be getting worse and worse all the time." Some observers blamed the extreme militancy not on the IWW, but on "unruly and undisciplined female elements." "Just as soon as women disregard constituted authority by catching and tearing officers' coats," bemoaned a Massachusetts judge, "why, then you have the foundation for all that follows." For many, the women's leader, Elizabeth Gurley Flynn, was the symbol of the ubiquitous female militant. "Partly a Joan of Arc, partly an Emma Goldman," explained one newspaper editor, "but Flynn is more than either, a reincarnation of the militant and maddened women who led the march of the Commune from Paris to Versailles."

Until recently, these women represented what historians defined as pre-political, even marginal actors in working-class political life, and their efforts have often been neglected in the historiography of worker militancy. Most did not belong to unions or political parties, and joined the IWW only during the strike, deserting it soon after. Although evidence is sketchy, most activists seem to have come to Lawrence from traditionally rural or recently industrializing areas, although there were important exceptions to this pattern.

It would be a mistake, however, to view these women as outside or peripheral to working-class militancy and consciousness. The bonds which nourished female friendships and alliances (often identified as characteristic of pre-industrial cultures) also helped sustain neighborhood networks in an industrial setting. Ties between women provided a necessary organizational base for collective efforts and helped to maintain strike discipline and promote class consciousness. In Lawrence, women's efforts in the neighborhoods broadened the critique of capitalist development to include not only wage disputes, but issues of daily community struggle. It was, after all, a strike for bread, and for roses too. The extensive scope of the strike, whereby nearly every mill in the city was shut down, demonstrated almost universal participation in strike activities, concretizing widely shared notions of commonality and justice – or what strikers labeled "a square deal." "We stick together now," explained one female mender, "all of us, to bring about a settlement according to our ideals, our ideas of what is right."

Understanding the role of working-class women in workers' struggles means exploring topics once eschewed by the labor historian: the family, the household and what historians of women have called the "bonds of womanhood." By placing women at the center of community struggle and collective actions, historians like Sheila Rowbotham and Temma Kaplan have begun to challenge the prevailing assumption that male-defined trade unionism is the essential form of working-class organization. Unlike the work of the new labor historians, which tends to neglect the role of the non-wage earner in class formation, these studies call attention to the importance of neighborhood activity and daily life in honing class consciousness and assessing power relations. By extending the definition of class beyond (but not necessarily excluding) relations of production, Kaplan and Rowbotham have located working-class political organization in the daily lives not only of the wage-earner, but also of those groups who, though "formally outside of capitalist production, are still part of the working-class social network."[2]

Since the Lawrence strike is a primary historical example of a workers' struggle which drew extensively on community networks, and since it involved such a large and disparate group of women, it offers a particularly good opportunity to explore the relationship between the traditional sphere of working women – the home, the marketplace and the streets – and working-class activism. What sorts of conditions allowed ordinary women, both housewives and wage-earners, collectively and militantly to protest their situation? How did women's collective efforts promote community cohesiveness and neighborhood discipline? How was women's traditional sphere used to mobilize community action and solidify class consciousness? And finally, did participation in the strike change women's consciousness of themselves? How did their activism alter their personal relationships and traditional subservience to men?

We can begin to answer some of these questions by reconstructing the experiences of women who participated in the Lawrence strike. This chapter draws on research into the lives of more than 114 working-class women who were active in the strike, culled from newspaper accounts, arrest records, hospital reports and government investigations. These women were the most militant of the rebels – those, as one striker put it, "who had drunk of the cup to the very dregs." This essay looks at collective action from the inside, examining the ways in which women's daily experiences and resources helped transform working-class neighborhoods into networks of militant, collective struggle.

The founders of the city of Lawrence had, from the start, envisioned an industrial boomtown and worked hard to insure high profits and maximum productivity. The machine-tending nature of the textile industry, which required increasingly less skill, encouraged management to establish patterns of labor recruitment and a system of social control that it hoped would provide the mills with a docile and vulnerable workforce. Semi-skilled and unskilled immigrants were actively recruited throughout Lawrence's history so that, in the decades before World War I, the city's neighborhoods contained large proportions of immigrant workers, the majority of whom were women. By 1910, Lawrence was one of the world's largest woolen textile centers and fully three-quarters of the city's 85,000 people directly depended on the mills for their livelihood. Of the 60 percent who actually toiled inside the factory gates, well over half were women and children.

Typically, these women lived in densely crowded neighborhoods which surrounded Lawrence's vast mill district. In the center of the working-class community, an area known as The Plains, a 1911 survey of five half-blocks revealed an average of between 300 and 600 people per acre. As one historian has pointed out, "Only 3 blocks in Harlem contained more densely crowded streets." Among the women who made these streets their home, most either worked in one of the city's mills, or lived in a household of textile operatives. Either way, women were essential breadgivers in Lawrence as few families could secure the "necessaries of life" without female labor. This was especially evident in immigrant families. Of 292 foreign-born homes surveyed in 1909, only 18 percent consisted of households in which the husband alone provided the family's entire income. While Lithuanian and Polish families tended to supplement income with boarders and lodgers, thereby utilizing female labor in laundering, sewing, cleaning and cooking for tenants, the French (77 percent), Syrians (42 percent) and Southern Italians (37.5 percent) relied heavily upon the mill earnings of wives and children. "In Lawrence," observed the *New York Call*, "all the family must work, if the family is to survive."

The selective nature of the immigration process also insured that households included a broad range of familial and non-familial social relationships. Government investigators found that defining these numerous entanglements was often tortuous, and eventually settled on describing a household in these neighborhoods as any arrangement "consisting of one or more families, with or without boarders or lodgers as well as all groups of persons living together, no family included, or various combinations of family, groups and boarders and lodgers." As one former striker explained:

> One of my life-long friends and I first met as bedsisters in a friend's place – you know, what they called a tenement. There was a saying, "The beds were never cold." Well, sure, back then you see this is how you lived – you slept in shifts. We all lived like one then. One kitchen we all used and we all knew each other.

Such collective living arrangements facilitated daily exchange and the sharing of goods, services, and mutual concerns. For women, traditional domestic responsibilities such as child care, laundry, food preparation, sewing and nursing, also encouraged mutual support among female neighbors and kin, and secured the household as well as other communal spaces as women's prerogatives. Both before and during the strike, those local centers of female activity – grocery stores, streets, stoops, bath houses, kitchens – also enhanced women's concepts of material rights and sustained efforts to negotiate and agitate for economic justice. As a former weaver who shared rooms with a girlfriend and her uncle commented:

> We met a few months before the strike, but both worked at different mills. We'd (all of us girls) be together sure, in the kitchen, wherever – and we talked. Of course, we all knew our pay, we compared all the time. Better pay, we'd go get it.

Comparing wages and prices was also a common ritual for women and girls who shared their daily commute to and from the factory gates:

> We'd all meet at a certain corner on our block in the morning, it was very dark, you know. We worked very early, came home in the dark too. Well, we'd get our girlfriends together and we'd walk each other to the mills. We'd talk about everything, but always, too, about our pay, oh sure.

Several women recalled shopping with their mothers or friends where grocery stores served as social centers as well as forums for price discussions. As one activist recalled:

> The shops had chairs and we'd take the chance to catch up. We compared prices with our neighborhood and the other Italian markets, then we'd go to the other grocery stores and do the same. Everyone was there, and the stores stayed opened till late at night.

Such spaces had important implications for popular organization during the strike. Street corners and stores were transformed into daily information and decision-making centers; for despite the disruption in wage patterns, women and girls continued domestic routines. As one striker put it, "We'd all want to know, 'what to do, what to do?' Everyone was out, so we'd meet, at our corner, and, oh, everywhere."

The sources of women's culture in the multi-ethnic neighborhoods of Lawrence began here, in the web of informal relationships that were nourished and sustained by women as they performed their customary tasks of mutual help, daily exchange, breadwinning and food preparation. The grocery, where mothers and daughters shared timely gossip as well as daily price indexes with other women, was a critical contact-point where a woman's aptitude for obtaining a "just price" underscored both her individual and public importance in regulating and adjudicating the community's moral economy. Prices and wages were discussed with keen and almost daily interest, and women held sharp and exacting notions of what one was entitled to. Finances were calculated to the penny and converted into hardheaded notions of worth. Several women recalled the Lawrence strike as "the strike for three loaves," and most remembered not only that the pay was short, but that it was precisely thirty-two cents short. The streets, which allowed for public scrutiny as well as space for personal exchange; the tenement stoops, where mothers patrolled their blocks and supervised community activity; and kitchens, where nurturance and communal cooperation occurred daily – all sustained close-knit, female-centered networks.

Often unencumbered by traditional sources of restraint, such as older siblings, grandparents, village life, or, in the case of the Lithuanians and Poles, the established church, their networks allowed women collectively to confront their situation from the focal-point of their lives as they straddled the challenges of womanhood and the demands of wage labor. Both the exigencies of migration and the harsh reality of Lawrence mill life intensified the need for mutual assistance and daily reciprocity. Bonds that were formed along informal networks were strengthened and reinforced in the constant struggle for survival so that sharing responsibilities, both in the home and in the workplace, helped provide a communal and holistic context for individual action. "We are not egged on by anyone or forced to go upon a picket line," explained one female striker. "We go there because we feel that it is but duty."

In no way was women's collective duty more vigorously expressed than in the daily attempts to discipline their neighborhoods and prevent community dissension. Both soldiers and scabs knew from personal experience that these networks could be transformed into effective sources of resistance and militancy. Of the 130 women formally arrested during the strike, almost 90 percent were charged with assault on an officer or intimidation. Guarding the streets from third- and fourth-floor windows, women at times poured scalding water on work-bound neighbors. Hanging out of these makeshift watchtowers, others joined in, throwing stones along with heated insults. The IWW shrewdly took advantage of these opportunities to prevent scabbing and provided several female leaders with cameras so that they could follow those neighborhood "traitors" and photograph them. Women shadowed their victims and then, amidst great hissing and hooting, ceremoniously hung his picture or her image in the local grocery store.

In most cases, however, sisterhood and communal unity were maintained in the household, where traditions of reciprocity and sharing were now systematized for political struggles. Among activist households, 23 percent were headed by women dependent on strikers' wages. Solidarity, it seems, overrode immediate financial losses. Mothers often converted their homes into soup kitchens for hungry strikers or provided child care while younger women picketed or paraded. One former striker recalled how her mother would open up the kitchen "to all the kids on the block. She'd make bread or pizza and everybody would be there – all during the strike. My brother was very active, so we didn't see too much of him, you know he was in jail or at the IWW. So my mother makes sure no one goes hungry or cold, not on our block." Others, less well off, served at soup kitchens or organized fund-raising drives at stores, restaurants, and other businesses, asking for money or food. "If they don't help you now in your hour of need," proclaimed a popular IWW leader, "you know how to treat them." And most women did. Unsympathetic stores were boy-cotted and any that refused credit or food found red scab signs on their front doors. On the whole, however, local shops contributed to the effort and ran soup kitchens as well as supplying food to strikers and their families.

During the strike, plans to care for children and thus prevent the "lash of youthful hunger" from driving women back to work utilized com-munal child-care patterns and established boarding practices already woven into workers' lives. Typically (before the strike) working mothers had turned to neighbors who took in children at modest fees, or, in some cases, had sent their young into the countryside during the work week and collected them again on Sundays. The famous strike tactic of send-ing Lawrence's children to socialist and anarchist sympathizers in New York and Philadelphia, the so-called "children's exodus," was in many ways an extension of this method of child care, successfully merging radical political strategy with customary practice.

The composition and structure of the women's networks had an important bearing on the character and effectiveness of the strike, as well. Ages of female activists ranged widely, from 13 to 48 years. The mean age was 26, with the 20–4 and 25–9 categories containing the highest concentrations. Alliances between generations of women forti-fied class solidarity and often inspired new forms of collective action. What often appeared to some observers as spontaneous and largely uncontrolled outbursts usually contained their own internal logic and organizational structure. Women often branched out from large parades and organized themselves into "endless human chains" by linking their arms together and encouraging others in the area to join in. They would then weave through the neighborhoods and business sections jeering, hooting, and hissing. At this point, wrote one careful observer, "They would rush out, as if on cue, and attack their enemy." Police, militia, unsympathetic priests and nuns, the houses of mill management and unfriendly city officials, were all booed, humiliated, and occasionally physically attacked. Several women hid scissors under their long cloaks and when troopers came into their ranks trying to separate them, they drew out their domestic sabers and cut the backs of the soldiers' uniforms, "exposing their yellow insides." At other times, female demonstrators would cut suspenders and collectively strip offenders while groups of women pointed and hooted as the victim made his escape from the streets. By linking arms and moving in groups, women were able to protect each other and avoid arrest. By creating chaotic scenes and constant noises they hoped to confuse officers and camouflage the identity of individual attackers.

Women also arranged their marches into horizontal lines so that the youngest girls were in the middle of their formation. In part, this was to protect the most vulnerable strikers but also women sought publicly to expose the abuses of child labor through this tactic. In Lawrence, fully one-half of the city's children worked in the mills, and their poor survival rate was a critical issue during the strike. Although city officials complained about the use of children in such demonstrations, nothing exceeded the outcry that accompanied the "children's exodus." Social workers from Boston loudly voiced their outrage against the "dragging of offspring into the matter." Calling these women "maudlin millionaires," Elizabeth Gurley Flynn struck home when she pointed out that "When mothers had to go into the mills and work hard and leave their children to other people's care, there was no outcry and no offers of sympathy for her or her kids." By relying on local custom and developing strategies to maximize their collective impact, working-class women used the sources at hand, and in so doing gave meaning, coherence and unity, where contemporaries saw only confusion and disorder.

Such efforts went far in promoting a consciousness of kind which often crossed ethnic boundaries, for close living and common domestic responsibilities made for frequent contact between immigrant women. While in the mill rooms, management sought to use ethnic loyalty to separate workers, female networks provided occasional opportunities to surmount interethnic antagonisms and distrust. Although the Italians and Jews of Lawrence had strong concentrations of "their own kind," Syrians, Poles, Lithuanians, Franco-Belgians and Scots, overlapped and spilled into their blocks. Courtyard arrangements in these heterogeneous districts often united women who shared only broken English but who offered mutual assistance and support. The cross-ethnic friendships that were nourished in this environment were sometimes hidden from male heads of households, but were important sources of strength for women. "My father," explained an Italian woman, "never knew our mother had

Syrian friends. They would visit each other in the day and eventually my mother could cook like a Syrian."

During the strike, when men and women needed to cooperate as a united force, such friendships helped to link disparate communities and offered an effective basis for multi-ethnic solidarity. Streets were patrolled by groups of girls from different immigrant backgrounds; when they found someone carrying the telltale lunchbox of a strike-breaker, similar language and culture could be brought to bear on the worker in an attempt to turn him or her back. If words failed, women united to brandish red pepper, rocks, clubs and other means at their disposal to minimize worker disunity.

Women also affirmed their sisterhood and commonality by assisting each other against the common oppressor, whether it be a scabbing neighbor, a policeman, a city official or, as one female striker described the militia, "those things in khaki suits." Consistently, women tried to help each other escape when being arrested, often crowding into police vans demanding that "everyone" or "no one" be hauled off to jail. Julia Yulla, a Syrian woman, was arrested for helping Irish-born Maggie Smith, "a notorious scab mugger," escape from Officer O'Brien. Both women had been shopping in the Italian section and possessed large quantities of red pepper under their cloaks. A third striker, Josephine Dimmock, who was from Poland, was also charged in the incident and relieved of a large piece of gas pipe she carried in her shawl. Women also tried to disguise personal liability during group actions. Instruments such as pipes, ten-pins and scissors, were quickly passed among assembled women just before arrest, making it almost impossible for the officer to prove who had used it.

Popular organization for the strike was decentralized, and much of the decision-making concerning collective action took place along these networks that criss-crossed local centers of activity. When town officials closed down the saloons, the public common and local union halls, and when mill management rented out all available private spaces including the town ballpark, male strikers found themselves increasingly confined to small shops and crowded ethnic halls. To reach the masses and mobilize effectively, they depended on women's use of female domains to maintain order, get out the news, transport and distribute circulars and dodgers, prevent defeatist rumors, and organize demonstrations. Stores, homes, back porches, streets, clubs, even Jewish bath houses, were used to distribute information. Women also decided daily strategy and even held elections on street corners deep within the immigrant communities, where "soldier boys" were loath to go. It was at such a meeting that Louise Zurwell saw a policeman shoot and kill 32-year-old Annie LoPizzo, an event which alerted officials to the importance of controlling the neighborhoods, and military orders that women and children keep off the streets quickly followed. Arrests dramatically increased, but shopping visits, social gatherings, communal meals and frequent street assemblies continued to be used as organizational meetings where women compared notes on scabs, needy families, fundraisers, child care, picket duty and soup kitchens.

Local leadership during the strike was seldom spontaneous, and both workers and radicals relied heavily on existing neighborhood resources. Known female activists whom the press dismissed as "petty leaders" were often either newly created militants or women who, as a result of their shrewdness, intelligence, strength and generosity of spirit, had long before earned a position of leadership in the local community. "Such women," complained the local press, "spring up from time to time and brief rallies would follow in the middle of the streets." One such woman had moved outside of Lawrence prior to the strike and along with her husband operated an egg farm. But her advice and support were eagerly sought by the strikers and she visited the city almost daily during the struggle, bringing food, news and comfort. Her farm also became known as a safe hiding place for agitators, a tradition which would continue long after the strike ended. Some, like Annie Welsenback, the only female member of the general strike committee, earned a reputation for strength and courage both on the shopfloor, where she earned more money than most male operatives, and in the community, where she cared for her sisters, husband and parents. Born in Canada, Annie was the daughter of Polish mill-workers and spoke several languages. When she was arrested for intimidating several male strike-breakers, local middle-class women's groups joined strikers to protest, and groups gathered outside the jail windows to demonstrate their support and outrage.

In marches and demonstrations, women sought to unify and connect their actions with the ideals of a republican America, and those of their oppressors with the international symbols of terror and brutality. Joining their male comrades, women of diverse ethnic heritages draped American flags around their shoulders or used them as shawls and banners. Leading a "monster" parade of about 2,000 people, 22-year-old Annie Kiami, a Syrian mill operative, carried a huge American flag. As the demonstrators passed the bayonetted soldiers, she would wait for the other women, some dressed in red, white and blue, to begin a ritualized "slow, dismal, groan" at the troopers. When the militia men looked nervous, Annie would point the flag and shout, "Cossacks," "Black Hundreds." "We protest," shouted one woman, "to somebody higher up!" "We couldn't believe it, you know," remembered one striker. "Here, this happening, in America. Oh, they were cruel."

This ritualized expression of discontent and the use of the neighbor-hoods in a general strike, allowed those who did not share similar relations of production to unite with workers. By organizing in the community, women insured that the focus of hostility was centered not on one employer, the American Woolen Company, but on the ruling, or as one striker put it, the "preying classes." Among the female activists whose occupations are known, only 68 percent actually worked in the mills at the time of the outbreak, while a large corps, 26 percent, were housewives. Others included shop clerks, wives of grocery store owners, a teacher and a midwife. In a city choked by pollution, where raw sewage flowed in the water system, where the mean age at death was fifteen years, and where thirty-six out of every 100 mill operatives died before their twenty-fifth birthday, women demanded that more than one boss or company be held accountable. By centering their hostility on those, as one strike leader put it, "who sought to defeat the democratic institutions...to satisfy an unholy greed," women helped define their community of interest and articulate class conscious-ness.

As in other multi-ethnic industrial cities in the years prior to World War I, the structure of the relations of production and the parameters of ethnic culture did much to influence and define the nature of Lawrence's working-class community. Yet the lives of these laboring women – espe-cially "those who had drunk...to the very dregs" – suggests the sig-nificance of female associational life in workers' efforts to confront economic oppression and improve their collective situation. Analyzing women's struggles in the neighborhoods also points to the importance of female bonds, and the informal community networks that sustained them, in the formation of working-class consciousness, worker militancy and communal cohesion. Utilizing resources at hand, women helped unite shopfloor struggles with neighborhood discontent. In so doing, as one striker put it, they "served a public indictment against the powers that prey not only upon the original producer...but on the ultimate consumer...who is fully cognizant of the wrongs inflicted upon them."

The women's culture that grew out of the heterogeneous and densely populated neighborhoods of Lawrence was shaped and nourished by female customary tasks and by the exigencies of immigration. Although it would be too simple to conclude (as Big Bill Haywood, leader of the IWW, did) that "the women won the strike," Lawrence's unemployed women, housewives and female wage-earners were critical to the com-munity's ability to assess power relations, maintain popular resistance and sustain worker militancy. Furthermore, the radicalization of "women's sphere" in 1912 and the political orientation of collective female efforts reveals a more creative and complex fabric of working-class politics than labor theorists have previously suggested. Often functioning as information centers, election headquarters, price exchanges, consumer and environmental forums, welfare centers, child-care facilities and support groups, women's spaces portray a shadowy but distinct form of class politics that highlights women's efforts to extend class interests beyond the relations of production, promoting solidarity among disparate members of the working-class social network. Here, women's position in the home and the neighborhood could combine with their labor-force experience to produce a radical consciousness and promote militancy in the public sphere.

Of course, the female bonds which entwined Lawrence's neighborhoods were not the only sources of workers' strength in the bitter struggle for a "square deal" in 1912. The city's rich radical culture, which overlapped male and female domains, and the impact of the IWW, are neglected here. But these more studied aspects of the strike rested upon the bedrock of laboring women's daily lives, which provided the critical support for worker militancy, ethnic solidarity and class consciousness. On the other hand, the associational life upon which the strike's success relied did not constitute a permanent form of labor organization, suggesting a more complex basis for the presumed "failure" of the IWW to provide a lasting presence.

Following female activists through their own neighborhoods at the height of labor–capital tensions also reveals the importance of local women's leadership in mass struggle. Mutual dependence and daily reciprocity strengthened women's ties with each other and helped identify trusted female neighbors. Such women were often vocal advocates for local interests and they supplied the working class with effective agitators, those whom New England mill management had often regarded as "radicals of the worst sort." By focusing on such "petty leaders," we can begin to tunnel beneath the wall that has traditionally separated the public and private lives of workers. Rather than diluting class antagonism, the linkage between the workplace and the "private" sphere helps untangle not only laboring women's place within the productive process but the complex relationship between gender, class and worker militancy. As one anonymous wage-earning woman wrote after an earlier struggle, "I only add the record of my experience as a possible atom of force to that lever which shall one day topple the rock out of our road." Analyzing such experiences suggests new questions concerning the role of women in working-class and ethnic history and provides a lever with which to unearth the varied and at times radicalized forms of women's consciousness, formed below the surface of official scrutiny, in the convoluted yet ordinary web of female daily life.

Notes

1 David Montgomery, "The 'New Unionism' and the Transformation of Workers' Consciousness in America, 1909–1922," *Journal of Social History* 7 (1974), pp. 509–29.
2 Sheila Rowbotham, *Women, Resistance and Revolution* (New York: Pantheon Books, 1973); Temma Kaplan, *Anarchists of Andalusia, 1868–1903* (Princeton, NJ: Princeton University Press, 1977).

Documents

Introduction to the Documents

In her article in this chapter, Ardis Cameron focuses on women's community solidarity and militance in the 1912 textile strike in Lawrence, Massachusetts. The first two documents complement her analysis with background on the workplace and the strike itself. Document One, from a United States Senate report on the strike, demonstrates that most workers before the strike earned less than 15 cents an hour and worked at least 56 hours weekly. More than a tenth of the workers were under 18, some as young as 14. Women, on average, made 3 cents an hour less than men. Document Two is the testimony before a US House committee of Victoria Wennaryzk, a 14-year-old who left school after fifth grade to enter the mills. The condescension of the questioners is evident, as are the problems that drove women, men, and youths to the picket lines in Lawrence.

Lawrence, the "Bread and Roses" strike, was not a battle for wages alone. Workers wanted a better life. They used elements of their diverse cultural backgrounds to dramatize their situation. Document Three shows lyrics, parodying a popular song of the era, that workers sang on the picket lines. ("Gurley Flynn" refers to Elizabeth Gurley Flynn, a charismatic IWW leader known as the "Rebel Girl" who came to Lawrence for the strike.) Document Four is by the early twentieth-century poet James Oppenheim. Although the poem itself appeared before this strike, women in Lawrence displayed the phrase "Bread and Roses" on their banners. The verses came to be identified with the strikers' idealism and aspirations for freedom and fulfillment. Later set to music, the song and the slogan continue as watchwords in labor and feminist struggles.

Wages and Working Conditions in the Textile Mills

Reprinted from "Wages and Hours of Labor and Conditions of Work in the Textile Mills," in *Report on Strike of Textile Workers in Lawrence, Mass., in 1912,* 62nd Congress, 2nd Session, Senate Document 870 (Washington, DC, 1912), pp. 71–5.

Summary of Wages and Hours of Labor

Data relative to wages and hours of labor were secured from the pay rolls of four woolen and worsted mills and three cotton mills in Lawrence. The period for which information was taken was the week ending nearest November 25, 1911. For weavers and a few other occupations information was secured for two or four weeks. Two of the four woolen and worsted mills allow a premium in some occupations, and in all cases where a premium was earned the amount of the earnings during the whole premium period and the amount of the premium were added to produce the total earnings. Overseers and clerks are not included in the tabulation.

The total number of textile employees for whom wages and hours were secured was 21,922, which was approximately two-thirds of the total number employed in the textile mills of Lawrence immediately preceding the strike. Of the 21,922 employees for whom data were secured, 12,150, or 55.4 per cent, were males, and 9,772, or 44.6 per cent, were females. The distribution of employees into sex and age groups was as follows:

[Table 1]

Sex and age groups	Number	Per cent distribution
Males, 18 years of age and over	11,075	50.5
Males, under 18 years of age	1,075	4.9
Total	12,150	55.4
Females, 18 years of age and over	8,320	38.0
Females, under 18 years of age	1,452	6.6
Total	9,772	44.6
Grand total	21,922	100.0

Eleven and one-half per cent of the total number of employees were under 18 years of age. The males under 18 formed 8.8 per cent of the total number of males and the females under 18 formed 14.9 per cent of the total number of females.

Approximately one-fourth (23.3 per cent) of the 21,922 textile-mill employees earned less than 12 cents per hour, and about one-fifth (20.4 per cent) earned 20 cents and over per hour. The average rate of earnings per hour was 16 cents.

Almost one-third (33.2 per cent) of the 21,922 employees earned less than $7, and approximately one-half as many, 17.5 per cent of the total, earned $12 and over during the week for which pay-roll data were secured. The average amount earned during the week was $8.76.

During the week for which pay-roll data were secured 19.9 per cent of the 21,922 employees worked more than 56 hours, 57.2 per cent worked 56 hours, and 22.9 per cent worked less than 56 hours. The average number of hours worked during the week was 54.4.

The table which follows [table 2] shows in summary form for the employees of each sex and within each age group data relative to rate of wages per hour and amount earned and hours worked during the week for which information was secured.

The summary table [table 3] shows for the employees of each sex and within each age group the average rate of wages and the per cent earning each classified rate per hour. The table also shows the per cent of employees working less than 56 hours during the week. The classified rates are shown in the form of cumulative percentages.

Less than 12 cents per hour was earned by 10.9 per cent of the males 18 years of age and over, 25.9 per cent of the females 18 and over, 72.8 per cent of the males under 18, and 66.3 per cent of the females under 18. Twenty cents and over per hour was earned by 32.4 per cent of the males 18 and over, 10.4 per cent of the females 18 and over, 0.4 per cent of the males under 18, and 1.7 per cent of the females under 18. Forty-nine per cent of the males and 69.1 per cent of the females earned less than 15 cents per hour.

The average rate earned by the 11,075 males 18 years of age and over was $0.179 per hour, which was $0.032 per hour above the average for the females 18 years of age and over. The average rate of earnings per hour of the 1,075 males under 18 years of age was $0.114, and of the 1,452 females under 18 years of age $0.117.

The summary table [table 4] shows for the employees of each sex and within each age group the average amount earned and the per cent earning each classified amount during the week for which data were secured. The classified amounts are shown in the form of cumulative percentages.

[Table 2]   ]Average rate of wages and average amount earned and hours worked during week for which data were secured, by sex and age groups: woolen and worsted mills and cotton mills

Sex and age groups	Total number of employees	Rate of wages per hour			Amount earned during week			Hours worked during week			
		Average	Per cent of employees earning –		Average	Per cent of employees earning –		Average	Per cent of employees working –		
			Under 12 cents	20 cents and over		Under $7	$12 and over		Under 56	56	Over 56
Males, 18 years and over	11,075	$0.179	10.9	32.4	$10.20	17.5	30.2	56.5	19.8	41.3	38.9
Males, under 18 years	1,075	0.114	72.8	0.4	6.02	80.2	0.3	52.5	20.8	76.7	2.4
Total	12,150	0.173	16.4	29.5	9.83	23.0	27.5	56.1	19.9	44.4	35.7
Females, 18 years and over	8,320	0.147	25.9	10.4	7.67	40.4	5.7	52.2	26.1	73.6	0.2
Females, under 18 years	1,452	0.117	66.3	1.7	6.02	77.1	0.3	51.5	29.8	69.7	0.6
Total	9,772	0.143	31.9	9.1	7.42	45.8	4.9	52.1	26.7	73.0	0.3
Grand total	21,922	0.160	23.3	20.4	8.76	33.2	17.5	54.4	22.9	57.2	19.9

[Table 3] Per cent of employees earning each classified rate of wages per hour, by sex and age groups: woolen and worsted mills and cotton mills

Sex and age groups	Employees		Average rate of wages per hour	Per cent of employees earning each classified rate of wages per hour				
	Total	Per cent working less than 56 hours during week		Under 12 cents	Under 15 cents	Under 20 cents	20 cents and over	
Males, 18 years and over	11,075	19.8	$0.179	10.9	44.3	67.6	32.4
Males, under 18 years	1,075	20.8	0.114	72.8	97.3	99.6	0.4
Total	12,150	19.9	0.173	16.4	49.0	70.5	29.5
Females, 18 years and over	8,320	26.1	0.147	25.9	65.1	89.6	10.4
Females under 18 years	1,452	29.8	0.117	66.3	92.3	98.3	1.7
Total	9,772	26.7	0.143	31.9	69.1	90.9	9.1
Grand total	21,922	22.9	0.160	23.3	58.0	79.6	20.4

[Table 4] Per cent of employees earning each classified amount during week, by sex and age groups – woolen and worsted mills and cotton mills

Sex and age groups	Employees		Average amount earned during week	Per cent of employees earning each classified amount during week				
	Total	Per cent working less than 56 hours during week		Under $5	Under $7	Under $10	Under $12	$12 and over
Males, 18 years and over	11,075	19.8	$10.20	5.0	17.5	56.4	69.8	30.2
Males, under 18 years	1,075	20.8	6.02	12.3	80.2	98.8	99.7	0.3
Total	12,150	19.9	9.83	5.6	23.0	60.2	72.5	27.5
Females, 18 years and over	8,320	26.1	7.67	8.7	40.4	86.5	94.3	5.7
Females, under 18 years	1,452	29.8	6.02	17.6	77.1	98.3	99.7	0.3
Total	9,772	26.7	7.42	10.0	45.8	88.2	95.1	4.9
Grand total	21,922	22.9	8.76	7.6	33.2	72.7	82.5	17.5

[Table 5] Per cent of employees working each classified number of hours during week for which data were secured, by sex and age groups – woolen and worsted mills and cotton mills

Sex and age groups	Number of employees	Average hours worked per week	Per cent of employees working each classified number of hours during week					
			Under 30 $\frac{3}{6}$	Under 40 $\frac{4}{6}$	Under 50 $\frac{5}{6}$	Under 56	56 and over	
Males, 18 years and over	11,075	56.5	4.1	6.5	12.1	19.8	80.2	
Males, under 18 years	1,075	52.5	5.4	8.1	13.8	20.8	79.2	
Total	12,150	56.1	4.2	6.6	12.3	19.9	80.1	
Females, 18 years and over	8,320	52.2	5.3	8.9	15.6	26.1	73.9	
Females, under 18 years	1,452	51.5	7.9	11.4	18.4	29.8	70.2	
Total	9,772	52.1	5.6	9.3	16.0	26.7	73.3	
Grand total	21,922	54.4	4.8	7.8	13.9	22.9	77.1	

During the week for which pay-roll data were secured less than $5 was earned by 7.6 per cent of the 21,922 employees, less than $7 by 33.2 per cent, less than $10 by 72.7 per cent, less than $12 by 82.5 per cent, and $12 and over by 17.5 per cent. Less than $5 was earned by 5 per cent of the males 18 years of age and over, 8.7 per cent of the females 18 and over, 12.3 per cent of the males under 18, and 17.6 per cent of the females under 18. Twelve dollars and over was earned by 30.2 per cent of the males 18 and over, 5.7 per cent of the females 18 and over, 0.3 per cent of the males under 18, and 0.3 per cent of the females under 18.

The [last] summary table [table 5] shows for the employees of each sex and within each age group the average number of hours worked and the per cent working each classified number of hours during the week for which data were secured. The usual division of the 56-hour week in the textile mills of Lawrence was $10\frac{1}{6}$ hours on Monday, Tuesday, Wednesday, Thursday, and Friday, and $5\frac{1}{6}$ hours on Saturday. The classified hours are shown in the form of cumulative percentages.

During the week for which pay-roll data were secured 56 hours and over were worked by 77.1 per cent of the 21,922 employees, under 56 hours by 22.9 per cent, under $50\frac{5}{6}$ hours by 13.9 per cent, under $40\frac{4}{6}$ hours by 7.8 per cent, and under $30\frac{3}{6}$ hours by 4.8 per cent. Less than 56 hours were worked by 19.8 per cent of the males 18 years of age and over, 26.1 per cent of the females 18 and over, 20.8 per cent of the males under 18, and 29.8 per cent of the females under 18. Fifty-six hours and over were worked by 80.2 per cent of the males 18 years of age and over, 73.9 per cent of the females 18 and over, 79.2 per cent of the males under 18, and 70.2 per cent of the females under 18.

Statement of Victoria Wennaryzk

Reprinted from *The Strike at Lawrence, Massachusetts, Hearings before the Committee on Rules of the House of Representatives... 1912*, 62nd Congress, 2nd Session, House Document 671 (Washington, DC, 1912), pp. 162–8.

MR. HARDWICK.   What is your name?
MISS WENNARYZK.   Victoria Wennaryzk.
MR. HARDWICK.   Say that again.
MISS WENNARYZK.   Victoria Wennaryzk.
MR. HARDWICK.   What is your nationality?
MISS WENNARYZK.   Polish.

MR. HARDWICK.   Polish. How old are you?

MISS WENNARYZK.   Fourteen years and five months.

MR. HARDWICK.   Fourteen years and five months? How many children are there in your family?

MISS WENNARYZK.   There are eight; my mother and my father is ten of us.

MR. HARDWICK.   Your mother and your father have eight children? Are you the youngest or the oldest?

MISS WENNARYZK.   No; I am the third from the oldest.

MR. HARDWICK.   You are the next to the oldest?

MISS WENNARYZK.   No; third from the oldest.

MR. HARDWICK.   Let us see; are you one of the strikers?

MISS WENNARYZK.   Yes, I am. [Laughter.]

MR. HARDWICK.   Were you in any of these police fights? Did you see any of these riots that the strikers had with the policemen and the soldiers, and so on?

MISS WENNARYZK.   Well, I saw others hurt, but I forgot all about it. I saw a lot of it, but I forgot how it was.

MR. HARDWICK.   You saw some of it, but you have forgotten how it was?

MISS WENNARYZK.   Yes, sir.

MR. POU.   You will have to remind yourself.

THE CHAIRMAN.   Do you think you can remember it now and tell us what you saw?

MISS WENNARYZK.   That was just the beginning –

MR. HARDWICK.   Can you tell us the beginning?

MISS WENNARYZK.   I saw only some of it.

MR. HARDWICK.   Tell us what you can.

MISS WENNARYZK.   The policemen were chasing the womens; and the womens were trying to get to the other women to tell them not to go to work; and the policemen were chasing them all around, and some of them were pushed and were falling over, and some of them were hurt.

MR. HARDWICK.   Now, let me see; you have said that so fast I could not understand. You said that the policemen were chasing the women?

MISS WENNARYZK.   The women, some of them were striking and the others were working, and these that were striking told the others not to go to work; and the policemen saw them in the crowd, and the policemen came and were chasing them all around, and the people were falling there and some of them got hurt.

MR. HARDWICK.   You say they were chasing them. What were they doing? Running after them? What did they do? Did they hit them?

MISS WENNARYZK.   I didn't see them hit them.

MR. HARDWICK.   What were they after them about, because they were trying to persuade these other people not to go to work?

MISS WENNARYZK.   I don't know.

MR. HARDWICK.   You don't know what these women were doing?

MISS WENNARYZK.   Well, they were hitting the others in the back and telling them not to go to work.

MR. HARDWICK.   Hitting the others in the back?

MISS WENNARYZK.   Hitting them in the back, and the policemen coming around and chasing them around.

MR. HARDWICK.   And that is how it got started?

MISS WENNARYZK.   Yes, sir.

MR. HARDWICK.   Did anybody hit you in the back?

MISS WENNARYZK.   No.

MR. HARDWICK.   Anybody tell you not to go to work?

MISS WENNARYZK.   No.

MR. HARDWICK.   How came it that you did not go to work then? Why didn't you go to work?

MISS WENNARYZK.   I didn't want to get hurt.

MR. HARDWICK.   Well, were you satisfied with your job? Did you have enough bread to eat?

MISS WENNARYZK.   Well, when we were all working I did. . . .

MR. HARDWICK.   Yes; when you were all working you did. Were you satisfied with your job and your pay, or not?

MISS WENNARYZK.   Well, I was not satisfied, for I didn't get what I wanted. I was working piecework.

MR. HARDWICK.   Oh, yes; so it depended on how much you did what you got?

MISS WENNARYZK.   They did not give me the right pay.

MR. HARDWICK.   They did not give you the right pay? Did you agree to strike before the strike was called, or did you just follow the strike to keep from getting into trouble? Were you consulted about whether you wanted to strike or not before the strike occurred?

MR. POU.   She does not understand.

MR. HARDWICK.   Did anybody ask you about whether you wanted to strike or not before the strike began?

MISS WENNARYZK.   No.

MR. HARDWICK.   You did not agree to strike before the thing started?

MISS WENNARYZK.   I didn't know there was going to be a strike.

MR. HARDWICK.   That is what I say; you did not know there was going to be a strike, and you were afraid if you did not go down there you would get hurt.

MISS WENNARYZK. They all went out, and I had to go out after them.

MR. HARDWICK. You had to go out after them?

MISS WENNARYZK. Yes.

MR. HARDWICK. All right. What company did you work for at the time this strike began?

MISS WENNARYZK. The woolen company.

MR. HARDWICK. American Woolen Co.?

MISS WENNARYZK. Yes.

MR. HARDWICK. How long had you worked for them?

MISS WENNARYZK. Five months.

MR. HARDWICK. Five years?

MISS WENNARYZK. Five months.

MR. HARDWICK. What was your job?

MISS WENNARYZK. Low spooling.

MR. HARDWICK. How much did you get for it?

MISS WENNARYZK. It was piecework, and was on how much I made. I made about $5, $4, or $3. The first time I went to work there, twice I got $6; the rest of the time they would not give me that even if I made it. They gave me $5.

MR. HARDWICK. The first time you got $6, the second time you made it, but they would not give to you?

MISS WENNARYZK. The first time I got $4; the second time I got $6; the third time I got $6. The rest of the times I got $5, $4, $3, and $2.

MR. HARDWICK. Five, four, three, and two? Why was that difference, according to the amount you worked or not? Why didn't they give you the same amount every week? Did you do less work some weeks than you did other weeks?

MISS WENNARYZK. No, I did not. Some weeks I make more and they do not give me that.

MR. HARDWICK. The weeks that you made $2 did you work as much as the weeks you made $5?

MISS WENNARYZK. Well, sometimes I did.

MR. HARDWICK. Sometimes you did not, too?

MISS WENNARYZK. Well, if it was slack and I didn't get yarn I couldn't make more pay.

MR. HARDWICK. If you did not get the yarn you could not make more. In other words, they did not give you enough work to make more?

MISS WENNARYZK. Yes; I had to wait half an hour for the work I was waiting for.

MR. HARDWICK. Was the work pretty hard?

MISS WENNARYZK.   Yes; you have got to run; it is pretty hard and I would sweat all day.

MR. HARDWICK.   You were pretty tired when you got home?

MISS WENNARYZK.   Yes; and as soon as I came home I had to go to sleep, I was so tired.

MR. HARDWICK.   Did they take any of your pay for water?

MISS WENNARYZK.   I worked about a month and a half and a man came to me and said he wanted a dime for water. I only paid once.

MR. HARDWICK.   What sort of water did they give you?

MISS WENNARYZK.   I drink water every day.

MR. HARDWICK.   Ice water?

MISS WENNARYZK.   They bring the water in bottles and they put the ice into it.

MR. HARDWICK.   And during that five months they charged you 10 cents for water?

MISS WENNARYZK.   Yes.

MR. HARDWICK.   Did they hold back a week's pay in the mill you worked for – hold back a week's pay – keep back a week's pay?

MISS WENNARYZK.   Yes.

MR. HARDWICK.   Have you any sisters that work in that mill?

MISS WENNARYZK.   I have a sister working in that mill.

MR. HARDWICK.   How many?

MISS WENNARYZK.   One.

MR. HARDWICK.   Have you got any other sister who works in any other mill?

MISS WENNARYZK.   Pemberton mill; yes; and my father works in the Everett mill.

MR. HARDWICK.   In the Everett mill? What does your father get for his work?

MISS WENNARYZK. $7.70 overtime.

MR. HARDWICK. $7.70 per week and overtime?

MISS WENNARYZK.   Yes.

MR. HARDWICK.   What does the overtime amount to?

MISS WENNARYZK.   He has to work Saturday overtime.

MR. HARDWICK.   How much does that amount to – $7.70?

MISS WENNARYZK.   That is all he gets.

MR. HARDWICK.   How much does your sister get?

MISS WENNARYZK.   The one in the Pemberton mill gets $6 and the other who works in the Wood mill gets $6 a week.

MR. HARDWICK.   How old are these two girls – your sisters?

MISS WENNARYZK.   The oldest one is 17 and the other one is 16.

MR. HARDWICK.   Yes; and they get about the same pay you do?

MISS WENNARYZK. Well, the oldest one here she gets $6 and a few cents.

MR. HARDWICK. The oldest one gets $6 a week? What country were you born in?

MISS WENNARYZK. Salem, Mass.

MR. HARDWICK. Where? Salem, Mass.? Your father was from Poland?

MISS WENNARYZK. Yes.

MR. HARDWICK. How long has he been in this country?

MISS WENNARYZK. Eighteen or seventeen years.

MR. HARDWICK. Seventeen or eighteen years?

MISS WENNARYZK. Yes.

MR. HARDWICK. Is he naturalized? Does he vote in the elections?

MISS WENNARYZK. Yes.

THE CHAIRMAN. Is that all? You can stand aside. Does any other member wish to ask a question?

MR. CAMPBELL. I would like to ask a few questions. You have been working about five months in the mill?

MISS WENNARYZK. Yes, sir. . . .

MR. CAMPBELL. You talked it over in the family about when you would go to work, did you?

MISS WENNARYZK. Yes.

MR. CAMPBELL. Tell us what you said about it.

MISS WENNARYZK. My mother said I would have to go to work, so we could earn our living.

MR. CAMPBELL. Your mother said you had to go to work?

MISS WENNARYZK. So we could earn our living.

MR. CAMPBELL. As soon as you were 14?

MISS WENNARYZK. I went to school; I was 14 on Wednesday, and I did not go to work until Monday.

MR. CAMPBELL. You quit immediately after you became 14?

MISS WENNARYZK. Yes, sir.

MR. CAMPBELL. To go to work in the mill?

MISS WENNARYZK. Yes, sir.

MR. CAMPBELL. What grade were you in?

MISS WENNARYZK. Fifth grade.

MR. CAMPBELL. Do you remember what your father and mother said about it when they were talking about your quitting school and going into the mill?

MISS WENNARYZK. No; I didn't hear anything that they said about it; but I heard my mother say that I would have to go to work because we did not have enough money; that was all my mother said.

MR. CAMPBELL.   Who went to the mill to see about getting a place for you?

MISS WENNARYZK.   I went.

MR. CAMPBELL.   You went down yourself? Whom did you see?

MISS WENNARYZK.   I saw a girl there; I asked could I get a job there, and she says, "Yes," and she was learning me.

MR. CAMPBELL.   Yes; did you go to work immediately after you quit school?

MISS WENNARYZK.   Yes.

MR. CAMPBELL.   Which would you rather do, go to school or go to the mill?

MISS WENNARYZK.   I would rather go to school.

MR. CAMPBELL.   How many rooms are in your house?

MISS WENNARYZK.   Four rooms.

MR. CAMPBELL.   Do you know how much rent you pay?

MISS WENNARYZK. $2.75.

MR. CAMPBELL. $2.75 a week?

MISS WENNARYZK.   Yes, sir.

MR. CAMPBELL.   Do you have water in the house?

MISS WENNARYZK.   Yes, sir.

MR. CAMPBELL.   How many stoves do you have in your house?

MISS WENNARYZK.   One....

MR. CAMPBELL.   You get up at 6 o'clock and dress and have your breakfast, and then do you go to the mill right away?

MISS WENNARYZK.   Yes, sir.

MR. CAMPBELL.   What time do you get home in the evening?

MISS WENNARYZK.   Well, before we came home at 6 o'clock; now we come home at half-past 5.

MR. CAMPBELL.   Do you go home at noon?

MISS WENNARYZK.   No.

MR. CAMPBELL.   You take your lunch with you to the mill?

MISS WENNARYZK.   Yes, sir.

MR. CAMPBELL.   How much rest do you have at noon? How long?

MISS WENNARYZK.   Well, as soon as – [sic] we stop at 1 o'clock.

MR. CAMPBELL.   You stop at 12 and rest until 1?

MISS WENNARYZK.   One o'clock.

MR. WLSON.   What do you have for your luncheon?

MISS WENNARYZK.   Pies and cakes, coffee or milk.

MR. WLSON.   And you take that with you from your home?

MISS WENNARYZK.   Yes.

MR. WLSON.   Do you remember any time when you were hungry and had no food in the house?

MISS WENNARYZK. Well, sometimes in the morning when I get up late, I didn't have enough time to have my breakfast.

MR. WLSON. Yes; but it was not – the reason was not because you didn't have it in the home, was it?

MISS WENNARYZK. No.

MR. WLSON. Just because you were a little late?

MISS WENNARYZK. Yes, sir.

MR. WLSON. How many times a week do you have meat?

MISS WENNARYZK. Once a week.

MR. WLSON. Don't you have it more than once a week?

MISS WENNARYZK. No. There are so much of us we could not get the money to buy the meat.

MR. WLSON. What day do you usually have it?

MISS WENNARYZK. Sunday we have meat.

MR. WLSON. Sunday.

MR. LENROOT. Do you know whether your father pays grocery bills by the week, or does he pay cash each time?

MISS WENNARYZK. Grocery bills?

MR. LENROOT. Yes.

MISS WENNARYZK. We pay by the week.

MR. LENROOT. Do you know about how much a week it runs?

MISS WENNARYZK. Well, we pay $4, $3.

MR. LENROOT. And do you know how much the meat bill is a week? Is that separate?

MISS WENNARYZK. Well, we don't have meat only on Sundays.

MR. LENROOT. But do you know how much it is? Does he pay cash for that – or don't you know?

MISS WENNARYZK. Do you mean how much the meat costs?

MR. LNROOT. Yes.

MISS WENNARYZK. Well, the meat was 18 cents a pound; I don't know how much it is now. My father buys it; I don't.

TIHE CHAIRMAN. You say you have pies and cakes and milk for lunch?

MISS WENNARYZK. Well, when we used to work; not now.

THE CHAIRMAN. You are doing pretty well; that is about all the Congressmen down here get for lunch.

MISS WENNARYZK. I don't think so.

THE CHAIRMAN. You can stand aside now.

Song: "In the Good Old Picket Line"

First published in *Solidarity*, June 29, 1912, reprinted from Joyce L. Kornbluh (ed.) *Rebel Voices: An I.W.W. Anthology* (Ann Arbor: University of Michigan Press, 1964), p. 180.

In the good old picket line, in the good old picket line,
The workers are from every place, from nearly every clime,
The Greeks and Poles are out so strong, and the Germans all the time,
But we want to see more Irish in the good old picket line.

In the good old picket line, in the good old picket line,
We'll put Mr. Lowe in overalls and swear off drinking wine,
Then Gurley Flynn will be the boss,
Oh Gee, won't that be fine,
The strikers will wear diamonds in the good old picket line.

James Oppenheimer, "Bread and Roses"

Reprinted from *The American Magazine* 73 (December 1911), p. 214.

As we come marching, marching, in the beauty of the day,
A million darkened kitchens, a thousand mill-lofts gray
Are touched with all the radiance that a sudden sun discloses,
For the people hear us singing, "Bread and Roses, Bread and Roses."

As we come marching, marching, we battle, too, for men –
For they are women's children, and we mother them again.
Our lives shall not be sweated from birth until life closes –
Hearts starve as well as bodies: Give us Bread, but give us Roses.

As we come marching, marching, unnumbered women dead
Go crying through our singing their ancient song of Bread;
Small art and love and beauty their drudging spirits knew –
Yes, it is Bread we fight for – but we fight for Roses, too.

As we come marching, marching, we bring the Greater Days –
The rising of the women means the rising of the race –
No more the drudge and idler – ten that toil where one reposes –
But a sharing of life's glories: Bread and Roses, Bread and Roses.

Suggested Reading

Ava Baron, *Work Engendered: Toward a New History of American Labor*, Ithaca, NY: Cornell University Press, 1991. An innovative collection of articles about work and gender, mostly dealing with the United States in the twentieth century.

Ardis Cameron, *Radicals of the Worst Sort: Laboring Women in Lawrence, Massachusetts, 1860–1912*, Urbana, IL: University of Illinois Press, 1993. Cameron, the author of the article in this chapter, finds that the interplay of migration, work, and community provided a context for women's labor radicalism in Lawrence.

Melvyn Dubofsky, *We Shall Be All: A History of the Industrial Workers of the World*, 2nd ed., Urbana, IL: University of Illinois Press, 1988. A comprehensive history of the IWW that stresses the organization's lack of ideological dogma and its roots in Western working-class life.

David J. Goldberg, *A Tale of Three Cities: Labor Organization and Protest in Paterson, Passaic and Lawrence, 1916–1921*, New Brunswick, NJ: Rutgers University Press, 1989. A comparative study of three textile manufacturing communities that concludes that it was difficult to maintain a radical labor presence after the great strike in Lawrence.

Alice Kessler-Harris, *Out to Work: A History of Wage-Earning Women in the United States*, New York: Oxford University Press, 1982. A broadly conceived history of women's paid labor throughout American history, sensitive to issues of race and ethnicity as well as social class.

David Montgomery, *Workers' Control in America*, Cambridge, UK and New York: Cambridge University Press, 1979. An influential interpretation of labor history and the "new unionism" of the years around World War I. See also the same author's *The Fall of the House of Labor: The Workplace, the State and American Labor Activism, 1865–1925*, Cambridge, UK and New York: Cambridge University Press, 1987.

The Michigan State University Library American Radicalism Collection has placed several important pamphlets and other documents about the Industrial Workers of the World on its website at:

http://www.lib.msu.edu/coll/main/spec_col/radicalism/index.html

The Industrial Workers of the World still exist. Their website is at:

http://www.iww.org/

(Note that URLs on the Web are often subject to change. These links were valid in August 2000.)

7

Black Communists in the Great Depression South

1917 Russian Revolution, Communists assume power.

1924 Communist Party of the United States of America (CPUSA) forms. Its membership remains very small during the prosperous 1920s.

1927 Soviet dictator Joseph Stalin claims that world capitalism has entered a period of crisis and that revolutionary conditions will prevail. CPUSA adopts this extreme leftist line and rejects cooperation with reform movements or other radical organizations.

October 1928 The Comintern (Communist International, world-wide group dominated by the Soviet Union) passes a resolution in favor of black "self-determination" in the Black Belt of the American rural South. American Communists are directed to consider organizing blacks in the South as a crucial revolutionary task.

1929 Onset of the Great Depression, a decade-long economic crisis.

March 25, 1931 Scottsboro incident. Two white women falsely accuse nine young black men of rape on a freight train near Scottsboro, Alabama. They are all convicted and all but one sentenced to death. The Communist Party and its affiliated International Labor Defense provide defense counsel and mobilize protests against the injustice. Eventually, the death penalty is blocked; the last defendant is released from prison in 1950.

Early 1930s Sharecroppers Union (SCU) organizes predominantly black tenant farmers in the deep South. Communists play a leading role in the SCU.

1934 Alabama Communist Party membership, 95 percent black, is about 1,000.

1935–9 Communist Parties around the world adopt more moderate "Popular Front" strategy of building alliances with other progressive movements and working for reforms. Although southern organizing continues, the CPUSA's main priority is building industrial unions within the newly-formed Congress of Industrial Organizations in basic manufacturing industries. The Sharecroppers' Union merges into a broader agricultural union coalition and declines in late 1930s.

Introduction to the Article

The history of the Communist Party of the United States of America still provokes heated controversy, all out of proportion to the power it wielded in American society. Anti-Communist historians portray the organization as utterly subservient to the totalitarian Soviet Union. Recent revelations that Moscow financed the party for decades and that some American Communists spied for the USSR have reinforced the party's reputation as a hostile agent of a foreign power. Historians such as Robin D. G. Kelley do not deny the party's unsavory aspects but they concentrate on the struggles of Communists and their allies at the grass-roots level, where they often were the most dedicated and implacable opponents of exploitation and discrimination.

The Communist Party of the United States of America never achieved a major role in the nation's political life. It certainly never could plausibly hope to lead a revolutionary transformation here. However, during the 1930s and World War II, with the nation encountering prolonged economic depression and then total war, the party played an important role in the efforts to organize unions of workers in basic American industries. During its peak years of influence, the Popular Front period of 1935–9, when they dropped its revolutionary rhetoric in favor of militant struggle for reforms, Communists and their sympathizers also made important inroads in American cultural and intellectual life. They cooperated, usually warily, but sometimes even warmly, with Franklin D. Roosevelt's New Deal and pushed American liberals into adopting measures such as Social Security and minimum wage legislation.

The party's determined opposition to racial segregation and discrimination won it the adherence of a significant number of African Americans. In the urban North, black intellectuals, politicians, and labor leaders saw Communists as allies in the battle against discrimination and sometimes joined the party themselves. In the Jim Crow South, as Kelley points out, African-American Communists risked their lives to fight white supremacy. In 1931, nine young black men were arrested, tried, and convicted of raping two white women who were traveling with them on a freight train near Scottsboro, Alabama. The evidence was flimsy and one of the women later recanted her accusations. The Communist Party spearheaded opposition to the death sentences eight of them received. Over the rest of the decade, Communists and their allies managed to save all of them from execution and, eventually, to win their release from prison. This case signaled the party's determination to fight racism.

Kelley draws upon the Italian Marxist Antonio Gramsci's theory of hegemony: ruling classes can never impose their will on society by force alone. They need as well a degree of cultural and intellectual dominance. In Karl

Marx's words, "the class which is the ruling material force of society is at the same time its ruling intellectual force." As Kelley observes, African-American cultural traditions have historically not been subservient to those dominant ideas. An "oppositional" black culture has been the seedbed of African-American radicalism. African-American Communists in the deep South brought their own cultural traditions and understanding of their situation into the party. While official Marxist dogma held that religion was the "opiate of the masses," designed to dull their opposition to exploitation, black Communists in Alabama found creative ways to combine their radical politics with Christian faith. The Bible provided both an interpretation of the injustice they experienced and a validation of revolt against oppression. Similarly, for these radicals, the Communist movement was part of a new war to carry out the unfinished business of Emancipation and Reconstruction. In a sense, the Soviet Union would play the same role as the North had in the Civil War.

The documents indicate some aspects of the party's approach to southern blacks. They raise some important questions. Along with rare courage and commitment to equality, Communists brought a Marxist vocabulary that must have sounded strange at best to most rural southerners in the 1930s. Would the party have succeeded more if it had come closer to speaking the language of the people it tried to organize? What did the radicalism Kelley describes owe to earlier black revolts in the South, such as their participation in the rural protest Lawrence Goodwyn describes? (see chapter 5). How did it differ? And what was its legacy for the great civil rights movement that finally brought down legalized segregation and white supremacy in the South after World War II?

"Comrades, Praise Gawd for Lenin and Them!"
Robin D. G. Kelley

Dating back to the "Cold War," historians of American Communism established an uncritical dictum that Afro-Americans were never seriously drawn to left-wing radical movements. Any isolated instances of

Reprinted from Robin D. G. Kelley, " 'Comrades, Praise Gawd for Lenin and Them!': Ideology and Culture among Black Communists in Alabama, 1930–1935," *Science and Society* 52/1 (Spring 1988), pp. 59–82. Reprinted by permission of Guilford Press, New York.

black support for the Communist Party during the depression were usually explained in terms of duplicity on the part of the Communists. In other words, ignorant and unaware of their true intentions, Afro-Americans were merely victims of Communist intrigue (Record 1951, 1964; Nolan 1951; Draper 1960: ch. 15; Klehr 1984: 324–48). This idea, however, has been challenged by radical historians, particularly those of the "New Left" school of historiography. Recent scholarship has revealed that Afro-Americans were drawn into the orbit of American Communism because of individual campaigns such as the campaign to free the Scottsboro Boys, the party's resolute position on racial equality, or the failure of middle-class reformist organizations to take up the struggles of the black working class (Lyons 1982: 77–84; Martin 1976, 1979, 1985; Naison 1978, 1981, 1983; Solomon 1972).

While recent work thoroughly refutes the notion that black supporters and adherents of the Communist Party were little more than innocent dupes of an organization they barely understood, the problem of analyzing ideology and consciousness has been a much more elusive area of study. Were blacks drawn to the party as "race conscious" nationalists who used the Communists to put through their own agenda? Were they, as the party often purported, the "most class conscious" section of the working class? And when they joined the party or any of its auxiliary organizations, to what extent had their ideas about politics, society, and economy changed?

The Communist experience in Alabama sheds a little light on the ideological complexities of Afro-American working-class radicals. The party in Alabama, based mainly in the Birmingham-Bessemer industrial complex and in the rural black belt, was overwhelmingly black and working class in its social composition. In 1934, the party's membership in the state of Alabama reached approximately 1,000, of whom about 95 percent were black (*DW* 1934f and 1934h). Afro-Americans were so prevalent, Alabama's Communists were commonly referred to as the "nigger party" (*DW* 1934f; C. Johnson 1986; Hudson 1986a). In fact, during the early to mid-1930s, the Communist Party had several times more members in Birmingham than the local NAACP. And when one considers the Communist-sponsored mass organizations, the party directly touched the lives of tens of thousands of black Alabamans.

While the numbers were never large in relation to the state's black population, a brief survey of the Alabama cadre should elucidate the underlying ideological and cultural currents of the party in Alabama during the "Third Period." In addition, this paper seeks to illustrate the party's impact in terms of developing a radical class consciousness through methods of pedagogy and praxis.

Italian Marxist Antonio Gramsci provides a valuable framework for understanding the social and cultural roots of radicalism. For Gramsci, force alone is not enough to sustain a ruling class in power. The existence and reproduction of a class is dependent on its ability to exercise cultural and ideological hegemony over the popular masses. Therefore, the development of a revolutionary working-class consciousness depends on a rejection of the dominant culture, requiring the construction of "counter-hegemonic" ideology and culture (Gramsci 1971: 52–60, 104–6, 206–8, 416–18).

Elements of Afro-American working-class culture and ideology, though by no means entirely "counter-hegemonic," were in many ways "oppositional" to the ideological foundations of the Southern ruling classes. As several scholars have pointed out, Afro-Americans have been able to preserve their cultural traditions, and thus maintain a separate, often oppositional, existence from the cultural and ideological hegemony exercised by the status quo (Robinson 1983; Franklin 1984). In Alabama, this radical grass-roots ideology and culture not only attracted blacks to the Communists and their allied organizations; to a large extent it also defined the party's radicalism.

Afro-American Communists shared with the rest of the black working-class community a grass-roots understanding of exploitation and oppression which was based more on scripture than anything else. The prophetic Christian tradition, so characteristic of the Afro-American experience, has historically contained a vehement critique of oppression. Ironically, this radical, prophetic tradition of Christianity was a major factor in drawing blacks into the Communist Party and its mass organizations.

References to God and the Bible were not uncommon among Alabama's black radicals. In 1933 the *Daily Worker* (13 April) received an interesting letter from a black Communist from Tallapoosa County, thanking "God and all the friends of the Negro race that are working for the defense and rights of the Negroes. I pray that we may succeed in our struggle for Bread, Land and Freedom." A black woman from Orrville, Alabama explained, "Your movement is the best that I ever heard of. God bless you for opening up the eyes of the Negro race. I pray that your leaders will push the fight.... I am praying the good Lord will put your program over" (*DW* 1935b). Even the party's literature in the South sometimes adopted, probably unwittingly, religious imagery and language. An article by Nat Ross, the party's district organizer for Alabama, declared that the Communists "can and will destroy this hell and build a heaven for the Southern working people right here in Dixie" (*SW* 1934). Furthermore, not only were most black Communists in Alabama churchgoing Christians; for quite some time, Communists in Montgomery opened all their meetings with a prayer (Hudson 1986b; Green 1935: 25).

To many blacks, the Communists represented a movement which believed in, and practiced, righteousness. The party's long-term goals – a non-racist, socialist society – were often seen as the fruits of redemption. In the words of John Garner, a black Birmingham Communist who remained in the party for over 51 years, "this whole world going to be ruled in righteousness, be somebody right here when it take place, plenty of folk.... There's gonna come a new heaven and a new earth, coming down from God to dwell forever.... And then we'll inherit all things new" (Garner 1984: 9). Angelo Herndon, then a young, unemployed miner who joined the party in Birmingham in 1930, originally viewed the role of the Communists in biblical terms. While at an unemployed meeting, he was reminded of a biblical phrase popular among Afro-Americans: "And the day shall come when the bottom rail shall be on top and the top rail on the bottom. The Ethiopians will stretch forth their arms and find their place under the sun" (Herndon 1937: 75).

What was perhaps most appealing to blacks, from a biblical standpoint, was the Communists' vigilance in the fight for equality and justice. Because of an ideological commitment, whites treated blacks with dignity and respect. To Lemon Johnson (1986), former secretary of the Share Croppers Union (SCU) in Hope Hull, communism and equality meant one and the same thing. "The Communists want, in short," he recalled, " 'you treat me like I treat you,' when you talking about color." According to Hosea Hudson (1986b), a leading black Communist in Birmingham throughout the 1930s and 1940s, the party gave working-class blacks a sense of dignity which even the black middle class and bourgeoisie denied them:

> The preachers and leaders was calling the Negroes the "low class." In order to get anywhere you had to be part of the "better class." This low class of people was the ones the police was killing what nobody saying nothing about. Outcasts! When the Party come out, these people were somebody. You took these people and made leaders out of them.

White party leaders on trial for sedition very often made strikingly bold statements in Alabama courtrooms. Blaine Owens, one of several Communists arrested and severely beaten in the 1934 post-May Day raids in Birmingham, told a crowded courtroom that he not only believed in social equality, he "would rather associate with Negroes than with police thugs and such elements as the prosecutor...." Laura Stark, the district secretary for the ILD who was also on trial with

Owens, was laughed at and nearly charged with contempt when she insisted that the court cease using the term "niggers" (*DW* 1934g).

Although the Communists never had a sympathetic ear from the larger, well-established black churches, several ministers and working-class congregations of smaller Baptist churches in and around Birmingham provided critical support for the Communists. In 1935, a group of black churches joined the Communists and the International Labor Defense in opposition to a state-wide anti-sedition bill. In fact, pastors from Peace Baptist Church, 45th Street Baptist Church, Friendship Baptist Church, the Church of Christ and Mt. Sinai Baptist Church each sent petitions to the Governor of Alabama branding the bill as "fascist" and an attack on "militant working-class organizations." Several church leaders actually sent petitions which resolved to "continue to organize a strong Communist Party in Alabama, as the political leader of the working class...." (Gov. Graves papers 1935b, 1935c, 1935d, 1935e, 1935f, 1935g, 1935h, 1935i).

Nevertheless, the party in Birmingham did not refrain from criticizing local black clergy. Often the severest criticisms came from local blacks, not Northern white Communists. Through the pages of the *Southern Worker*, Alabama's Communists attacked corrupt preachers who used the church for personal gain, or clergy who preached against labor organization, or any form of militant, mass action (for example, *SW* 1931a, 1931c, 1931e, 1931f, and 1931h). In Birmingham, the party's criticisms were not too far off the mark. The city had a long history of incidents in which preachers not only opposed union organizing, but were subsidized by companies to do so. Therefore, the recollections of Dobbie Sanders, a black ILD member active in Birmingham, probably reflect the sentiments of a considerable portion of Alabama's black working class in the 1930s:

> Man, them preachers is a mess. Most of em ain't no good. Brainwashing, that's what they all about. They should have been race leaders, but instead they are race hold-backers.... These preachers go around here charging people to keep them looking back. (Parham and Robinson 1985: 233)

The black churches were not always the focus of criticism. The religious institutions of the "oppressor" provided an occasion to elucidate the uses and "misuses" of Christianity. In a poem entitled "The Modern Church," an unemployed Communist contributed to the *Southern Worker* (1931b) a scathing expose of "status quo" religion. The protagonist, a tired and hungry unemployed worker, was told to find salvation in Jesus. After attending a local church service, he:

... failed to find Jesus there,
Instead I found a cruel judge,
    Who sent six men to the chair.
I also found a lawyer,
    Who, for the love of gold,
Had put a widow's only son
    In a prison gray and cold.
And above me sat a sheriff,
    Who, just the other day,
Had drawn a gun on his fellow-man,
    And taken his life away.
And over here a landlord,
    Who, because she could not pay,
Had thrown a woman out of doors,
    Only yesterday. . . .

Since working-class blacks did not attend the same church as the local authorities, landlords and white industrialists, highly religious party members could still empathize with "The Modern Church." Consequently, the party's critique of religion, as manifested in more localized and popular forms of propaganda, rarely attacked black Communists' grass-roots "theology." When the party's literature exhibited opposition to Christianity as a belief, its appeal was usually not based on materialist discourse. A moving example is a 1932 poem entitled "Stop Foolin' Wit' Pray," published in the *Liberator* (1932):

Sistern an' Brethern,
Stop foolin' wit' pray;
When black face is lifted
Lawd turnin' 'way.

Heart filled wit' sadness,
Head bowed down wit' woe;
In the hour of trouble
Where's a black man to go?

We're buryin' a brother,
They kill for the crime
Tryin' to keep
What was his all the time. . . .

Challenges to religious beliefs frequently surfaced in personal conversations and arguments within the party. Such challenges did not only come from white Communists; they were common among some leading blacks. What Hosea Hudson's recollections reveal is that attacks on religion often had little bearing on politics or theory. He was rebuked by comments such as "Ain't no God. . . . Nobody ever seen God. How you know it's a God?" When he cited the Bible as his witness, he recalled a common retort was, "The white man wrote the Bible" (Hudson 1986b; Painter 1979: 134–5). In other words, black Communists who questioned the viability of religion had concerns kindred to a good portion of working-class blacks throughout the United States. Therefore, we cannot assume that the party experience itself was the sole reason for "atheism" practiced by a small minority of Communists in Alabama. On the contrary, it is likely that blacks who questioned the existence of an omnipresent God or were simply fed up with clerical corruption, were drawn to the party *because* of its scathing critique of the church.

The Afro-American tradition of Christianity does not fully explain what attracted these individuals to the party in the first place. Why had they not formed their own organization? Why did they risk their lives to join a party so hated and repressed by local police, industrialists and landlords? While the party's program was surely appealing to the black working class, it alone cannot explain what initially drew them to the Communists. Evidence leads me to suggest that a black folk interpretation of history played a supplemental role in attracting some blacks to the party. Afro-Americans throughout the South had their own oral tradition of Reconstruction and the role of the so-called "carpet-baggers" in the struggle for a democratic South. There was a general folk belief that the "Yankees" would return in order to complete the Reconstruction. Many believed that another Civil War would be waged in the South (see also Naison 1973: 55). When the party began to organize in Birmingham, Hosea Hudson (1986b) observed:

> The Negro began to look. Something's gonna happen now. Man, them folks in the North, them folks in New York, in Russia. We thought we was looking to have a war in the South. And when the organizers of the Party came in there representing what these organizations what the Negro been reading about in the paper and the Governor getting letters about them, this is what brought the Negroes into the organization. . . . They thought the North was coming back and they was going to have another war.

When Angelo Herndon was first discovered by the Communists in Birmingham, he experienced a similar realization. "Conditions were so bad," he wrote, "that many people believed that the only way they could ever get better was to start a new war. As I read the handbill I very naively was under the impression that the Unemployed Council was calling all Negro and white workers to a new war" (Herndon 1937: 73).

It seems as though the central difference between this "new war" and the folklore of the Civil War and Reconstruction was that the former took on an international dimension. The Russians became the "new Yankees," and for some, Stalin became the new "Lincoln." The Soviet Union was perceived as a powerful element fighting on behalf of black folks. Southern propaganda which portrayed the Communists as being "Soviet agents" often worked to the party's advantage in the black community. With the collapse of biracial unionism in Birmingham in the twentieth century, and the failure of black middle-class organizations to create a viable and effective movement, a large portion of the black working class had little confidence in their ability to initiate and sustain a movement without outside assistance. Outnumbered and outgunned, thousands chose migration over militant organization, which many saw as potentially suicidal. But the idea of Soviet and Northern radical support provided a degree of psychological confidence for those blacks intending to wage the long-awaited revolution in the South. A black woman from Orrville, Alabama saw the party as an underground movement organized and led by Northern radicals. "We need some help in pushing this movement here. We will keep all your orders secret. Tell us what we must do. Let me hear from you folks up there" (*DW* 1935b). John Garner (1984: 2–4) honestly believed that the party in Alabama was started by Soviet agents who were sent to Alabama by Stalin. Likewise, Lemon Johnson (1986) felt that without Russian support, they probably could not have organized the SCU. He also believed that all the leaflets, handbills and newspapers were actually printed in Russia.

Alabama's Communists transformed the "framework" of the Communist Party into a radical movement which was more a reflection of their culture and world view than anything else. But the party, as an international movement based on the principles of Marxism-Leninism, also transformed Alabama's radicals. Their indigenous world view was given form and definition through praxis and pedagogy.

When the Communists first became active in Birmingham in 1930, establishing a party school was a top priority (U.S. Congress, House 1930b and 1930c; *SW* 1930a; Allen 1984: 62). But Tom Johnson, the district organizer for Alabama, realized from the beginning that black southerners were not well suited for a "workers' school" in the traditional sense. In a letter to the party's Agitational Propaganda Department, he pointed out that Alabama's predominantly black membership

are not old sympathizers of the party who have been on the fringe of the movement for some time and have absorbed some of our theory and philosophy. They are raw green workers, with a much lower educational standard than northern workers. Many are illiterate. They have not the slightest idea when they come into the party of how the party operates. (U.S. Congress, House 1930a: 106–7)

Since illiteracy was a problem, Alabama's Communists made it the responsibility of literate members to teach others how to read (*DW* 1935a; Hudson 1986b). While being used as literacy tools, the *Southern Worker*, the *Daily Worker* and the *Liberator* were central to their radicalization. Articles provided relevant information about the world that could not be found in the mainstream press. This was attractive to blacks who had an interest in Africa and other places where people of color were engaged in similar struggles. To Charles Smith (1986), a member of the SCU in Lowndes County, the *Southern Worker*

> had some either direct or indirect bearing on the conditions we found ourselves in. The white power structure had somehow gotten themselves planted in these several African countries and they was taking it over. In some cases they take the lands from these black folks, just like here.

Communist support for self-determination in the black belt was actually a factor, although a minor one, in attracting Afro-Americans. When the *Liberator*, the newspaper of the League of Struggle for Negro Rights, was distributed in Alabama, it was usually the most sought after reading material among blacks. The *Liberator* dealt directly with self-determination and issues affecting blacks throughout the world (Hudson 1986b; Murphy 1933: 81). Whether or not they believed that self-determination in the black belt could actually be achieved, the idea that they shared a common identity appealed to them. Black Communists and people in the mass organizations saw things in terms of color *and* class. Frequently, black Communist rhetoric in the South was hardly distinguishable from the literary expressions of Garveyism. In 1931 for instance, a black Communist from Birmingham wrote,

> Every chance is used to keep the black man in his "place." Let a Negro raise his voice. Let him resent a kick in the shins, let a black man stand up straight – he'll be kept put. Get a rope, hang him, burn him, get a gang and beat him to a raw steak in a pool of blood. (*SW* 1931e)

Circulation of the party press, in actual numbers, was never great. But subscriptions and individual sales were not a true reflection of its readership. In Alabama, people simply could not afford to buy the paper, so "every copy is handed around until it is worn out" (*DW* 1934i). James Allen, the founding editor of the *Southern Worker*, recalled that in the black community, "a single copy would often serve an entire block, to be passed from hand to hand or read aloud to a group" (Allen 1984: 56). Furthermore, because of "criminal anarchy" laws and seditious literature ordinances, possession of Communist publications often could lead to a six-month jail sentence and a heavy fine. In the black belt, distribution was particularly problematic. A member of the SCU Executive Committee wrote to the *Daily Worker* (1933b), "It is not easy for us to get the *Daily Worker*, but we sneak it in our cabins. One copy goes from one man to his neighbor. We hide it anywhere we think is safe."

The party press was only a portion of the literature Alabama's Communists distributed and read. Irrespective of one's level of literacy, study groups were formed where they read works in pamphlet form, ranging from James S. Allen's *Negro Liberation*, Lenin's *What Is to Be Done?*, to Marx and Engels's *Communist Manifesto*. By the middle of 1934, the Bessemer section of the party decided to devote one half-hour of each meeting to study – fifteen minutes of reading and fifteen minutes devoted to discussing and studying the works they read. The ore mine units in Bessemer were reading Earl Browder's "Report to the Eighth National Convention," as well as the *Communist Manifesto*. There were about five to nine workers in each study group (Hudson 1986; *DW* 1934k).

A few Communists from Alabama were occasionally given the opportunity to study at the Workers' School in New York, or in some cases, at the Lenin School in Moscow. Hosea Hudson, who was himself illiterate at the time, had a real interest in obtaining an education. He and two other Communists hoboed all the way to New York in the dead of winter to attend a ten-week training school. Hudson left New York with what he considered a clearer understanding of capitalism and a sharper theoretical perspective. This increased his confidence as a party organizer. As he put it, "I felt like I'm somebody. . . . I'm talking about political economy, about the society itself, how it automatically would breed war and fascism. I'm discussing about the danger of imperialist war" (Painter 1979: 224).

Regardless of how much one learned at party school, the trip itself made a substantial impact on the lives of blacks, many of whom had never been outside of the rural South. Between 1932 and 1934, at least five black Alabamans traveled to the Soviet Union to study at the Lenin School (Howell 1932; C. Johnson 1986; Hudson 1986b; Painter 1979: 115, 124). Even when traveling did not involve education in a direct sort of way, it still greatly impacted the lives of black Communists. Capitola Tasker and her husband, James Tasker, started out as poor sharecroppers in Montgomery County. Soon after joining the party, Capitola suddenly found herself in Paris, France addressing the Women's

International Congress Against War and Fascism on behalf of the Women's Auxiliary of the SCU (*DW* 1934j; Bloor 1940: 256). Afterward she described to renowned Communist leader, "Mother" Ella Bloor, her impressions of the trip and the conference:

> Mother, when I get back to Alabama and go out to that cotton patch of our little old shack, I'll stand there thinking to myself, "Capitola, did you really go over there to Paris and see all those wonderful women and hear all those great talks, or was it just a dream that you were over there?" And if it turns out that it really wasn't a dream, why Mother, I'm just going to broadcast all over Alabama all that I've learned over here, and tell them how women from all over the world are fighting to stop the kind of terror we have in the South, and to stop war. (Bloor 1940: 256)

Through a real grass-roots pedagogy, many of Alabama's Communists were able to obtain a basic understanding of Marxism. The party's leadership, during this period, never tried to "fool" its supporters into believing that it was anything else but a radical organization. Nor were black Communists reluctant to introduce non-party working people to a whole new world of Marxist theory. Even the barber shop became a forum for Alabama's cadre of black Communists. As Hosea Hudson (1986b) recalls,

> I'd be discussing socialism in the barber shop.... We'd start the conversation off, then we'd talk about socialism, and how the workers conditions would be improved under socialism. That barber shop, boy, I had a lot of contacts. They'd sit down there...wouldn't interrupt what I'm saying. They wanted to see what I had to tell.

The combination of praxis, theory, and a pre-existing "radical" world view, created an outlook which incorporated a clearer critique of capitalism, an inchoate vision of a new world and new economic system to replace the old, and for some, advocacy of militant class struggle. Through letters to the *Daily Worker*, Alabama's black militants exhibited a somewhat clearer understanding of class distinctions and capitalism as a system. Viola Cobb, the wife of Ned Cobb, revealed a keen understanding of the problems of "New Deal" capitalism. In a letter published in the *Daily Worker* (1934a) thanking the ILD for sending money to her incarcerated husband, she described the present situation as she understood it:

> The government say that it is doing everything it can to help the poor people but the landlords gets all the profits for they rents the land at top prices and then draw the government money. And the storekeepers sell

their stuff at double price and at that rate the government won't have to help us long because we all will be perished and froze to death.

Alabama's Communists were convinced that black sharecroppers and workers could never improve their conditions merely through a change of conscience on the part of "good white people." Rather, they viewed change as a struggle for power – a struggle which they believed the Communist Party was capable of leading. The Communists experienced enough repression and violence to recognize the importance of force as a factor in transforming society. John Garner, a devout Christian and devout Communist, did not minimize the importance of force. He explained that any oppressed people must free themselves by force. "You can't set still and let it go on forever. And you might call it rebellion. But you got to punch your way out..." (Garner 1984: 4). Similarly, a Communist from Dadeville, Alabama, wrote, "I hope to see the day, when we all get together and fight, so we workers will be strong enough to take the land, have plenty of bread and clothing and all. Let the damn bosses know what we really mean" (*DW* 1934c).

Fighting oppression and what was perceived as "fascism" in Alabama was the "good fight" for Afro-American militants. Alabama's black militants very often took the position that even minor campaigns had long-term significance for revolutionary change. A group of black Birmingham workers, organized by the Communists to protest the state anti-sedition bill, passed a resolution warning the Governor that if the bill became law, "you are [going] to start a Revelushon up on ya Bosses. [W]e will not stand for more fasices terror..." (Gov. Graves papers, 1935a). A black woman from Dadeville who had organized a group of unemployed women in 1931 in an attempt to obtain relief from the local welfare office, was convinced that militant, mass struggles were the only means for achieving even the most basic demands. "Comrades," she wrote, "all I see now is mass action, and go to them just like you would fight fire, and let them know we are humanity just like them. Let them know we are organizing the masses in such a way as to smash this dirty, lowdown Southern ruling class" (*DW* 1934d).

Smashing the "lowdown Southern ruling class" was only part of the chore which lay ahead. Capitalism had to be replaced with some form of economic "justice." A black Communist from Tallapoosa County wrote, "[W]e cannot make it without a change. The capitalists have everything clenched in their hands and we must fight to weaken their tight grip and then we can eat and wear as the ruling class does.... We must organize into stronger masses and demand the bosses to give us what we want" (*DW* 1934b).

While the party's Marxist-Leninist understanding of the world partially contributed to the formation of a radical consciousness, the combination of black and white Southern cultural mediums and socialist ideology influenced the party's culture. The development of a radical folk music tradition combined with Communist activity in the South had its roots in the North Carolina textile strikes and the Kentucky coal miners' struggles of the early 1930s. Ella May Wiggins, a young white textile worker who was felled by a bullet during the Gastonia textile strike, "Aunt" Molly Jackson and Florence Reece, natives of Kentucky who were active in the National Miners Union, left a wealth of radical folk songs, blues and spirituals describing and praising the activities of the Communists and the ILD in the South (Greenway 1971: 245–75; Denisoff 1971: 19–26; Larkin 1929: 3–4; Reece 1972: 23–4; Hevener 1978: 61, 67–8).

By the early 1930s, the Communists "discovered" a revolutionary tradition in Afro-American music. Spirituals were treated by Communist cultural theoreticians as the most basic and class-conscious genre of protest in black music (Frank 1929: 28–9; Gellert 1930: 10–11; Denisoff 1971: 37; Gellert and Siegmeister 1936). The "revolutionary spirit" of black religious music was recognized in Alabama as well. During the ore miners' strike of 1934, the Communist-led Unemployed Local of the International Union of Mine, Mill and Smelter Workers in Bessemer staged a show in order to raise enough money to send a delegate to the union's national convention. Black women provided the singing, consisting mainly of spirituals and gospel hymns, "which express the deep revolutionary spirit of an oppressed people" (DW 1934l)

Perhaps the most commonly used spiritual was the ever so popular "Give Me That Old Time Religion." The verse was changed to "Give Me That Old Communist Spirit," and party members closed out each stanza with "It was good enough for Lenin, and it's good enough for me." Closer to home, Ralph Gray, the first SCU martyr, replaced Lenin in the final line of the phrase (DW 1934e, 1935c; SW 1936a; SFL 1936a, 1936b). This same melody was also transformed into "The Scottsboro Song":

> The Scottsboro verdict,
> The Scottsboro verdict,
> The Scottsboro verdict,
> Is not good enuf for me.
>
> Its good for big fat bosses,
> For workers double-crossers,
> For low down slaves and hosses.
> But it ain't good enough for me...
> (SW 1931g)

"A Stone Came Rolling Out of Babylon," a classic black gospel song, went on to become the "official" ILD song in the South. Renamed "We Got a Stone," the words were written by a black woman in Birmingham. The chorus was changed to "Come a-rollin' through Dixie/ Come a-rollin' through Dixie/ A-tearing down the Kingdom of the boss." The verses referred to the militant example of the ILD and the role of workers in the class struggle (*DW* 1933a; Denisoff 1971: 37; Preece 1938: 14).

Some gospel songs to which words were adapted subsequently became popular songs of the civil rights movement. "We Shall Not Be Moved" was one of those songs. Known as the "theme song" of the SCU, it was renamed "Alabama" by party members in the black belt. The song actually remained the same, with the exception of the first line of each verse. "I'm on my way to glory" was replaced by phrases such as "We're from Alabama," "We fight against evictions," and "We fight against terror." Each verse concluded exactly like the original: "Just like a tree that's planted by water/ We shall not be moved" (Johnson Papers 1936).

The blues were treated as an efficacious example of resistance. Although it is really not clear, it appears that readers of the *Southern Worker* and party members sent in transcriptions of blues they may have heard or wrote themselves. One of the earliest editions of the *Southern Worker* (1930b) carried a piece entitled, "Autumn Blues":

> The 'baccer ain't a sellin'
> The corn is dryin' up,
> There ain't a bit of tellin'
> Where the army worms will sup.
>
> The weevil eats the cotton,
> The beetle eats the beans,
> Do you think it's any wonder,
> There's nothing in my jeans?

The blues were also utilized to describe the conditions of industrial workers in the urban areas, especially Birmingham. A woman who labored as a bedspread maker provided the *Southern Worker* (1936b) with just such a melodic expression entitled "The Bedspread Blues":

> Work from early morning
> Until ten at night;
> All the dishes dirty;
> Kitchen in a sight;
> Landlord comes a-knocking
> Says he wants his rent,

All that I can tell him
Haven't got a cent.
I've got the blues;
I've got the blues,
The tufted bedspread blues . . .

"Autumn Blues" and "The Bedspread Blues" mirror the traditional style of black musical expression in their description of real conditions. There were other songs which paralleled the party's notion of class struggle much more directly. Authored by "A Comrade," the song "Money Gettin' Small" (*SW* 1930c) exemplifies the radicalism characteristic of the Communist Party in Alabama:

Greenbacks are gettin' smaller,
Times is gettin' harder;
If there ain't no change we'll be a horse
Eatin' corn an fodder.

The bosses have all the money
They shut down on us tight,
If they don't turn the money loose,
We'll whack them out of sight.

Despite these examples, the development of a radical cultural movement in the South was not stressed by party leadership during this period. The day-to-day frustrations of organizing an underground movement in the face of repression dominated the work of the party. Nevertheless, these songs are representative of a radical consciousness, articulated through media common to Alabama's working people.

Our brief investigation of Afro-American thought and the Communist experience in Alabama is but a tiny example of the complex relationship between left-wing radicalism and black urban and rural working people. What this small group of black Alabama radicals represents is the confrontation and combining of two different traditions. A handful of working-class blacks from Birmingham and the black belt joined and/or supported an organization whose purported principles were based on Marxism-Leninism and "proletarian internationalism." But when one looks at the social character of the party's recruits, the majority of black Communists were semi-literate, devout Christians. They saw within the party a venue for improving their day-to-day conditions in the short run, and possibly an essential element in achieving some form of "deliverance" in the long run. Although the party's interpretation of Marxism added to that which already characterized the Afro-American working-class experience, blacks in turn transformed the party into an institution which mirrored their own culture and ideology. In short, the dynamic of an overwhelmingly black, working-class Communist Party in the deep South, rooted in the cultural traditions of the Afro-American South, gave rise to complex ideological constructions which defy simple categorization. For Alabama's black Communists, the party meant much more than jobs, relief and freedom for the Scottsboro Boys.

Note

The paper's title is derived from a statement made by Hosea Hudson during my interview with him. In the original phrase, he was explaining the actions of the Communists in Montgomery, Alabama. In his own words, "Man, them folks down there! They used to start the meeting with a prayer, just like they's in church, be thanking God for Browder and Lenin and Stalin and them" (Hudson 1986b).

References

Abbreviations:
> DW   Daily Worker
> SFL   Southern Farm Leader (Share Croppers Union)
> SW   Southern Worker
> NAACP   National Association for the Advancement of Colored People

Allen, James S., 1984, "Communism in the Deep South: The Opening, 1930–31 – A Political Memoir." Unpublished manuscript, copyright James S. Allen. In possession of the author's estate.

Bloor, Ella Reeve, 1940, We Are Many: An Autobiography. New York: International Publishers.

Browder, Earl, 1934, Papers. Party Membership, Chart D, "Organizational Status of the Party, [1934]." Microfilm, reel 3.

Daily Worker, 1933a, 7 November.
—— 1933b, 14 November.
—— 1934a, 9 March.
—— 1934b, 22 March.
—— 1934c, 29 March.
—— 1934d, 5 April.
—— 1934e, 7 April.
—— 1934f, 4 May.
—— 1934g, 18 May.
—— 1934h, 31 May.
—— 1934i, 12 June.
—— 1934j, 25 July.
—— 1934k, 11 August.
—— 1934l, 18 August.

—— 1935a, 19 January.

—— 1935b, 4 July.

—— 1935c, 17 July.

Denisoff, R. Serge, 1971, *Great Day Coming: Folk Music and the American Left.* Urbana: University of Illinois Press.

Draper, Theodore, 1960, *American Communism and Soviet Russia*, New York: Viking Press.

Frank, Richard, 1929, "Negro Revolutionary Music." *New Masses*, 10 (15 May), 28–9.

Franklin, V. P., 1984, *Black Self-Determination: A Cultural History of the Faith of Our Fathers.* Westport: Lawrence Hill and Co.

Garner, John, 1984, Interview with John Garner, conducted by Cliff Kuhn, July 20, 1984, unpublished transcript, *Working Lives Collection*, Archives of American Minority Cultures, University of Alabama.

Gellert, Lawrence, 1930, "Negro Songs of Protest." *New Masses*, 6 (November), 10–11.

Gellert, Lawrence and Siegmeister, Elie, 1936, *Negro Songs of Protest.* New York: American Music League.

Gramsci, Antonio, 1971, *Selections from Prison Notebooks*, edited and translated by Quentin Hoare and Geoffrey Nowell Smith. New York: International Publishers.

Graves, Governor Bibb, 1935a, Papers. "800 White and Negro Workers," Birmingham, Alabama to Governor Graves, 20 February. Alabama Department of Archives and History, Montgomery, Alabama.

—— 1935b, Papers. Resolution from Peace Baptist Church, Powderly, Alabama, 17 February.

—— 1935c, Papers. Resolution from St. John BYPU, 17 February.

—— 1935d, Papers. Resolution from St. John Sunday School, 17 February.

—— 1935e, Papers. Resolution from the Church of Christ, 10 February.

—— 1935f, Papers. Resolution from Rev. J. H. Thomas, Friendship Baptist Church, Birmingham, 14 March.

—— 1935g, Papers, Resolution from Rev. G. W. Reed, Forty Fifth Street Baptist Church, 11 March.

—— 1935h, Papers. Resolution from Mt. Sinai Baptist Church, n.d.

—— 1935i, Papers. Resolution from Woodlawn Sunday School, n.d.

Green, Gil, 1935, "Report from Gil Green for the National Bureau to a Meeting of the Enlarged National Executive Committee held in New York, February 23, 1935." *International of Youth* (March), 25.

Greenway, John, 1971 [1953], *American Folksongs of Protest.* Reprint, New York: Octagon Books.

Herndon, Angelo, 1937, *Let Me Live.* New York: International Publishers.

Hevener, John, 1978, *Which Side Are You On?: The Harlan County Coal Miners, 1931–1939.* Urbana: University of Illinois Press.

Howell, R. M., 1932, Memorandum by R. M. Howell, 1 November, File 10110–2664, U.S. Military Intelligence Reports, microfilm, reel 28, Tamament Institute, New York University.

Hudson, Hosea, 1986a, Interview with author, Gainesville, Florida, 15 November.

Hudson, Hosea, 1986b, Interview with author, Gainesville, Florida, 16 November.

Johnson, Clyde L., 1936, Papers. Harold Preece to Anne Johnson, 25 December. Microfilm edition, part of *The Green Rising: Supplement to the Southern Tenant Farmers' Union Papers*, reel 13.

—— 1986, Interview with author, Berkeley, California, 21 December.

Johnson, Lemon, 1986, Interview with author, Hope Hull, Alabama, 8 December.

Klehr, Harvey, 1984, *The Heyday of American Communism: The Depression Decade*. New York: Basic Books.

Larkin, Margaret, 1929, "The Story of Ella May." *New Masses*, 5 (November), 3–4.

Liberator, 1932, 18 March.

Lyons, Paul, 1982, *Philadelphia Communists, 1936–1956*. Philadelphia: Temple University Press.

Martin, Charles, 1976, *The Angelo Herndon Case and Southern Justice*. Baton Rouge: Louisiana State University Press.

—— 1979, "Communists and Blacks: The ILD and the Angelo Herndon Case." *Journal of Negro History*, 64 (Spring), 131–41.

—— 1985, "The International Labor Defense and Black America." *Labor History*, 26: 2, 165–194.

Murphy, Al., 1933 [Comrade "M"], "Agrarian Work: From a Speech of Leading Comrade of Sharecroppers' Union." *Party Organizer*, 6 (August–September), 80–2.

Naison, Mark D., 1973, "Black Agrarian Radicalism in the Great Depression: The Threads of a Lost Tradition." *Journal of Ethnic History*, 1: 3 (Fall), 47–65.

—— 1978, "Historical Notes on Blacks and American Communism: The Harlem Experience." *Science & Society*, 42: 3 (Fall), 324–43.

—— 1981, "Communism and Harlem Intellectuals in the Popular Front: Anti-Fascism and the Politics of Black Culture." *Journal of Ethnic Studies*, 9: 1 (Spring), 1–25.

—— 1983, *Communists in Harlem During the Depression*. Urbana: University of Illinois Press.

Nolan, William, 1951, *Communism versus the Negro*. Chicago: Henry Regnery Co.

Painter, Nell Irvin, 1979, *The Narrative of Hosea Hudson, His Life as Negro Communist in the South*. Cambridge: Harvard University Press.

Parham, Groesback and Robinson, Gwen, 1985, " 'If I Could Go Back...' An Interview with Dobbie Sanders by Groesback Parham and Gwen Robinson." In *Blacks in Appalachia*, edited by William H. Turner and Edward J. Cabbell. Lexington: University of Kentucky Press.

Preece, Harold, 1938, "Folk Music of the South." *New South*, 1: 2 (March), 14.

Record, Wilson, 1951, *The Negro and the Communist Party*. Chapel Hill: University of North Carolina Press.

—— 1964, *Race and Radicalism: The NAACP and the Communist Party in Conflict*. Ithaca: Cornell University Press.

Reece, Florence, 1972, "Which Side Are You On? An Interview with Florence
    Reece." *Mountain Life and Work*, 48 (March), 23–4.
Robinson, Cedric, 1983, *Black Marxism: The Making of the Black Radical Tradi-
    tion*. London: Zed Press.
Smith, Charles, 1986, Interview with author, Hope Hull, Alabama, 8 December.
Solomon, Mark, 1972, "Red and Black: Negroes and Communism, 1929–
    1932." Ph.D. dissertation, Harvard University.
Southern Farm Leader, 1936a, July.
—— 1936b, August.
Southern Worker, 1930a, 20 September.
—— 1930b, 20 October.
—— 1930c, 8 November.
—— 1931a, 21 February.
—— 1931b, 4 April.
—— 1931c, 18 April.
—— 1931d, 12 June.
—— 1931e, 20 June.
—— 1931f, 4 July.
—— 1931g, 18 July.
—— 1931h, 5 August.
—— 1934, 10 February.
—— 1936a, July.
—— 1936b, September.
U.S. Congress, House, 1930a, "Proposals for Party Training in the South
    (District 17)" [copy], *Special Committee on Communist Activities in the U.S.,
    Investigation of Communist Propaganda*, 71st Congress, 2nd Session, pt. 6,
    vol. 1.
U.S. Congress, House, 1930b, Samuel A. Darcy to District 17, Communist
    Party, April 28, 1930 [copy], *Special Committee on Communist Activities in the
    U.S., Investigation of Communist Propaganda*, 71st Congress, 2nd Session, pt.
    6, vol. 1.
U.S. Congress, House, 1930c, Tom Johnson to Sam Darcy, May 8, 1930 [copy],
    *Special Committee on Communist Activities in the U.S., Investigation of Commun-
    ist Propaganda*, 71st Congress, 2nd Session, pt. 6, vol. 1.

Documents

Introduction to the Documents

Robin D. G. Kelley's account of black Communists in Alabama shows both the
depths of racial oppression and the creative ways some African Americans
combined cultural and religious traditions with "foreign" Marxist ideology in
order to combat racism. Document One shows one of Alabama's leading

Communists, Hosea Hudson, in Birmingham at the beginning of the Depression, working in a foundry. Hearing about the Scottsboro case and an attack on black sharecroppers at Camp Hill, Alabama, Hudson was receptive to the party's uncompromising message. Party membership meant sacrifice and danger, but it did not remove him from community life. Hudson, who was active in amateur baseball and singing groups, combined these interests with his political commitment.

Document Two is an excerpt from the autobiography of another African-American Communist, Angelo Herndon. The party sent Herndon, barely 20 years old, to Atlanta, Georgia to organize unemployed workers. He distributed a leaflet calling for a hunger march and was arrested and charged with "insurrection," under a state law dating from the Reconstruction era. He was swiftly convicted and sentenced to twenty years in jail. The sentence was not overturned until the US Supreme Court declared the Georgia law unconstitutional in 1937. Herndon's speech to the trial jury is appended to his autobiography. Note both his description of the treatment he endured and his forthright call for unity of white and black workers and the unemployed.

Document Three, taken from the autobiography of Nate Shaw (a pseudonym for Ned Cobb), a black Alabama tenant farmer, describes his first encounter with the Communist-led Sharecroppers' Union. Simply to meet and organize was dangerous for African Americans in the segregated South. Shaw's comments on churches indicate how central religion was, and how racist practices shaped it. Later, Shaw was to block the efforts of a white sheriff to seize a neighbor's livestock; arrested, he served a long jail term.

Document Four, an early work by Muriel Rukeyser, one of America's leading poets, was first published in 1935. Rukeyser, a white northerner who was sympathetic to the Communist Party, had come down to Alabama to observe one of the Scottsboro trials. She weaves Scottsboro into an evocation of black resistance and revolt against slavery and of a revolutionary tradition stretching back to the Roman empire.

Nell Irvin Painter, from The Narrative of Hosea Hudson

Reprinted from "Joining the Communist Party," in *The Narrative of Hosea Hudson* (Cambridge, MA: Harvard University Press, 1979), pp. 80–7.

In the late 20's I didn't have any mind about racial issues, but I always did resent injustice and the way they used to treat Negroes, whip them and mob them up and run them with hounds. I came up to that from a kid. I always did feel that if the older people got together, we could stop that kind of stuff. My grandmother used to talk about these things. She was very militant herself, you know. I didn't have no understanding on the race question, but I did wonder why the Negroes were doing the same work as the whites and yet the whites getting more pay than the Negroes. I couldn't understand that. I used to talk with John Beidel about that. . . .

At the same time, the Communist Party was putting out leaflets, but I didn't know nothing about the Party. I'd pick up the leaflets, but I didn't pay them much attention, because I was only interested in singing. Several leaflets came by. The people were always putting them around the community, but I didn't know who they was. They'd drop by at night and you'd pick them up in the morning – there'd be a leaflet on your porch. Sometimes I'd get my wife to read it, because at that time I couldn't read. But she never was too interested in politics, even when I got real all out into it.

The Party people, they first came into Birmingham I think it was along about in 1930 when they had the first meeting. They went to the officials of the city for a permit to hold a meeting in the park, and told them what they planned, what everything was, and they give them a permit to hold the meeting. The whites was ignorant about it too. So when these Party guys got out, right in the Depression, and started speaking about the unemployed conditions, talking about the bosses and the capitalist system, and Negro-white unity and the rights of the Negro people, the officials told them, "Now you all leave these niggers off," they said. "You all get the white folks together, we'll take care of the niggers."

So the Party people said, "No, we have to organize the Negroes too."

The city officials wouldn't give in on that question. They said, "Well, now if you won't leave the niggers off, we going to fight you."

"You'll just have to fight, cause that's our Party policy. We can't go back on the policy." Then the police broke up the meeting, run them out the park. They went to hounding them and trying to arrest them. Then the Party went to going underground, to stay in Birmingham. All that was before my time.

I didn't pay no attention to any leaflets till the Scottsboro case, when they took the boys off the train, and then the sharecroppers' struggle in Camp Hill. Those two was about the first thing that claimed my interest. I don't remember which one of these cases broke first, but I know well how I felt.

The first break I know about the Scottsboro boys was in the Birmingham *News* on Sunday morning – had big, black headlines, saying nine nigger hoboes had raped two white women on the freight train, and

Attorney General Knight said he was going to ask for the death penalty for eight of them. The boy, twelve years old, he was going to turn him over to the juveniles, and when he come of age, eighteen, then he'd try him for his life. That was the first of my knowing about it. I began to buy the papers then, so my wife could read the paper and see what was going on – the Birmingham *News*, I hadn't seen any other newspapers.

Whenever Negroes was frame-up, I always would look for somebody else to say something about it. I wouldn't say nothing because I didn't think there was nothing I could say. I'd look to some of the better-class white folks. Dr. Edmunds, he was the leading white minister in Birmingham, he'd always come out with some nice statement about race relations, so I didn't figure the better class of whites as being the enemies of Negroes. I thought it was the poor whites, and that was the regular stand. "It ain't these better class of people," you hear it even now every once in awhile, "it's this here poor class of whites doing things." I didn't see the hidden hand was doing the devilment. So I was looking to the whites. Sometimes it was some white woman would come out and make a statement. But it wouldn't amount to nothing, because they would continue to do the same things they was doing, until the Scottsboro case, when these people from all over the world began to talk. Then I could see some hope. . . .

Then they had this gun battle, these Negroes down there had that shoot-out at Camp Hill. The papers came out about it, and about fifteen of the leading Negroes, preachers and some businessmen, issued a statement in the paper condemning the action of the sharecroppers' union down there in Camp Hill. They put up a $1500 cash award for the capture and conviction of the guilty party who was down there "agitating and misleading our poor, ignorant niggers." (Later I learnt that Mack Coad was the man who was down there, that they put up the $1500 reward for, and he was a steelworker, Negro, from the country just like me, couldn't read and write.) I thought the better class ought to been putting up the money trying to help the Negroes who's trying to help themselves. I had some wonder about it. I couldn't understand it.

They had filled the jails at Camp Hill full of these Negroes, and telegrams began to come in from all over, demanding they not be hung. I wanted to know what's happening to them, what's going to happen to them, what's going to be done? It was the first time I ever known where Negroes had tried to stand up together in the South. I tried to keep up with it, asking people about it, and "what you think about it?" – getting other people's opinions among my friends and people of my stature, all working people. I didn't have no contact with no better class of Negroes. A whole lot of them was sympathetic to the sharecroppers. They wanted to see something done, too, to break up the persecution against the Negro people.

Everybody in the community had seen the Party leaflets, but nobody was much involved. The general word was it was "these Reds." It was the Reds' leaflets. We'd pick them up and try to read them. They'd sound good, but so far as I was concerned, it didn't never jell in my mind. I was sympathetic to the Scottsboro boys, but I still didn't grapple with it to try to find out, cause, as I say, I'm concerned about singing. "Where we going to sing at tonight?" or "Where we going to sing at tomorrow?" We had went on the radio in 1927, and this here was in '31. And I was very popular and having fun with the girls. I had to push them off.

At first I just look at the leaflets and keep going. I wasn't scared of the Reds, never was scared of the Reds, but I just wasn't interested. Other people were scared, said, "better not fool with that mess, you'll lose your job." But I never was scared of losing a job. I lost five jobs.

Somebody approached me, that's how I became interested. I met a guy who had been working in the shop, Al Murphy. I think he was about twenty-six years old. He was slender, not skinny, but slender, and about 5 1/2 feet tall. Somewhere along the line before I met him, he had got a pretty good education. I don't know whether he got his like I got mine, in the Party, but I think he had more schooling than me. Murphy was with Herndon and them one time in Birmingham. They got arrested once in a meeting. Now that was along there in 1930, but I didn't know nothing about the Party then.

The first time I met him to come to know him was somewhere along about 1930 or '31, there in the shop. He wasn't a molder. He worked in the coal room. You know if you be around a long time, you see a guy, you say "hello, hello." You don't know his name, but you know his face. So I had done knowing him long enough to recognize him when I met him in the street. Whether I knowed his name then or not, I don't remember. I hadn't seen him in a good while and I ran into him, asked him, "You ain't working in the shop now?"

"No, they fired me."

"Fired you, what they fire you for?"

He said, "They fired me because I was participating in that organization for the defense of the Scottsboro boys." He said, "I just came from New York."

I said, "Yeah? What is they saying?" Now I'm looking for somebody to say something. I'm looking to see what is going to be said out of all these telegrams. "What is they saying about us?"

Murphy said, "They asking why the Negroes won't organize. I told them they wasn't organized because they don't have nothing to fight with. So they asked me which is it easier to do, organize or fight, and I told them it was easier to organize. They said, 'Well, you go back down there and organize, and then if you get when you need guns, we'll see what we can do about helping you to get some guns.' "

When he said that, I said, "You all got an organization here?" Up until then, so far as organization, I never heard anything about no organization. No NAACP, no nothing, no union. I only know I had heard them talk about the railroad union in Atlanta when the railroad workers went on strike, and I heard them talk about the coal miners' union when the coal miners went on strike along about '22 in Birmingham. I said, "You all got something here?"

He said, "Yeah, we have meetings here in Birmingham."

"Is that what you a member of?"

He said yeah.

I said, "When you going to have another meeting?"

He said, "I'll let you know." Then he became suspicious of me. Everytime I'd see him, I'd say, "When you going to have the meeting?"

"I'll let you know." He became suspicious, and he shunned me a good while. He told me years after that he thought I was one of the company stoolpigeons.

Finally he came by and left word, came by my house. He done got fired, now, and I'm living in the company house. That shows you how much damage people who's inexperienced in the Party can do to a person who has a job. Now here I'm living in Stockham row, and all the company stoolpigeons on here too.

Here's Tom Truss, the guy in the dispenser's office, call hisself "Dr. Truss." On the same row is George Smiley, the custodian around the office. And here is John Mitchell, he's on the head of the ball club and the YMCA at the shop. All these are stoolpigeons. This here is just one block. It wasn't no long neighborhood, just one block, and all these houses on one side the street. Out here is the ball diamond, over here the houses. And here come this guy Murphy they done fired out the shop. He know he been spotted, they know who he is. And he come busting up to my house and yard with an armful of papers in broad daylight. He brought me papers, come strutting up the street, everybody know him, ain't nowhere to hide, and he come there, leave me a paper. So I take the paper, try to read it. It was called the *Liberator*, on the right of self-determination for the Negro people in the Black Belt of the South.

Then he told me there was a meeting that night and I went on to the meeting. It was just over there across the shop. I'm living on this side the shop, and you go around one block, turn over there, come right down over on that side. That's where we had our meeting. We went to a small house of the man who had the meeting, and he was working at the shop. When I got there, it was two guys I didn't know, and the rest of them, like Beidel and Anderson Harris, all the others I knowed. They was working there in the shop with me. I didn't say anything, but I'm a little let down, cause I'm looking for a big something, important people. And here's the guys working in the shop with me, regular guys. Those other two were working in the U.S. Pipe Shop, up there in the same community.

We was sitting there, and Murphy got to outlining about the role of the Party and the program of the Party – the Scottsboro case and the unemployed and the Depression and the imperialist war. You had all that he was talking about that night. In the biggest part, I didn't know what he was saying. All I know is about the Scottsboro case. He was explaining about how the Scottsboro case is a part of the whole frame-up of the Negro people in the South – jim crow, frame-up, lynching, all that was part of the system. So I could understand that all right, and how speed-up, the unemployment, and how the unemployed people wouldn't be able to buy back what they make, that they was consumers and that it would put more people in the street. He went through all that kind of stuff, and I understood it. I understood that part. He took the conveyer, up there where we mold, took that and made a pattern, said, "How many men been kicked out in the street after they put that conveyer machine in there?" I could see that.

That was the beginning. I didn't do much thinking about it. When it come ready to join, I join, that night. Everybody there that night signed up, right there that night, the 8th of September, 1931. I don't know how it came to be, but I didn't never kick against nothing. They elected me as organizer – they didn't call it chairman – they elected me as organizer of the unit.

Angelo Herndon, Speech to the Jury

Reprinted from Angelo Herndon, Let Me Live (New York: Random House, 1937), pp. 342, 344–7.

Gentlemen of the Jury: I would like to explain in detail the nature of my case and the reason why I was locked up. I recall back about the middle of June 1932, when the Relief Agencies of the City of Atlanta, the County Commission and the city government as a whole, were cutting both Negro and white workers off relief. We all know that there were citizens who suffered from unemployment. There were hundreds and thousands of Negroes and whites who were each day looking for work, but in those days there was no work to be found.

The Unemployment Council, which has connection with the Unemployed Committees of the United States, after 23,000 families had been dropped from the relief rolls, started to organize the Negro and white workers of Atlanta on the same basis, because we know that their interests are the same. The Unemployment Council understood that in order to get relief, both races would have to organize together and forget about the question whether those born with a white skin are "superior" and those born with a black skin are "inferior." They both were starving and the capitalist class would continue to use this weapon to keep them further divided. The policy of the Unemployment Council is to organize Negroes and whites together on the basis of fighting for unemployment relief and unemployment insurance at the expense of the state. The Unemployment Council of Atlanta issued those leaflets after the relief had been cut off, which meant starvation for thousands of people here in Atlanta. . . .

On Monday, July 11, 1932, I went to the post office to get mail . . . and was arrested by detectives, Mr. Watson and Mr. Chester. I had organized unemployed workers, Negro and white, of Atlanta, and forced the County Commissioners to kick in $6,000 for unemployment relief. For this I was locked up in the station house and held eleven days without even any kind of charges booked against me. I was told at the station house that I was being held on "suspicion." Of course, they knew what the charges were going to be, but in order to hold me in jail and give me the dirtiest kind of inhuman treatment that one could describe, they held me there eleven days without any charge whatsoever until my attorney filed a writ of habeas corpus demanding that they place charges against me or turn me loose. It was about the 22nd of July, and I still hadn't been indicted; there had been three sessions of the grand jury, and my case had been up before them each time, but still there was no indictment. This was a deliberate plot to hold me in jail. At the habeas corpus hearing, the judge ordered that if I wasn't indicted the next day by 2.30, I should be released. Solicitor Hudson assured the judge that there would be an indictment, which, of course, there was. Ever since then I have been cooped up in Fulton County Tower, where I have spent close to six months – I think the exact time was five months and three weeks. But I want to describe some of the horrible experiences that I had in Fulton Tower. I was placed in a little cell there with a dead body and forced to live there with the dead body because I couldn't get out of the place. The man's name was William Wilson, who fought in the Spanish-American war for the American principles, as we usually call it. He was there on a charge of alimony. His death came as a result of the rotten food given to all prisoners, and for the want of medical attention. The county physician simply refused to give this man any kind of attention whatsoever. After three days of illness, he died, and I was forced to live there with him until the undertaker came and got him. These are just some of the things that I experienced in jail. I was also sick myself. I could not eat the food they gave me as well as hundreds of other prisoners. For instance, they give you peas and beans for one dinner, and at times you probably get the same thing three times a week. You will find rocks in it, and when you crack down on it with your teeth, you don't know what it is, and you spit it out and there it is. They have turnip greens, and just as they are pulled up out of the ground and put in the pot, with sand rocks and everything else. But that's what you have to eat, otherwise you don't live. For breakfast they feed grits that look as if they were baked instead of boiled, a little streak of grease running through them, about two strips of greasy fatback. That is the main prison fare, and you eat it or else die from starvation. I was forced to go through all of this for five months without a trial. My lawyers demanded a trial time after time, but somehow the state would always find a reason to postpone it.

They knew that the workers of Atlanta were starving, and by arresting Angelo Herndon on a charge of attempting to incite insurrection the unity of Negro and white workers that was displayed in the demonstration that forced the County Commissioners to kick in with $6,000, would be crushed forever. They locked Angelo Herndon up on such charges. But I can say this quite clearly, if the State of Georgia and the City of Atlanta think that by locking up Angelo Herndon, the question of unemployment will be solved, I say you are deadly wrong. If you really want to do anything about the case, you must go out and indict the social system. . . .

After being confined in jail for the long period of time that I have already mentioned, I was sick for several weeks. I asked for aid from the county physician and was refused that; the physician came and looked through the bars at me and said: "What's the matter with you?" I told him, "I'm sick, can't swallow water, my chest up here is tight and my stomach absolutely out of order, seems as if I am suffering with ulcers or something." He would answer: "Oh, there's nothing the matter with you, you're all right." I explained: "I know my condition. I know how I'm feeling." He said: "You will be all right." Through friends I was able to get some medicine; otherwise I would have died.

On Christmas Eve I was released. My bail was once $3,000 but they raised it to $5,000 and from that up to $25,000, just in order to hold me in jail, but you can hold this Angelo Herndon and hundreds of others, but it will never stop these demonstrations on the part of Negro and white workers, who demand a decent place to live in and proper food for their kids to eat.

I want to say also that the policy of the Unemployment Council is to carry on a constant fight for the rights of the Negro people. We realize that unless Negro and white workers are united together, they cannot get relief. The capitalist class teaches race hatred to Negro and white workers and keep it going all the time, tit for tat, the white worker running after the Negro worker and the Negro worker running after the white worker, and the capitalist becomes the exploiter and the robber of them both. We of the Unemployment Council are out to expose such things. If there were not any Negroes in the United States, somebody would have to be used as the scapegoat. There would still be a racial question, probably the Jews, or the Greeks, or somebody. It is in the interest of the capitalist to play one race against the other, so greater profits can be realized from the working people of all races. It so happens that the Negro's skin is black, therefore making it much easier for him to be singled out and used as the scapegoat.

I don't have to go so far into my case, no doubt some of you jurymen sitting over there in that box right now are unemployed and realize what it means to be without a job, when you tramp the streets day in and day out looking for work and can't find it. You know it is a very serious problem and the future looks so dim that you sometimes don't know what to do, you go nuts and want to commit suicide or something. But the Unemployment Council points out to the Negro and white workers that the solution is not in committing suicide, that the solution can only be found in the unity and organization of black and white workers. In organization the workers have strength.

Nate Shaw, from All God's Dangers

Reprinted from *All God's Dangers*, compiled by Theodore Rosengarten, first published 1974 (New York: Vintage Books, 1989), pp. 295–8.

A heap of families, while I was livin on the Tucker place down on Sitimachas, was leavin goin north. Some of my neighbors even picked up and left. The boll weevil was sendin a lot of em out, no doubt. I knowed several men went north, some with their families and some without; they sent for their families when they got to where they was goin. More went besides what I knowed of, from all parts of this southern country. They was dissatisfied with the way of life here in the south – and when I was livin on the Pollard place it come pretty wide open to me and touched the hem of my garment. But my family was prosperin right here, I didn't pay no attention to leavin. I wanted to stay and work for better conditions. I knowed I was in a bad way of life here but I didn't intend to get out – *that* never come in my mind. I thought somehow, some way, I'd overcome it. I was a farmin man at that time and I knowed more about this country than I knowed about the northern states. I've always been man enough to stick up for my family, and love them, and try to support em, and I just thought definitely I could keep it up. In other words, I was determined to try.

And durin of the pressure years, a union begin to operate in this country, called it the Sharecroppers Union – that was a nice name, I thought – and my first knowin about this union, this organization, that riot come off at Crane's Ford in '31. I looked deep in that thing, too I heard more than I seed and I taken that in consideration. And I knowed what was goin on was a turnabout on the southern man, white and colored; it was somethin unusual. And I heard about it bein a organization for the poor class of people – that's just what I wanted to get into, too; I wanted to know the secrets of it enough that I could become in the knowledge of it. Now I heard talk about trucks comin into this country deliverin guns to the colored people but I decided all that was talk, tryin to accuse the niggers of gettin into somethin here that maybe they weren't – and maybe they were. But didn't no trucks haul no guns to nobody. Colored people hadn't been armed up for nothin; it was told like that just to agitate the thing further. Of course, some of these colored folks in here had some good guns – you know a Winchester rifle is a pretty good gun itself. But they didn't have nothin above that. It weren't nothin that nobody sent in here for em to use, just their own stuff.

Well, they killed a man up there, colored fellow; his name was Adam Cole. And they tell me – I didn't see it but I heard lots about it and I never did hear nothin about it that backed me off – Kurt Beall, the High Sheriff for Tukabahchee County, got shot in the stomach. He run up there to break up this meetin business amongst the colored people and someone in that crowd shot him. That kind of broke him up from runnin in places like that.

And these white folks woke up and stretched themselves and commenced a runnin around meddlin with niggers about this organization. And it's a close thing today. One old man – and he was as big a skunk as ever sneaked in the woods – old man Mac Sloane, come up to me one day – he didn't come to my home, he met me on the outside – old man Mac Sloane come to me hot as a stove iron, "Nate, do you belong to that mess they carryin on in this country?"

I just cut him off short. I didn't belong to it at that time, but I was eager to join and I was aimin to join, just hadn't got the right opportunity.

"No, I don't belong to nothin."

Mac Sloane, white man, said, "You stay out of it. That damn thing will get you killed. You stay out of it. These niggers runnin around here carryin on some kind of meetin – you better stay out of it."

I said to myself, "You a fool if you think you can keep me from joinin." I went right on and joined it, just as quick as the next meetin come. Runnin around and givin me orders – he suspected I might be the kind of man to belong to such a organization; put the finger on me before I ever joined. And he done just the thing to push me into it – gived me orders not to join.

The teachers of this organization begin to drive through this country – they couldn't let what they was doin be known. One of em was a colored fella; I disremember his name but he did tell us his name. He wanted us to organize and he was with us a whole lot of time, holdin meetins with us – that was part of his job. We colored farmers would meet and the first thing we had to do was join the organization. And it was said, we didn't want no bad men in it at all, no weak-hearted fellows that would be liable to give the thing away. It was secret with them all that joined it; they knowed to keep their mouths shut and meet the meetins. And this teacher said – don't know where his home was; he had a different way of talkin than we did – "I call em stool pigeons if they broadcast the news about what's happenin." And said, if a nigger, like myself, went and let out any secrets to the white folks about the organization, the word was, "Do away with him."

Had the meetins at our houses or anywhere we could have em where we could keep a look and a watch-out that nobody was comin in on us. Small meetins, sometimes there'd be a dozen, sometimes there'd be more, sometimes there'd be less – niggers was scared, niggers was scared, that's tellin the truth. White folks in this country didn't allow niggers to have no organization, no secret meetins. They kept up with you and watched you, didn't allow you to associate in a crowd, unless it was your family or your church. It just worked in a way that the nigger wasn't allowed to have nothin but church services and, O, they liked to see you goin to church, too. Sometimes white people would come into the Negro church and set there and listen at the meetin. Of course, it weren't nothin but a church service goin on. But if a nigger walked into a white church, he'd just be driven out, if they didn't kill him. But if a Negro was a servant for white people, then they'd carry him to church with em, accept him to come in and take a seat on the back seat and listen at the white people. But if you was a independent Negro you better stay away from there. But if you was a white man's dear flunky, doin what he said do, or even on the woman's side, if they was maids for the white people, well thought of, they'd take em out to their home churches, dupe em up in a way. They knowed they weren't goin to cause no trouble – and if they did, they'd just been knocked out of the box and called in close question. But they never did act disorderly; just set there and listened at the white folks' meetin quiet as a lamb. And when the white folks would come in the colored churches, good God, the niggers would get busy givin em first class seats – if there was any in that buildin the white folks got em. They was white people; they classed theirselves over the colored and the colored people never did do nothin but dance to what the white people said and thought. White people was their bosses and their controllers and the colored people went along with it. White men, white women – I been there – go in colored churches and be seated. Nigger aint got nothin to do but run around there and give em the nicest seats.

Muriel Rukeyser, "The Trial"

Reprinted from *Theory of Flight* (New Haven, CT: Yale University Press, 1935), pp. 47–9.

The South is green with coming spring ;   revival
flourishes in the fields of Alabama.   Spongy with rain,
plantations breathe April :   carwheels suck mud in the roads,
the town expands warm in the afternoons.   At night the black boy
teeters no-handed on a bicycle, whistling The St. Louis Blues,
blood beating, and hot South.   A red brick courthouse
is vicious with men inviting death.   Array your judges; call your
     jurors; come,
here is your justice, come out of the crazy jail.
Grass is green now in Alabama; Birmingham dusks are quiet
relaxed and soft in the park, stern at the yards:
a hundred boxcars shunted off to sidings, and the hoboes
gathering grains of sleep in forbidden corners.

In all the yards   :   Atlanta, Chattanooga,
Memphis, and New Orleans, the cars, and no jobs.

Every night the mail-planes burrow the sky,
carrying postcards to laughing girls in Texas,
passionate letters to the Charleston virgins,
words through the South   :   and no reprieve,
no pardon, no release.

A blinded statue attends before the courthouse,
bronze and black men lie on the grass, waiting,
the khaki dapper National Guard leans on its bayonets.
But the air is populous beyond our vision:
all the people's anger finds its vortex here
as the mythic lips of justice open, and speak.

Hammers and sickles are carried in a wave of strength, fire-tipped,
swinging passionately ninefold to a shore.
Answer the back-thrown Negro face of the lynched, the flat forehead
      knotted,
the eyes showing a wild iris, the mouth a welter of blood,
answer the broken shoulders and these twisted arms.
John Brown, Nat Turner, Toussaint stand in this courtroom,
Dred Scott wrestles for freedom there in the dark corner,
all our celebrated shambles are repeated here   :   now again
Sacco and Vanzetti walk to a chair, to the straps and rivets
and the switch spitting death and Massachusetts' will.
Wreaths are brought out of history
   here are the well-nourished flowers of France, grown strong on blood,
   Caesar twisting his thin throat toward conquest, turning north from
         the Roman laurels,
   the Istrian galleys slide again to sea.
   How they waded through bloody Godfrey's Jerusalem   !
   How the fires broke through Europe, and the rich
   and the tall jails battened on revolution   !
   The fastidious Louis', cousins to the sun, stamping
   those ribboned heels on Calas, on the people;
   the lynched five thousand of America.
   Tom Mooney from San Quentin, Herndon   :   here
   is an army for audience
                         all resolved
to a gobbet of tobacco, spat, and the empanelled hundred,

a jury of vengeance, the cheap pressed lips, the narrow eyes like
    hardware;
the judge, his eye-sockets and cheeks dark and immutably secret,
the twisting mouth of the prosecuting attorney.
Nine dark boys spread their breasts against Alabama,
schooled in the cells, fathered by want.
    Mother : one writes : they treat us bad.   If they send us
    back to Kilby jail, I think I shall kill myself.
    I think I must hang myself by my overalls.

Alabama and the South are soft with spring;
in the North, the seasons change, sweet April, December and the air
loaded with snow.   There is time for meetings
during the years, they remaining in prison.
                                        In the Square
a crowd listens, carrying banners.
Overhead, boring through the speaker's voice, a plane
circles with a snoring of motors revolving in the sky,
drowning the single voice.   It does not touch
the crowd's silence.   It circles.   The name stands :
Scottsboro

Suggested Reading

Dan T. Carter, *Scottsboro: A Tragedy of the American South*, rev. ed., Baton
    Rouge, La.: Louisiana State University Press, 1979. A detailed narrative of
    the Scottsboro case that situates it in the context of Southern race rela-
    tions in the 1930s.
Michael Denning, *The Cultural Front: The Laboring of American Culture in the
    Twentieth Century*, New York: Verso, 1996. A broad study that argues that
    Marxist and other pro-labor values and ideals played a key role in shaping
    American culture in the 1930s and beyond.
James Goodman, *Stories of Scottsboro*, New York: Pantheon Books, 1994. A
    retelling of the Scottsboro incident and its aftermath from a variety of
    participants' perspectives.
Robin D. G. Kelley, *Hammer and Hoe: Alabama Communists during the Great
    Depression*, Chapel Hill, NC: University of North Carolina Press, 1990. A
    path-breaking account of African-American radicalism in the deep South, by
    the author of this chapter's article.
Mark Naison, *Communists in Harlem during the Great Depression*, Urbana, Ill.:
    University of Illinois Press, 1983. Emphasizes the resourcefulness and

adaptability of Communists in New York's leading African-American neighborhood and the responses of Harlem's residents.

Fraser M. Ottanelli, *The Communist Party of the United States: From the Depression to World War II*, New Brunswick, NJ: Rutgers University Press, 1991.

The Michigan State University Library American Radicalism Collection has
placed several important pamphlets and other documents about the
Scottsboro case on its website at:

     http://www.lib.msu.edu/coll/main/spec_col/radicalism/index.htm

The Famous American Trials website has a section devoted to the legal
issues in the Scottsboro trials. The URL is

    http://www.law.umkc.edu/faculty/projects/FTrials/scottsboro/scottsb.htm

(Note that URLs on the Web are often subject to change. These links were
valid in August 2000.)

8
Spiritual Roots of New Left Radicalism

1945 German theologian Dietrich Bonhoeffer is executed by Nazis for his role in plotting Hitler's overthrow. Bonhoeffer's combination of existentialist theology and political engagement influences student activists in the late 1950s and early 1960s.

1952 The Christian Faith-and-Life Community is founded at the University of Texas, Austin. Under the leadership (1956–62) of Reverend Joseph Wesley Mathews, the Community becomes a forerunner of New Left organizing in Austin.

1955–6 Montgomery, Alabama bus boycott is one of the most dramatic examples of nonviolent direct action against segregation.

1957 Confrontation in Little Rock, Arkansas. President Eisenhower calls out federal troops to escort nine African-American students into Central High School against the opposition of segregationist Governor Orval Faubus.

1960 Students for a Democratic Society (SDS) is founded. It becomes the most prominent student New Left organization in the following decade.

1962 SDS issues its "Port Huron Statement," analyzing society from the standpoint of young people "bred in at least modest comfort" and calling for "participatory democracy."

August 28, 1963 At the civil rights march on Washington, Rev. Dr. Martin Luther King Jr. delivers his "I have a dream" speech.

March 1965 The first US ground combat troops arrive in Vietnam. The US troop build-up reaches over half a million by 1968.

1965–8 Rapid growth of SDS and other New Left movements.

1966 The formation of the Black Panther Party is a sign of growing black militance and a shift away from civil rights and integration to a movement for Black Power.

1969 SDS comes apart in factional disputes. A small group (which came to be known as the Weather Underground) turns to terrorist tactics.

Spring 1970   Following US invasion of Cambodia and killings of protesting students at Kent State (Ohio) and Jackson State (Mississippi) Universities, demonstrations and student strikes shut down nearly five hundred colleges and universities.

Introduction to the Article

The outburst of radical protest in the 1960s was one of the great surprises in American history. That college students were at the center of a new era of radical protest was even more unexpected, following as it did an era when students were labeled "the uncommitted" and a "silent generation." For more than a generation, historians and other commentators have combined hindsight and scholarship to explain the upheaval their predecessors failed to predict.

Virtually everyone agrees that the New Left depended on the inspiration and the experience of the African-American movement for civil rights. The struggle in the South highlighted the continuing gap between American claims of democracy and equality and the reality of segregation, disenfranchisement, and racial discrimination. It is also accepted that there were stirrings of youthful cultural discontent in the seemingly placid 1950s: the Beat movement, some rebellious strains in the popular music, films, and television of those years, a sense of alienation and anxiety about the threat of nuclear weaponry, for example. Intellectuals who questioned the dominant consensus – sociologist C. Wright Mills, radical historian William Appleman Williams, and essayist Paul Goodman were some of the best-known – were also beginning to have an impact in the early sixties. In an important book, *If I Had a Hammer* (Basic Books, 1987), Maurice Isserman has found more links between the Old Left of the 1930s and 1940s and the emerging New Left.

Most of the research on the origins of radicalism in the sixties has focused on major urban centers and elite colleges and universities: New York, Boston, the Bay Area; Columbia, Harvard, Berkeley. Douglas Rossinow, on the other hand, studies the "heartland": Austin, Texas, and the giant public university there. And unlike most previous analysts, he has emphasized the importance of religious values and church-related organizations, in particular groups professing a Christian version of existentialist philosophy. Several local ministers and the staff at the Austin YMCA/YWCA upheld a political and religious liberalism that put them in conflict with the conservative status quo. The Christian Faith-and-Life Community, a campus religious education center, became the center of campus activism. Influenced in particular by the anti-Nazi German pastor Dietrich Bonhoeffer, members of the community sought both personal spiritual transformation and engagement with political concerns.

This study helps us to understand one of the characteristics distinguishing the New Left from the Old, its insight that "the personal is political." Sixties radicals stressed that how individuals lived their lives should reflect the social ideals the movement strived for. Of course, radicals did not always live up to this principle. Later in the decade, the sexism in interpersonal relations of many male activists spurred the growth of the women's liberation movement. Rossinow also helps us to understand some of the affinities between the politically-minded New Left and the decade's emerging counter-culture. Both emphasized personal authenticity and sought release from what they saw as the stifling, unnatural demands of the social mainstream. But if the radicals were disaffected from the dominant society, they also had much in common with it. Their spiritual quest resonated with themes deeply embedded in American society.

Rossinow's important insights balance interpretations of the New Left which focus on secular concerns. But do they contradict them? Perhaps the paths to political activism in the 1960s varied widely depending on place, background, and circumstance. Did religious concerns continue to motivate New Leftists in Austin? Did they turn away from mainstream faiths and embrace new forms of spirituality? Or did they adopt a more secular and materialist outlook as Marxist rhetoric infused the movement during the sixties? Was it the drive for ever higher levels of personal commitment at the end of that turbulent decade that led a small segment of the New Left into destructive actions that split the movement and brought down heavy repression on radical activists?

"The Break-through to New Life"

Doug Rossinow

Historians have long recognized Christianity's connections to democratic reform and radical movements in the North American past.
From the American Revolution to abolitionism, from the social gospel
and Debsian socialism to the civil rights movement, opponents of earthly
inequalities have appealed to the leveling authority of the Christian God.
Recent writing on the history of American radicalism has made room
for more diffuse traditions of spirituality and perfectionism, as well as for
more strictly Judeo-Christian prophetic religion. As historians of the Left
in the United States approach more recent movements, however, their
accounts become more secularized. In works on the "new left" – the
white youth movement against racism and imperialism and for radical
democracy that flourished on American campuses in the 1960s – religion
is absent from the historical picture altogether. Students of religion are
aware of the intellectual and political ferment that shook religion in the
United States during the 1960s. Some have connected that religious
upheaval to broader cultural currents, but scholars of political radicalism
during that period have rarely, if ever, cast a glance at the world of
religion. Yet, throughout the depths of the cold war and into the
1960s, connections persisted between the realms of religion and political
activism. Religion and spirituality remained rich repositories of oppositional values in these years, and political historians of the period might
do well to follow the example of historians of earlier American reform
and radicalism by putting religion back into "the sixties."

If we keep religion in our field of vision when we trace the history of
reform and radicalism to the cold war, a changed picture of the new left's
emergence takes shape. This revision is particularly valuable because,
despite several studies published in the last decade on the subject, the
new left remains largely unconnected to the broader contours of American cultural and political history. Previous accounts have contained this
political movement within an autonomous history of American radicalism that is isolated from larger historical currents or have suggested that

Reprinted from Douglas Rossinow, " 'The Break-through to New Life': Christianity and
the Emergence of the New Left in Austin, Texas, 1956–1964," *American Quarterly* 46/3
(September 1994), pp. 309–31. © 1994, the American Studies Association. Reprinted by
permission of the Johns Hopkins University Press.

the new left emerged spontaneously from powerful ideas and thinkers. These unlikely explanations of the new left's origins, and the concomitant neglect of the religious factor in the story, are in some measure due to the empirical biases of the existing literature on the new left. By correcting these biases, we can embed the new left in a broader historical terrain.

The empirical biases are regional, ethnocultural, and elitist. Almost all the scholarly work on the new left has been based on the experiences and memories of northern activists. The founding elite of this movement was largely from northern, metropolitan areas where the influence of the strongly materialist old left of the 1930s and 1940s was relatively strong. Many of the most widely read studies of the new left either were written by members of this "old guard" or focused on their experiences. Even those accounts that do not center entirely on the old guard still focus on the national leadership of students for a democratic society (SDS), the largest new left organization, whose elite was always tilted strongly toward the North. The old guard included many young Jews for whom religious identity had become a secular ethnic identity, and the relative religious-ethnic diversity of the old guard discouraged any emphasis on religion in their politics. This disinclination has passed into most accounts of the new left's origins. Examination of a southern environment, as well as of a less elite group within the emerging student movement of the 1960s, clarifies the role of religion, specifically Christianity, in the new left's emergence.

Looking to the South during the 1950s and 1960s reveals that the obvious connection between religion and democratic political activism lies in the civil rights movement. The centrality of Christian religion in the civil rights movement is well established institutionally and intellectually, but, for the most part, historians have associated religion specifically with *black* civil rights activism. Virtually no one has considered seriously that religion may have motivated and shaped *white* participation in the civil rights movement. Some scholars have documented the roots of the new left in this white civil rights activism. (Interestingly, however, those narratives of the new left that focus on the old guard of SDS underplay the role of the civil rights movement.) I suggest that the important role religion played in mobilizing white civil rights activism in the South indicates a religious element in the formation of the new left. In the South, both an old tradition of Christian liberalism and a newer force, Christian existentialism, played important roles in the emergence of white youth radicalism in the 1960s.

The role of Christian existentialism is noteworthy to historians of the cold war for existentialism of various kinds was evident in radical thought throughout the country during this period. Unfortunately, historians of the new left have mentioned existentialism merely to disparage it. Whatever one thinks of it, existentialism was a crucial element in the creation of the new left. Indeed, the presence of existentialism may have been so pervasive among American youth in the late 1950s and 1960s that, ultimately, historians will ask not why the new left became so influenced by existentialism but why so much youth existentialist sentiment in the 1960s took the form of *leftist* existentialism. In the South, the existentialist element often appeared in a specifically Christian form.

A close examination of a local environment, Austin, Texas, reveals the way in which all these factors – Christian existentialism, Christian liberalism, and civil rights activism – interacted with one another. My study of Austin, home of the University of Texas (UT) and the largest center of white youth radicalism in the South during the 1960s, demonstrates the convergence of all these forces in the years around 1960. The watershed of white student participation in civil rights protests in Austin occurred in the year between the fall of 1960 and the fall of 1961. Christian liberalism and Christian existentialism, in various ways, motivated, organized, and influenced the white participation in this activity. In turn, these traditions combined with the experience of political activism to result in the radicalization of many participants and to point the way toward a new left in the South.

The University Y and Christian Liberalism

The political environment in Texas during the first decade of the cold war, from the late 1940s to the late 1950s, was characterized by an exaggerated version of the conservative trend apparent nationwide, an exaggeration rooted in regional and local history. Here, liberals found themselves on the defensive and were easily accused of communist sympathies or race treason when they advanced programs that enjoyed greater legitimacy in other parts of the country. Liberalism was a far more politically oppositional force in Texas than in less Right-leaning areas. In a sea of conservatism, the main island of liberalism was the University of Texas in Austin; it was also the state capital. Administrators and professors of liberal inclinations at UT found some degree of refuge in the tradition of academic freedom. Their insulation from the regional political culture was far from complete, however, as they learned from the case of Homer Rainey, the liberal president of the university who was fired in 1944 after he tried to protect some liberal faculty members from political persecution. Rainey passed into local folklore as a hero of civil liberties and free discussion, which became key issues dividing liberals from conservatives in Texas.

Within the university environment, the least vulnerable center of liberalism was the local church network. Through the 1940s and 1950s, a group of ministers from churches surrounding the university was "right up there on the front edge" of political liberalism, as one protegé said. The most politically active of the group was Blake Smith at University Baptist Church, who was known for his view that "racial segregation is a betrayal of democracy, an affront to human dignity, and an insult to God." These ministers occasionally testified at legislative hearings at the capitol in support of liberal positions on free speech and other issues; they took a firm position favoring the rigid separation of church and state. In a politically and culturally conservative environment, political liberalism enjoyed its widest legitimacy when it was lent the authority of Christian religion.

Most students came to the university from churchgoing backgrounds; they were usually from congregations that were both theologically and politically conservative. Once at UT, however, they encountered a different combination: theological and political liberalism. Jim Neyland, who became prominent among liberal Christian activists at UT in the early sixties, recalled that he and his friends were "concerned about" both "religious hypocrisy" and "political and social hypocrisy." For young people who chafed at a fundamentalist heritage that increasingly seemed to belong to another era, Christian liberalism offered a way to remain in the Christian fold. Austin ministers presented this accommodating religion to them, in the tradition of the social gospel, as inextricably bound to political liberalism, particularly on the issue of race.

For UT students, the center of both theological liberalism and political activity was the university YMCA/YWCA (Y), which had its own building located directly across the street from the campus, on Guadalupe, the retail strip known as "the Drag." Y activities involved hundreds of students each school year, and the Y formed undergraduates into study and discussion committees on subjects ranging from "Psychology and Religion" and "Contemporary Literature" to "Race Relations" and "Pacifism and Disarmament." Each committee was cochaired by a woman and a man. This institutionalization of gender equality afforded women opportunities to rise to leadership positions that they did not enjoy in other settings. Women who became leaders in the Y at UT because of its binary structure, and who subsequently became leaders in the civil rights activity off-campus, included Dorothy Dawson and Sandra "Casey" Cason in the late 1950s and Vivien Franklin in the early 1960s. The Y structure and atmosphere seemed inviting to women generally; as of December 1961, the overall student membership of the Y at UT was nearly two-thirds women.

For all its varied activities, the Y was, more than anything else, an outpost of free speech and discussion, where speakers who could not appear on campus – from George Washington Carver to Norman Thomas and the one-time Communist John Gates – were invited to present their views. The excitement generated by the unusually broad range of views expressed at the Y continually attracted students to speeches and panel discussions, which typically focused on issues such as race relations or world affairs.

This worldly focus was very much in keeping with the traditions of theological liberalism. As Frank Wright – the executive secretary of the university YMCA starting in 1954 – put it, "in the Y, we start with the issues of life – no holds barred – and work toward the issues of faith." The conception of Christianity that the Y promoted was highly practical and not very theistic. It was pragmatic, in a philosophical sense, and to Jim Neyland, who was president of the YMCA in the 1960–61 school year, this pragmatism required an atmosphere of free discussion. "To be liberal in the way the 'Y' is liberal," he said, "is to be willing to hear all sides of an issue and to refuse to accept at face value the 'standard' interpretation of what is happening in the world. It means to refuse to accept any value without . . . testing and applying it to life." For students who felt they came from provincial backgrounds, the Y was an oasis of open-mindedness.

The Y played this role at UT largely because of the efforts of its staff. "We've tried to show that Christianity isn't just something for Sunday exercise, that Christianity is something that has to do with living seven days a week if it's worth a hoot, that it has something to do with your treatment of people," said Block Smith, who ran the Y from 1921 until his retirement in 1954. One student in the mid-1950s called him "a primitive Christian" for the simplicity of his egalitarian outlook. Rosalie Oakes and Frank Wright sought to preserve this legacy. They embodied the most militant aspects of Christian liberalism in the United States in the middle decades of the twentieth century. Oakes, the executive secretary of the YWCA in the late fifties, had been active in the student Y movement since her college days during the late 1930s. Before coming to Austin, she worked as a traveler throughout the southeast. Visiting campus Ys with a black coworker, she saw Jim Crow up close. Frank Wright took over Block Smith's job and held it through the 1960s. Wright had performed alternative service in mental hospitals during World War II as a conscientious objector. Firmly committed to the pacifist and socially conscious traditions of midwestern Protestant clergy, he perpetuated this tradition in the 1960s in his own work with the local American Friends Service Committee, the Central Texas chapter of the ACLU, and other groups.

Smith, Oakes, and Wright guarded their autonomy from larger institutional forces jealously, for they knew it was the key to their political
freedom. The university Y was hardly related at all to the downtown
Austin Y, which was not politically active. Within the regional and
national student Y structures, individual campus Ys had a great deal of
autonomy. The UT-Y staffers carefully maintained their financial independence from the UT administration. They strove to be free from
university control in order to serve the university better. They aspired
to the role of "gadfly," exactly the role that prominent theologian
Harvey Cox recommended to student Ys in 1959. Cox, who wrote *The
Secular City* in 1965 and popularized liberal and radical theology that
was already at work in the nation's seminaries, spoke frequently to
student Y audiences from the mid-1950s onward and was well known
to the Austin group. Cox urged student Y activists to function as a "loyal
opposition" on the nation's campuses. Cox called this gadfly stance a
new kind of "radicalism," and it was a kind of radicalism that liberal
students could live with. Mary Gay Maxwell, president of the YMCA
during the 1959–60 school year, wrote that the Y was used to "taking
stands" on political issues but that the ultimate goal of such activity was
to promote an "exchange of ideas" and thus to serve the campus
intellectually.

Two issues that epitomized the university Y's political and intellectual
role on campus were internationalism and civil rights. The Y, as a world-
wide organization, had an international perspective built into it. For
liberal students in Texas, a concern about international issues was a
variation on the larger theme of cosmopolitanism versus provincialism.
Through its frequent speakers and discussions on world affairs, the Y
broadened political discussion on the Austin campus. In 1961, for
example, UT professors and black South African students spoke at the
Y about politics in South Africa, and representatives from student Christian groups in the United States and Cuba discussed relations between
their countries.

Equally important, students active in the Y had opportunities to travel
abroad with Christian student groups, and these experiences often
became formative political moments. They visited third world countries
and, most unusually, Eastern Europe. Consequently, they were able to
put a human face on socialism, the greatest cold war bogey. In 1961,
Susan Reed went to Poland and returned still anticommunist but convinced that socialism had helped the Polish people. Another student
visited Russia and reported on his return that the Russians "want
peace more than any [sic] people in the world." Vivien Franklin went
to the Soviet Union and several Eastern Bloc countries. She came back
and began telling people that she now thought "business interests" in

the United States were "blocking disarmament for political reasons." Travels such as these drew some liberal student activists to the left flank of American liberalism and led to expressions of dissent from cold war orthodoxy, which many Texans found alarming indeed.

The 1958–59 National Student Assembly of the Ys (NSAY – a quadrennial gathering), held at the University of Illinois at Urbana, passed resolutions that clearly expressed such dissent from the "'standard' interpretation" of social and political issues. Casey Cason of the UT contingent chaired the section titled "In Search of World Community." These students saw a "shocking" ignorance of world affairs, of foreign cultures, and of the activities of the U.S. government abroad among the American public. They suggested the American government and press could not be trusted when it came to reporting foreign affairs. They urged a nonbelligerent approach to international relations, which in itself was a form of dissent from the cold war.

Expressions of sympathy for civil rights were equally controversial. Students who became involved in the Y in Austin came into contact with people who told them, by both word and example, that they thought racism contradicted simple Christian belief. The few black students at the school – UT started to admit a trickle of black undergraduates starting in 1956, but, by the early 1960s, there were still fewer than two hundred African-American students in a university of over twenty thousand – were more welcome at the Y than in any official UT building. A few black students became quite involved in Y activities. Action in behalf of an integrationist viewpoint by Y activists in Austin quickened after the 1958–59 NSAY, which Jim Neyland also attended. The assembly turned into a civil rights rally, with three thousand attendees, white and black, joining hands and singing "Kumbaya" and "We Shall Overcome" at the closing session. Back in Austin, the UT delegation was inspired to try their hands at sitting-in. Neyland's first sit-in was at a downtown bus station cafe with Jennie Franklin and Gwen Jordan, two black women. The manager closed the shop rather than serve them. The students were left with a feeling of "liberation and exhileration [sic]," Neyland remembered. "It was a victory for us, because we now knew that 'Christian non-violence' could work; we did not know how long it would take, but we were certain our rectitude would eventually wear down the opposition."

The participating students called themselves "the fellowship of sitters." The mainstream Christian groups at UT endorsed their actions. The UT-Y Cabinet expressed its approval in the classic terms of liberal Christianity: "The Y sees value in this project as one in which a student can take action 'in behalf of' the values he is beginning to affirm." In keeping with their practical conception of Christianity, the local Y leadership asserted that values were no good unless one put them into action. "The greatest need of both education and religion today is to have more ways in which we can put our muscles into support of our thoughts, emotions, and our convictions."

Y activists thought they had to take action in the world to affirm their values, and they thought they needed to affirm their values in order to live meaningful lives. "Only in the enactment of [a student's] values in concrete life experience," the UT-Y leaders wrote in spring 1962, "does he divulge his faith to himself and others." This was crucial, for the "major task" of the University of Texas Y, a student reporter wrote after interviewing its staff, was "that of confronting all persons in the University with the necessity of choosing what they will value." Neyland wrote, "Real personal commitment is the goal of the 'Y,' as it encourages a free and open search for meaning." Values, commitment, meaning – these were the things that students should search for, said the Y activists. In the years around 1960, for many of these activists, the search ended in the civil rights movement.

The concern to find meaning in life underlay all the discussion and activity of Y activists. Student Y activists constantly invoked the student "search for meaning" in both their internal literature and their publicity materials. They felt this was a real longing among their contemporaries; it was not just a search that they, as activists, recommended. Another liberal student at UT in the late fifties, *Daily Texan* editor Robb Burlage, thought he heard among his generation "a new call for a meaningful life, as if it sprang from the heart of meaninglessness." Actually, the search for meaning implied a commitment neither to political activism nor to political liberalism. But student Y activists strove mightily to hitch that search to their political vision. Liberal activists of all kinds were making this connection at this time, but, in Austin, Y activists, who developed the connection in the context of Christian liberalism, made it most consistently.

Some historians have portrayed twentieth-century liberal Protestantism as a tradition that was unable to speak to such inner longings. Some have portrayed it as a conservative tradition as well, intellectually tepid and politically complacent. The story of the university Y in Austin suggests how simplified this version of twentieth-century American religious history is. It is crucial that historians consider the political history of religious institutions, as well as the history of religious ideas, in order to evaluate the political role of religion in the industrial United States. Liberal Protestantism certainly could be conservative, but it also could be socially engaged and could encourage a critical perspective on society. It could be as worldly as secular liberalism – but it could also be deeply spiritual as it answered the call for meaning in life that many young white people were expressing in the late 1950s. In Austin, white student support for civil rights might never have been mobilized had it not been for the "free space" that the university Y provided on the edge of campus. This was a space where women and men who questioned the "standard interpretation" of things felt free to explore any issue they chose, and it was also a space where their personal longings were validated. Most of all, it was a place where their worldly concerns and their personal yearnings were linked, for many of them inseparably.

The Christian Faith-and-Life Community and Christian Existentialism

Despite this fusion of the personal and the political, the university Y was best known on the UT campus for its concern with political issues. The Christian Faith-and-Life Community (CFLC) – or "the community," as its members tended to call it – was the place on campus most closely associated during those same years with expressly theological discussion, and the discussion that occurred there placed personal concerns front and center. This residential and religious education center was part of the campus's liberal political culture. Between 1958 and 1963, many university Y leaders who became involved in civil rights activism and other liberal or radical politics lived for some time at the community. Dick Simpson, who lived at the CFLC for a year and who was president of the YMCA in 1962–63, wrote that there was "no place else in conservative Texas quite like [the community]." These student activists came in contact with new ideas at the CFLC that spoke powerfully to their cultural situation, ideas that imparted a radical experimentalism to their thought and action. This was Christian existentialism.

Like the more diffuse "search for meaning" that pervaded youth discussion around this time, existentialism implied a sympathetic response to neither political liberalism in general, the civil rights movement in particular, nor certainly to leftist radicalism. However, in this time and place, it is clear that these themes *did* contribute to the development of white youth liberalism and radicalism, which was crystalized in the crucible of civil rights protest. In a conservative environment such as that in Texas, people of both conservative and critical inclinations were likely to associate all forms of dissidence with one another. This imparted a political tenor to theological and intellectual dissent that it might not have acquired in different circumstances.

The community did not seem likely to nurture any type of radicalism at its inception in 1952. Because the CFLC's "mission," as the staff put it, was framed in terms of theological study, it received the blessings of many local establishment figures, including the UT administration, from the start. It was the task of W. Jack Lewis, the Presbyterian campus minister who founded the CFLC and a man firmly rooted in mainstream Texas culture – as an undergraduate at UT in the 1930s he had been chief "yeller," or cheerleader, for pep rallies – to round up and maintain this kind of establishment approval for his experiment. The CFLC became well known among campus clergy and others involved in lay education around the country, even around the world; ultimately, clergy at many other schools, such as Duke and Brown Universities and the Universities of Montana and Wisconsin, modeled their own campus centers after the CFLC.

Lewis traveled to the Iona intentional Christian community in Scotland in the early fifties and was impressed with the members' attempts to answer what he saw as the spiritual questions of the day, questions that he thought traditional campus ministry was, in contrast, not addressing. He resolved to duplicate the experiment in Austin. By forming an explicit and intentional "covenant" that expressed their collective purpose in living and studying together, he believed, students could ease the sense of social and spiritual alienation that, many social observers in the 1950s claimed, plagued American youth. As the "Moral Covenant" averred, "Authentic, self-consciously disciplined community does not swallow the individual; it rather creates the very possibility of personhood by pushing the individual against the necessity to decide for himself."

Men and women lived in separate residences, but they had a more coeducational experience than any other students at UT. They took community classes together, ate Friday dinners together, and attended lectures and prayer services together. Judy Schleyer Blanton, who lived at the community in 1960, remembered students there sneaking in and out of bedroom windows, but, in general, there is little reason to believe that more sex went on in the CFLC than elsewhere around campus at the time. Female students there remembered functioning as equals with men in the classroom. Numerous participants in the civil rights protest of 1960–61 remembered Cason, who lived in the women's residence starting in 1958, as the driving force in their group, the initial "mover." In years afterward, she felt that, during her time in Austin, she had been part of an "incipient women's network" that was very different in style from the northern-dominated, and male-dominated, environment of the National Student Association (NSA) and SDS that she encountered later. This "women's network" existed in such Christian groups as the Y and the community, as well as elsewhere. This setting encouraged the development of strong female leadership in the student body at UT generally and in the group of liberal activist students that coalesced around 1960 specifically.

Cason's mentor at the community was Joseph Wesley Mathews, whose arrival as head of curriculum in 1956 decisively changed the course of the "Austin experiment." Until he departed for Chicago in 1962, Mathews's teaching and personality were an omnipresent influence on the character of life and study at the CFLC. Jack Lewis conducted rather conventional Bible-study classes for the residents during the first four years of the experiment but felt that this curriculum lacked an "existential 'bite.' " He hired Mathews to develop a curriculum with sharper teeth. Mathews instituted a rigorous course of study that used not only biblical texts but also contemporary plays and stories and, most heavily, avant-garde Protestant theology – much of it written since the 1920s, much of it imported from Germany, much of it existentialist. The most important theologians to whom he introduced students in Austin were Rudolf Bultmann; Paul Tillich; and, perhaps the greatest influence politically, Dietrich Bonhoeffer.

Mathews had started his career as an evangelical preacher with fundamentalist leanings, but he had undergone a spiritual and intellectual crisis as a chaplain during World War II, when he found his simple religious precepts could not help him cope with the death all around him. After the war he went to Yale Divinity School to study with H. Richard Niebuhr, and he became immersed in existentialism. After this, Mathews combined the evangelistic zeal of his American Protestant tradition with the European theology he had adopted at Yale, and it proved a combustible mix. He became a local celebrity at Perkins Theological Seminary in Dallas and was well known for his iconoclastic sermons, during which he was known to rip pages out of a church's Bible to illustrate his belief that the book was not sacred. Mathews also became renowned at UT for his public performances. In the mid-1950s, he and the liberal philosophy professor John Silber engaged in a series of debates, which drew hundreds of students, over the question, "What is the most important thing in life?" The two later debated the meaningfulness (or meaninglessness) of Beckett's *Waiting for Godot*. Cason, like others, found in Mathews someone sympathetic to her questioning spirit. She lived in a women's dorm when she first came to UT and hated it. She did not feel she could reveal this reaction to most authority figures on campus, but she felt she could talk about it with Mathews. There was "a lot of façade everywhere" in the 1950s, she remembered, and Mathews was one of the few people who seemed to be trying to strip the façade away from things and people. He wanted to ask, "What's eating at the core of people?" It was a question she was also ready to ask.

It was as if Mathews wanted his young charges at the community to experience some of what he had experienced: a crisis of belief, a crisis of identity. What he hoped to accomplish by boring toward a person's "core" was a "breakthrough" – perhaps the pivotal idea of the community. This concept was rooted in both Protestant theology and modern psychological theory. It meant a rebirth into a new life, just as Mathews had started a new life – a personal breakthrough, which, if duplicated enough times, could produce a social breakthrough. According to this concept, breakthrough could occur only by means of break*down*. Crisis led to salvation, as Jack Lewis suggested:

> A breakthrough is a gift that we acknowledge when we have been broken through. Ask those who have returned from the valley of the shadow in mental illness, alcoholism, family disruption, business failure and other personal or social crises.

Both Joe Mathews's followers and detractors saw him trying to induce this kind of personal crisis among students at the community. "Breaking people down" was important to him, Casey Cason Hayden remembered. For some people, breakdown did not lead to breakthrough. At least one or two students in the community ended up in mental hospitals, and some blamed Mathews, at least in part. His critics more typically just saw him as domineering, intimidating, autocratic – some said he attracted "a little cult" around him. Dorothy Dawson Burlage found him "extreme, doctrinaire, zealous," though "brilliant." To him, "nothing was sacred."

The idea of breakthrough came most directly from the writings of Tillich and Bonhoeffer. Tillich combined psychoanalytic theory with Christian theology to develop a life-affirming ontology of love. In a discussion of Tillich's ideas, James Moeser, an undergraduate in the community who shared an apartment with Jim Neyland in the 1960– 61 school year in which many of the planning meetings for political activities took place, emphasized that the experience of grace only arrived in moments of profound crisis. "It comes to us in our darkest moments of deepest despair. It strikes our consciousness just at the moment that we realize our own inadequacy to deal with our existence." This was what Tillich called "the human boundary-situation," which followed the archetype of Jesus's experience on the cross.

The grace received during this kind of crisis meant "reunion," said Moeser. It meant the end of the human experience of "estrangement," of "separation – separation from all other men, separation from the self, and separation from the Ground of Being." This "estrangement" was the basic existentialist concept of alienation, which Tillich thought was the great problem of twentieth-century culture. He identified alienation from God with a sense of alienation from one's true or potential self and recast God as "the Ground of our Being." Furthermore, he identified alienation with sin and preached that grace would bring the opposite of alienation – it would bring self-acceptance and community.

In Tillich's hands, the political implications of the idea of breakthrough as basically an end to alienation were ambiguous. But for students at the CFLC, the concept of breakthrough received a clear political emphasis from the life and work of Dietrich Bonhoeffer. Bonhoeffer is best known not for his life but for his death, in a German prison camp in 1945. He was executed for his involvement in the indigenous German anti-Nazi resistance. For some students in Austin around 1960, Bonhoeffer's influence helped tether the promise of a personal breakthrough to the prospect of political breakthrough. His account of his experience overseeing a renegade Lutheran seminary in Germany in the 1930s, *Life Together*, became a model for the CFLC's "common life together." In *Life Together*, he spoke of a "break-through to new life." Bonhoeffer asserted that the new life in Christ would be a communal life and that the "break-through to new life" would also be a "break-through to community." This breakthrough to community, he said, would occur most clearly in the process of confession. "Confession in the presence of a brother is the profoundest kind of humiliation," he wrote, and this was exactly its usefulness. As it had for Jesus, abasement had to precede breakthrough. Like Tillich, Bonhoeffer drew on the drama of the crucifixion for his discussion of the contemporary human prospect.

Bonhoeffer's vision of community seemed to harbor considerable appeal for the young people gathered at the CFLC. One student there called on her contemporaries, in 1962, to "face the breakdown of authentic human relations in [our] marriages and homes." Perceiving this kind of social alienation, the CFLC stated that its goal was the development of "new and creative modes of corporate existence." Where "the struggle" to create such "creative modes" occurs, they said, "there is the breakthrough. There is the future alive in the present." In a way both personal and social, out of "breakdown," a "breakthrough" could arrive.

Breakthrough to the future, metaphorically, meant a rebirth as a "new man." The experience of rebirth would clear one's thinking and acting of the old ways; one would face the new world with the "simplicity and straightforwardness" for which Bonhoeffer called. For illustration he used the image of the child – a literal image of rebirth. He longed for "the eschatalogical possibility of the child," who might be "the new man of the future," he wrote. The remarks of Lois Boyd, a student who came to the CFLC for a "spiritual retreat" in 1962, suggest the currency of this image within the community. She described the Austin students communicating the idea of rebirth to her: " 'Come on,' They shouted at us, 'You can LIVE.... You have Cosmic Permission to LIVE!'" She compared her breakthrough experience to a butterfly emerging from a chrysalis – and to a child emerging from the womb. She wrote rapturously, "our Lives were so very new ... and birth is such a delicate, fragile thing – and violent – and personal. But good! Only the newly Alive can know how good!"

The new life into which the students and staff at the CFLC hoped to be reborn would not be merely a sensorium of personal discovery, however. They, like Bonhoeffer, made it clear that the "worldliness" of the new life was to be a political participation in the world. In their prayer services, they prayed for strength "to be responsible" in "politics ... the social order ... education ... vocation." Students at the community expressed disdain for those so caught up in their own selves that they refused to take action in the world around them. Although they read a great deal of psychoanalytic theory, some of them – Carol Darrell, for example – derided the type of student whom she thought was *too* fond of psychology or who was so analytic that he "assumed the posture of a mere spectator." Like students active in the Y, she thought action, in addition to thought, was necessary. In some cases, only a decision to take action would clarify thought. Although the two Christian groups offered different paths to this conclusion, the familiar tradition of Christian liberalism and the newer tradition of Christian existentialism did indeed converge on this point – the need for action.

At the community as at the Y, this call to action had a politically oppositional orientation. Casey Hayden recalled the importance of the image of the "tragic hero or heroine," which she and her friends took from both Christian existentialists, such as Bonhoeffer, and atheist existentialists on the near Left, such as Albert Camus. She though it was important to take action in behalf of one's beliefs, in spite of the risks – perhaps because of the risks. Like Bonhoeffer at his life's end, the community members vowed solidarity with the downtrodden. In a prayer service in early 1961, the students said, "let us take upon ourselves the urgencies of this world." They pleaded,

> may we have compassion for
>   the starving
>   the sick
>   the estranged
>   the oppressed
>   the imprisoned.

The title of this section of the service was "The Life," and it followed some morbid comments on "death" and "fragmentation." The new life that overcame fragmentation, finally, was a life of commitment to the oppressed.

If the students wanted to make a commitment to the oppressed, in the South, the challenge of combating racial oppression presented itself to them, especially after the beginning of the civil rights movement in the mid-1950s. In fact, community members on several occasions expressed solidarity with African Americans. Allen Lingo remembered preaching at local, small-town, white churches in favor of civil rights for blacks as part of his training as a member of the CFLC's staff. As a student resident at the community, another student there had challenged Lingo to protest the annual blackface minstrel show at UT, and he had done so. He did not think a student anywhere else on campus would have challenged him in this manner. The CFLC as a whole took a stand for racial equality when, in 1954, they admitted a black woman and became the only racially integrated student housing at UT. Students remembered this move as a conscious political decision by the group, and it cost the community some sorely needed financial support. Other black students, like Robert Bell, lived there in subsequent years; he remembered it as "a real enjoyable place to live...people were real friendly." Solidarity with black students continued at the community, most dramatically when, in 1960, a large group of students went "en masse" to join the civil rights protests occurring just off campus. More than anything else, race was the focus of the political efforts that emerged from the CFLC in the 1956–62 period.

Many students who spent time at the CFLC went on to further political activity, and their politics often retained a spiritual aspect. Casey Hayden became heavily involved in the Student Nonviolent Coordinating Committee (SNCC) and worked in the Deep South in conditions far riskier than any she experienced in Austin. In later years, she became involved in the women's liberation movement and in the counterculture. Dorothy Dawson Burlage also worked with SNCC and other civil rights and antipoverty groups until 1970, when she returned to school and ultimately became a child psychotherapist. Claire Johnson Breihan has worked for over two decades in the Austin Independent School District as a specialist in racial integration. Allen Lingo pursued a radical inner-city organizing agenda with Joe Mathews in Chicago after Mathews split with Jack Lewis and left the CFLC in 1962. Dick Simpson became a scholar of African politics, a prominent activist in Chicago city politics, and finally an ordained minister. For these people and many others who shared their college experiences, personal quest and social mission were thoroughly interwined.

The 1962 split in the community came over the question of the balance between the personal and the political. Joe Mathews's goal,

Judy Schleyer Blanton thought, was to "infiltrate" the mainline Protestant churches and use them as a base for the pursuit of a "social justice agenda." Jack Lewis though Mathews was scaring away the financial donations that the community needed and still sought from well-heeled Texans. He resolved to bring the CFLC back to a conventional religious education curriculum. To avoid dismissal, Mathews quit and seven of the twelve staff members left with him. This split broke the creative tension between personal and political concerns that the CFLC had cultivated, and, in the mid-1960s, it became not a religious study center but a human potential workshop and experimented with the various therapeutic techniques that arrived from the West Coast. Lewis, no longer in control, left soon after Mathews. The community veered fully into the search for a personal breakthrough that was unconnected to political breakthrough and thus revealed the political ambiguity of the former.

For many students before 1962, though, the CFLC reinforced the possibility of stringing personal quests tightly to social concerns. Like the university Y, it was a "free space" where, as one student said, he felt the "freedom to talk about my questions" – questions of self, of God, and of life. To one sympathetic observer of the CFLC, the community spoke "a message of courage, of gameness . . . of earnest concern for the problems of one's own self, of others one is with, and of the world at large." Both the Y and CFLC encoded and legitimated the connection between personal and political concerns in a Christian vocabulary; while the Y dealt first and foremost with the wordly side of the formula, the community explored the spiritual and theological side more deeply. Both prepared students to take political action in defiance of established power.

The "Stand-Ins"

For white student activists at UT, the two turning points that led toward civil rights agitation were the 1958–59 NSAY and the beginning of the black student sit-in movement in February 1960. As discussed earlier, an interracial group of Y activists began sitting in at whites-only restaurants in the spring semester of 1959. In early 1960, the wave of sit-ins that swept through the historically black colleges of the South inspired student activists in Austin to continue their efforts. Black students at Bishop College and historically black Wiley College in Marshall, Texas, conducted a series of militant sit-ins, which were animated by the philosophy of Gandhian nonviolence. A coalition of mostly black students from UT, Huston-Tillotson – a historically black college in Austin – and a couple of local seminaries staged demonstrations soon afterward against segregation in Austin. By May 1960, over thirty lunch counters and cafes in Austin had desegregated in response to these and other pressures.

Activists at the Y then decided to step up their activity. The student activists at Bishop had contacts with the Y in Austin; in April, a woman representing the Bishop students came to the Y to recount the events in Marshall. The Y activists at UT felt that they, too, should be part of the student movement for civil rights, and, in the summer of 1960, they started to plan more concerted action. Cason spent part of that summer in New York City working as a tutor in a parish in East Harlem. In August, she attended an NSA seminar on civil rights and stayed for the NSA Congress in Minneapolis, where she first came to national attention among young activists by delivering a dramatic speech challenging the gathered students to risk their own security by commiting civil disobedience in behalf of racial equality. Here she, like Dorothy Dawson and Robb Burlage, came in contact with the Liberal Study Group within the NSA, which included Al Haber and Tom Hayden of the University of Michigan and which formed the nucleus of SDS. By September 1960, a circle of activists that included Cason, Houston Wade – "one of the evangels of the new left" and the only member of the group from an old left family – Jim Neyland, Jennie Franklin, and others settled on a strategy of protests directed at the two movie theaters on the Drag that did not admit blacks. Holding all their planning meetings at the Y, they insulated the Y politically and gave themselves complete autonomy by organizing as a non-Y, nonuniversity group – even though most of them were UT students and Y activists. They called themselves Students for Direct Action (SDA).

Starting in early November, SDA organized "stand-ins" at the two theaters in the evenings, often several times a week. White students would line up at the ticket windows to buy tickets if the theaters would also admit their black friends; when they were refused, they would go to the back of the line and wait to do the same thing again. The black students simply asked to buy tickets for themselves and, of course, were likewise refused. This strategy succeeded in clogging up the ticket line and, thus, slowing ticket sales; it also drew a great deal of attention both from passersby and from the local media. Eleanor Roosevelt wrote one of her daily "My Day" columns about the stand-ins. The protestors, 70 percent to 80 percent of them white, received a fair amount of petty harassment and verbal threats, but no one suffered violence during the stand-ins; an early planning meeting in the Y basement was interrupted by a lame bombing incident in which no one was hurt. In November 1960, Glenn Smiley, who worked for the pacifist organization the Fellowship of Reconciliation, visited the UT-Y and delivered a talk on the methods of nonviolent resistance. The students in SDA practiced nonviolence but not nonviolent resistance to authority; there were no planned arrests. For six months, SDA regularly put between forty and two hundred people on the streets for this evening activity; the turnout reached five hundred at the high point of protest in February 1961. This perhaps attested to the organizational skills acquired by the leaders in the varied activities of the student Y. As noted earlier, a large number of participants, as well as leaders, came from the CFLC. Couples sometimes went to the stand-ins for a cheap date. Students avoided complete boredom by singing made-up songs, such as "When the Saints Go Standing In." After each evening's actions, they returned to the Y for a follow-up group meeting; sometimes they sang as they went. Their humor and good spirits reflected their belief that they were part of a vibrant movement for change and that ultimately they would win.

Indeed, by September 1961, they won their demand; the theaters promised to integrate. The protests had put into practice the idea that action was required to affirm one's values, to make life meaningful, and to exercise the human potential for freedom. This activity satisfied the imperatives of both Christian liberalism and existentialism. Furthermore, it left an influential legacy of direct action to subsequent waves of student activists. Real freedom, real community, new life – young activists in the 1960s came to believe that these things could not be achieved if one's politics remained just talk. These convictions were established firmly, and the path to radicalization was opened, by the civil rights activism that erupted on campuses all over the country in the early 1960s.

The experience of the stand-ins spun the white participants onto several different trajectories. Some, including Jim Neyland and Vivien Franklin, continued their interracial civil rights activism in and around Texas; Franklin moved further to the Left than Neyland. Some worked with Frank Wright to form Austin for Peaceful Alternatives, which advocated an end to the arms race and superpower confrontation. Neyland continued to work through the Y, which came under attack in the spring of 1962. The conservative *Dallas Morning News* ran a series of exposé-style articles discussing the liberal-Left politics of the staff and student activists at the Y. As a result, the student government at UT removed the Y from their annual fundraising effort. Neyland and Dick Simpson started an alternative, liberal campus political party in 1960–61; after some initial success, in spring 1962, they were defeated in campus elections, and, in a symbolic renunciation of liberal activism, the student government then withdrew UT from membership in the NSA. As liberals began to find the campus mainstream less hospitable, and as a self-conscious student Left emerged in the 1960s, the Y lost its position on the Left "cutting edge" of student activism in Austin.

The SDA circle was "plugged into the nascent radical movement" of the early sixties, recalled Chandler Davidson, SDA's official chairman in 1960–61. The wedding of Casey Cason and Tom Hayden in the fall of 1961 symbolized these connections in Austin. Joe Mathews performed the ceremony at the CFLC. Neyland and Vivien Franklin, who had been dating for some time, were the legal witnesses. Cason and Hayden read passages from Ecclesiastes and Camus. Houston Wade and Robb and Dorothy Burlage attended, as did Al Haber and others involved in the foundation of SDS. Some later claimed that the idea of the Port Huron Conference, where SDS really began, grew out of the political discussion that continued late into the night after the wedding. Tom Hayden argued with Jim Neyland and told him that social change could come only from "outside the system," while Neyland wanted to continue working inside mainstream institutions. Afterward, on their way to further adventures, the new couple left town. Vivien Franklin attended the Port Huron Conference and organized a civil rights conference for SDS in Dallas.

As with all social movements, not all the participants continued along a single path. While some young white civil rights activists moved Left and intensified their political involvement, others shouldered the human cost of personal and political upheaval. By late 1963, Neyland had left the state and Vivien Franklin had left the country; they were both psychologically unable to continue political work. The attacks on the Y compounded a personal crisis Neyland was experiencing, and he suffered a breakdown that did not lead to breakthrough.

Christianity did not *cause* the involvement of these young people in civil rights protest or in the new left. A compound of political and cultural forces moved them in those directions, a compound that was forged in the heat of activism. However, the important role of Christian religion and Christian institutions in the emergence of white youth activism in Austin during this time is unmistakable. It is possible that the stand-in activity of 1960–61 would not have occurred had it not been for the safe haven that the university Y provided. There, students, white and black, who were supportive of civil rights could come together without fear of disapproval or harassment to plan their actions and to reinforce one another's commitments. The institutional role that the university Y played in fostering civil rights activism supports the view of Harry Boyte and Sara Evans concerning the importance of "free spaces" where discussion and planning can occur in the development of movements for democratic social change. Moreover, the university Y's connection to larger institutional networks of Christian liberal activism gave those who represented an embattled viewpoint in their local settings a sense of empowerment and expanded political possibility.

The intellectual role Christianity played in this story is more complex. Christian liberalism taught students to practice, as well as preach, religious beliefs. It taught that an affirmation of one's values could bring meaning and coherence to one's life. Existentialism gave a name to the feelings of meaninglessness and incoherence that some young white people sought to assuage, and that name was alienation. Christian existentialism searched for ways of replacing alienation with feelings of wholeness, authenticity, and community. One can see these longings in a Christian liberal context like the student Y, but, at a place like the CFLC, these longings received more elaborate expression and deeper exploration. At this historical moment, these two intellectual and political frameworks worked well together; existentialism gave liberalism intellectual grounding, and liberalism helped to keep existentialism politically engaged. In other places, this configuration may have appeared in throughly secular settings and terms, but, in Austin, the discussion took place in a Christian idiom.

Furthermore, existentialism gave a politically fateful twist to the idea of putting one's values into practice for it encouraged the belief that meaningful action was risky action. This was politically important because it was in such risky situations, in defiance of authority, that the process of radicalization often occurred. It became axiomatic on the Left in the years to come that action precipitated political breakthroughs that were also personal breakthroughts. The fate of the CFLC in itself suggests the political ambiguity of the search for a personal breakthrough. Nonetheless, it should be clear from this study that it is a serious mistake to view such personal searches simply or always as depoliticizing forces for, at the University of Texas around 1960, the quests for meaning and for breakthrough acted as politicizing forces. The personal and the political were fused from the start of "the sixties."

Finally, it was this intersection of Christian liberalism and Christian existentialism that helped push some young white people in this time and place into the strange territory to the Left of liberalism. Christian liberalism, since the time of the social gospel movement, had harbored a critical perspective on industrial capitalist society, in both social and spiritual terms. Ironically this liberal tradition afforded a critical perspective on the liberal politics that represented a reconciliation with that society. This critical perspective received new life in the student Y movement during the civil rights era and ended, for many young Americans, in an estrangement from political liberalism and mainstream institutions. Existentialism, on the other hand, was an intellectual force with scant moorings in liberal traditions. Christian existentialism emphasized a search for new methods, new thinking, in all matters. Liberalism drew strength from a tradition of political competition, but Christian existentialism looked to a "new world" and a "new man." It made what was familiar seem timid and compromised. It advocated not a breaking away from this world but a breaking through to a new life in this world, and whatever else the politics of this breakthrough would be, if it were really new, it seemed clear to some that it could only be radical.

Resonating with North American Protestant traditions of evangelism and individual regeneration, Christian existentialism was a body of ideas from foreign soil that spoke to the situation of these youths in the American South. In the future, we will have to inquire searchingly into the cultural history of the twentieth-century United States if we wish to understand why it spoke to them so. Only by seriously considering the hollowness that white middle-class youth perceived at the center of their good fortune will we comprehend their desire to embark on radical campaigns for change in the society and culture they inherited and to which they looked "uncomfortably." By recognizing the religious component in the new left's beginnings, we can see that this emptiness they saw was, to them, spiritual as well as psychological. Their search for meaning, authenticity, and social justice stands as a reflection on the culture of advanced industrial capitalism in the United States, and it is here that their movement's abiding historical significance may lie.

Documents

Introduction to the Documents

The documents in this section indicate some of the spiritual and ethical dimensions of New Left activism. As Douglas Rossinow points out in his study of Austin, Texas, liberal Christianity and existentialism propelled some of the University of Texas's most serious and talented students into radical politics. In Document One, an autobiographical excerpt, Dick Simpson recounts his upbringing in conservative white middle-class Texas in the fifties and his encounters with the Christian Faith-and-Life Community and the student YMCA/YWCA. Politicized as an undergraduate, Simpson went on to an activist career in Chicago grass-roots politics, and peace and social justice movements. After college, he withdrew from organized religion but in the 1980s a spiritual reawakening led him to become an ordained minister.

It is clear that the struggle against racial segregation in the South was the great moral cause for the students Rossinow describes. Document Two, the Founding Statement of the Student Nonviolent Coordinating Committee (SNCC), shows the religious roots of the foremost predominantly black direct action group. SNCC renounced the statement in 1966, when it turned to a Black Power philosophy. Document Three, an article by SNCC leader Charles McDew, points out that southern racism was a sharp contradiction of "precepts learned in church and in democratic family life." For the white students at Texas, however, recognizing the contradictions of racism led them to engage with causes and ideas that took them beyond their families of origin or the churches of their childhood.

Among the leaders of the incipient Austin New Left was Casey Hayden. Deeply involved in the civil rights movement, she and her friend Mary King drafted a private statement in 1965 to point out how the devaluation of women's roles in the movement compromised the ideals of those struggling for justice and equality. They permitted their "kind of memo" (Document Four) to be published in the pacifist magazine *Liberation* the next year. It struck a chord with many women in the New Left, whose experiences with their male colleagues' sexism stimulated the growth of the women's liberation movement in the late sixties.

Dick Simpson, from The Politics of Compassion and Transformation

---

Reprinted from Dick Simpson, "Afterword," in *The Politics of Compassion and Transformation* (Athens, OH: Swallow Press/ Ohio University Press, 1989), pp. 251–5.

I was born in Houston, Texas, in 1940. Like everyone, I am product of a long, complicated family history. Both my parents came from large Anglo-Saxon families that had settled in Texas and Arkansas. My Grandfather, Will Simpson, was a farmer and horse tamer who committed suicide before I was born. My Grandfather Felts, who had a great impact on me, was a Nazarene preacher who rode the circuit of small churches in Oklahoma and Arkansas. There is a long history of preachers, teachers, frontiersmen, and Indian squaws in both families but more of businessmen and women in my parents' generation.

My mother was a member of the Methodist church and took me to Sunday school. My father preferred the golf course to Sunday worship.

He was a Texas oilman with the drive and pride for which they are known. We were upper-middle-class but not rich. My parents' political views were characterized by tolerance, with mother being more liberal and father more conservative. My father held the bigoted views of the region and those Texas businessmen with whom he associated.

I grew up with the idealized view of the world common to a comfortable middle-class home in the 1940s and 1950s. My father left us when I was three to go to fight in World War II and returned a war hero when I was five. I received extra love and attention from my parents as I was an only child and I achieved early success with their support. I was an Eagle Scout by the time I was fourteen. I soon added the God and Country, Silver Explorer Award, and Order of the Arrow recognition from Scouting.

In my teenage years at junior high and high school I was a loner. I did well enough in grades to graduate with honors, well enough at golf and poker to hold my own at the country club, and I learned the social graces of bridge and dancing. I usually felt more at home with adults than with my peers. Like all fast-growing teenagers, I was shy and awkward. Scouting gave me an outlet, a chance to excel, and the opportunity of being a leader of other kids even when I was young.

By college I began developing my own distinctive religious and political path. I went to a military school, Texas A&M, set to become the nuclear physicist my parents believed would be a good career for me. My father had gone to A&M, which had trained him in petroleum engineering and in the arts of war. He had been a lieutenant colonel in the Battle of the Bulge in World War II. Naturally, he thought A&M would be perfect for me. After high school, I worked in the oil fields for my father's company for six months and then enrolled at A&M. All I knew about the school was that it had good sports teams and school spirit, and the students wore ROTC uniforms all the time. What I did not know was that A&M, in the practical everyday life within the Corps of Cadets, was anti-intellectual, inhumane, and antireligious. Nor did I know that I wasn't meant to be a nuclear physicist. My personal confrontations at A&M were to change me profoundly and to set my life on a different course. . . .

When the year came to an end, I decided to leave A&M and go to its archrival and infinitely better school, the University of Texas. There I experienced a virtual explosion of intellectual and emotional growth. I simultaneously grew in four different dimensions – religion, politics, love, and work. When I moved to the University of Texas, I moved into the Christian Faith and Life Community, a Protestant reform group that studied modern theologians like Tillich and Bultman and created its own worship services. It was an intentional community with covenants, reflection, and a sense of purpose. It sought to reform individuals, through them the local Protestant churches, and through these churches, the entire culture. There was really no place else in conservative Texas quite like it. More than anything else it taught me at what an intense level a community of people could live together and what a deep commitment such a group of people could sustain.

Supplementing the Christian Faith and Life Community was the student YMCA with which I had begun my journey to consciousness at Texas A&M. The YMCA/YWCA at the University of Texas was the meeting place and institutional sponsor of the sit-in and stand-in movement for racial integration. It was the subject of a laudatory newspaper column by Eleanor Roosevelt in the national press and a front-page series of "hatchet-jobs" in the *Dallas Morning News*. The student YMCA/YWCA served as a local support group translating general Christianity into social action, and the national student YMCA made me a national officer and sent me to Africa, Europe, the Soviet Union, and Japan. These exposures to foreign cultures and subsequent culture shock widened my understanding of the world. They made me fundamentally different from Americans who have not traveled abroad or those who have gone overseas only as casual tourists. The YMCA helped to make me a world citizen.

Growing up in Texas in the 1950s and 1960s, I learned to hold controversial social and political positions against intense opposition and even hatred. Within a few months of moving to the University of Texas, I joined the civil rights movement. At our first organizing meeting, a pipe bomb was set off in an attempt to end our movement. But it failed, only blowing a few bricks off the building. Gangs of high school toughs would ride by in cars shouting threats while we stood in demonstrations outside movie theaters we were trying to integrate. But I was never harmed or even arrested in the civil rights movement.

Texas was a state in which the few hundred "liberals" all knew each other. Certainly the hundred of us who participated in the civil rights demonstrations at movie theaters knew one another. There were not many black students at the university in those days, but blacks and liberal whites banded together to break the entrenched segregation patterns. And we succeeded.

Moving from protest movements to politics was easy. I became president of the local student YMCA/YWCA, a national YMCA officer, and a U.S. delegate to international meetings. I began a new student political party and helped elect a liberal-dominated student government. I became a part of the National Student Association, played a role electing others to national office, and was an effective delegate to international student meetings.

I switched my major from sociology to political science and graduated from the University of Texas with honors. I moved on to graduate school with every prospect of success. I learned to think – not just in the pragmatic calculations required for narrow politics – but also to consider the interplay of forces and ideas. Politics and the study of politics seemed glorious and exciting and I was on the winning side in student politics. It seemed in those years as if students, in cooperation with other progressive forces in society, would succeed in turning the country around. All things were possible. The marching, protests, music, and the voting were moving history. We were winning.

I was no longer an adolescent. I had become a man and I came to know love as an adult. I had dated in high school but mostly by having a regular bridge partner and going to formal dances. While at A&M I began "to fall in love." At the University of Texas I had several romances that lasted about a year each. I learned that I could love and be loved, which was perhaps the most important lesson of my college years. I also learned to take the risks that love requires.

Student Nonviolent Coordinating Committee Founding Statement

SNCC Founding Statement, October 1960, reprinted from Massimo Teodori (ed.) *The New Left: A Documentary History* (Indianapolis: Bobbs-Merrill, 1969), pp. 99–100.

We affirm the philosophical or religious ideal of nonviolence as the foundation of our purpose, the presupposition of our belief, and the manner of our action.

Nonviolence, as it grows from the Judeo-Christian tradition, seeks a social order of justice permeated by love. Integration of human endeavor represents the crucial first step towards such a society.

Through nonviolence, courage displaces fear. Love transcends hate. Acceptance dissipates prejudice; hope ends despair. Faith reconciles doubt. Peace dominates war. Mutual regards cancel enmity. Justice for all overthrows injustice. The redemptive community supersedes immoral social systems.

By appealing to conscience and standing on the moral nature of human existence, nonviolence nurtures the atmosphere in which reconciliation and justice become actual possibilities.

Although each local group in this movement must diligently work out the clear meaning of this statement of purpose, each act or phase of our corporate effort must reflect a genuine spirit of love and good-will.

Charles McDew, "Spiritual and Moral Aspects of the Student Nonviolent Struggle in the South"

First published in *The Activist* 1 (1961), reprinted from Mitchell Cohen and Dennis Hale (eds.) *The New Student Left*, rev. ed. (Boston: Beacon Press, 1966), pp. 51–7.

The Nature of Our Opposition

The system of Southern Tradition is a fabrication of wishful thinking, self-delusion, false values, outmoded beliefs, and pig-headed, deliberate ignorance. White supremacy is the foundation stone of the entire system. Our white supremacists forget that it was a doctrine of racial superiority that set off World War II, which killed more than 10,000,000, and from which many other millions will never recover. No doctrine of racial superiority will hold up in the court of modern world opinion.

I say that the system of Southern Tradition is fabricated upon wishful thinking and self-delusion because our detractors insist on believing that Negroes are satisfied with second-class citizenship and inadequate wages and education and opportunities. They say this even in the face of our demonstrations, our intelligent use of the franchise, and our evident love for democracy.

I say that the system of Southern Tradition is founded on pig-headed deliberate ignorance because they [the white supremacists] legislate their prejudices, prostitute justice – where Negroes and whites are involved – and will not even consider the idea that Negroes share the same quality of humanity which they possess. . . .

In our section half-truth is taken as truth, patronage masquerades as friendship, chauvinism is called democracy, and God is thought of as a Southern white man.

This is the situation – the system which we feel obligated to correct not only because it disadvantages Negroes, but because it blights everything it touches; it stunts the growth of a third of the States of this nation; it prevents realization of the American dream for millions of our citizens; it jeopardizes the good name of America around the world; and it causes the Southern white man to lose his soul – for he says something bad about God.

What is the nature of our opposition? In the words of the Apostle Paul: "We wrestle not against flesh and blood, but against principalities, against powers, against the rulers of the darkness of this world; against spiritual wickedness in high places" (Ephesians 6: 12).

Now this quotation brings us to our next major question:

What is the Nature of Our Fight?

It may be stated in many ways. Dr. Martin Luther King, Jr. . . . calls it "the withdrawal of support from evil." In other terms it is called "seizing the moral initiative," "the use of moral force against immoral force," and "the attempt to create the beloved community" or to "build the city of God." The organization called "The Fellowship of Reconciliation" refers to our process as introducing a redemptive element into an otherwise explosive or "intolerably immoral situation."

At this point I'm reminded that a minister friend told me recently that the "sit-in" dates at least as far back as the times of Christ, for, one day he sat down beside a well in Samaria and when a woman came to draw, he said: "Please give me a drink of water" and this simple request shook both her life and her society to the very foundations. "How is it that you, being a Jew, and a man, say to me, who am a Samaritan and a woman, 'Give me a drink.' Don't you know that Jews and Samaritans have no dealings?" And Jesus saw immediately the evil of this situation, and its potential explosiveness, and spoke these redeeming words: "If you knew the gift of God you could not feel this way." And what is this "gift of God?" The gift of eyes that see life as others see it. The gift of ears that hear the hidden rebuffs as the underprivileged hear it. The gift of heart that feels another's care. "If you knew the gift of God, you'd know that there is enough water in this well for both of us, and that God blesses us with blessings which would enrich us both if we shared them."

Jesus asked for a drink of water, and all the old antagonisms of the centuries came to the surface. Negro students in our South can walk into a drug store and ask for a cup of coffee – and the entire fabric of our Southern civilization trembles to the foundations.

Now, it is axiomatic that you cannot draw a man to you by striking him a blow. Neither a left uppercut nor a right cross nor even a haymaker can win a man's love or admiration or cooperation. On the other hand, we go along with the Book when it says, "A soft answer turneth away wrath; but grievous words stir up anger." The story is told of an officer who once faced a personal enemy who, in an impulsive moment of anger, spat in his face.... But instead of striking back, the officer calmly reached into his pocket for his handkerchief, wiped off the spittle, and said, "If I could wipe your blood off of my soul as easily as I can wipe your spit off my face, I'd kill you." The angry one repented and the two became fast friends. "A soft answer," indeed, "turneth away wrath," but a blow by the officer would have made them enemies for life.

Our fight is not against persons, but persons are involved in the promotion and perpetuation of the system we would revise. The present system is an affront to the Christian doctrine of man – or perhaps I should say "the Judeo-Christian doctrine of man." The affirmations that "God created man in his own image" as Genesis 1: 27 says, and "The Lord God formed man of the dust of the earth, and breathed into his nostrils the breath of life; and man became a living soul" as Genesis 2: 7 declares, are foundations of our belief in the dignity and worth of each man and all men. The Southern doctrine of white supremacy calls Genesis a lie, and the man who excludes me from his lunch counter says something bad about God, for he says that God created me unworthy to be with certain others of His creatures in the universal need to fill the stomach with food. The man is saying: "God shouldn't have made you that way. If He'd made you like me I'd let you in." No conscientious Christian can stand idly by and see God demeaned in such a way.

This mention of the dignity of man as conferred by God's creation reminds me of something a minister said at one of Dr. Martin King's meetings last year. This was not the most handsome man you ever saw, so it was very striking to see him stand until everyone was absolutely quiet, and then say in a booming voice: "I want you to know that when God made me, He was at His very best." Audience reaction was tremendous and prolonged. Now, this is just where we students stand! When God made us, He was at His level best. And we want to create a society which will both offer the best and bring out the best in us. We believe that a society that keeps us out of the best schools, hotels, culture centers, the best jobs, housing, hospitals, libraries and recreation places, churches, and organizations is one which does not deserve to live, for it dehumanizes us by such stupid discrimination.

Now let us turn to another facet of our struggle. We are often accused of engaging in a fad – like the hula-hoop craze, says Governor Hollings of South Carolina. But I have seen with my own eyes evidences that the spiritual roots are deep, and that young students are more sincere about the Christian faith than they have ever been before....

It seems that the fell clutch of circumstance closes in upon the Negro family about the time a child learns that he is colored and that there is a certain limit to his freedoms imposed by the color of his skin. The parents' explanations are always a contradiction of precepts learned in church and in democratic family life. The child's idealism is shattered. His natural ambition becomes belligerence. His dream becomes a nightmare. And his budding Christian faith receives a serious jolt. This "killing of the dream," as Lillian Smith calls it, occurs in preadolescence. And by the time he comes to college, the Negro student is in dire need of a faith which he can practice as a part of his growth and his daily adventure. The sit-ins offered the students a chance for the "word to become flesh," as it were. The sit-ins have promoted a challenging philosophy – the philosophy of love overcoming hate, of nonviolence conquering violence, of offering oneself as a sacrifice for a valuable cause. The sit-ins, too, offer adventure and an opportunity to live out the demands of decency and dignity. And who knows but that these same sit-ins may be the means by which the walls of Southern Tradition shall crumble far sooner than most of us had imagined.

The sit-ins have inspired us to build a new image of ourselves in our own minds. And, instead of sitting idly by, taking the leavings excreted by a sick and decadent society, we have seized the initiative, and already the walls have begun to crumble.

The nonviolent approach is designed to leave our opponent a face saving device so that there will be little bitterness when the fight is over.

The nonviolent struggle challenges us to live out the Golden Rule.

It has given us a new perspective and a new purpose – a sense of mission, as it were.

And I can promise you, in the name of the militant Negro students of the South, that we shall not be satisfied until every vestige of racial segregation and discrimination are erased from the face of the earth.

Casey Hayden and Mary King, "Sex and Caste: A Kind of Memo"

First published in *Liberation* 11/2 (April 1966), pp. 35–6; reprinted from Judith Clavir Albert and Stewart Edward Albert (eds.) *The Sixties Papers* (Westport, CT: Praeger, 1984), pp. 133–6.

We've talked a lot, to each other and to some of you, about our own and other women's problems in trying to live in our personal lives and in our work as independent and creative people. In these conversations we've found what seems to be recurrent ideas or themes. Maybe we can look at these things many of us perceive, often as a result of insights learned from the movement:

Sex and Caste

There seem to be many parallels that can be drawn between treatment of Negroes and treatment of women in our society as a whole. But in particular, women we've talked to who work in the movement seem to be caught up in a common-law caste system that operates, sometimes subtly, forcing them to work around or outside hierarchical structures of power which may exclude them. Women seem to be placed in the same position of assumed subordination in personal situations too. It is a caste system which, at its worst, uses and exploits women.

This is complicated by several facts, among them: (1) The caste system is not institutionalized by law (women have the right to vote, to sue for divorce, etc.); (2) Women can't withdraw from the situation (à la nationalism) or overthrow it; (3) There are biological differences (even though those biological differences are usually discussed or accepted without taking present and future technology into account so we probably can't be sure what these differences mean). Many people who are very hip to the implications of the racial caste system, even people in the movement, don't seem to be able to see the sexual caste system and if the question is raised they respond with: "That's the way it's supposed to be. There are biological differences." Or with other statements which recall a white segregationist confronted with integration.

Women and Problems of Work

The caste system perspective dictates the roles assigned to women in the movement, and certainly even more to women outside the movement. Within the movement, questions arise in situations ranging from relationships of women organizers to men in the community, to who cleans the freedom house, to who holds leadership positions, to who does secretarial work, and who acts as a spokesman for groups. Other problems arise between women with varying degrees of awareness of themselves as being as capable as men but held back from full participation, or between women who see themselves as needing more control of their work than other women demand. And there are problems with relationships between white women and black women.

Women and Personal Relations with Men

Having learned from the movement to think radically about the personal worth and abilities of people whose role in society had gone unchallenged before, a lot of women in the movement have begun trying to apply those lessons to their own relations with men. Each of us probably has her own story of the various results, and of the internal struggle occasioned by trying to break out of very deeply learned fears, needs, and self-perceptions, and of what happens when we try to replace them with concepts of people and freedom learned from the movement and organizing.

Institutions

Nearly everyone has real questions about those institutions which shape perspectives on men and women: marriage, child rearing patterns, women's (and men's) magazines, etc. People are beginning to think about and even to experiment with new forms in these areas.

Men's Reactions to the Questions Raised Here

A very few men seem to feel, when they hear conversations involving these problems, that they have a right to be present and participate in them, since they are so deeply involved. At the same time, very few men can respond non-defensively, since the whole idea is either beyond their comprehension or threatens and exposes them. The usual response is laughter. That inability to see the whole issue as serious, as the strait-jacketing of both sexes, and as societally determined, often shapes our own response so that we learn to think in their terms about ourselves and to feel silly rather than trust our inner feelings. The problems we're listing here, and what others have said about them, are therefore largely drawn from conversations among women only – and that difficulty in establishing dialogue with men is a recurring theme among people we've talked to.

Lack of Community for Discussion

... The reason we want to try to open up dialogue is mostly subjective. Working in the movement often intensifies personal problems, especially if we start trying to apply things we're learning there to our personal lives. Perhaps we can start to talk with each other more openly than in the past and create a community of support for each other so we can deal with ourselves and others with integrity and can therefore keep working.

Objectively, the chances seem nil that we could start a movement based on anything as distant to general American thought as a sex-caste system. Therefore, most of us will probably want to work full time on problems such as war, poverty, race. The very fact that the country can't face, much less deal with, the questions we're raising means that the movement is one place to look for some relief. Real efforts at dialogue within the movement and with whatever liberal groups, community women, or students might listen are justified. That is, all the problems between men and women and all the problems of women functioning in society as equal human beings are among the most basic that people face. We've talked in the movement about trying to build a society which would see basic human problems (which are now seen as private troubles) as public problems and would try to shape institutions to meet human needs rather than shaping people to meet the needs of those with power. To raise questions like those above illustrates very directly that society hasn't dealt with some of its deepest problems and opens discussion of why that is so. (In one sense, it is a radicalizing question that can take people beyond legalistic solutions into areas of personal and institutional change.) The second objective reason we'd like to see discussion begin is that we've learned a great deal in the movement and perhaps this is one area where a determined attempt to apply ideas we've learned there can produce some new alternatives.

Suggested Reading

Alexander Bloom and Wini Breines (eds.) *Takin' it to the Streets: A Sixties Reader,* New York: Oxford University Press, 1995. A broad-gauged collection of primary source documents on the social movements of the 1960s.

Wini Breines, *Community and Organization in the New Left, 1962–1968: The Great Refusal,* New York: Praeger, 1982. An intriguing analysis of the tension between creating a powerful movement and building a "beloved community" of people living out their ideals.

Todd Gitlin, *The Sixties: Years of Hope, Days of Rage,* rev. ed., New York: Bantam Books, 1993. Gitlin, a sixties activist who became a leading sociologist, provides a detailed history that stresses the fragmentation and decline of 1960s radicalism.

Jim Miller, *"Democracy is in the Streets": From Port Huron to the Siege of Chicago,* New York: Simon&Schuster, 1987. A thoughtful interpretation of Students for a Democratic Society and its concept of participatory democracy.

Doug Rossinow, *The Politics of Authenticity: Liberalism, Christianity and the New Left in America*, New York: Columbia University Press, 1998. Rossinow looks at the origins of student radicalism through a detailed study of activism around the University of Texas. He finds a strong religious component among early New Leftists.

The Michigan State University Library's American Radicalism collection has a significant number of documents of 1960s radicalism from Students for a Democratic Society, the Black Panther Party and other groups on its website at:

    http://www.lib.msu.edu/coll/main/spec_col/radicalism/index.html

(Note that URLs on the Web are often subject to change. This link was valid in February 2000.)

9

New Social Movements: The Case of AIDS Activism

June 27–8, 1969 Late on Friday night, police raid a gay bar, the Stonewall Inn, in New York's Greenwich Village. The customers resist and riots continue in the area on successive nights. "Stonewall" becomes a symbol of the origins of the modern movement for gay liberation.

July 1969 Gay Liberation Front forms in New York. The group undertakes actions to bring visibility to demands for gay rights.

October 1973 National Gay Task Force (later renamed National Gay and Lesbian Task Force) formed "to bring gay liberation into the mainstream of American civil rights."

December 1973 American Psychiatric Association removes homosexuality from its list of psychiatric disorders.

October 14, 1979 National March on Washington for Lesbian and Gay Rights draws an estimated 75,000.

1981–2 A new disease associated with unprotected male homosexual activity is diagnosed and labeled as Gay Related Immunodeficiency Disease (GRID); the name is soon changed to Acquired Immune Deficiency Syndrome (AIDS).

1981–9 During President Ronald Reagan's eight years in office, he makes no public mention of the AIDS crisis.

1982–95 Steady growth in deaths in US from AIDS, reaching 26,355 by 1989 and 48,250 in 1995.

1983 Reverend Jerry Falwell proclaims that AIDS is "the judgment of God" for the "perverted lifestyle" of homosexuals.

March 10, 1987 New York gay activists, angered by government inaction and public bigotry, form Aids Coalition to Unleash Power (ACT UP). Using the slogan "Silence = Death," ACT UP stages dramatic protests against the stigmatization of people with AIDS and the repression of gay sexuality.

1992 Bill Clinton elected President. With openly gay advisers, Clinton pledges during his campaign to end the ban on homosexuals serving in the armed forces. After his election and strong objections from military officers and politicians, he retreats to a policy of "Don't ask, don't tell." **Mid-1990s** Newly available drugs prolong the lives of people with AIDS and death rates in the US begin to fall. The drugs are very expensive, and deaths from AIDS become increasingly concentrated among the poor and racial minorities.

Introduction to the Article

Sometimes, we can find a social movement's "birthday." The early hours of Saturday, June 28, 1969, when hundreds of gay men resisted a police raid on the Stonewall Inn, a gay bar in New York's Greenwich Village, usually mark the start of the contemporary struggle for equal rights for, and transformed attitudes about, gay men and lesbians. Until then, homosexual groups had pursued goals such as ending police harassment and employment discrimination through quiet, non-confrontational means. After Stonewall, the movement became more radical as it grew, demanding more than mere toleration and adopting militant tactics for change.

By the 1980s, however, gay liberation was being put on the defensive. In the first place, certain religious right-wingers had branded homosexuality as a menace and had launched counter-campaigns against equal rights or public acceptance. Moreover, a new disease, Acquired Immune Deficiency Syndrome, first identified in 1982, was bringing disease and death to gay men. Gay men were not, though, the only people with AIDS. (By the late 1990s other at-risk groups constituted the majority of newly-diagnosed people with AIDS. In much of the rest of the world, heterosexual transmission was the main mechanism by which the disease spread.) However, the syndrome was first diagnosed among gay men, and the impact on gays was disproportionately severe.

The conservative Reagan administration, medical professionals, and others responded to the AIDS crisis hesitantly and ungenerously. Gays, furious that mainstream institutions had failed to combat the disease aggressively and had often stigmatized people with AIDS and blamed them for their illness, came together to form the group ACT UP in 1987. Joshua Gamson provides an account of the organization's San Francisco group both as a researcher and as an activist in the group. His participation provided him with insights which would probably be unavailable to a scholar studying the movement from the outside.

ACT UP in many respects fits the pattern of what sociologists call new social movements. Gamson lists their characteristics: "a (broadly) middle-class membership and a mix of instrumental, expressive, and identity-oriented activities ... Rather than exclusively orienting itself towards material distribution, ACT UP uses and targets cultural resources as well." The new movements depart from older ones, which stressed demands for equal rights (typically in the nineteenth century) or (in the twentieth) a more equal distribution of wealth, income, and political power. With their goal of acceptance and honor for diverse identities, new social movements call into question older goals of inclusion for dispossessed groups. Radical gay and lesbian activists, for example, reject the sexual norms of the dominant heterosexual culture and seek validation of alternative values. Participants in new social movements often also suggest that older styles of political action are inadequate. In a society of images and appearances, self-presentation becomes a way of "doing" radical politics; new social movements often find innovative ways to dramatize their views.

Gamson points out three issues that ACT UP was facing in its effort to challenge AIDS complacency and homophobia. First, who was the audience for their theatrics? Second, how could the group combine the need to combat the anti-gay prejudice behind the mainstream response to the disease with its desire to be inclusive of all people with AIDS? And finally, how could ACT UP emphasize that AIDS was a gay issue without submerging the politics of AIDS into the broader range of gay activism? At the heart of these problems, he maintains, was the fact that the movement faced both identifiable and invisible enemies. Drawing on the highly influential ideas of the French theorist Michel Foucault, Gamson notes that power acts to categorize the "abnormal" and differentiate them from the "norm." In doing so, power itself "becomes increasingly abstracted and invisible, while the dominated ... becomes the focus of attention."

For both scholars and activists, Gamson's account raises intriguing questions. On some levels, ACT UP functioned much as earlier movements had, demanding an end to discrimination, insisting that more resources needed to be channeled to helping people with AIDS. In other ways, though, the group's emphasis on identity and pride stressed difference more than inclusion. This marks a change. How much do new social movements have in common with their predecessors? In what ways are they truly new? What are the possibilities of alliances and coalitions among varied social movements, each attempting to assert a distinct identity? And how do the broad divisions of race and class that still remain important in American society affect the strategies, successes, and failures of social movements, new and old?

Silence, Death, and the Invisible Enemy

Josh Gamson

Shea Stadium is packed. As the Mets play the Astros, New York AIDS activists scream and shout along with the rest of the fans. Their cheers are somewhat unusual: "ACT UP! Fight back! Fight AIDS!" Their banners, unfurled in front of the three sections they have bought out, shout plays on baseball themes: "No glove, no love," "Don't balk at safer sex," "AIDS is not a ball game." The electronic billboard flashes some of their messages as well. The action gets wide coverage the following day. Later, in a *Newsweek* (1988a) article on the activist group ACT UP, a baseball fan complains, "AIDS is a fearful topic. This is totally inappropriate."

The fan is right, on both counts; in fact, I would suggest, he inadvertently sums up the point of the action. He also calls attention to the oddities: Why fight AIDS at a baseball game? Why mix fear and Americana? Who or what is the target here?

Susan Sontag and others have noted that the AIDS epidemic fits quite smoothly into a history of understanding disease through the "usual script" of the plague metaphor: originating from "outside," plagues are visitations on "them," punishments of both individuals and groups, they become stand-ins for deep fears and tools for bringing judgments about social crises. "AIDS," Sontag (1988: 89) suggests, "is understood in a premodern way."

Yet the plague of AIDS has brought with it understandings and actions that are hardly "premodern": civil disobedience at the Food and Drug Administration protesting the sluggish drug approval process, guerrilla theater and "die-ins," infiltrations of political events culminating in the unfurling of banners protesting government inaction, media-geared "zaps," illegal drug research and sales, pickets and rallies. AIDS has given rise to a social movement. This is not, in fact, part of the usual script.

Perhaps, then, AIDS can be understood as part of a different script as well. Much has been written in the past decade about "new social movements" (NSMs); perhaps AIDS activism follows an outline parti-

Josh Gamson, "Silence, Death, and the Invisible Enemy: AIDS Activism and Social Movement 'Newness'," © 1989 by The Society for the Study of Social Problems. Reprinted from *Social Problems* 36/4 (October 1989), pp. 351–67, by permission.

cular to contemporary movements. This classification presents its own difficulties: social movements literature has a hard time clarifying exactly what is "new" about contemporary social movements and can, through its fuzziness, easily accommodate yet another social movement without shedding new light.

In this paper, I examine AIDS activism – by which I mean an organized "street" response to the epidemic – through the activities of ACT UP (the AIDS Coalition to Unleash Power), its most widespread and publicly visible direct-action group.

ACT UP, which began in New York, has chapters in Chicago, Boston, Atlanta, Los Angeles, Houston, Rochester, Madison, Nashville, San Francisco, and a number of other cities. The groups are loosely federated under the umbrella of the AIDS Coalition to Network, Organize and Win (ACT NOW). New York is by far the largest ACT UP, with weekly meeting attendance in the hundreds and membership estimated at nearly 3,000, while the others are smaller. San Francisco, with a membership of over 700, averages 50 people at general meetings. My comparisons between ACT UP in San Francisco and chapters in New York and other cities are based on a national conference in Washington, DC, internal publications, informal discussion and interviews, and newspaper reports.

Using data from six months of participant-observation research (September 1988 through February 1989) in San Francisco's ACT UP, coupled with local and national internal documents and newspaper writings about the group, I develop an analysis intended both to sharpen focus on the struggle over the meaning of AIDS and to challenge some of the hazy understandings of social movement newness. The analysis here treats ACT UP not as an exemplar but rather as an anomaly, asking what unique conditions constitute the case and how the case can aid in a reconstruction of existing theory. Micro- and macro-level analyses are linked through seeking out an "explanation for uniqueness" such that "we are compelled to move into the realm of the 'macro' that shapes the 'micro' that we observe in face-to-face interaction" (Burawoy 1989: 7).

In the first part of the paper I briefly review approaches to contemporary social movements, locating ACT UP within this literature. I then turn to ACT UP's activities and internal obstacles, looking at their response to the plague script, the alternative scripts they propose and their strategies for doing so, and the difficulties they face in this process. I argue that asking "who is the enemy?" provides a fruitful direction for making sense of these dynamics because ACT UP members often have trouble finding their "enemies." The paper continues with an examination of why this may be so, and what light it may shed on contemporary movements. Borrowing from Michel Foucault (1979), I turn to an examination of the forms of domination to which ACT UP members respond. I argue that, in addition to visible targets such as government agencies and drug companies, much of what ACT UP is fighting is abstract, disembodied, invisible: control through the creation of abnormality. Power is maintained less through direct force or institutionalized oppression and more through the delineation of the "normal" and the exclusion of the "abnormal." I suggest that this "normalizing" process, taking prominence in a gradual historical shift, is increasingly unlocked from state oppression in recent decades. State figures and institutions – though certainly still deeply involved in this domination – are now less apt to contribute to the production and dissemination of labels, making the process itself, abstracted, the focus of protest. The paper then traces how responses to normalization play themselves out in ACT UP activities: activists use the labels to dispute the labels, use their abnormality and expressions of gay identity to challenge the process by which this identity was and is defined. Finally, I suggest directions this framework provides for analyzing contemporary movements.

The Theoretical Context: What's New?

Among the shifts provoked by the rise of massive social movements in the 1960s and 1970s was a rupture in theorizing about social movements. Until that time, the dominant paradigm of collective behavior theory treated noninstitutional movements as essentially nonrational or irrational responses by alienated individuals to social strain and breakdown (for example, Smelser 1963). Many 1960s activists did not fit the mold. Neither anomic nor underprivileged nor responding to crises with beliefs "akin to magical beliefs" (Smelser 1963: 8), they in fact came together largely from the middle class, with concrete goals and rational calculations of strategies. The predictions of classical social movement theory regarding who made up social movements and how they operated had broken down (see Cohen 1985; McAdam 1982).

In the last two decades, attempts to retheorize social movements have moved in two major directions. North American resource mobilization theory accounts for large scale mobilizations by emphasizing rational calculations by actors, focusing on the varying constraints and opportunities in which they operate and the varying resources upon which they draw (see McCarthy and Zald 1977; Oberschall 1973; Tilly 1978; and Jenkins 1981). This paradigm, directly challenging the assumptions of collective behavior theory, insists on the rationality of collective action. European theorists, on the other hand, have argued that rational-actor models are inappropriately applied to new groups seeking identity and autonomy. The movements of the 1960s and their apparent descendants

– the peace movement, for example, or feminist, ecological, or local-autonomy movements – have been taken together by theorists as "new" phenomena to be accounted for; it is their nonrational focus on identity and expression that these theories emphasize as distinctive. They attempt to outline the characteristics shared by contemporary movements and to discern the structural shifts that might account for new dimensions of activity (see Kitschelt 1985; Cohen 1985; Eder 1985; Habermas 1981; Offe 1985; and Touraine 1985).

With some exceptions (see, for example, Doug McAdam's 1982 study of black insurgency), American theory, with its insistence on instrumental rationality, tends to pass over these distinctive characteristics – feminist attention to "consciousness," for example, and black and gay "pride" – to which European theories of "new social movements" (NSMs) direct attention. The European literature, then, in that it attempts to explain these apparently new characteristics found also in AIDS activism, provides the stronger conceptual tools with which to approach ACT UP. Yet what is actually "new" according to European NSM theory is both disputed and unclear. Most agree that a middle-class social base is distinctive (see Eder 1985 and Kreisi 1989); indeed, the fact that NSMs are *not* working-class movements focused primarily on economic distribution seems to be a characteristic on which there is clarity and agreement. From here, the range of characteristics expands and abstracts; NSMs claim "the sphere of 'political action within civil society' as [their] space" (Offe 1985: 832); they use different tactics from their predecessors (Offe 1985); their conflicts concern not "problems of distribution" but "the grammar of forms of life," arising in "areas of cultural reproduction, social integration and socialization" (Habermas 1981: 33); they "manifest a form of middle-class protest which oscillates from moral crusade to political pressure group to social movement" (Eder 1985: 879); they are "both culturally oriented and involved in structural conflicts" (Touraine 1985: 766), involve a "self-limiting radicalism" that "abandons revolutionary dreams in favor of the idea of structural reform, along with a defense of civil society that does not seek to abolish the autonomous functioning of political and economic systems" (Cohen 1985: 664).

Common to this list is a recognition that the field of operation has shifted, broadly put, to "civil society" and away from the state; that culture has become more of a focal point of activity (through "lifestyle" and "identity" movements, for example); and that this shift has to do with broad changes in the "societal type" to which movements respond and in which they act. Common to the list is also an unclear answer to the question of how new the shift really is; as Jean Cohen (1985: 665) points out, the theme of defending civil society does not in itself imply something new – the question "is whether the theme has been connected to new identities, forms of organization, and scenarios of conflict." New social movement theorists – even those like Touraine and Cohen who address these questions directly – seem to be unclear on what these shifts and changes really are: What exactly is the "cultural field" of "civil society" and what do these movements actually do there? What is it that is different about contemporary society that accounts for the characteristics of new social movements? When and how did these changes take place?

ACT UP as a New Social Movement

ACT UP provides an opportunity both to examine some of these issues concretely and to offer new hypotheses. The AIDS activist movement appears to share the most basic characteristics of "new social movements": a (broadly) middle-class membership and a mix of instrumental, expressive, and identity-oriented activities. Rather than exclusively orienting itself towards material distribution, ACT UP uses and targets cultural resources as well. What, this examination asks, does ACT UP do on the cultural terrain? What light does their activity shed on the question of "newness"? How can a study of this group contribute to an understanding of shifts in the nature of social movements and in the nature of the social world in which they operate?

The answer begins with the group's overall profile. ACT UP/San Francisco grew out of the 1987 San Francisco AIDS Action Pledge, becoming ACT UP in the fall of that year after New York's ACT UP began to gain recognition. In addition to planned and spontaneous actions, the group meets weekly in a church in the predominantly gay Castro neighborhood. ACT UP/San Francisco is made up almost exclusively of white gay men and lesbians, mostly in their 20s and 30s. The core membership – an informal group of about 25 activists – draws from both established activists (gay rights, Central American politics, etc.) and those newly politicized by AIDS.[1] Some, but by no means all, of ACT UP's membership has either tested positive for HIV antibodies or been diagnosed with AIDS. As one member said, "I'm here because I'm angry and I'm tired of seeing my friends die." The membership is typically professional and semi-professional: legal and health care professionals, writers, political organizers, students, artists with day jobs. ACT UP/New York and ACT UPs in other cities exhibit similar profiles (Green 1989).

Self-defined in their flyers and media kits as "a nonpartisan group of diverse individuals united in anger and committed to direct action to end the AIDS crisis" (ACT UP 1988a), ACT UP pushes for greater access to treatments and drugs for AIDS-related diseases; culturally sensitive, widely available, and explicit safe-sex education; and well-funded research that is "publicly accountable to the communities most affected" (ACT UP 1988a). Moreover, the group pushes for the participation of people with AIDS (PWAs) in these activities (ACT UP 1989). The idea here is to change the distribution of resources and decision-making power; the principle guiding actions is strategic, aimed at affecting policy changes. "People have been fighting for social justice in this country for centuries," says one member (September 1988). "We're going to get aerosol pentamidine [a treatment drug for pneumocystis pneumonia] a lot quicker than we're going to get social justice."

ACT UP is also often involved in actions, however, whose primary principle is expressive. They focus inward on "building a unified community" (the gay and lesbian community and, increasingly, a sub-community of PWAs and the HIV- infected), and on the "need to express the anger and rage that is righteous and justified" from the community outward. They organize at times around actions in which AIDS is not the central issue or in which AIDS activism is incorporated into the project of "recreating a movement for gay and lesbian liberation." This orientation towards identity and expression, while not excluding older-style strategic action, is one key characteristic cited by students of post-60s social movements.

Most interestingly, though, one hears and sees in ACT UP a constant reference to theater. ACT UP operates largely by staging events and by carefully constructing and publicizing symbols; it attacks the dominant representations of AIDS and of people with AIDS and makes attempts to replace them with alternative representations. At times, ACT UP attacks the representations alone; at times the attack is combined with a direct one on cultural producers and the process of AIDS-image production.

Another action principle weaves through ACT UP. As *Newsweek* (1988a) puts it, ACT UP has often "deliberately trespassed the bounds of good taste": throwing condoms, necking in public places, speaking explicitly and positively about anal sex, "camping it up" for the television cameras. This trespassing or boundary-crossing – and we can include in it the infiltration of public and private spaces (the Republican national convention, for example, where activists posing as participants unfurled banners) – both uses and strikes at the cultural field as well. In this case, rather than reacting to images of AIDS, activists use a more general tactic of disturbing "good taste" – and, in a point *Newsweek* quite characteristically misses, calling attention to the connection between cultural definitions and responses to AIDS. Boundary-crossing, along with theatrical and symbolic actions, makes clear that ACT UP operates largely on the cultural field where theorists situate new social movements.[2] It also suggests that an examination of the specific patterns of culturally oriented actions may be especially revealing. By focusing on the cultural activities of AIDS activists as a key *distinctive* element, I by no means want to suggest that this activism is primarily cultural. In fact, treatment issues, needle-exchange programs, and access to health care, for instance, are all common subjects of action. Pursuing this examination via ACT UP's peculiarities, I hope to generate possibilities for grounding and developing social movement theory.

ACT UP's Internal Obstacles

The examination turns, then, to ACT UP's distinctive characteristics. ACT UP's strong cultural orientation has already been noted. In addition, buried in its various strategies are three fundamental confusions. First, ACT UP's orientation towards theatrics suggests a clear delineation of performer from audience, yet actions are often planned by ACT UP members without an articulation of whom they're meant to influence. If one wants to affect an audience – for example, by invoking a symbol whose meaning is taken for granted and then giving it a different meaning – one clearly needs a conception of who that audience is. In ACT UP planning meetings, there is often an underlying confusion of audiences, and more often the question of audience is simply ignored. When activists in New York infiltrated a Republican women's cocktail party and later unfurled banners ("Lesbians for Bush," read one), the response of the cocktail partiers, a defensive singing of "God Bless America" (reported in "Workshop on Creative Actions," ACT NOW Conference, Washington, DC, October 8, 1988), was important not for what it showed about the Republicans' AIDS consciousness, which came as no surprise. Instead, it was important for what it showed the activists about their own power. They were, in effect, their own audience, performing for themselves and making others perform for them. In "brainstorms" for new actions, there is almost never a mention of audience, and action ideas with different audiences proliferate. ACT UP protested Dukakis, for example, with no media coverage, Dukakis nowhere in sight, and no one to witness the protest but passing cars (San Francisco, September 30, 1988). In the meetings I observed, I commonly heard suggestions for actions that bypassed any actual event, heading straight for the at-home audience through "photo opportunities," mixed in with suggestions for actions that almost no one would see. Much of this confusion is exacerbated by an openness of exchange and decentralized decision making born of ACT UP's democratic structure (in San Francisco, decisions are made consensually). The loose organizational structure acts against focussed planning and action. I argue, however, that the roots are deeper.

A second point of confusion is that, while ACT UP professes to be inclusive, and ideas are often brought up that target non-gay aspects of AIDS (issues of concern to intravenous drug-users, for example, or access to health care for those who cannot afford it), there are few signs that ACT UP in fact succeeds at including or actively pursues non-gay members. This does not mean that the membership is exclusively gay men; in fact, a good portion of the activists are women. The formation of coalitions is sometimes brought up as a good idea – "we need to join with others in solidarity around common suffering and common enemies," said the key-note speaker at the ACT NOW conference in October 1988 – but generally not effected. Cooperative actions with other groups generate little excitement in San Francisco meetings. Actions are aimed mainly at targets with particular relevance to lesbians and gays; there are few black or Hispanic members, gay or straight. Despite the goal of inclusiveness, ACT UP continues to draw from and recreate the white, middle-class gay and lesbian community.

A third and related problem is perhaps even more fundamental: AIDS politics and gay politics stand in tension, simultaneously associated and dissociated. ACT UP is an AIDS activist organization built and run by gay people. Historically, this is neither surprising nor problematic; among the populations first hit hardest by AIDS, gay people were alone in having an already established tradition and network of political and self-help organizations. Still, this tradition has meant that "AIDS groups have found it very difficult to establish themselves as non-gay, even where they have deliberately presented themselves as such" (Altman 1986: 90). AIDS activists find themselves simultaneously attempting to dispel the notion that AIDS is a gay disease (which it is not) while, through their activity and leadership, treating AIDS as a gay problem (which, among other things, it is).

While this dilemma is in part due to the course the disease itself took, how it plays itself out in ACT UP is instructive. For some, particularly those members who are not newly politicized, ACT UP *is* gay politics, pure and simple, a movement continuous with earlier activism. They emphasize the need for "sex positive" safe-sex education, for example, linking AIDS politics to the sexual liberation of earlier gay politics. The main organizer of a November 1988 election night rally in San Francisco's Castro district for the gay community to "Stand Out and Shout" about results envisioned it as a return to the good old days of gay celebration. In planning speakers for the rally, he and others quickly generated a long list of possibles – from the gay political community. Here, AIDS issues often get buried.

For others, it's important to maintain some separation, albeit a blurry one, between the two sets of issues. In New York, for example, when a newspaper calls ACT UP a "gay organization," ACT UP's media committee sends out a "standard letter" correcting the error ("Media Workshop" at ACT NOW Conference in Washington, DC, October 8, 1988). The ACT UP agenda, when the balance is towards distinctive AIDS politics, often focuses more narrowly on prevention and treatment issues as in, for example, a San Francisco proposal for an "AIDS treatment advocacy project" which argued that "whether it is an entire family with AIDS in Harlem or an HIV+ gay man in San Francisco, treatment is ultimately the issue they are most concerned with" (ACT UP 1988b: 1). More commonly, though, ACT UP actions don't fall on one side or the other, but combine an active acceptance of the gay-AIDS connection with an active resistance to that connection.

Visible and Invisible Enemies

Why do these particular confusions occur? They eventually will come to make sense as the particularities of ACT UP's actions are examined. These three confusions within ACT UP, which seem to give its action a somewhat unfocused character, in fact will prove to be core elements of the group's being. Explaining ACT UP's confusions, and those of social movements like it, hinges on the answer to a pivotal question: Who is the enemy? Asking this question of ACT UP, one often finds that the enemies against which their anger and action are directed are clear, familiar, and visible: the state and corporations. At other times, though, the enemy is invisible, abstract, disembodied, ubiquitous: it is the very process of "normalization" through labelling in which everyone except one's own "community" of the de-normalized (and its supporters) is involved. At still other times, intermediate enemies appear, the visible institutors of the less visible process: the media and medical science.

This second enemy forms the basis of my core theoretical claim: that ACT UP is responding to a gradual historical shift towards a form of domination in which power is maintained through a normalizing process in which "the whole indefinite domain of the non-conforming is punishable" (Foucault 1979: 178). Through labelling, or socially organized stigmatization, behaviors and groups are marked as abnormal; in the last two centuries, the norm has largely replaced the threat of violence as a technique of power. As Michel Foucault (1979: 183) argues, individuals are differentiated

> in terms of the following overall rule: that the rule be made to function as a minimum threshold, as an average to be respected or as an optimum

towards which one must move. It...hierarchizes in terms of values the abilities, the level, the "nature" of individuals. It introduces, through this "value-giving" measure, the constraint of a conformity that must be achieved. Lastly, it traces the limit that will define difference in relation to all other differences, the external frontier of the abnormal.

In this process, the dominator becomes increasingly abstracted and invisible, while the dominated, embodied and visible (and, importantly, "marked" through stigmatization), becomes the focus of attention. In effect, people dominate themselves; rather than being confronted with a punishment (physical, material) as a mechanism of control, they confront themselves with the threat of being devalued as abnormal.

These ideas are not incompatible with those put forward by the sociology of deviance and discussions of stigmatization (e.g., Lemert 1967; Goffman 1963), which, of course, call attention to the process of labelling and its impact on the "deviant." However, the various forms of labelling theory have also been challenged by collective action since the 1960s. Those theories, by studying how one "becomes deviant," and the defensive reaction of "deviants" to an identity defined for them – the "management of spoiled identities" (Goffman) and "secondary deviation" as a "means of defense" against the "problems created by the societal reaction to primary deviation" (Lemert 1967: 17) – are ill-equipped to explain the organization of the stigmatized into social movements. As John Kitsuse (1980: 5) argues, the accommodative reactions analyzed by deviance sociology (retreat into a subculture, nervously covering up or denying aberrations) do not "account for, nor do they provide for an understanding of, the phenomenal number of self-proclaimed deviant groups that have visibly and vocally entered the politics" of recent decades. Earlier theories are hard-pressed to account for historical change, and for the assertive building of collective movements based on self-definitions that *reject* the dominant definitions. Foucault, on the other hand, treats pressure for conformity not as a given problem for the "deviant," but as a technique of power with a variable history.

Identity strategies are particularly salient and problematic within this domination form. When power is effected through categorization, identity is often built on the very categories it resists. ACT UP's expressive actions, in this light, are part of a continuing process of actively forging a gay identity while challenging the process through which it is formed *for* gay people at a time when the stigma of disease has been linked with the stigma of deviant sexuality. ACT UP members continue to organize around the "deviant" label, attempting to separate label from stigma.

Identity-oriented actions accept the labels, and symbolic actions disrupt and resignify them.

Identity actions and representational strategies thus stand in awkward relationship: they are increasingly linked in the attack on the normalization process itself. In a simpler identity politics – in the celebration of gay liberation, for example – labels are important tools for self-understanding. That sort of politics involves what John Kitsuse (1980: 9) calls "tertiary deviation," the "confrontation, assessment, and rejection of the negative identity . . . and the transformation of that identity into a positive or viable self-conception." ACT UP members, however, push past this "new deviance" to use stigmas and identity markers as tools against the normalization process. The representation of oneself as abnormal now becomes a tool for disrupting the categorization process; the labels on which group identity is built are used, in a sense, against themselves.

Why, though, is this response to normalizing power coming into its own now? Stigmatization is certainly not new. Foucault, in *Discipline and Punish*, traces a shift in the eighteenth and nineteenth centuries, a shift that takes place primarily in technologies of control: the rise of surveillance techniques and the constitution of the subject by "experts" and scientific discourse. This shift has arguably solidified in this century in Western societies. Yet, while state institutions and actors in the twentieth century certainly have still been involved in the normalization process (as well as in direct repression), they have evidently been less involved in the latter half of this century (or, stated less strongly, less visibly involved). One sees this in the history of civil rights: racism continues while state-sponsored racism and racist policies become less acceptable (see Omi and Winant 1986: 89ff.). Similarly, state definitions of women's "roles" have been liberalized, as the state has withdrawn somewhat from prescribing "normal" female behavior. One sees this as well in the response to AIDS; the federal government, while conservative or split in its policies, has over time become somewhat more liberal in terms of labelling. Public health officials advertise AIDS as an "equal opportunity destroyer"; the Surgeon General warns against treating AIDS as a gay disease and argues in favor of protections against discrimination; the Presidential Commission calls for "the reaffirmation of compassion, justice, and dignity" and indicts, among other things, "a lack of uniform and strong antidiscrimination laws" (Johnson and Murray 1988). State institutions increasingly refuse to "discriminate," that is, to set policies based on social labels. As the state becomes less directly involved in normalization, the process itself necessarily becomes more an independent point of attack by the de-normalized and resisted as a process. It is within this overall historical shift in methods of domination, this study proposes, that ACT UP's social movement activity makes sense.

ACT UP and Normalization

How does this resistance play itself out? What is the link between enemies and actions? Let's begin with the old forms of domination, which are very much still at work. The state is certainly involved in the domination of people with AIDS, as it is in the repression of sexual minorities. For example, the Federal Food and Drug Administration approves drugs and has been sluggish in approving AIDS-related drugs; it is perceived as allowing bureaucracy to get in the way of saving or prolonging lives (*Newsweek* 1988b). In October 1988, ACT NOW organized a conference, teach-in, rally, and day of civil disobedience in Washington, DC, to "seize control of the FDA" (Okie 1988; Connolly and Raine 1988). The Reagan and Bush administrations have been notoriously inattentive to the AIDS epidemic. Reagan first mentioned AIDS publicly at a time when over 36,000 people had already been diagnosed and over 20,000 had died from the disease. While subsequently calling AIDS "America's number one health problem," the administration consistently avoided initiating a coordinated, adequately financed attack on that problem (see Shilts 1988). Reagan and Bush have become common targets of ACT UP "AIDSgate" signs and t-shirts, of "zaps," of posters charging that "the government has blood on its hands," of disruption and protest during campaign speeches. In this case, specific state institutions and actors are targeted, mostly through conventional protest actions and media-geared actions. In these cases, it is quite clear who is responsible for needless death and who is controlling resources, and ACT UP functions as a pressure group to protest and effect policy decisions. Here, AIDS politics and gay politics are quite separable and separated.

Similarly, pharmaceutical companies are manifest enemies; they control the price of treatment drugs and make decisions about whether or not to pursue drug development. That drug company decisions are guided by considerations of profit (Eigo et al. 1988) is a direct and visible instance of oppression and represents an embodied obstacle to the physical survival of people with AIDS. For example, AZT (azidothymidine, the only drug approved at this writing for treatment of AIDS illnesses) cost $13,000 a year in 1987. Again, ACT UP attacks these targets with pressure tactics: boycotting AZT manufacturer Burroughs-Wellcome, zapping that company and others with civil disobedience actions, publicizing government–drug company relations (Eigo et al. 1988). In this example, again, the focus is specifically on issues of relevance to all people with AIDS.

Yet AIDS has also been from the outset a stigma, an illness constructed as a marker of homosexuality, drug abuse, moral deficiencies – stigmas added to those of sexual transmission, terminal disease and, for many, skin color.[3] AIDS has

> come to assume all the features of a traditional morality play: images of cancer and death, of blood and semen, of sex and drugs, of morality and retribution. A whole gallery of folk devils have been introduced – the sex-crazed gay, the dirty drug abuser, the filthy whore, the blood drinking voodoo-driven black – side by side with a gallery of "innocents" – the hemophiliacs, the blood transfusion "victim," the new born child, even the "heterosexual." (Plummer 1988: 45)

Associated most commonly with the image of the male homosexual or bisexual AIDS "victim" or "carrier" who is vaguely responsible through deviant behavior for his own demise, AIDS has been appropriated to medicalize moral stances: promiscuity is medically unsafe while monogamy is safe; being a member of certain social groups is dangerous to one's health while being a member of the "general population" is dangerous only when the un-general contaminate it. As Simon Watney (1987: 126) notes, in AIDS "the categories of health and sickness... meet with those of sex, and the image of homosexuality is reinscribed with connotations of contagion and disease, a subject for medical attention and medical authority."

The construction and reconstruction of boundaries has been, then, an essential aspect of the story of AIDS. The innocent victim is bounded off from the guilty one, pure blood from contaminated, the general population from the AIDS populations, risk groups from those not at risk. Those who span the boundaries arguably become the most threatening: the promiscuous bisexual, the only one who can "account for and absolve the heterosexual majority of any taint of unlawful desire" (Grover 1987: 21) and the prostitute, with her longstanding position as a "vessel" of disease (Grover 1987: 25).

Who achieves this demarcation of boundaries? Who has made AIDS mean what it does? Who is the enemy? Two manifest producers of stigmas appear (in addition to certain public figures who disseminate them): the mass media, on whose television screens and newspaper pages the stigmatized are actually visible, and medical science, which translates the labels into risk-group categories. ACT UP thus challenges the medical establishment, largely by undermining the expertise claimed by them. Activists keep up to date on and publicize underground and foreign treatments (e.g., Eigo et al. 1988), sell illegal treatment drugs publicly, yell the names of known AIDS-illness drugs in front of the

FDA ("Show them we know!" the organizer calls). They wear lab coats and prepare a "guerilla slide show" in which they plan to slip slides saying "He's lying" and "This is voodoo epidemiology" into an audio-visual presentation by a health commissioner.

ACT UP also sets up challenges to the media. An ongoing San Francisco battle had ACT UP shutting down production and members negotiating with producers over the script of an NBC drama, "Midnight Caller." In that script a bisexual man with AIDS purposely infects others and is shot and killed in the end by one of his female partners. It was objected to by ACT UP members as playing on "the great fear of the 'killer queer'" and implying that, as an ACT UP representative put it, "basically it's justifiable to kill a person with AIDS" (Ford 1988). A similar response has been discussed for the San Francisco filming of Randy Shilts's *And the Band Played On*, a controversial history of the American AIDS epidemic. The media are usually treated by ACT UP as allies in the public relations operation of garnering coverage. As one New Yorker put it (October 1988), "the media aren't the enemy, the media are manipulated by the enemy, and we can manipulate them too." When actively involved in the labelling of people with AIDS as murderers, however, the media become the enemies to be fought. This ambivalence makes sense: the media, as the institutional mechanism through which normalization is most effectively disseminated, are both a visible enemy and a necessary link to a more abstract form of domination.

The question of who is behind the generation and acceptance of stigmas, though, for the most part doesn't get asked as activists plan and argue, perhaps because the answer is experienced daily: everyone and no one. No one actually does it and everyone participates in it – your family and your neighbors as well as the blatant bigots far away. It's a process that appears usually as natural, as not-a-process.

Playing with Labels, Crossing the Boundaries

Fighting this largely hidden process calls for different kinds of strategies, mostly in the realm of symbols. Examining the symbolic maneuverings of ACT UP, we can begin to see how fighting the process calls for parti-cular strategies. ACT UP's general strategy is to take a symbol or phrase used to oppress and invert it. For example, ACT UP makes explicit chal-lenges, guided by other AIDS activists and particularly PWAs, on the kind of language used to discuss AIDS. In place of the "AIDS victims" they speak of "people with AIDS" or "people living with AIDS." In place of "risk groups," they insert the category of "risk practices." They talk about blood and semen rather than "bodily fluids," and they chal-lenge the exclusionary use of "general population" (see Grover 1987).

The strategy runs much deeper than speech, however. The visual symbol most widely publicized by American AIDS activists – "SILENCE = DEATH" written in bold white-on-black letters beneath a pink triangle, the Nazi emblem for homosexuals later co-opted by the gay movement – provides a snapshot look at this process. Here, ACT UP takes a symbol used to mark people for death and reclaims it. They reclaim, in fact, control over defining a cause of death; the banner connects gay action to gay survival, on the one hand, and homophobia to death from AIDS, on the other. ACT UP's common death spectacles repeat the inversion. In AIDS commentary death is used in a number of ways (Gilman 1987); it is either a punishment (the image of the withered, guilty victim), an individual tragedy (the image of the lonely, abandoned dying), or a weapon (the image of the irresponsible "killer queer"). A "die in," in which activists draw police-style chalk outlines around each other's "dead" bodies, gives death another meaning by shifting the responsibility: these are deaths likened to murders, victims not of their own "deviance," but shot down by the people controlling the definition and enforcement of normality. You have told us what our deaths mean, their actions say, now we who are actually dying will show you what they mean.

A similar shift of responsibility takes place around the symbol of blood. In popular discussions, blood is talked about in terms of "purity" and a benevolent medical establishment working to keep "bad blood" out of the nation's blood supply. In many ACT UP activities, "blood" is splattered on t-shirts (San Francisco, October 3, 1988) or doctor's uniforms (Washington, DC, October 11, 1988). Members want to shoot it out of squirt guns, blood-balloon it onto buildings, write "test this" with it on walls ("Creative Actions" workshop, Washington, DC, October 8, 1988). Here, on one level, they use the established discourse of purity against its users as an angry weapon: "infected" blood is everywhere. On another level, though, the frame is shifted from purity (in which the blood supply is "victimized") to crime (in which PWAs are victimized). The blood becomes evidence not of infection, but of murder; the activists are blood-splattered victims, as was made explicit in posters originally directed at Mayor Koch in New York and later translated into an indictment of the federal government. "The government has blood on its hands," the sign says, "One AIDS death every half hour." Between the two phrases is the print of a large, bloody hand. In a San Francisco rally against Rep. William Dannemeyer's Proposition 102 (October 3, 1988), which would have required by law that doctors report those infected and those "suspected" of infection, require testing at the request of doctors, employers or insurers, and eliminate confidential testing, ACT UP carried a "Dannemeyer Vampire" puppet. The vampire, a big ugly head on a stick, with black cape and blood pouring from its fangs, was stabbed with a stake later in the action. Here, ACT UP activates another popular code in which blood has meaning – the gore of horror movies – and reframes blood testing as blood sucking. It's not the blood itself that's monstrous, but the vampire who would take it. By changing the meaning of blood, ACT UP activists dispute the "ownership" of blood; more importantly, they call attention to the consequences of the labels of "bad" blood and "purity" and implicate those accepting the labels in the continuation of the AIDS epidemic.

Boundary-crossing, though tactically similar, goes on the offensive while inversions are essentially reactive. The spectacle of infiltration and revelation runs through real and fantasized ACT UP actions. Members speak of putting subversive messages in food or in the pockets of suit jackets, of writing messages on lawns with weed killer, of covering the Washington monument with a giant condom, of replacing (heterosexual) bar ashtrays with condom-shaped ashtrays. They place stickers saying "Touched by a Person with AIDS" in phone booths and stage a mock presidential inauguration through the San Francisco streets during rush hour (January 1989). The idea, as one activist put it, is to "occupy a space that's not supposed to be yours," to "usurp public spaces." San Francisco's underground graffiti group, specializing in "redecorating" targeted spaces, sums up the principle in its humorous acronym, TANTRUM: Take Action Now to Really Upset the Masses.

The ideas that charge brainstorming sessions and the eventual choices for visual and theatrical activity at actions are not arbitrary. The selections are revealing. Spaces and objects are chosen that are especially American (that is, middle American – lawns, cocktail parties, baseball games, patriotic symbols, suits) and presumably "safe" from the twin "threats" of homosexuality and disease. ACT UP here seizes control of symbols that traditionally exclude gay people or render them invisible, and take them over, endowing them with messages about AIDS; they reclaim them, as they do the pink triangle, and *make them mean* differently. In so doing, they attempt to expose the system of domination from which they reclaim meanings and implicate the entire system in the spread of AIDS.

It is important to notice that ACT UP's identity-oriented actions often revolve around boundary-crossing and label disruption. These are strategies for which these mostly white, middle-class gay people are particularly equipped, largely because their stigma is often invisible unlike, for example, the stigmatized person of color. They can draw on a knowledge of mainstream culture born of participation rather than exclusion and, thus, a knowledge of how to disrupt it using its own vocabulary. Here the particular cultural resources of ACT UP's membership become important; they are resources that other movements (and gay people from other races or classes) may not have to the same degree or may not be able to use without considerable risk.

Gay campiness, raunchy safe-sex songs in front of the Department of Health and Human Services, straight-looking men in skirts wearing "Fuck Me Safe" t-shirts (Washington, DC, October 1988), lesbians and gay men staging "kiss-ins," a general outrageousness that "keeps the edge" – these actions simultaneously accept the gay label, build a positive gay identity, challenge the conventional "deviant" label, connect stigmatization to AIDS deaths, and challenge the very process of categorization. This is the power of the pink triangle and "SILENCE = DEATH"; the building of an identity is linked with the resistance of a stigma as the key to stopping the AIDS epidemic. "We are everywhere," says a sign at a DC ACT NOW rally, a sign common at gay political demonstrations, and the noisy expressions of collective anger and identity add up to the same claim. Here, the gay "we" and the AIDS "we" are melded; the destabilizing effect of the suddenly revealed homosexual is joined with the fear that suddenly no space is safe from AIDS. A chant at several San Francisco protests captures the link between asserting an identity and challenging the labels: "We're fags and dykes," the activists chant, "and we're here to stay." Meaning: we are what you say we are, and we're not what you say we are. "We're here," they chant, "We're queer, and we're not going shopping."

What exactly is being challenged in these symbolic inversions? Certainly, in symbols like the Dannemeyer vampire and the bloody hand attributed to the government, the old and consistent enemy, the state, is mixed in; but it isn't exclusive. ACT UP disrupts symbolic representation, heeding the call to "campaign and organize in order to enter the amphitheater of AIDS commentary effectively and unapologetically on our own terms" (Watney 1987: 54). It does so, moreover, often through symbols that are not tied to the state but to "mainstream" American culture. In the case of inversions, AIDS and gay labels are not necessarily linked: any oppressive marker is taken over. In the case of boundary-disruption, AIDS and gay labels are connected; the fear of gay people and the fear of AIDS, now linked in the normalization process, are used to call attention to themselves. In both cases, the *process* of stigmatization, by which symbols become markers of abnormality and the basis for decisions about "correcting" the abnormal, is contested.

Strategies and Obstacles Revisited

The mix of strategies, then, can be seen in terms of the visibility of enemies. More familiar, instrumental pressure-group strategies attempt to change the distribution of resources by attacking those visibly controlling distribution. Identity-forming strategies are particularly crucial and problematic when the struggle is in part against a society rather than a visible oppressor. Label disruption – contained in identity-forming strategies, and the core of symbolic strategies – is a particular operation on the cultural field. It is made necessary by a form of domination that operates through abstractions, through symbols that mark off the normal. (I am not suggesting, of course, that these are discrete types in concrete actions; actions are always mixed exactly because the forms of domination are simultaneous.)

We can also make sense of ACT UP's internal obstacles through this lens. It's not surprising that the question of audience becomes a difficult one to address. First of all, the audience often is the group itself when identity formation becomes a key part of struggle. Yet at the same time, we have seen that identity struggles involve pushing at the very labels on which they're based, and here the audience is the entire society. Actions are thus often founded on a confusion of audiences. More commonly, the question of audience is simply lost because the underlying target of action is the normalization process. While it might be more "rational" for ACT UP activists to try to spell out the particular audience each time they design an action, the struggle in which they are involved makes the particularity of an audience difficult to see. When stigmatization is being protested, the audience is the undifferentiated society – that is, audience and enemy are lumped together, and neither is concretely graspable.

Understanding that ACT UP is attacking this particular form of domination, we can also see why ACT UP is caught between the association and dissociation of AIDS politics from gay politics. Clearly, PWAs and gay people are both subject to the stigmatization process; this process, as it informs and supports responses to AIDS, has become literally lethal for PWAs, gay and non-gay, and dangerous for those labelled as "risk group" members, gay men (and often by an odd extension, lesbians), drug users, prostitutes, blacks, and Hispanics. Socially organized labels that, before AIDS, were used to oppress, are now joined with the label of "AIDS victim." This form of domination is *experienced* by ACT UP members as a continuous one. AIDS is a gay disease because AIDS has been made to attribute viral disease to sexual deviance. Separating AIDS politics from gay politics would be to give up the fight against normalization.

Yet joining the two politics poses the risk of losing the fight in that it confirms the very connection it attempts to dispel. This is a familiar dilemma, as Steve Epstein (1987: 19) points out, and one that is not at all limited to the gay movement: "How do you protest a socially imposed categorization, except by organizing around the category?" Organizing around a resisted label, in that it involves an initial acceptance of the label (and, in identity-oriented movements, a celebration of it), can tend to reify the label. Identity politics thus contain a danger played out here: "If there is perceived to be such a thing as a 'homosexual person,' then it is only a small step to the conclusion that there is such a thing as a 'homosexual disease,' itself the peculiar consequence of the 'homosexual lifestyle'" (Epstein 1987: 48). The familiarity of the dilemma, though, should not obscure its significance. This is neither a dilemma attributable simply to the random course of AIDS nor to mistakes on the part of activists, but to the form of domination to which social movements respond.

In this light, it's not surprising that ACT UP has difficulty including non-gays and forming coalitions. In some ways, ACT UP is driven towards inclusiveness since AIDS is affecting other populations and since the fight includes more broad-based struggles over resources. But, as we have seen, resistance to labelling involves accepting the label but redefining it, taking it over. Group identity actions are bound up with this resistance. This drives ACT UP strongly away from inclusiveness. The difficulty in walking these lines – between confirming and rejecting the connection between gay people and AIDS, between including and excluding non-gays – is built into the struggle against normalization in which ACT UP is involved.

Bodies and Theories

I have argued that ACT UP responds to the script of the AIDS plague by undermining that script, resisting the labelling through which contemporary domination is often effectively achieved. This seems to be missed by most observers of AIDS, who interpret the politics of AIDS on the model of conventional politics. Randy Shilts's 1988 best-seller, for example, ignores the development of grassroots AIDS activism even in its updating epilogue. AIDS serves as a particularly vivid case of disputed scripts in American politics in that the epidemic of disease, as others have noted, has occurred simultaneously with an "epidemic of signification"; AIDS exists "at a point where many entrenched narratives intersect, each with its own problematic and context in which AIDS acquires meaning" (Treichler 1987: 42, 63). ACT UP illustrates this, treating the struggle over the narratives opened and exposed by AIDS as potentially life-saving.

ACT UP also illustrates major effects of an historical shift. If, as I've proposed in drawing on Foucault, domination has gradually come to operate less in the form of state and institutional oppression and more in the form of disembodied and ubiquitous processes, it is hardly surprising that diseased bodies become a focal point of both oppression and resistance. As the enemy becomes increasingly disembodied, the body of the dominated – in this case, primarily the diseased, gay male body – becomes increasingly central. The AIDS epidemic itself fits this process so well as to make it seem almost inevitable: the terror of the disease is that it is an enemy you cannot see, and, like the labels put to use in normalizing power, it is spread invisibly. AIDS activism in part struggles against this disembodied type of power by giving that body – its death, its blood, its sexuality – new, resistant meanings. The plague script meets here with the script of new social movements.

But what does this tell us about theorizing new social movements? First, it calls into question the value of "newness" as a reified category of analysis. In suggesting that the history of enemies and types of domination is central to understanding ACT UP, this study points to a gradual shift rather than a radical break in movement activity; "newness" militates towards a focus on a moment (the 1960s) rather than a history that reaches back into, for example, the eighteenth and nineteenth centuries (as in the historical transformation that Foucault describes). It obscures what may be instructive continuities across time. Secondly, this study points towards ways of distinguishing *among* contemporary movements. To assert that ACT UP exemplifies contemporary movements would clearly be to overstate the case; rather, this analysis demonstrates the insufficiency of analyzing different movements as like phenomena simply because of a shared cultural and identity focus. Operating on the "cultural field" means something more specific than focusing on problems that "deal directly with private life" (Touraine 1985: 779) or even targeting and using narrative and artistic representation. ACT UP's cultural strategies reclaim and resignify oppressive markers. Orienting actions towards identity formation means something more specific than "defend[ing] spaces for the creation of new identities and solidarities" (Cohen 1985: 685). Identity assertions in ACT UP point up boundaries, using the fear of the abnormal against the fearful. These are specific operations that may be shared by other contemporary social movements – those subject to stigmatization, for example, and which are also in a position to "shock" – and not by others. Stigmatization, moreover, may take different forms and give rise to different types of movement activity. Whether in Shea Stadium or at the FDA, discerning the types of enemies to whom movements are responding is a task for analysts of social movements as well as for activists within them.

Notes

1 Unless otherwise noted, quotations and descriptions of actions are drawn from the author's field notes from September 1988 through January 1989 (ACT UP

weekly general meetings; Media Committee weekly meetings and activities, and other committee meetings; ACT NOW AIDS Activism Conference, October 8–11, 1988, Washington, DC; ACT UP/San Francisco actions).

2 By way of comparison, it's important to notice that most AIDS politics does not operate according to this description, but according to a more conventional political model. "Most AIDS politicking," as Dennis Altman (1986: 105) describes it, "has involved the lobbying of federal, state and local governments... [This] has meant dependence upon professional leaders able to talk the language of politicians and bureaucrats."

3 The activist response of black communities to AIDS has, though, differed greatly from that in gay communities, and this merits careful examination not allowed for here. The lag in black and Hispanic activism has been attributed by one observer to a combination of lack of material and political resources (minority PWAs are disproportionately lower class or underclass) and "denial" on the part of minority leadership (because of the dangers posed by feeding racism with the stigma of disease, and because of strong anti-gay sentiments in black and Hispanic cultures). (See Goldstein 1987.)

References

ACT UP/San Francisco, 1988a, "Our goals and demands." Informational flyer.
—— 1988b, "The AIDS treatment advocacy project." Proposal drafted for ACT NOW Conference. September.
—— 1989, "ACT UP PISD caucus." Informational flyer.
Altman, Dennis, 1986, *AIDS in the Mind of America*, Garden City, NY: Anchor Press/Doubleday.
Burawoy, Michael, 1989, "The extended case method." Unpublished manuscript.
Cohen, Jean L., 1985, "Strategy or identity: new theoretical paradigms and contemporary social movements," *Social Research* 52: 663–716.
Connolly, Mike and George Raine, 1988, "50 AIDS activists arrested at FDA," *San Francisco Examiner*, October 11: A1.
Eder, Klaus, 1985, "The 'new social movements': moral crusades, political pressure groups, or social movements?", *Social Research* 52: 869–90.
Eigo, Jim, Mark Harrington, Iris Long, Margaret McCarthy, Stephen Spinella, and Rick Sugden, 1988, "FDA action handbook." Unpublished manuscript prepared for October 11 action at the Food and Drug Administration.
Epstein, Steven, 1987, "Gay politics, ethnic identity: the limits of social constructionism," *Socialist Review* 17: 9–54.
Ford, Dave, 1988, "'Midnight Caller' script provokes gay activists' ire." *San Francisco Sentinel*, October 21: 4–5.
Foucault, Michel, 1979, *Discipline and Punish*, New York: Vintage Books.
Gilman, Sander, 1987, "AIDS and syphilis: the iconography of disease," in Douglas Crimp (ed.) *AIDS: Cultural Analysis/Cultural Criticism*, Cambridge, MA: MIT Press, pp. 87–107.
Goffman, Erving, 1963, *Stigma: Notes on the Management of Spoiled Identity*, Englewood Cliffs, NJ: Prentice-Hall.

Goldstein, Richard, 1987, "AIDS and race," *Village Voice*, March 10: 23–30.

Green, Jesse, 1989, "Shticks and stones," *7 Days*, February 8: 21–6.

Grover, Jan Zita, 1987, "AIDS: keywords," in Douglas Crimp (ed.) *AIDS: Cultural Analysis/Cultural Criticism*, Cambridge, MA: MIT Press, pp. 17–30.

Habermas, Jürgen, 1981, "New social movements," *Telos* 49: 33–7.

Jenkins, J. Craig, 1981, "Sociopolitical movements," in Samuel Long (ed.) *Handbook of Political Behavior*, New York: Plenum Press, pp. 81–153.

Johnson, Diane and John F. Murray, 1988, "AIDS without end," *New York Review of Books*, August 18: 57–63.

Kitschelt, Herbert, 1985, "New social movements in West Germany and the United States," *Political Power and Social Theory* 5: 273–324.

Kitsuse, John I., 1980, "Coming out all over: deviants and the politics of social problems," *Social Problems* 28: 1–13.

Kreisi, Hanspeter, 1989, "New social movements and the new class in the Netherlands," *American Journal of Sociology* 94: 1078–116.

Lemert, Edwin, 1967, *Human Deviance, Social Problems, and Social Control*, Englewood Cliffs, NJ: Prentice-Hall.

McAdam, Doug, 1982, *Political Process and the Development of Black Insurgency 1930–1970*, Chicago: University of Chicago Press.

McCarthy, John and Mayer Zald, 1977, "Resource mobilization and social movements: a partial theory," *American Journal of Sociology* 82: 1212–40.

Newsweek, 1988a, "Acting up to fight AIDS," June 6: 42.

—— 1988b, "The drug-approval dilemma," November 14: 63.

Oberschall, Anthony, 1973, *Social Conflict and Social Movements*, Englewood Cliffs, NJ: Prentice-Hall.

Offe, Claus, 1985, "The new social movements: challenging the boundaries of institutional politics," *Social Research* 52: 817–68.

Okie, Susan, 1988, "AIDS coalition targets FDA for demonstration," *Washington Post*, October 11: A4.

Omi, Michael and Howard Winant, 1986, *Racial Formation in the United States*, New York: Routledge and Kegan Paul.

Plummer, Ken, 1988, "Organizing AIDS," in Peter Aggleton and Hilary Homans (eds.) *Social Aspects of AIDS*, London: Falmer Press.

Shilts, Randy, 1988, *And the Band Played On: Politics, People and the AIDS Epidemic*, New York: Penguin Books.

Smelser, Neil, 1963, *Theory of Collective Behavior*, New York: Free Press.

Sontag, Susan, 1988, "AIDS and its metaphors," *New York Review of Books*, October 27: 89–99.

Tilly, Charles, 1978, *From Mobilization to Revolution*, Reading, MA: Addison-Wesley.

Touraine, Alain, 1985, "An introduction to the study of social movements," *Social Research* 52: 749–87.

Treichler, Paula A., 1987, "AIDS, homophobia, and biomedical discourse: an epidemic of signification," in Douglas Crimp (ed.) *AIDS: Cultural Analysis/Cultural Criticism*, Cambridge, MA: MIT Press, pp. 31–70.

Watney, Simon, 1987, *Policing Desire: Pornography, AIDS and the Media*, Minneapolis, MN: University of Minnesota Press.

Documents

Introduction to the Documents

Joshua Gamson, in the preceding article, provides a participant-observer's perspective on the militant AIDS organization, ACT UP. Document One is a feature story on this organization's first demonstration which appeared in the mainstream *Los Angeles Times*. Like Gamson, Zonana shows ACT UP putting its anger to creative uses. At the same time, "establishment" figures in politics, medicine, and even gay and lesbian organizations expressed discomfort over ACT UP's aggressive tactics. "We are not out to make friends," replied one member. Note that even as the group strived to include women, blacks and Latinos as well as white gay men, the spokespeople cited had high-level professional and managerial backgrounds. "We come from the system we are trying to change," one commented. Where power is diffuse, impersonal, and often invisible, it is not surprising that some people "in" the system would seek radical change.

Document Two presents three vivid graphics. These posters and stickers, which blanketed neighborhoods in New York, San Francisco, and elsewhere, exemplify the dramatic, confrontational style of ACT UP. The "Silence = Death" poster appropriates the pink triangle, originally the emblem gays were forced to wear in Nazi Germany, both to symbolize gay pride and to equate government inaction on AIDS to Hitler's murderous regime. In the second poster, ACT UP invokes gay history, bracketing the Stonewall riot and the AIDS crisis. The third points out that people with AIDS are predominantly gay, black, Latino, and poor, attacking racism and class oppression along with homophobia.

That AIDS is a women's issue is the theme of Document Three. In it, an activist group demands that health-care professionals at an international conference recognize the devastating impact of the disease on the women who contract it, and on those who are caregivers to people with AIDS. Note the argument that AIDS heightens the need for expanded reproductive rights for women around the world.

Finally, Document Four is a challenge to ACT UP's perspective by a well-known gay author. Joshua Gamson's article commented on the uncertain relationship between AIDS activism and gay and lesbian politics. Rist maintains that the two directions are "violently incompatible." He complains that obsessive worry about AIDS has diminished attention to other concerns of gay men, lesbians, and their allies. Implicitly, he asks whether the militance of groups like ACT UP disguised a defensive conservatism that steered gay activists away from broader demands for liberation.

Victor F. Zonana, "New Fronts in the AIDS War"

Reprinted from Victor F. Zonana, "New Fronts in the AIDS War; An Activist Group for the '80s Aims to 'Shame People into Action'," *Los Angeles Times*, April 4, 1989, Part 5, p. 1.

Peter Staley, a $200,000-a-year bond trader, was on his way to work on Wall Street one morning when he ran across a group of boisterous demonstrators. Many carried black signs bearing pink triangles – the symbol of Nazi oppression of homosexuals – and the words "SILENCE = DEATH." Others dramatized their rage at the slow testing of potential drugs for acquired immune deficiency syndrome by "hanging" an effigy of U. S. Food and Drug Administration chief Dr. Frank Young. A handful blocked traffic on lower Broadway and were arrested.

"ACT UP! FIGHT BACK! FIGHT AIDS!" the 250 men and women shouted. "ACT UP! FIGHT BACK! FIGHT AIDS!" "That night, when I turned on the TV, I was blown away by how they were able to transmit their anger to an entire nation," said Staley, diagnosed with an AIDS-related condition in 1985. "I decided that these were my people."

That was two years ago. Staley, 28, since has left Wall Street to become the unpaid fund-raising chairman of the AIDS Coalition to Unleash Power, a burgeoning alliance of elite professionals and street activists "united in anger and committed to direct action to end the AIDS crisis." The group includes art directors who design eye-catching posters, television producers who teach demonstrators to talk in "sound bites" and lawyers who defend group members arrested for acts of civil disobedience. There is even a pharmaceutical chemist, Dr. Iris Long, who critically analyzes research protocols for clinical trials of experimental drugs.

Taking Fight to Streets

At a time when other AIDS groups lobby quietly behind the scenes or tend to dying patients, ACT UP is taking the AIDS battle into the streets. Its members say they are fed up with a system they are convinced is not doing all it can to prevent the carnage. Its activities range from guerrilla theater – tossing condoms at officials who oppose safe-sex education, say, or staging "die-ins" at offices of companies making exorbitant priced drugs – to elaborately choreographed acts of civil disobedience like last week's siege of New York's City Hall, where 200 were arrested.

ACT UP has supporters and detractors among other AIDS activist groups and the public. Critics say its tactics may do as much harm as good by alienating people. "We are not out to make friends," Staley said. "We are out to shame people into action."

As the movement has grown, it has come to encompass women, blacks and Latinos, as well as the gay white men who launched the group two years ago. "We have tapped into the fear, anger and grief surrounding the epidemic, and have turned it into action," said Avram Finkelstein, the art director who designed ACT UP's SILENCE = DEATH logo.

Life-and-Death Stakes

It is as if the passion and activism of the '60s have been updated for the careerist and entrepreneurial decade of the '80s. And it all comes with an intensity of energy that could only be justified by the life-or-death stakes. "I am getting tired of candlelight vigils when, in fact, blow torches may be necessary," said Mark Sikorowski, 37, a managing partner of a New York design firm. Actually, while ACT UP members court arrest, the group eschews violence, preferring nonviolent civil disobedience in the Gandhi tradition. Before last week's demonstration in New York, its biggest action occurred in October, when demonstrators surrounded and shut the FDA headquarters in Rockville, Md., and 187 people were arrested.

Born, appropriately, in New York City, ACT UP now has chapters in two dozen cities and perhaps 5,000 adherents who regularly attend meetings and take part in its actions.

Trying to Change System

"We come from the system that we are trying to change," explained Ken Woodard, an art director for DDB Needham Worldwide who designs advertisements for Volkswagen and Seagrams by day and for ACT UP by night. Though of the system, ACT UP's members work within and outside the system to achieve group goals. ACT UP's initial goal was to increase availability of experimental treatments to people with AIDS and those infected with the virus. More recently, the group has sought better prevention and treatment services from cities like New York.

Woodard's latest creation for ACT UP, which ran as a full- page ad in last week's *Village Voice*, is an arresting portrait of New York Mayor Edward I. Koch in front of a sea of graves. "What does Koch plan to do about AIDS?" the ad asks. "Invest in marble and granite." Koch has drawn the activists' ire for refusing to meet with them in the epidemic's early years and for presiding over a crumbling health-care system in which patients must sometimes wait days for a bed in overcrowded hospitals.

Impact of the Group

While ACT UP has been unable to bring forth a cure for AIDS, whose death toll is approaching 50,000 in this country, some of its chapters around the country have started to have an impact:

- In Los Angeles, the County Board of Supervisors voted to speed creation of a 20-bed AIDS ward at County-USC Medical Center after ACT UP staged a seven-day, around-the-clock vigil at the hospital.
- In San Francisco, producers of the television drama "Midnight Caller" revised a script after ACT UP disrupted filming an episode that activists claimed would incite violence against gays.
- In Boston, the John Hancock Mutual Life Insurance Co. reversed its policy and began paying for treatments of aerosol pentamidine to prevent pneumocystis pneumonia, the biggest killer of AIDS patients, after ACT UP members blocked an entrance at the insurer's headquarters.
- And in New York, a sit-in at the offices of a Japanese pharmaceutical firm ensured that supplies of a potentially promising anti-viral drug sold over the counter in Japan would continue to flow to the U.S. The group's ubiquitous posters and stickers have also forced into the public consciousness an epidemic that most New Yorkers would rather not think about.

Altered AIDS Debate

Perhaps more importantly, ACT UP has helped to alter terms of the national debate on AIDS. "We have refocused the discussion to the rights of people with AIDS to gain access to drugs and decent health care," said Ann Northrop, a former CBS News producer and ACT UP member who trains fellow activists to deliver pithy sound bites.

Indeed, earlier this year, Dr. Anthony S. Fauci, director of the National Institute on Allergies and Infectious Diseases, took the unprecedented step of publicly urging the FDA to ease its restrictions on a pair of drugs that appear to prevent AIDS patients from going blind. "You had Tony Fauci, the nation's top AIDS official, sounding like ACT UP," said Steve Morin, an aide to Rep. Nancy Pelosi (D-San Francisco). The FDA has also unveiled reforms aimed at speeding drugs to critically ill patients, though activists claim the changes are largely cosmetic.

Though mainstream AIDS groups sometimes cringe at ACT UP's confrontational tactics, especially its penchant for personal attacks, they generally support it. "The people with the power to change things must be made to know the extent of the anger and sadness and frustration," said Dr. Mathilde Krim, the founding chair of the American Foundation for AIDS Research. "In a democracy, it is almost a necessity, a duty, to speak out."

"Rocks the Boat"

Urvashi Vaid, communications director of the National Gay and Lesbian Task Force, added: "There's a certain complacency that sets in as the epidemic drones on and on. ACT UP rocks the boat, and that is good. But tactics that confront and provoke can alienate too."

FDA chief Young – who was hanged in effigy at ACT UP's first rally two years ago – has mixed feelings about the group. "On one hand, seeing demonstrators can make people realize some of the deep, deep concerns," he said. "I worry, on the other hand, that scientific decisions won't be made objectively if they are subjected to political pressure. And that might slow things down." Still, he said, he fully understands the demands of AIDS patients and people infected with the human immunodeficiency virus for access to experimental drugs. "I had a melanoma myself. If it ever mestatasizes (spreads), do I want to have access to experimental drugs? Yes."

ACT UP traces its roots to March 10, 1987, when playwright and activist Larry Kramer delivered a fiery speech to about 70 people at the Gay and Lesbian Community Center as part of its monthly speakers series. He had long felt that the gay community's political energy was being sapped by grief and denial. His goal was to shatter denial about the magnitude of the epidemic – with a sledgehammer, if necessary. "Two-thirds of this room could be dead within five years," Kramer thundered. "How many dead brothers have to be piled up in front of your faces in a heap before you learn to fight back and scream and yell and demand and take some responsibility for your own lives?"

ACT UP Graphics

Reproduced from Douglas Crimp, *AIDS Demo Graphics* (Seattle: Bay Press, 1990), pp. 30, 99, 108.

Politicized Gay Men

While Kramer supplied the rhetoric, art director Finkelstein had begun a separate effort to politicize gay men using visual imagery. He and a group of five friends came up with the idea of using the pink triangle, which homosexuals were forced to wear in Hitler's concentration camps, over the words SILENCE = DEATH.

When Finkelstein's group learned about ACT UP, the two groups joined forces. ACT UP printed 1,000 SILENCE = DEATH buttons for $160 and sold them for $1 apiece, clearing an $840 profit, "enough to finance a good-sized demo," Finkelstein noted with satisfaction. "The logo has turned out to be quite marketable," said Staley, the former Wall Street bond trader. "We've put it on T-shirts, sweat shirts and, now, tank tops." Staley has used his financial acumen to build ACT UP into a $300,000 a year group, deriving roughly equal amounts from merchandising, direct mail and benefits and foundation grants.

More New Members

The group is constantly renewing itself with new members. In New York, about 4,000 people are on ACT UP's mailing list and 300 to 400 attend its weekly meetings, where chaos often reigns; ACT UP has no president or board of directors and tries to operate by consensus. Meetings are sometimes punctuated by the announcement that a member has died, reminding people why they are there. "I am HIV-positive," said Gregg Bordowitz, who trains ACT UP members for civil disobedience, "and I feel, very simply, that a war is being played out in my body. One of the ways I can wrest power from that situation is to literally put my body on the line, to be arrested. So let them drag me through the streets, take my fingerprints, put me in court. Because I am not going away."

 OUR GOVERNMENT CONTINUES TO IGNORE THE LIVES, DEATHS AND SUFFERING OF PEOPLE WITH HIV INFECTION BECAUSE THEY ARE GAY, BLACK, HISPANIC OR POOR. BY JULY 4, 1989 OVER 55 THOUSAND WILL BE DEAD. TAKE DIRECT ACTION NOW. FIGHT BACK. FIGHT AIDS.

The International Working Group on Women and AIDS, an Open Letter

From *PWA Coalition Newsline* 25 (July–August 1987), reprinted from Douglas Crimp (ed.) *AIDS: Cultural Analysis/ Cultural Activism* (Cambridge, MA: MIT Press, 1988), pp. 166–8.

An Open Letter to the Planning Committees of the Third International Conference on AIDS

AIDS is a women's issue.

- In the US, women are proportionately the fastest growing group of people with AIDS.
- In NYC, AIDS is the primary cause of death for women 25–29 years old.
- In the US, 51 percent of all women with AIDS are black and 21 percent are Latina, although blacks make up only 18 percent of the total US population, and Latinos 11 percent.
- The number of children with AIDS is doubling every 8–9 months; over 90 percent of affected children under 5 years old are children of color.
- 50 percent of people with AIDS in Africa and the Caribbean are women.
- In Western Europe, women comprise 9 percent of cases; in Africa, the male-to-female ratio is almost 1:1.

AIDS is a women's issue, with a particularly devastating and disproportionate impact on the lives of women who have the disease, who have family or who live in communities beset with the disease, and who care for the people who are sick with the manifestations of HIV infection.

Throughout the world, women are the caretakers of the family and of the sick. Women comprise about 90 percent of all the nurses, social workers, educators, home health aides, and health workers. Women are the most poorly paid of all health workers and frequently are recruited from the populations already most severely affected by HIV-related disease.

Throughout the world, the burden of unpaid health services has always fallen to wives, mothers, grandmothers, sisters, aunts, daughters, and women friends. Volunteerism is increasingly seen as the answer to the escalating costs of caring for those with AIDS and ARC, without regard for the enormous burden this illness already places on those communities with the least support and resources from the health care delivery system.

Furthermore, AIDS offers a paradigm for all of the critical issues which impact on women:

- Deeply ingrained societal racism and sexism.
- Inadequate quality and inaccessibility of health care, including outpatient, hospice, and respite care as well as more traditional facilities.
- Absence of decent affordable housing, particularly for female-headed households, the impoverished, and the working poor.
- Insufficient child-care facilities and support services for raising children.
- Unequal educational opportunities and illiteracy.
- Underemployment and low paying jobs which enforce dependency on social service agencies.
- Devaluation of female sexuality as an important element of health and a part of our life experience, which has been suppressed and distorted by cultural insensitivities and overt discrimination.

Of particular concern is the paternalistic and cavalier disregard for the reproductive rights of women at highest risk for HIV infection. Because, historically, women of color have been repeatedly subject to forced sterilization and coerced family planning decisions, it is essential that all public health measures respect the dignity and autonomy of the pregnant woman. No meaningful reproductive options exist in the absence of adequate nutrition, prenatal and medical care, or without day care, education, and schooling for all children, including those born with disease or HIV positivity, and the availability of abortion on demand for women who choose it.

Women cannot be subject to compulsory, mandatory, "routine," or any other testing which is not entirely informed and voluntary. Testing mandates adequate counseling in a culturally sensitive manner using appropriate language. Anonymous testing and counseling must be available to women on request.

In this third international conference on AIDS, which has been a major forum for the discussion and definition of issues and problems involving AIDS, women are largely invisible except in two roles: as vectors for transmission either perinatally or (putatively) through prostitution. Even in those sessions that have focused on issues impacting on women's lives, for example heterosexual transmission, women are not adequately represented on the panels.

The International Women and AIDS Caucus insists that:

1 Women participate on the organizing, steering, and program committees for the international AIDS conferences in significant numbers.
2 A series of sessions on issues of concern to women be planned for the next international AIDS conferences.
3 Women's perspectives be represented in all sessions that address topics impacting on women and children.
4 Services be expanded to ensure accessibility to the conferences, including child care and sliding scale based on income, and travel subsidies.

We recognize that other affected groups have been similarly disenfranchised by the conference organizers and therefore support similar inclusion for all who have been excluded.

We believe that these recommendations carry the possibility of bringing us all closer to our mutual goal: victory over this devastating epidemic – the foremost public health challenge of our lifetime.

Darrell Yates Rist, "AIDS as Apocalypse: The Deadly Costs of an Obsession"

Reprinted from The Nation, February 13, 1989, pp. 181, 196, 198–200.

> In seasons of pestilence, some of us will have a secret attraction to the disease – a terrible passing inclination to die of it. And all of us have like wonders hidden in our breasts, only needing circumstances to evoke them.
>
> Charles Dickens, *A Tale of Two Cities*

Not long ago, while I was researching a book on the lives of gay men across America, a writer friend offered me an unsettling view of gay San Francisco. Rob Goldstein had no use for the polish and smugness of the Castro, the Promised Land for homosexuals; he toured me instead through the disenfranchised Latino gay life of the Mission district and the destitution of the Tenderloin. In the Tenderloin, I met homeless gay

men with AIDS and gay teenage runaways who risked their lives bartering sex for meals and drugs, hustling on every street corner.

I had just spent a night among those abandoned adolescents when, at
a dinner in the Castro, I listened to the other guests talk about nothing
but AIDS, the dead, the dying – which to their minds included every gay
man in the city: fashionable hysteria. "This," one of them actually said,
"is the only thing worth fighting for." Not long before, I'd heard Larry
Kramer, playwright and AIDS activist, say something like that too, and
had felt, in that suffocating moment, that finally we'd all gone suicidal,
that we'd die of our own death wish.

Though I tried above all to empathize with my tablemates' wretchedness, the other images of San Francisco kept importuning. I described
what I'd seen in their hometown and recalled the gay youth agency I
knew best, New York City's Hetrick-Martin Institute, its dreary facilities,
small staff and paltry budget. "Shouldn't we start worrying again about
all those issues we've forgotten in the epidemic? Gay kids?" I ventured –
as though we'd ever really cared. "Even if they don't get AIDS, what are
we giving them to *live* for?"

The guests fell silent. Across from me sat an elder of the city's gay
community, a man of money and influence. He stared at me in utter
disbelief, his face suspended above the pork roast. "How *can* we?" he
rasped. "We're *dying*!"

There's an oily sentiment among gay men and lesbians these days that
– amid the din of a culture that keeps us in our place – we've matured;
that we've grown aggressive in defense of our lives since fate, with some
harsh wisdom, sent us AIDS. We produce abundant evidence of sacrifice
to prove the claim: For most of this decade we've frantically been
building AIDS organizations, draining our pockets poor with AIDS
donations, exhausting our strength as AIDS volunteers, doing battle
with AIDS bigots, creating mayhem in the streets, nurturing, mourning,
worrying about infection till we're sick, dying with a desperate hold on
dignity. We've been full of AIDS – gay men, lesbians, our parents, our
newly sympathetic heterosexual friends. We've all had heart, in fact, for
nothing else.

Even lesbians, none of whom, according to the U.S. Centers for
Disease Control (C.D.C.), have contracted AIDS making love to a
woman, have taken to keening that the whole gay community is dying
– so compulsive is the human need to partake in the drama of cata-
strophe. And this panicky faith that all of us are doomed cries down the
sobering truth that it is only a minority of homosexuals who've
been stricken or ever will be, leaving the rest of us to confront not so
much the grief of dying as the bitterness, in an oppressive world, of
staying alive.

No one has influenced (or parroted) the gay community's views on AIDS more than Larry Kramer and his organizational offspring, New York's AIDS Coalition to Unleash Power (ACT UP) – chic street protesters with clones, albeit autonomous ones, in nearly every major city. The numbers they use to pronounce universal death on the gay community's men are immoral because they are panic-mongering, insidious because they are specious. They fall within some extreme theoretical realm of possibility, and therefore prey on the frightened; they willfully propagate the worst that medical science can imagine, regardless of the improbability, regardless of maddening contradictions in epidemiologic definitions and data.

Neither Kramer nor anyone else has any hard national figures on the prevalence of infection with HIV, the virus assumed to cause AIDS. But most activists, and the media, seem to have swallowed the C.D.C.'s estimate of 1 million to 1.5 million men, women and children. These numbers, unchanged since 1986 despite the luridly publicized "spread" of HIV, ludicrously derive not from national seroprevalence surveys but in great part from mythical assumptions about the population size and sexual practices of gay men....

Data on the homosexual population and AIDS will change in time and yield more truth – or less. But no imprecision in the numbers has sobered the gay apocalyptics for a moment. And their fantasy of wholesale mortality gives us yet a new excuse to desert the business of living and ignore the most vulnerable among us. Certainly when it comes to kids, even the homosexual heart for AIDS beats false; it beats only for men of a certain age, a certain color – in fact, a certain social class.

Since its founding in 1981, New York's pre-eminent AIDS service organization, the Gay Men's Health Crisis (G.M.H.C.), with an annual budget of almost $11 million – and $1 million more in material donations for new office furnishings last year – has never funded outreach of any kind to gay and lesbian youth. I've been told again and again the organization is fearful of being accused of proselytizing, that most vicious imputation afflicting homosexuals. So children die while we dance to the songs of bigots....

But even concerns more immediate than gay children fail to engage our self-interest. The battle against anti-gay violence languishes while assaults have soared specifically as a backlash to the disease. According to the New York City Gay and Lesbian Anti-Violence Project (A.V.P.), in the city alone there were 609 reported queer-bashings last year, reflecting a more than 300 percent increase since 1984, when AIDS stories began to saturate the media. Moreover, the A.V.P. reports that 90 percent of anti-gay and -lesbian crimes nationwide are never reported: Victims are afraid of being forced from the closet and demeaned by the police or made to face, in many states, the legally sanctioned discrimination of sodomy laws. Despite New York's huge gay and lesbian population at risk of assault, the A.V.P. could muster a budget last year of a mere $150,000, just $10,000 of which was donated by the community.

The epidemic of violence has been long, brutal and often fatal. David Wertheimer, director of A.V.P., describes the hatred vented in anti-gay attacks as "unimaginable." Speaking about a series of murders in New York's Chelsea neighborhood that began in 1985, he said, "The victim is commonly found stabbed twenty or thirty times, sometimes with his castrated penis stuffed in his mouth." Yet there has not been a sustained outcry from the gay community against this violence.

Why are we so callous about these attacks? Can no threat but AIDS ignite our indignation? Why do we care so little, in fact, even for the sanctity of our relationships? Why is there no ACT UP specifically to protest laws forbidding same-sex marriage, banned in every state? Why no marathon protests at marriage license bureaus, no sit-ins at state legislatures, no class action suits? Why doesn't such brutality against our love incite our anger? Are we such demoralized creatures that only the threat of extinction can stir our collective will? When a car wreck left Sharon Kowalski a quadraplegic, her homophobic father had her quarantined by a court from Karen Thompson, her lover. Is the murder of their relationship at the hands of American law less of a horror than losing one's lover to a virus? . . .

The ruse that comforts us is that the fight against AIDS and the struggle for gay rights are the same. Last year, a gay Chicago newspaper headlined, "Riverside [California] Supports Gay Rights." The story below read: "The Riverside City Council unanimously approved an ordinance that bans discrimination against people with AIDS." It's in this very sort of thing that we're deceived. What good do those laws do for most lesbians, who certainly are not suffering from AIDS? Or for the average homosexual or bisexual man, who, whatever our hysteria, would not test positive for HIV either? Or for those who have been exposed to the virus but are asymptomatic, not all of whom will sicken and die, however fantastic the latest rumors? What's the benefit of such legislation to gay men with AIDS themselves if the excuse to abuse their rights isn't AIDS but homosexuality? Any benefit that gay men and lesbians get from the legislated rights of people with AIDS is second-handed grace: You have to claim to be dying to receive it.

But our failure is far more iniquitous than mere dereliction. For, though the constituencies of gay rights and AIDS activism may overlap, the politics – as conceived – are often violently incompatible. At the October 1987 National March on Washington for Lesbian and Gay Rights, an uncommon show of militant self-respect among homosexuals, at least a half-million of us paraded not just against AIDS but for all the rights and privileges that heterosexuals enjoy. Yet, even as we rallied, I sat in a meeting of national AIDS activists who fretted over the possibility that the event would become a political embarrassment for AIDS lobbyists. The symbolic public same-sex wedding the Saturday before the march, a demonstration for spousal rights, was a particular sore point. The director of a powerful national AIDS umbrella organization especially complained that when the wedding hit the news a disgusted Congress would renege on AIDS funding. She and her colleagues still hoped desperately that last-minute maneuvers would kill the thing – treachery bartering away gay liberation.

Some angry lesbians question whether bourgeois gay men ever wanted more than comfortably closeted sex anyway – and now wonder if they want more than a quick cure for AIDS in order to get back to the old days. Some ask more bitterly yet whether men, who demand center stage for AIDS, would sacrifice a pittance of their politics or pleasures if lesbians were the ones dying. Yet, there always have been gay men who've wanted more than sex and obsequious privacy, whose cause has been politically radical and impolite. They've been largely shouted down by the politics of this epidemic. And the more the AIDS movement divorces itself from the demands of gay rights, the more it becomes a route to respect for homosexuals not open to unapologetic gay activists. AIDS is the cause célèbre, and, insidiously, we are drawn in, chumming with the Liz Taylors and even the William F. Buckley Jrs. (who've contributed charitably to the fight against AIDS, though Bill has called for tattooing infected gay men's asses). Gossip columnists boldface AIDS activists' names among mentions of the socially registered. New York's artsy Bessie Committee even gave ACT UP a performance citation last year for its street protests, unlikely applause for genuine revolutionaries.

But even homophobes who'd never want to see a homosexual holding a lover's hand, especially in front of the children, can cry (and contribute) at the thought of so many gay men dying. They're with us on AIDS: Dying and preoccupied with dying, we're less of a threat, our radical potential diverted to mere survival. Through a marriage with disease we've arrived. But to live with our apostasy we've also had to hide from the damning truth that our patrons in the fight against AIDS are seldom dear friends when we're not being sick, just homosexual.

It isn't a virus that for centuries has deprived us gay men and lesbians of our freedom, nor is it this epidemic that now most destroys our lives. Nor is it bigotry. It's our own shame, a morbid failure of self-respect and sane, self-righteous anger. If we care about nothing but AIDS now, it is because identifying with sexually transmitted death plays to some dark belief that we deserve it.

In the midst of death, we are confronted with a choice of life that so far we've only dallied with, the terrible responsibility of living free. For wholeness demands more than arguing with bigots, more than crying for acceptance, more than fighting against disease. It asks that we abandon selfishness, self-pity and every compromise of our self-worth. It insists that we nurture the dying, more selflessly than we ever have, but care as much for the promise of life. It compels us to understand that silence equals death not only in the middle of an epidemic, but that it always has killed us and will continue its genocide when AIDS is gone. And wholeness forces us to forsake AIDS as our dark obsession, as the sum of our lives. For this disease is at least as fatal to our hearts as to our blood. Our devotion to it will kill us more surely than a virus ever could.

Suggested Reading

Dudley Clendinen and Adam Nagourney, *Out for Good: The Struggle to Build a Gay Rights Movement in America,* New York: Simon & Schuster, 1999. Two reporters for the *New York Times* provide a detailed history of gay and lesbian activism since the Stonewall revolt of 1969.

Douglas Crimp (ed.) *Aids: Cultural Analysis/Cultural Activism,* Cambridge, MA: MIT Press, 1988. A collection of essays about how the disease called AIDS is "constructed" by the dominant culture and how activists have fought discrimination and stigmatization of people with AIDS.

Barbara Epstein, *Political Protest and Cultural Revolution: Nonviolent Direct Action in the 1970s and 1980s,* Berkeley: University of California Press, 1991. An activist historian describes and analyzes new social movements, stressing the significance of feminism and new forms of spirituality in direct action protests.

Elizabeth Fee and Daniel M. Fox (eds.) *AIDS: The Making of a Chronic Disease,* Berkeley: University of California Press, 1992. Articles by historians and others discuss social and political aspects of the history of AIDS.

Eric Marcus, *Making History: The Struggle for Gay and Lesbian Equal Rights 1945–1990, an Oral History,* New York: HarperCollins, 1992. A series of several dozen first-hand accounts by gays and lesbians describing their personal and political involvement with the gay and lesbian liberation movement.

Randy Shilts, *And the Band Played On: Politics, People and the AIDS Epidemic,* New York: St. Martin's Press, 1987. An angry journalist's controversial history of the AIDS epidemic that blames government, the medical establishment, and the gay men's movement itself for failure to confront the crisis.

Index

CPSIA information can be obtained
at www.ICGtesting.com
Printed in the USA
LVHW021320210121
677028LV00006B/119